THE AMERICAN LECTURES
ON THE HISTORY OF RELIGIONS.

I. **Buddhism.**—The History and Literature of Buddhism. By T. W. RHYS-DAVIDS, LL.D., Ph.D.

II. **Primitive Religions.**—The Religions of Primitive Peoples. By D. G. BRINTON, A.M., M.D., LL.D., SC.D.

III. **Israel.**—Jewish Religions. Life after the Exile. By Rev. T. K. CHEYNE, M.A., D.D.

IV. **Israel.**—Religion of Israel to the Exile. By KARL BUDDE, D.D.

V. **Ancient Egyptians.**—The Religion of the Ancient Egyptians. By G. STEINDORFF, Ph.D.

VI. **Religion in Japan.**—The Development of Religion in Japan. By GEORGE W. KNOX, D.D.

VII. **The Veda.**—The Religion of the Veda. By MAURICE BLOOMFIELD, Ph.D., LL.D.

VIII. **Babylonia and Assyria.**—Aspects of Religious Belief and Practice in Babylonia and Assyria. By MORRIS JASTROW, JR., Ph.D.

G. P. PUTNAM'S SONS
NEW YORK AND LONDON

AMERICAN LECTURES ON THE
HISTORY OF RELIGIONS

NINTH SERIES, 1910

Aspects of Religious Belief and Practice in Babylonia and Assyria

By

Morris Jastrow, Jr., Ph.D.

Professor of Semitic Languages in the University of Pennsylvania.

*With 54 Illustrations and a Map
and
Chronological Lists
of the
Rulers of Babylonia and Assyria*

46150.

G. P. Putnam's Sons
New York and London
The Knickerbocker Press

1911

The Knickerbocker Press, New York

Pl. 1. Map of Babylonia and Assyria, Showing Sites of Principal Cities.

To

HORACE HOWARD FURNESS

TO WHOSE LOVING AND ENDURING FRIENDSHIP

I OWE MORE THAN WORDS CAN TELL,

THIS VOLUME IS AFFECTIONATELY DEDICATED.

" More is thy due, than more than all can pay."

PREFACE

WHEN the American Committee for Lectures on the History of Religions kindly invited me to deliver a course of lectures under its auspices, I hesitated at first for various reasons, but was led to accept by the consideration that the invitation would afford an opportunity to summarise in a popular and (I trust) a readable form the results of recent researches on some aspects of the religion of Babylonia and Assyria, in which I was privileged to have a share. The importance of the extensive omen literature of Babylonia and Assyria, very imperfectly known until a few years ago, is now generally recognised, and I feel that no apology is necessary for devoting two of the lectures to the two chief aspects of this literature—divination through the liver, and divination through the observation of the heavens. Both forms of divination have wide and significant bearings on the general history of religious rites and beliefs. Through hepatoscopy, a definite link has been established between the Euphratean culture and the Etruscan civilisation, with the Hittites, apparently, as the mediating factor. The Babylonian astrologers

are the "fathers" of all who seek to read the future
in the stars; and as I write these lines, Prof. Franz
Cumont's valuable paper on "Babylon und die
Griechische Astronomie" (*Neue Jahrbücher für das
Klassische Altertum*, 1 Abt., Band XXVII., pp. 1–10)
comes to hand, to emphasise the debt that even Greek
astronomy owes to the results obtained by the Babylonian priests, actuated though these were, at least
up to a late period, solely by the supposed bearings of
the study of the movements of heavenly bodies on
human destinies.

So steady is the increase in the material for the
study of the Babylonian-Assyrian religion, and so
unceasing is the activity of the band of scholars in
this country and Europe who are devoting themselves to the interpretation of this material, that it
becomes necessary from time to time to recast our
views of the pantheon and the cult. I have, therefore, availed myself of this opportunity to present
in outline a picture of the chief deities in the systematised pantheon, with due regard to the manner in
which the original traits of these deities were overlaid with the attributes accorded to them because of
the political position assumed by the centres in which
they were worshipped. While many problems still
remain to be worked out, I venture to hope that my
presentation of the pantheon will be regarded as an
advance upon previous attempts.

Our knowledge of the local cults in the earlier periods before the tendency towards centralisation set in is still very defective, but the broad subdivisions of the cult are now clear; and we are also in a much better position than some years ago to sketch the general character of the temple architecture of both Babylonia and Assyria, thanks, chiefly, to the work done at Nippur, Babylon, and Kalah-Shergat (or Ashur). Through the Hammurapi Code, in conjunction with the numerous business documents of all periods, we are able to trace the development of ethics, and the application of ethical principles to the practical affairs of life. So far as the limitations of a single lecture allow, I have tried to do this in the concluding chapter, which may therefore be regarded as an illustration of the actual influence exerted by the religion upon the life and thought of the people. Throughout, I have kept in mind to distinguish between the popular religion and the somewhat artificial form given to it in the official cult, largely through the attempts of the priests to bring the current beliefs into accord with theological speculations, unfolded in the schools attached to the temples. How far I have succeeded in doing so, it will be for others to judge, but I am convinced that for a proper understanding of the religion under discussion, we must differentiate more sharply than has hitherto been done between these two currents of thought—

the popular and the speculative. In the views of life after death, the contrast between what the people believed and the way in which the priests partly justified and partly modified these beliefs is particularly instructive.

The illustrations have been carefully chosen and will, I trust, aid in elucidating the subject. Special attention should be called to the explanatory comments added to the illustrations in which I have endeavored to give the data necessary for their interpretation.

My profound thanks are due to my esteemed friend Prof. C. H. Toy for the careful revision that he has given to my manuscript, in the course of which he made a large number of valuable suggestions, bearing both on the matter and on the form of presentation, while that dearest and rarest of men, who has been my "guide, philosopher, and friend" during my career, and who has permitted me to grace this volume by inscribing his name on the dedication page, has added to the heavy debt that I already owe him—a debt too large for me to even pay the interest thereof—by submitting the manuscript to a final and critical examination. How much this has meant, those who know Dr. Furness need not be told.

My thanks are also due to Dr. George B. Gordon, the efficient director of the Museum of Archæology of the University of Pennsylvania, for his kindness in placing at my disposal the Museum material for a large number of the illustrations in this volume.

The index is the work of my pupil, Dr. B. B. Charles, Research Fellow in Semitic Languages at the University of Pennsylvania, to whom I am under many obligations for the care, time, and thought that he has bestowed on the task.

My wife has, as on former occasions, read proof and assisted in various other ways in the preparation of the volume. Deep as are my obligations to her for this direct aid, what she has done by her loving and continuous sympathy with my work has been a help and a source of strength too great (and too close to my heart) to be expressed in words

Lastly, as I write these lines I recall with pleasure and gratitude the sympathetic audiences that listened to the story of the long-forgotten past, now so largely restored to us. If some of my hearers should also be among my readers, I hope that the written word will strengthen the bond of sympathy created by the spoken one.

M. J., Jr.

UNIVERSITY OF PENNSYLVANIA,
March, 1911.

ANNOUNCEMENT

THE American Lectures on the History of Religions are delivered under the auspices of the American Committee for Lectures on the History of Religions. This Committee was organised in 1892, for the purpose of instituting "popular courses in the History of Religions, somewhat after the style of the Hibbert Lectures in England, to be delivered by the best scholars of Europe and this country, in various cities, such as Baltimore, Boston, Brooklyn, Chicago, New York, Philadelphia, and others."

The terms of association under which the Committee exist are as follows:

1. The object of this Association shall be to provide courses of lectures on the history of religions, to be delivered in various cities.

2. The Association shall be composed of delegates from institutions agreeing to co-operate, with such additional members as may be chosen by these delegates.

3. These delegates—one from each institution, with the additional members selected—shall constitute themselves a Council under the name of the

"American Committee for Lectures on the History of Religions."

4. The Council shall elect out of its number a Chairman, a Secretary, and a Treasurer.

5. All matters of local detail shall be left to the co-operating institution under whose auspices the lectures are to be delivered.

6. A course of lectures on some religion, or phase of religion, from an historical point of view, or on a subject germane to the study of religions, shall be delivered annually, or at such intervals as may be found practicable, in the different cities represented by this Association.

7. The Council (a) shall be charged with the selection of the lecturers, (b) shall have charge of the funds, (c) shall assign the time for the lectures in each city, and perform such other functions as may be necessary.

8. Polemical subjects, as well as polemics in the treatment of subjects, shall be positively excluded.

9. The lectures shall be delivered in the various cities between the months of September and June.

10. The copyright of the lectures shall be the property of the Association.

11. The compensation of the lecturer shall be fixed in each case by the Council.

12. The lecturer shall be paid in instalments after each course, until he shall have received half of the

entire compensation. Of the remaining half, one half shall be paid to him upon delivery of the manuscript, properly prepared for the press, and the second half on the publication of the volume, less a deduction for corrections made by the author in the proofs exceeding 15% of the cost of the plates.

The Committee as now constituted is as follows: Prof. Crawford H. Toy, Chairman, 7 Lowell St., Cambridge, Mass.; Rev. Dr. John P. Peters, Treasurer, 227 W. 99th St., New York City; Prof. Morris Jastrow, Jr., Secretary, 248 S. 23rd St., Philadelphia, Pa.; Prof. Richard Gottheil, Columbia University, New York City; Prof. Robert F. Harper, University of Chicago, Chicago, Ill.; Prof. Paul Haupt, Johns Hopkins University, Baltimore, Md.; Prof. E. W. Hopkins, Yale University, New Haven, Conn.; Prof. F. W. Hooper, Brooklyn Institute, Brooklyn, N. Y.; Prof. G. W. Knox, Union Theological Seminary, New York City; Prof. Edward Knox Mitchell, Hartford Theological Seminary, Hartford, Conn.; President F. K. Sanders, Washburn College, Topeka, Kan.; Prof. H. P. Smith, Meadville Theological School, Meadville, Pa.

The lecturers in the course of American Lectures on the History of Religions and the titles of their volumes are as follows:

1894–1895:—Prof. T. W. Rhys-Davids, Ph.D. Buddhism.

1896–1897:—Prof. Daniel G. Brinton, M.D., LL.D.
Religions of Primitive Peoples.

1897–1898:—Rev. Prof. T. K. Cheyne, D.D.
Jewish Religious Life after the Exile.

1898–1899:—Prof. Karl Budde, D.D
Religion of Israel to the Exile.

1904–1905:—Prof. George Steindorff, Ph.D.
The Religion of the Ancient Egyptians.

1905–1906:—Prof. George W. Knox, D.D., LL.D.
The Development of Religion in Japan.

1906–1907:—Prof. Maurice Bloomfield, Ph.D., LL.D.
The Religion of the Veda.

1907–1908:—Prof. A. W. Jackson.
The Religion of Persia.[1]

The present course of lectures, the ninth of the series, was delivered by Prof. Morris Jastrow, Jr., Ph.D., Professor of Semitic Languages at the University of Pennsylvania, who has devoted many years of special study to the Religion of Babylonia and

[1] This course, by special arrangement with the Committee, will form part of Prof. Jackson's volume on the Religion of Persia in the series of "Handbooks on the History of Religions," edited by Prof. Morris Jastrow, Jr., and published by Messrs. Ginn & Company of Boston. The volume is expected to appear in 1912.

Assyria. In 1898 Prof. Jastrow published the first comprehensive work on the "Religion of Babylonia and Assyria" as Volume I. of the "Handbooks on the History of Religions" edited by him. In 1903 he began the publication of the revised German translation, which is practically a new work. The one volume of the English edition has been enlarged to two substantial volumes in the German form, in order to embody the additional material brought to light during the last decade. It is the intention of Prof. Jastrow to follow the German edition by a supplemental volume, to be published simultaneously in English and German, on "The Temples, Cult, and Myths of Babylonia and Assyria." Besides a large number of papers on special points connected with the religious beliefs of Babylonia and Assyria, or with the elucidation of religious texts, Prof. Jastrow is also the author of the article on the "Religion of Babylonia and Assyria" in the supplemental volume of Hastings's *Dictionary of the Bible*.

Other publications of Prof. Jastrow include *The Study of Religion*, London, 1901; *The Grammatical Works of Abu Zakarijja Hajjug*, Leiden, 1897; and a large number of philological and archæological articles, bearing chiefly on Assyrian, Hebrew, and Arabic, and published in technical journals of this country and Europe.

The lectures in this course were delivered before

the Lowell Institute, University of Chicago, Meadville Theological School, Union Theological Seminary, Brooklyn Institute, Drexel Institute, and the Johns Hopkins University.

JOHN P. PETERS,

C. H. TOY,

Committee on Publication.

February, 1911.

CONTENTS

Contents

Contents

ILLUSTRATIONS

xxi

Illustrations

Illustrations

Aspects of Religious Belief and Practice in Babylonia and Assyria

---

LECTURE I

CULTURE AND RELIGION

I

FIFTY or sixty years ago the task of a lecturer called upon to deliver a course of six lectures on the religion of Babylonia and Assyria would have been comparatively simple. He could have told all that was known or that he knew in a single lecture, and could have devoted the remaining lectures to what he did not know—an innocent form of intellectual amusement, sometimes indulged in by lecturers of all times. During the past five or six decades, however, the material for the study has grown to such an extent that it is no longer possible, even were it desirable, to present the entire subject in a single course of lectures.[1] It is my purpose, therefore, in

[1] This full treatment has already been furnished by the author

I

the present course to restrict myself to setting forth
the more salient features in the beliefs and practices of a religion of antiquity that well merits the
designation—remarkable. Its great age is of itself
sufficient to call forth respect and interest. Although
the civilisation that once flourished in the region of
the Euphrates and Tigris is not so ancient as not
many years ago it was fondly supposed to be
by scholars whose enthusiasm outran their judgment,[1] yet we may safely say that three thousand
years before our era, civilisation and religion in the
Euphrates Valley had reached a high degree of
development.

At that remote period some of the more important
centres had already passed the zenith of their glory.
Since the course of civilisation in this region flowed from
south to north, it follows that the cities of the south
are older than those of the northern part of the val-

---

in his work, *The Religion of Babylonia and Assyria*, (Boston, 1898),
to which, and to the enlarged and rewritten German edition
(*Die Religion Babyloniens und Assyriens*, 2 vols., Giessen, 1905–
1911), which gives a practically complete view of the material,
the reader is referred for details. In the German edition the
myths and legends and the cult have not been dealt with. The
writer proposes to do this in a separate work, to be published
simultaneously in English and German.

[1] It was claimed, *e.g.*, that the foundation of the city of Nippur could be referred to 7000 years B.C., but inscriptions that
were at first ascribed to *ca.* 4500 B.C. are now dated with more
accuracy at *ca.* 2500 B.C. See Meyer, *Geschichte des Altertums*,
i., 2, p. 457.

ley; and this assumption is fully confirmed by the results of excavations, as well as by historical data now at our disposal. The Babylonians themselves recognised this distinction between the south and the north, designating the former as Sumer (more correctly Shumer, though we shall use the simpler form)—which will at once recall the "plain of Shinar" in the Biblical story of the building of the tower[1]— and the latter as Akkad. The two in combination cover what is commonly known as Babylonia, but Sumer and Akkad were at one time as distinct from each other as were in later times Babylonia and Assyria. They stand, in fact, in the same geographical relationship to one other as do the latter; and it is significant that in the title "King of Sumer and Akkad," which the rulers of the Euphrates Valley, from a certain period onward, were fond of assuming to mark their control of both south and north, it is Sumer, the designation of the southern area, which always precedes Akkad.

[1] Genesis, chap. xi. The circumstance that in the Biblical story of the dispersion of mankind, Shinar and not Akkad or Babylon, is the designation of the Euphrates Valley is a valuable indication of the antiquity of the kernel of the tradition, even though, in its present form, representing, as it does, the combination of two folk-tales, one in regard to the building of a city (Babylon), the other in regard to the building of a tower, it betrays its late redaction. See an article by the writer, "The Tower of Babel," *The Independent*, 1905, vol. lvii., pp. 822–826.

More important, however, than any geographical distinction is the ethnological contrast presented by Sumerians and Akkadians. To be sure, the designations themselves, applied in an ethnic sense, are purely conventional; but there is no longer any doubt of the fact that the Euphrates Valley from the time that it looms up on the historical horizon is the seat of a mixed population. The germ of truth in the time-honoured Biblical tradition, that makes the plain of Shinar the home of the human race and the seat of the confusion of languages, is the recollection of the fact that various races had settled there, and that various languages were there spoken. Indeed, we should be justified in assuming this, *a priori;* it may be put down as an axiom that nowhere does a high form of culture arise without the commingling of diverse ethnic elements. Civilisation, like the spark emitted by the striking of steel on flint, is everywhere the result of the stimulus evoked by the friction of one ethnic group upon another. Egyptian culture is the outcome of the mixture of Semitic with Hamitic elements. Civilisation begins in Greece with the movements of Asiatic peoples—partly at least non-Aryan—across the Ægean Sea. In Rome we find the old Aryan stock mixed with a strange element, known as Etruscan. In modern times, France, Germany, and England furnish illustrations of the process of the commingling of diverse ethnic elements leading to advanced forms of civilisation, while in our own country the process is proceeding on so large a scale as to have suggested to a modern playwright the title of "The Melting Pot" for a play, depicting a new type of culture springing from the mixture of almost innumerable elements.

A pure race, if it exist at all outside of the brain of some ethnologists, is a barren race. Mixed races, and mixed races alone, bring forth the fruit that we term civilisation,—with social, religious, and intellectual progress. Monuments also bear witness, in ethnic types, in costumes, and in other ways, to the existence of two distinct classes in the population of the Euphrates Valley—Semites or Akkadians, and non-Semites or Sumerians. The oldest strongholds of the Semites are in the northern portion, those of the Sumerians in the southern. It does not, however, necessarily follow that the Sumerians were the oldest settlers in the valley; nor does the fact that in the oldest historical period they are the predominating factor warrant the conclusion. Analogy would, on the contrary, suggest that they represent the conquering element, which by its admixture with the older settlers furnished the stimulus to an intellectual advance, and at the same time drove the older Semitic population farther to the north.

We are approaching a burning problem in regard to which scholars are still divided, and which, in some of its aspects, is not unlike the Rabbinical quibble whether the chicken or the egg came first. It is the lasting merit of the distinguished Joseph Halévy of Paris to have diverted Assyriological scholarship from the erroneous course into which it was drifting a generation ago, when, in the older Euphratean culture, it sought to differentiate sharply between Sumerian and Akkadian elements.[1] Preference was given to the non-Semitic Sumerians, to whom was attributed the origin of the cuneiform script. The Semitic (or Akkadian) settlers were supposed to be the borrowers also in religion, in forms of government, and in civilisation generally, besides adopting the cuneiform syllabary of the Sumerians, and adapting it to their own speech. *Hic* Sumer, *hic* Akkad! Halévy maintained that many of the features in this syllabary, hitherto regarded as Sumerian, were genuinely Semitic; and his main contention is that what is known as Sumerian is merely an older form of Semitic writing, marked by the larger use of ideographs or signs to express words, in place of the

[1] Besides his numerous special monographs, Halévy's views will be found set forth in the pages of his periodical, *Revue Sémitique*. A survey of the situation will also be found in my paper, "A New Aspect of the Sumerian Question," in the *American Journal of Semitic Languages*, vol. xxii., pp. 89–109, though since then I have somewhat modified my views.

later method of phonetic writing wherein the signs employed have syllabic values.[1]

While an impartial review of the still active controversy demands the conclusion that Halévy has not succeeded in convincing scholars that there is no such thing as a Sumerian language, yet, in addition to demonstrating that, even in its oldest phase, the cuneiform syllabary contains unquestionable Semitic elements, he has also made it clear that many texts— particularly those of a religious character—, once regarded as Sumerian originals, are Semitic in character. The "Sumerian" form of writing was intended purely for the eye, and represented the ideographic method of writing such texts, further complicated by a super-layer of more or less artificial devices. This applies even to votive and other inscriptions of the oldest period. To maintain in reply that the pure Sumerian period lies still further back, is to beg the question.

On the other hand, the existence of a Sumerian people (or whatever name we may propose to give to the earliest non-Semitic settlers) being an un-

---

[1] By the "ideographic" method is meant the use of signs to express words, whereas in the "phonetic" method, the signs are used as syllables constituting the component parts of a word. The "mixed" method employs signs for words together with signs used as phonetic complements. Recent researches appear to show that the Sumerian already employs the "mixed" method to a limited extent.

deniable fact in view of the ethnic evidence furnished by the monuments,[1] we must perforce assume that there was also a Sumerian language; and we are certainly justified in looking for traces of this language in inscriptions coming from the strongholds of the Sumerians. Making full allowance for possible, or probable, Semitic elements in the oldest "Sumerian" inscriptions, there yet remain many features not to be satisfactorily accounted for on the supposition that they are artificial devices, introduced in the course of the adaptation of a hieroglyphic script to express greater niceties of thought. A substratum remains requiring the assumption that side by side with the ideographic method of writing the old Semitic speech, developing in the course of time to a phonetic and mixed phonetic-ideographic script, we have also inscriptions which must be regarded as non-Semitic, and that likewise show two varieties—ideographic and phonetic modes of expression.

But in accepting this conclusion we have not yet settled the question whether the script is due to the Semitic or to the non-Semitic settlers. Like every other script, the cuneiform characters revert to a purely hieroglyphic form. The pictures represented,

[1] Gathered by Eduard Meyer in his monograph, *Sumerier und Semiten in Babylonien*, Berlin, 1906. See also King, *History of Sumer and Akkad*, pp. 40-52.

Pl. 2.   Sumerian Types, Ur-Ninâ, Patesi of Lagash (*c.* 3000 B.C.), and his Family.

Limestone votive tablet found at Telloh and now in the Louvre. See De Sarzec, *Découvertes en Chaldée*, Pl. 2 *bis*, Fig. 1, and pp. 168–170; Heuzey, *Catalogue des Antiquités Chaldéennes*, pp. 96–100. Two similar votive tablets of this ruler and his family have been found at Telloh. One of these is also in the Louvre; the other in the Museum at Constantinople. See De Sarzec *Découvertes*, Pl. 1 *bis*, Fig. 2, and Pl. 2 *bis*, Fig. 1, pp. 171–172. Ur-Ninâ—naked to the waist—is represented in the upper row with a workman's basket on his head, symbolising his participation in the erection of a sacred edifice. In the accompanying inscription he records his work at the temples of Ningirsu and of Ninâ and other constructions within the temple area of Lagash. Behind him stands a high official—presumably a priest—with a libation cup in his hand, and before the king are five of his children. The lower row represents the king after the completion of the work pouring a libation. Behind him again the attendant, and before him four other children. The figure with the basket on the head became a common form of a votive offering (see Pl. 29) and persisted to the end of the Assyrian empire as is shown by the steles of King Ashurbanapal and his brother, Shamash-shumukin with such baskets. (See Lehmann, *Shamash-shumukin*, Leipzig, 1892.)

Ur-Ninâ, King of Lagash (c. 3100 B.C.) and I. Frontispiece

so far as these have been determined, do not carry us outside of the Euphrates Valley. A form of writing in the earliest pictorial style being applicable to any language, it is conceivable that the script of the Euphrates Valley may have been used by Semites and non-Semites alike; or, in other words, the pictorial representation of facts or ideas might have been read or translated into either non-Semitic Sumerian or Semitic Akkadian, using these terms for the languages of the two ethnic groups. The period of differentiation would set in when it became necessary to express thoughts or abstract ideas more definitely, and in nicer shades than is possible in a purely pictorial script, which has obviously definite limitations. Granting that the origin of the Euphratean civilisation is due to the combination of the Semitic and non-Semitic elements of the population, the script would likewise be the joint product of these two elements; and it is conceivable that, starting in this way, writing should develop in two directions—one calculated to adapt the script to express the greater niceties of thought in Sumerian, the other to express them in Akkadian, while both Sumerian and Akkadian would retain many elements in common in the general endeavour to give expression to thought in writing. At the same time, the two modes would exert upon each other an influence commensurate with the general process of mixture that gives to the religion and culture the harmonious combination of diverse factors. Some such theory as this, which would make the developed script the result of the intellectual activity of both elements of the population, and not the exclusive achievement of one and adopted by the other, may be eventually found to satisfy best the conditions involved, though it must be admitted that as yet neither this theory nor any other can be advanced as absolutely definite and final. The development of the script in two directions would not necessarily proceed *pari passu*. The one or the other might be accelerated or retarded by various factors. Throughout the different phases of development, there would always be at each stage the tendency to a mutual influence, until finally, with the definite predominance in the culture of one element—which in the case in question proved to be the Semitic,—the development in one direction would be arrested, while in the other it would proceed uninterruptedly.

It is perhaps idle to indulge the hope of ever being able to follow details of a process so complicated as the transformation of a script from its oldest hieroglyphic aspect to a form verging closely on an alphabetic system. The task is particularly hopeless in the case of the cuneiform script, because of this commingling of Sumerian with Akkadian elements which we encounter from the beginning. While, naturally, it is reasonable to expect that further progress to-

wards the solution of the problem will be made—
and indeed unexpected material throwing light on
the subject may at any time be discovered,—it is
safe to predict that this progress will serve also to
illustrate still further the composite character of
the Euphratean civilisation as a whole.

II

The earliest historical period known to us, which,
roughly speaking, is from 2800 B.C., to 2000 B.C.,
may be designated as a struggle for political ascendency between the Sumerian (or non-Semitic), and the
Akkadian (or Semitic) elements.   The strongholds of
the Sumerians at this period were in the south, in
such centres as Lagash, Kish, Umma, Uruk, Nippur,
and Ur, those of the Semites in the north, particularly
at Agade, Sippar, and Babylon, with a gradual extension of the Semitic settlements still farther north
towards Assyria.   It does not follow, however, from
this that the one element or the other was absolutely
confined to any one district.   The circumstance that
even at this early period we find the same religious
observances, the same forms of government, the same
economic conditions in south and north, is a testimony to the intellectual bond uniting the two districts,
as also to the two diverse elements of the population. * The civilisation, in a word, that we encounter
at this earliest period is neither Sumerian nor Akkad-

ian but Sumero-Akkadian, the two elements being so combined that it is difficult to determine what was contributed by one element and what by the other; and this applies to the religion and to the other phases of this civilisation, just as to the script.

When the curtain of history rises on the scene, we are long past the period when the Semitic hordes, coming probably from their homes in Arabia,[1] and the Sumerians, whose origin is with equal probability to be sought in the mountainous regions to the east and north-east of the Euphrates Valley,[2] began to pour into the land. The attraction that settled habitations in a fertile district have for those occupying a lower grade of civilisation led to constant or, at all events, to frequent reinforcements of both Semites and non-Semites. The general condition that presents itself in the earliest period known to us is that of a number of principalities or little kingdoms in the Euphrates Valley, grouped around some centre whose

[1] This statement must, of course, be considered merely as a general one and it is quite possible, and even probable, as King, *History of Sumer and Akkad*, p. 55, also believes, that the first permanent settlements of Semites may have been made by groups entering the Euphrates Valley from the north-west after traversing the Syrian district, *i.e.*, from Amurru.

[2] On the possible bearings of the recent explorations in Turkestan, and more particularly the important work of the Pumpelly expeditions under the auspices of the Carnegie Institution, see the appendix to King, *History of Sumer and Akkad*, pp. 351–358.

Pl. 3. Statue of Gudea, Patesi of Lagash (*c.* 2350 B.C.).

Diorite statue found at Telloh and now in the Louvre. The head was found by De Sarzec in 1881 (De Sarzec *Découvertes*, Pl. 12, Fig. 1) and through the discovery of the body in 1903 by Captain Cros, the statue was completed. See Heuzey, "Une Statue complete de Goudea," in *Revue d'Assyriologie*, vol. vi., pp. 18–22, and *Nouvelles Fouilles de Telloh*, pp. 21–25 and Pl. 1. Ten other such diorite statues of Gudea (minus the heads) have been found at Telloh, covered with dedicatory and historical inscriptions. See De Sarzec, *Découvertes*, Pls. 9–11; 14; 16–20; and Heuzey, *Catalogue* pp. 169–188.

Gudea, Patesi of Lagash
(*c.* 2350 B. C.)

religious significance always kept pace with its political importance, and often surpassed and survived it.
Rivalry between these centres led to frequent changes
in the political kaleidoscope, now one, now another
claiming a certain measure of jurisdiction or control
over the others. Of this early period we have as
yet obtained merely glimpses. Titles of rulers with
brief notices of their wars and building operations
form only too frequently the substance of the information to be gleaned from votive inscriptions, and
from dates attached to legal and business documents.
This material suffices, however, to secure a general perspective. In the case of two of these centres, Lagash
and Nippur, thanks to extensive excavations conducted there,[1] the framework can be filled out with

---

[1] Excavations at Telloh—the site of Lagash—were begun by
Ernest de Sarzec in 1881, and continued after his death in 1901
by Gaston Cros and others. See de Sarzec and Heuzey, *Découvertes en Chaldée*, (Paris, 1883), to date, Cros, *Nouvelles Fouilles
de Tello*, (Paris, 1909), and Heuzey's Catalogue of the Louvre
collections (*Collection des Antiquités Chaldéennes*, Paris, 1902).
At Nippur, excavations were conducted under the commission
of the University of Pennsylvania, by Messrs. Peters and Haynes
from 1888 to 1900. For a little over two months in 1900, the
excavations were conducted by Prof. Hilprecht. An account of
the two campaigns 1888–1890 was given by Dr. John P. Peters,
the organiser and first director, in two volumes under the title
Nippur (New York, 1897); Prof. Hilprecht in *Explorations in
Bible Lands* (Philadelphia, 1903), pp. 289–568 (republished as the
official history of the expedition under the title, *Excavations in
Assyria and Babylonia*), has given an account of all the work
done at Nippur from 1888 to 1900. The value of Prof. Hil-

numerous details. The general conditions existing at Lagash and Nippur may be regarded as typical for the entire Euphrates Valley in the earliest period.

The religion had long passed the animistic stage when all powers of nature were endowed with human purposes and indiscriminately personified. The process of selection (to be explained more fully in a future lecture) had singled out of the large number of such personified powers a limited number, which, although associated in each instance with a locality, were, nevertheless, also viewed as distinct from this association, and as summing up the chief Powers in nature whereon depended the general welfare and prosperity. Growing political relationships between the sections of the Euphrates Valley accelerated this process of selection, and furthered a combination of selected deities into the semblance, at least, of a pantheon partially organised, and which in time became definitely constituted. The patron deities of cities that rose to be centres of a district absorbed the local *numina* of the smaller places. The names of the latter became epithets of the deities politically more conspicuous, so that, *e.g.*, the sun-god of a

---

precht's account has been seriously impaired by charges of *animus* in belittling the work of Messrs. Peters and Haynes, and of direct misrepresentations—charges which have not been, it is thought, successfully refuted. Fortunately, the value of work actually accomplished at Nippur and of the material there obtained is not affected by these misrepresentations.

Pl. 4. Stone Libation Vase of Gudea, Patesi of Lagash (*c.* 2350 B.C.).

A votive offering to the god Ningishzida. The elaborately sculptured design consists of two serpents entwined around a staff, backed by two fantastic figures, winged monsters with serpents' heads and tails ending in a scorpion's sting. Green steatite. Found at Telloh and now in the Louvre. See De Sarzec, *Découvertes*, Pl. 44, Fig. 2, and pp. 234–236; Heuzey, *Catalogue*, pp. 280–284.

Libation Vase of Gudea
Patesi of Lagash
(*c.* 2350 B. C.)

centre like Lagash became almost an abstract and general personification of the sun itself. Similarly, the moon-god of Ur received the names and attributes of the moon-gods associated with other places.

A marked and deep religious spirit pervades throughout the culture of the time. The rulers held their authority directly from the patron deities— "by the grace of God," as we should now say. They do not generally go so far as to claim divine descent, but they closely approach it. They regard themselves as chosen by the will of the gods. Their strength is derived from Ningirsu, they are nourished by Nin-Kharsag, they are appointed by the goddess Innina. When they go to war the gods march at their side, and the booty is dedicated to these protecting powers. The political fortunes, and indeed the general culture, are thus closely bound up with the religion. Each centre had a chief deity whose position in the pantheon kept pace with the political growth of the centre. At Lagash this chief deity was Ningirsu, a solar deity; at Nippur it was Enlil, originally a personification of the storm; at Cuthah, it was Nergal, likewise a solar deity, and at Ur it was Sin, the moon-god. The chief edifice in the capital of the principality is the temple of the patron deity, alongside of which are smaller sanctuaries within the sacred area, dedicated to the gods and goddesses associated with the main cult. Art is developed around the cult. Such artistic skill was largely employed in the fashioning of votive objects; and even where the rulers erected statues of themselves, these were dedicated to some deity and intended to symbolise the pious devotion of the god's representative on earth. As further emphasising the bond between religious and secular conditions we find the palaces of rulers at all times adjoining the temple.

The architecture of both temple and palace is massive and, in consequence of the lack of a hard building-material in the Euphrates Valley, it is perhaps natural that the brick constructions developed in the direction of hugeness rather than of beauty. The drawings on limestone votive tablets and on other material during this early period are generally crude. More skill is displayed in incisures on seal cylinders[1] of various kinds of material, bone, shell, quartz, chalcedony, lapis-lazuli, hematite, marble, and agate. Though serving the purely secular purpose of identifying an individual's personal signature to a business document—written on clay as the usual writing-material—these cylinders incidentally illustrate the bond between culture and religion by their engraved designs, which are invariably of a religious character, —such as the adoration of deities, sacrificial scenes, or

[1] See W. H. Ward, *Seal Cylinders of Western Asia* (Washington, 1910), for the most thorough and exhaustive study of the material. Illustrations on Plates 6 and 7.

Pl. 5. Specimens of Early Babylonian Art.

Fig. 1. Silver Vase (with copper base) of Entemena, Patesi of Lagash (*c.* 2850 B.C.).

A votive offering to his god Ningirsu, deposited in the temple E-Ninnu. The central design of which only one face is shown in the illustration consists of four lion-headed eagles, of which two seize a lion with each talon, and a third eagle seizes a couple of deer and the fourth a couple of ibexes. The eagle appears to have been the symbol of Ningirsu, while the lion,—commonly associated with Ishtar—may represent Bau, the consort of Ningirsu—the Ishtar of Lagash. The combination would thus stand for the divine pair. Dr. Ward (*Seal Cylinders of Western Asia*, p. 34 *seq.*) plausibly identifies this design with the bird Im-Gig, designated in the inscriptions of Gudea as the emblem of the ruler. This vase, considered to be the finest specimen of early metal work of Babylonia, was found at Telloh, and is now in the Louvre. See De Sarzec, *Découvertes*, Pl. 43 and 43 *bis* and pp. 261–264; Heuzey, "Le Vase d'Argent d'Entemena" (*Monuments Piot*, ii., p. 5 *seq.*, and Pl. 1, and Heuzey, *Catalogue*, pp. 372–80). The same design of the lion-headed eagle seizing two lions is found on other monuments of Lagash. See Heuzey, *Catalogue*, Nos. 7 and 12. See also Nos. 234 and 239.

Fig. 2. Sculptured Base.

Decoration in stone (dark green steatite), forming the support of some larger piece. There are seven small squatting figures (each with a tablet on his knees) distributed in a circle around the stone and intended, presumably, as a decorative design. Found at Telloh. Now in the Louvre. See De Sarzec, *Découvertes*, Pl. 21, Fig. 5, and pp. 161–162; Heuzey, *Catalogue*, pp. 255–256.

Fig. 1.   Silver Vase of Entemena
Patesi of Lagash (*c.* 2850 B. C.)

Fig. 2.   Sculptured Base

Pls. 6 and 7. Seal Cylinders of Various Periods. See De Sarzec, *Décou-*
vertes, Pl. 30 and 30 *bis* and pp. 276–324.

These two plates of seal cylinders—all found at Telloh—may
be taken as typical of the illustrations found on these objects,
which served the purpose of personal seals, used by the owners as
their signatures to business documents. They were rolled over
the clay tablets on which business transactions were inscribed.
Presumably the cylinders were also used as amulets. (See Herodotus, Book I, § 195, who says that every Babylonian "carries a
seal.") The design in the centre of Pl. 6 represents Gilgamesh,
the hero of the Babylonian Epic, attacking a bull, while another
figure—presumably Enkidu (though different from the usual type)—
is attacking a lion. This conflict with animals which is an episode
in the Epic (see Pl. 33) is very frequently portrayed on seal cylinders in a large number of variations. See Ward, *Cylinders of*
Western Asia, Chap. X. Another exceedingly common scene portrays a seated deity into whose presence a worshipper is being led
by a priest—or before whom a worshipper directly stands—followed
by a goddess, who is the consort of the deity and who acts as interceder for the worshipper. On Pl. 6 there are three specimens of this
scene; on Pl. 7 likewise three. An altar, tree, or sacrificial animal—
and sometimes all three—are added to the design. The seated
god is commonly Shamash, the sun-god, but Sin, the moon-god,
Ea, and Marduk, Adad, Ningirsu (and probably others) are also
found, as well as goddesses. See Ward *op. cit.*, Chaps. XVI. and,
XXXIX. The seated god with streams issuing from both sides
on Pl. 7 (5th row to the right) is certainly Shamash; so also the one
in the opposite corner with rays protruding from his shoulders.
See Ward, *op. cit.*, Chap. XIV. Instead of the seated god, we
frequently find the god in a standing posture of which Pl. 7 contains three examples. The one on the lowest row to the left is
Shamash, the sun-god, with one leg bare and uplifted—symbolising
the sun rising over the mountain; the other in the fourth row to
the right is probably the god Marduk with the crook (or scimitar)
standing on a gazelle, while the third—on the third row in the centre
—is interesting as being, according to the accompanying inscription,
a physician's seal. The deity represented is Iru—a form or messenger of Nergal, the god of pestilence and death, which suggests a
bit of grim (or unconscious) humour in selecting this deity as the

emblem of the one who ministers unto disease. The accompanying emblems have been conjectured to be the physician's instruments, but this is uncertain. We have also two illustrations of the popular myths which were frequently portrayed on these cylinders—both on Pl. 7. The one in the centre on the second row is an episode in a tale of Etana—a shepherd—who is carried aloft by an eagle to the mountain in which there grows the plant of life; the second— on the fourth row in the centre—represents Nergal's invasion of the domain of Ereshkigal, the mistress of the lower world, and his attack on the goddess—crouching beneath a tree. The other scene on the cylinder seems to be an offering to Nergal, as the conqueror and, henceforth, the controller of the nether world. (See p. 369 and Ward *op. cit.*, Chap. XXIII.) The remaining designs similarly have a religious or mythical import. The seals of the Neo-Babylonian and Persian periods show a tendency to become smaller in size and to embody merely symbols (like the one on Pl. 7, 2nd row, right corner) instead of a full scene.

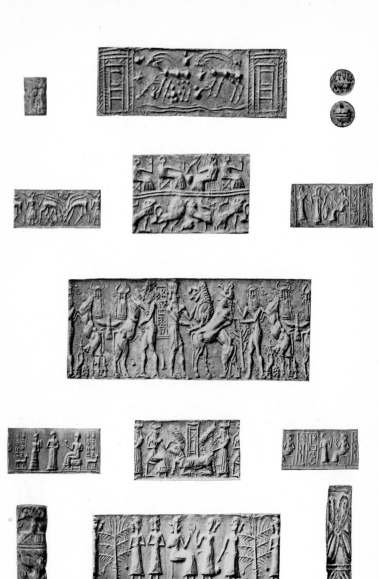

Seal Cylinders of Various Periods

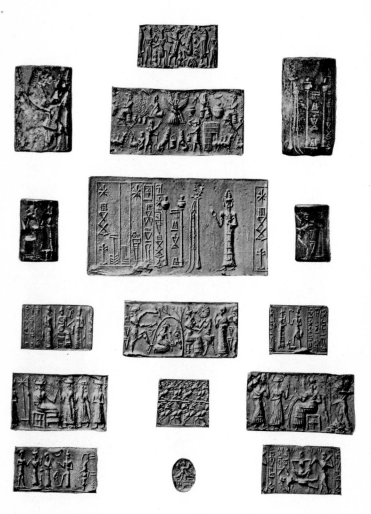

Seal Cylinders of Various Periods

representations of myths or mythical personages. Though marred frequently by grotesqueness, the metal work—in copper, bronze, or silver—is on the whole of a relatively high order, particularly in the portrayal of animals. The human face remains, however, without expression, even where, as in the case of statues chiselled out of the hard diorite,[1] imported from Arabia, the features are carefully worked out.

The population was largely agricultural, but as the cities grew in size, naturally, industrial pursuits and commercial activity increased. Testimony to brisk trading in fields and field products, in houses and woven stuffs, in cattle and slaves is furnished by the large number of business documents of all periods from the earliest to the latest, embracing such a variety of subjects as loans, rents of fields and houses, contracts for work, hire of workmen and slaves, and barter and exchange of all kinds. Even in the purely business activity of the country, the bond between culture and religion is exemplified by the large share taken by the temples in the commercial life. The temples had large holdings in land and cattle. They loaned money and engaged in mercantile pursuits of various kinds; so that a considerable portion of the business documents in both the older and the later periods deal with temple affairs, and form part of the official archives of the temples.[2]

[1] See the statue of Gudea, Plate 3. [2] See p. 276 *seq.*

2

The prominent influence exerted by religion in the oldest period finds a specially striking illustration in the position acquired by the city of Nippur—certainly one of the oldest centres in the Euphrates Valley. So far as indications go, Nippur never assumed any great political importance, though it is possible that it did so at a period still beyond our ken. But although we do not learn of any jurisdiction exercised by her rulers over any considerable portion of the Euphrates Valley, we find potentates from various parts of Babylonia and subsequently also the Assyrian kings paying homage to the chief deity of the place, Enlil.[1] To his temple, known as E-Kur, "mountain house," they brought votive objects inscribed with their names. Rulers of Kish, Uruk, Ur, Lagash, Agade are thus represented in the older period, and it would appear to have been almost an official obligation for those who claimed sovereignty over the Euphrates Valley to mark their control by some form of homage to Enlil, the name of whose temple became in the course of time a general term for "sanctuary."[2] The patron deities of other centres, such as Ningirsu of Lagash, Nergal of Cuthah, Sin of

---

[1] Or Ellil. See p. 67 note 1.

[2] The term Ekur, "temple," passes beyond the domain of the Euphrates Valley and survives apparently under the form *Igûrâ* in Aramaic papyri of the fifth century B.C. See Sachau, *Drei Aramäische Papyrusurkunden aus Elephantine* (Berlin, 1908), pp. 24 *seq.*

Ur, Shamash of Sippar, and Marduk of Babylon, were represented by shrines or temples within the sacred quarter of Nippur; and the rulers of these centres rarely failed to include in their titles some reference to their relationship to Enlil and to his consort Ninlil, or, as she was also called, Nin-Kharsag, "the lady of the mountain."

The position thus occupied by Nippur was not unlike that of the sacred places of India like Benares, or like that of Rome as the spiritual centre of Christendom during the Middle Ages. Sumerians and Semites alike paid their obeisance to Enlil, who through all the political changes retained, as we shall see, the theoretical headship of the pantheon. When he is practically replaced by Marduk, the chief god of the city of Babylon, after Babylon had become the political centre of the entire district, he transfers his attributes to his successor. As the highest homage paid to Marduk, he is called the *bêl* or "lord" *par excellence* in place of Enlil, while Marduk's consort becomes Ninlil, like the consort of Enlil.

The control of Nippur was thus the ambition of all rulers from the earliest to the latest periods; and the plausible suggestion has been recently made that the claim of divinity, so far as it existed in ancient Babylonia,[1] was merely intended as an expression

[1] See Kugler, *Sternkunde und Sterndienst in Babel*, ii., 1, pp. 144–149. Sargon of Agade and his son Naram-Sin are the first

of such control—an indication that a ruler who had secured the approval of Enlil might regard himself as the legitimate vicegerent of the god on earth, and therefore as partaking of the divine character of Enlil himself.

This close relationship between religion and culture, in its various aspects—political, social, economic, and artistic,—is thus the distinguishing mark of the early history of the Euphrates Valley that leaves its impress upon subsequent ages. Intellectual life centres around religious beliefs, both those of popular origin and those developed in schools attached to the temples, in which, as we shall see, speculations of a more theoretical character were unfolded in amplification of popular beliefs.

III

As already pointed out, even in the oldest period to which our material enables us to trace the history of the Euphrates Valley, we witness the conflict for political control between Sumerians and Akkadians (that is between non-Semites and Sem-

---

to affix the sign for deity to their names. Their example is followed by the kings of Ur, Isin, and Larsa, though not by all of them. With the rise of Babylon as the centre of the united states of the Euphrates Valley under Hammurapi (*ca.* 2000 B.C.), the custom appears to have disappeared, probably as a concession to Marduk, whose position as the practical head of the pantheon was jealously guarded by the rulers of Babylon.

ites). Lagash, Nippur, Ur, and Uruk are ancient
Sumerian centres, but near the border-line between the
southern and the northern sections of this valley a
strong political centre is established at Kish, which
foreshadows the growing predominance of the Semites. The rulers sometimes assume the title of
"king," sometimes are known by the more modest
title of "chief,"[1] a variation that suggests frequent
changes of political fortunes. The population is
depicted on the monuments as Sumerian, and yet
among the rulers we find one bearing a distinctly
Semitic name,[2] while some of the inscriptions of the
rulers of Kish are clearly to be read as Semitic, and
not as Sumerian. It is, therefore, not surprising to
find the Semitic kings of Akkad, *circa* 2500 B.C.,
and even before the rise of Kish, reaching a position
of supremacy that extended their rule far into the
south, besides passing to the north, east, and west,
far beyond the confines of Babylonia and Assyria.

There are two names in this dynasty of Akkad with
its centre at Agade that stand forth with special
prominence—Sargon, and his son Naram-Sin. Sar-

[1] Pa-te-si, the Semitic equivalent of which is *ishakku*, literally "the strong one"; it became, however, the designation of
a ruler who was dependent upon some powerful lord. The
Sumerian term is composed of three elements, conveying the
sense of "holding the staff of authority"; it points to the time
when rulership combined priestly with lay functions.

[2] Enbi-Ishtar. See Meyer, *Geschichte des Altertums*, i., 2,
p. 443.

gon[1] in fact marks an epoch in the history of the
Euphrates Valley. He is the first conqueror to in-
augurate a policy of wide conquest that eventually
gave to Babylonia and subsequently to Assyria a
commanding position in the ancient world. While
retaining his capital at Agade, he brings into prominence the neighbouring Sippar by devoting himself
to the service of the sun-god Shamash at that place;
and he either founds or enlarges the city Babylon
which a few centuries later became the capital of the
United Euphrates Valley; its fame was destined to
outlast the memory of all the other centres of the
south, and to become synonymous with the culture
and religion of the entire district. The old enemy of
Sumer on the east, known as Elam, with which
Sumerian rulers had many a conflict, was forced
to yield to the powerful Sargon. Far to the north
the principality of Subartu—the later Assyria—and
still farther north the district known as Guti acknowledged the rule of Sargon and of his successors.
The land to the west up to the Mediterranean coast,
known under the general designation of Amurru,[2]

[1] His fuller name was Shar-gani-sharri. On this form and its
relationship to Sharru-kin (the name of an earlier ruler of Kish)
see King, *History of Sumer and Akkad*, pp. 216–228.

[2] Identical in form with the Biblical Amorite, though the
Amorites in the Old Testament constitute, primarily, the inhabitants of the mountainous district and high plateaus of
northern Palestine and Syria.

Pl. 8. Stele of Naram-Sin, King of Agade (*c.* 2470 B.C.).

It represents the king conquering enemies in a mountainous district. The peak of the mountain is pictured as rising to the stars. Some of the king's foes are fleeing, others are pleading for mercy. Found at Susa, whither it was presumably carried as a trophy by the Elamites in one of their incursions into Babylonia, perhaps by Shutruk-Nakhunte, king of Elam, *c.* 1160 B.C. See *Délégation en Perse Mémoires*, i., pp. 144–158 and Pl. X. and ii., pp. 53–55. Now in the Louvre.

Stele of Naram-Sin, King of Agade
(*c.* 2500 B. C.)

Pl. 9. Bas-Relief of Naram-Sin (basalt).

Found in 1891 near Diarbekr; now in the Imperial Ottoman Museum at Constantinople. It records the victories of the king which he attributes to the aid of Ea, and pronounces curses on any one who destroys or removes this monument of himself. See Scheil and Maspero in *Recueil de Travaux*, vol. xv., pp. 62–66.

Plate 9.   Bas-Relief of Naram-Sin

was also claimed by Sargon. The rulers of Lagash humbly call themselves the "servants" of the powerful conqueror; Cuthah, Uruk, Opis, and Nippur in the south, Babylon and Sippar in the north, are among the centres in the Euphrates Valley, specifically named by Sargon as coming under his sway. He advances to Nippur, and, by assuming the title "King of Akkad and of the Kingdom of Enlil," announces his control of the whole of Sumer and Akkad.

The times must have been ripe for a movement on so large a scale. As so often happens, the political upheaval was followed by a strong intellectual stimulus which shows itself in a striking advance in Art. One of the most remarkable monuments of the Euphrates Valley dates from this period. It depicts Naram-Sin, the son of Sargon, triumphing over Elam; and it seems an irony of fate that this magnificent sculptured stone should have been carried away, centuries later, as a trophy of war by the Elamites in one of their successful incursions into the Euphrates Valley.[1] In triumphant pose Naram-Sin is represented in the act of humiliating the enemy by driving a spear through the prostrate body of a soldier, plead-

[1] Found in the course of the French excavations at Susa under the superintendence of Jacques de Morgan, to which we owe the famous code of Hammurapi, and the superb series of Boundary Stones—all carried to Elam as the booty of war in the 11th century B.C. See de Morgan, Scheil, Gautier, etc., *Delegation en Perse* (10 vols. of *Mémoires* already issued).

ing for mercy. The king wears the cap with the upturned horns that marks him as possessing the attributes of divine power. He continues the conquests of his father, and penetrates even into Arabia,[1] so that he could well lay claim to the high-sounding title which he assumes of "King of the Four Regions."[2] The glory of this extensive kingdom thus established by Sargon and Naram-Sin was, however, of short duration. Agade was obliged, apparently, to yield first to Kish. This happened not long after Naram-Sin's death but, what is more significant, within about two centuries the Sumerians succeeded in regaining their prestige; and with their capital at Ur, an ancient centre of the moon-cult, Sumerian rulers emphasise their sovereignty of both south and north by assuming the title "King of Sumer and Akkad." Ur-Engur, the founder of the dynasty (*ca.* 2300 B.C.), which maintained its sway for 117 years, is the first to assume this title, which, to be sure, is not so grandilo-

[1] Known as Magan, which appears to have been at the time the designation of Eastern Arabia, though the name has not yet been satisfactorily explained. It was from Magan that the hard diorite for statues was obtained by Gudea. See King, *History of Sumer and Akkad*, p. 241 *seq.*

[2] The four regions meant are Akkad, Subartu, Elam, Amurru —representing south, north, east, and west respectively. The term, however, became a general one to convey the idea of universal sway without reference to any particular countries. In the inscriptions of the Assyrian rulers it is replaced by the title *shar kishshati*, which may be rendered by "King of Universal Rule."

quent as that of "King of the Four Regions," but rests on a more substantial foundation. It represents a realm that could be controlled, while a universal empire such as Sargon and Naram-Sin claimed was largely nominal—a dream in which ambitious conquerors from Sargon to Napoleon have indulged, and which could at the most become for a time a terrifying nightmare to the nations of the world.

With Sargon and Ur-Engur we thus enter on a new era. Instead of a rivalry among many centres for political supremacy over the south or the north, we have Semites and Sumerians striving for complete control of the entire valley, with a marked tendency to include within their scope the district to the north of Akkad. This district, as a natural extension consequent upon the spread of the Sumero-Akkadian culture, was eventually to become a separate principality that in time reversed the situation, and began to encroach upon the independence of the Euphrates Valley.

Two new factors begin about this time, and possibly even earlier, to exercise a decided influence in further modifying the Sumero-Akkadian culture; one of these is the Amoritish influence, the other is a conglomeration of peoples collectively known as the Hittites. From the days of Sargon we find frequent traces of the Amorites; and there is at least one deity in the pantheon of this early period who was imported into the Euphrates Valley from the west, the home of the Amorites. This deity was a storm god known as Adad,[1] appearing in Syria and Palestine as Hadad. According to Professor Clay,[2] most of the other prominent members of what eventually became the definitely constituted Babylonian pantheon betray traces of having been subjected to this western influence. Indeed, Professor Clay goes even further and would ascribe many of the parallels between Biblical and Babylonian myths, traditions, customs, and rites to an early influence exerted by Amurru (which he regards as the home of the northern Semites) on Babylonia, and not, as has been hitherto assumed, to a western extension of Babylonian culture and religion. It is too early to pronounce a definite opinion on this interesting and novel thesis; but, granting that Professor Clay has pressed his views beyond legitimate bounds, there can no longer be any doubt that in accounting for the later and for some of the earlier aspects of the Sumero-Akkadian civilisation this factor of Amurru must be taken into account; nor is it at all unlikely that long before the days of Sargon, a wave of migration from the north and north-west to the south

[1] See p. 117 *seq.*

[2] *Amurru, the Home of the Northern Semites* (Philadelphia, 1909), a monograph distinguished for learning and ingenuity, in which the thesis is set forth of a very extensive influence on the religious conceptions, and on the myths of the Euphrates Valley.

and south-east had set in, which brought large bodies of Amorites into the Euphrates Valley as well as into Assyria. The circumstance that, as has been pointed out, the earliest permanent settlements of Semites in the Euphrates Valley appear to be in the northern portion, creates a strong presumption in favour of the view which makes the Semites come into Babylonia from the north-west.[1]

Hittites do not make their appearance in the Euphrates Valley until some centuries after Sargon, but since it now appears[2] that *ca.* 1800 B.C. they had become strong enough to invade the district, and that a Hittite ruler actually occupied the throne of Babylonia for a short period, we are justified in carrying the beginnings of Hittite influence back to the time at least of the Ur dynasty. This conclusion is strengthened by the evidence for an early establishment of a Hittite principality in north-western Mesopotamia, known as Mitanni, which extended its sway as early at least as 2100 B.C. to Assyria proper.

Thanks to the excavations conducted by the German expedition[3] at Kalah-Shergat (the site of the

[1] See above, p. 12, note 1.

[2] See a paper by the writer, "The Hittites in Babylonia," in the *Revue Sémitique*, vol. xviii., pp. 87–96, and Meyer's *Geschichte des Altertums*, i., 2, p. 577.

[3] Results published in the *Mitteilungen der Deutschen Orient-Gesellschaft*, issued at regular intervals of a few months. Since the beginnings of the excavations in 1901, some fifty numbers have been published.

old capital of Assyria known as Ashur), we can now trace the beginnings of Assyria several centuries further back than was possible only a few years ago. The proper names at this earliest period of Assyrian history show a marked Hittite or Mitanni influence in the district, and it is significant that Ushpia, the founder of the most famous and oldest sanctuary in Ashur, bears a Hittite name.[1] The conclusion appears justified that Assyria began her rule as an extension of Hittite control. With a branch of the Hittites firmly established in Assyria as early as *ca.* 2100 B.C., we can now account for an invasion of Babylonia a few centuries later. The Hittites brought their gods with them, as did the Amorites, and, with the gods, religious conceptions peculiarly

---

[1] See Ungnad's interesting discussion in his monograph, "Urkunden aus Dilbat," in the *Beiträge zur Assyriologie*, vol. vi., pp. 8–21. That the Mitanni are a branch of the Hittites is generally admitted; nor is there any longer reason to doubt that the "sons of Heth" from whom Abraham buys the cave of Machpelah (Genesis, chap. xxiii.) are genuine Hittites, who had passed far into the south of Palestine as they had penetrated into the Euphrates Valley. In the 18th century we find the centre of Hittite power in northern Asia Minor with the capital at Boghaz-Keui, where Winckler has found important remains including large numbers of clay tablets. See *Mitteilungen der Deutschen Orient-Gesellschaft*, Nr. 35. This more northern settlement appears to be due to the gradual retreat of the Hittites before the growing power of Semitic Assyria. On explorations in Hittite districts and the general status of our present knowledge about the Hittites, see Garstang, *The Land of the Hittites*, (New York, 1910).

their own. Traces of Hittite influence are to be seen
e.g., in the designs on the seal cylinders, as has been recently shown by Dr. Ward,[1] who, indeed, is inclined to
assign to this influence a share in the religious art, and,
therefore, also in the general culture and religion, much
larger than could have been suspected a decade ago.

Who those Hittites were we do not as yet know.
Probably they represent a motley group of various
peoples, and they may turn out to be Aryans. It is
quite certain that they originated in a mountainous
district, and that they were not Semites. We
should thus have a factor entering into the Babylonian-Assyrian civilisation—leaving its decided traces
in the religion—which was wholly different from the
two chief elements in that civilisation—the Sumerian and the Akkadian.

The Amorites have generally been regarded as
Semites. Professor Clay, we have seen, would regard Amurru as, in fact, the home of a large branch of
the Semites; yet the manner in which the Old Testament contrasts the Canaanites—the old population
of Palestine dispossessed by the invading Hebrews—
with the Amorites, raises the question whether this
contrast does not rest on an ethnic distinction. The
Amoritish type as depicted on Egyptian monuments [2]

---

[1] *Cylinders of Western Asia*, chaps. xxvi and xlii–liv.

[2] See Flinders Petrie, *Types from the Egyptian Monuments*,
London, 1887.

also is distinct from that of the Semitic inhabitants of Palestine and Syria. It is quite within the range of possibility that the Amorites, too, represent another non-Semitic factor further complicating the web of the Sumero-Akkadian culture, though it must also be borne in mind that the Amorites, whatever their original ethnic type may have been, became commingled with Semites, and in later times are not to be distinguished from the Semitic population of Syria.

Leaving these problems regarding Amorites and Hittites aside as not yet ripe for solution, we may content ourselves with a recognition of these two additional factors in the further development of the political and religious history of the Euphrates Valley and of its northern extension known as Assyria.

IV

For some time after Ur-Engur had established a powerful dynasty at Ur, the Sumerians seem to have had everything their own way. His son and successor, Dungi, wages successful wars, like Sargon and Naram-Sin, with the nations around and again assumes the larger title of "King of the Four Regions." He hands over his large realm, comprising Elam on the one side, and extending to Syria on the other, to his son Bur-Sin. We know but few details of the reign of Bur-Sin and of the two other members of the Ur dynasty that followed him, but the indications are that the Sumerian reaction, represented by the advent of the Ur dynasty, though at first apparently complete, is in reality a compromise. Semitic influence waxes stronger from generation to generation, as is shown by the steadily growing preponderance of Semitic words and expressions in Sumerian documents. The Semitic culture of Akkad not only colours that of Sumer, but permeates it so thoroughly as largely to eradicate the still remaining original and unassimilated Sumerian elements. The Sumerian deities as well as the Sumerians themselves adopt the Semitic form of dress.[1] We even find Sumerians bearing Semitic names; and in another century Semitic speech, which we may henceforth designate as Babylonian, became predominant.

On the overthrow of the Ur dynasty the political centre shifts from Ur to Isin. The last king of the Ur dynasty is made a prisoner by the Elamites, who thus again asserted their independence. The title "King of the Four Regions" is discarded by the rulers of Isin, and although they continue to use the title "King of Sumer and Akkad," there are many indications that the supremacy of the Sumerians is steadily on the wane. They were unable to prevent the rise of an independent state with its centre in the city of Babylon under Semitic control, and about the year 2000 B.C., the rulers of that city begin to assume the

[1] See Meyer, *Sumerier und Semiten*, p. 53, *seq.*

title "King of Babylon." The establishment of this so-called first dynasty of Babylon definitely foreshadows the end of Sumerian supremacy in the Euphrates Valley, and the permanent triumph of the Semites. Fifty years afterward we reach another main epoch, in many respects the most important, with the accession of Hammurapi[1] to the throne of Babylon as the sixth member of the dynasty. During his long reign of forty-two years (ca. 1958–1916 B.C.), Hammurapi fairly revolutionised both the political and the religious conditions.

The name of Hammurapi deserves to be emblazoned in letters of gold on the scroll of fame. His predecessors, to be sure, had in part paved the way for him. Availing themselves of the weakness of the south, which had again been split up into a number of independent principalities—Ur, Isin, Larsa, Kish, and Uruk,—they had been successful not only in warding off attacks from the outside upon their own district, but in forcing some of these principalities to temporary subjection. Still, there was much left for Hammurapi to do before he could take the titles "King of Sumer and Akkad" and "King of the Four Regions"; and it was not until the thirtieth year of his reign that, by the successful overthrow of the old-time enemy, Elam, and then of his own and his

[1] This form appears to be more correct than the current Hammurabi.

Pl. 10. Semitic Types.

Fig. 1. Two portraits of Hammurapi, king of Babylonia (*c.* 1958–1916 B.C.) (a) Bas-relief on a clay tablet, recording the homage of a high official Itur-Ashdum to Hammurapi and to the goddess Ashratum—a designation of the consort of the "Amorite" deity Adad. Now in the British Museum. See King, *Letters and Inscriptions of Hammurabi*, vol. iii. Frontispiece and pp. 194–196. (b) From the design at the head of the famous Code of Hammurapi. (See Pl. 34.)

Fig. 2. Assyrian Type.

Found by Layard at Nimroud and designated by him as the head of a winged figure. See Layard, *Monuments of Nineveh*, i., Pl. 92.

Semitic Types
Fig. 1. Two Portraits of Hammurapi, King of Babylonia
(*c.* 1958–1916 B. C.)

Fig. 2. Assyrian Type

father's formidable rival Rim-Sin, the king of Larsa, he could claim to be the absolute master of the entire Euphrates Valley, and of the adjoining Elam.[1] After that, he directed his attention to the north and north-west, and before the end of his reign his dominion embraced Assyria, and extended to the heart of the Hittite domain in the north-west. But Hammurapi is far more than a mere conqueror. He is the founder of a real empire—welding north and south into a genuine union, which outlasts the vicissitudes of time for almost fifteen hundred years. The permanent character of his work is due in part at least to the fact that he is not only "the mighty king, the king of Babylon," but also "the king of righteousness," as he calls himself, devoted to promoting the welfare of his subjects, and actuated by the ambition that every one who had a just cause should come to him as a son to a father. He establishes the unity of the country on a firm basis by the codification of the existing laws and by a formal promulgation of this code throughout his empire as the authoritative and recognised guide in government. The importance of this step can hardly be overestimated. If from this time on we speak of a Babylonian empire which,

[1] For a survey of the political history of Babylonia during the first dynasty of Babylon, we now have Dr. Arno Poebel's excellent sketch, based on a renewed study of the period, in his work *Legal and Business Documents from the Time of the First Dynasty of Babylon* (Philadelphia, 1909), pp. 113–122.

despite frequent changes of dynasties, despite a control of Babylonia for over half a millennium (*ca.* 1750–1175 B.C.), by a foreign people known as the Cassites, survived with its identity clearly marked, down to the taking of Babylon by Cyrus in 539 B.C., and in some measure even to the advent of Alexander the Great in 331 B.C.,—it is due, in the first instance, to the unifying power exerted by Hammurapi's code, the fortunate discovery of which in 1891[1] has contributed so much to our knowledge of the conditions of culture and religion in ancient Babylonia. It is no exaggeration to say that this code created the Babylonian people, just as, about six centuries later, the great leader Moses formed the Hebrew nation out of heterogeneous elements by giving them a body of laws, civil and religious.[2]

[1] Found at Susa (see above, p. 23 note 1), and first published in 1894 with a transliteration and translation by Professor Vincent Scheil of Paris. Since then various translations have appeared in English and German, the latest and most correct being the one by Kohler and Ungnad, *Hammurabi's Gesetz* (Leipzig, 1909). A convenient form in English is C. H. W. Johns' *Oldest Code of Laws in the World* (Edinburgh, 1903); a more complete edition is that of R. F. Harper, *The Code of Hammurabi* (University of Chicago, 1904), though both Johns' and Harper's renderings require correction now in many particulars. See Plate 34 for an illustration of the monument.

[2] While none of the codes now distinguished in the Pentateuch go back to the days of Moses, there are regulations in all of them that can be traced back to the beginnings of the Hebrew nation; and it seems to my mind a reasonable inference that the tradition which assumes Moses to have been a lawgiver rests

The code established a bond of union between Sumer and Akkad of a character far more binding than could be brought about by the mere subjection of the south to the north.   Through this code whatever distinctions still existed between Sumerians and Akkadians were gradually wiped out.   From the time of Hammurapi on, we are justified in speaking of Babylonians, and no longer of Sumerians and Akkadians.

The code illustrates in a striking manner the close relationship between culture and religion in the Euphrates Valley which forms our main theme in this lecture.   The eloquent introduction will illustrate the spirit that pervades it:

When the supreme Anu, king of the Annunaki, and Enlil, the lord of heaven and earth, who fixes the destiny of the land, had committed to Marduk, the first-born of Ea, the rule of all mankind, making him great among the Igigi, gave to Babylon his supreme name, making it pre-eminent in the regions (of the world), and established therein an enduring kingdom, firm in its foundation like heaven and earth—at that time they appointed me, Hammurapi, the exalted ruler, the one who fears the gods, to let justice shine in the land, to destroy the wicked and unjust that the strong should not oppress the weak, that I should go forth like the sun over mankind.

Hammurapi then passes on to an enumeration of all that he did for the various cities of his realm—for Nippur, Durilu, Eridu, Babylon, Ur, Sippar, Larsa,

---

on a sound basis, even though it is no longer possible to reconstruct the code that he compiled for the government of his people.

Uruk, Isin, Kish, Cuthah, Borsippa, Dilbat, Lagash, Adab, Agade, Nineveh, and the distant Hallab.[1] It is significant that he refers to his conquests only incidentally, and lays the chief stress upon what he did for the gods and for men, enumerating the temples that he built and beautified, the security that he obtained for his subjects, the protection that he granted to those in need of aid. "Law and justice," he concludes, "I established in the land and promoted the well-being of the people."[2]

The religious and ethical spirit is thus the impelling power of the most important accomplishment in Hammurapi's career; and the interdependence of culture and religion finds another striking illustration in the changed aspect that the pantheon and the cult assumed after the period of Hammurapi. He names at the beginning of his code the two deities, Anu and Enlil. Both were, originally, local gods, Anu the patron deity of Uruk, Enlil the chief deity of Nippur. Through a process that will be set forth in detail in the next lecture, Anu and Enlil became in the course of time abstractions, summing up, as it were, the chief manifestations of divine power in the universe. Anu, from being originally a personification of the sun, becomes the god of heaven, while Enlil,

[1] The modern Aleppo.

[2] The code itself will be more fully discussed in the last lecture as an illustration of the ethics of the Babylonians and Assyrians.

starting out as a storm-god, takes on as the theoretical head of the pantheon the traits of other gods, and becomes the god in control of the earth and of the regions immediately above it. The two therefore stand for heaven and earth, and to them there is joined, as a third member, Ea. Originally, the local deity of another ancient centre (Eridu, on or nearby the Persian Gulf[1]) and a god of the water, Ea became the symbol of the watery element in general. Anu, Enlil, Ea, presiding over the universe, are supreme over all the lower gods and spirits combined as Annunaki and Igigi, but they entrust the practical direction of the universe to Marduk, the god of Babylon. He is the first-born of Ea, and to him as the worthiest and fittest for the task, Anu and Enlil voluntarily commit universal rule. This recognition of Marduk by the three deities, who represent the three divisions of the universe—heaven, earth, and all waters,—marks the profound religious change that was brought about through the advance of Marduk to a commanding position among the gods. From being a personification of the sun with its cult localised in the city of Babylon, over whose destinies he presides, he comes to be recognised as leader and director of the great Triad. Corresponding, therefore, to the political predominance

[1] Owing to the steady accumulation of soil, Eridu is at present some ninety miles inland.

attained by the city of Babylon as the capital of
the united empire, and as a direct consequence thereof, the patron of the political centre becomes the
head of the pantheon to whom gods and mankind alike pay homage. The new order must not,
however, be regarded as a break with the past, for
Marduk is pictured as assuming the headship of the
pantheon by the grace of the gods, as the legitimate
heir of Anu, Enlil, and Ea. There are also ascribed
to him the attributes and powers of all the other great
gods, of Ninib, Shamash, and Nergal, the three chief
solar deities, of Sin the moon-god, of Ea and Nebo,
the chief water deities, of Adad, the storm-god, and
especially of the ancient Enlil of Nippur. He becomes like Enlil "the lord of the lands," and is known
pre-eminently as the *bêl* or "lord." Addressed
in terms which emphatically convey the impression that he is the one and only god, whatever
tendencies toward a true monotheism are developed in the Euphrates Valley, all cluster about
him. The cult undergoes a correspondingly profound change. Hymns, originally composed in
honour of Enlil and Ea, are transferred to Marduk.
At Nippur, as we shall see,[1] there developed an
elaborate lamentation ritual for the occasions when
national catastrophes, defeat, failure of crops, destructive storms, and pestilence revealed the dis-

[1] See p. 321, *seq*. V.

pleasure and anger of the gods. At such times earnest endeavours were made, through petitions, accompanied by fasting and other symbols of contrition, to bring about a reconciliation with the angered Powers. This ritual, owing to the religious pre-eminence of Nippur, became the norm and standard throughout the Euphrates Valley, so that when Marduk and Babylon came practically to replace Enlil and Nippur, the formulas and appeals were transferred to the solar deity of Babylon, who representing more particularly the sun-god of spring, was well adapted to be viewed as the one to bring blessing and favours after the sorrows and tribulations of the stormy season, which had bowed the country low. Just as the lamentation ritual of Nippur became the model to be followed elsewhere, so at Eridu, the seat of the cult of Ea, the water deity, an elaborate incantation ritual was developed in the course of time, consisting of sacred formulas, accompanied by symbolical rites for the purpose of exorcising the demons that were believed to be the causes of disease and of releasing those who had fallen under the power of sorcerers.[1] The close association between Ea and Marduk (the cult of the latter, as will be subsequently shown,[2] having been transferred from Eridu to Babylon), led to the spread of this incantation ritual to other parts of the Euphrates Valley. It was adopted

[1] See p. 312, *seq.* V.   [2] See p. 93.

as part of the Marduk cult and, as a consequence, the share taken by Ea therein was transferred to the god of Babylon. This adoption, again, was not in the form of a violent usurpation by Marduk of functions not belonging to him, but as a transfer willingly made by Ea to Marduk, as his son.

In like manner, myths originally told of Enlil of Nippur, of Anu of Uruk, and of Ea of Eridu, were harmoniously combined, and the part of the hero and conqueror assigned to Marduk. Prominent among these myths was the story of the conquest of the winter storms, pictured as chaos preceding the reign of law and order in the universe. In each of the chief centres the character of creator was attributed to the patron deity, thus in Nippur to Enlil, in Uruk to Anu, and in Eridu to Ea. The deeds of these gods were combined into a tale picturing the steps leading to the gradual establishment of order out of chaos, with Marduk as the one to whom the other gods entrusted the difficult task. Marduk is celebrated as the victor over Tiamat—a monster symbolising primeval chaos.[1] In celebration of his triumph all the gods assemble in solemn state, and address him by fifty names,—a procedure which in ancient phraseology means the transfer of all the attributes involved in these names. The name is the essence, and each name spells additional

[1] See also below p. 100 *seq.*

power. Anu hails Marduk as "mightiest of the gods," and, finally, Enlil and Ea step forward and declare that their own names shall henceforth be given to Marduk. "His name," says Ea, "shall be Ea as mine," and so once more the power of the son is confirmed by the father.

V

There is only one rival to Marduk in the later periods, and he is Ashur, who, from being the patron deity of the ancient capital of the Assyrian empire, rises to the rank of the chief deity of the warlike Assyrians. It is just about the time of Hammurapi that Assyria begins to loom into prominence. It was at first merely an extension of Babylonia towards the north with a strong admixture of Hittite and also Amoritish elements, and then a more or less dependent province; later its *patesis* exchanged the more modest title, with its religious implication,[1] for *sharru*, "king," and acquired a practically independent position at the beginning of the second millennium before this era. Within a few centuries, the Assyrians became formidable rivals to their southern cousins.

The first result of the rise of Assyria was to limit the further extension of Babylonia. The successors of Hammurapi, partly under the influence of the

[1] See above p. 21, note 1.

loftier spirit which he had introduced into the country during the closing years of his reign, partly under the stress of necessity, became promoters of peace. Instead of further territorial expansion we find the growth of commerce, which, however, did not hinder Babylonia itself from becoming a prey to a conquering nation that came (as did the Sumerians) from the mountainous regions on the east. Native rulers are replaced by Cassites who, as we have already indicated, retain control of the Euphrates Valley for more than half a millennium. It is significant of the strength which Assyria had meanwhile acquired, that it held the Cassites in check. Alliances between Assyrians and Cassites alternated with conflicts in which, on the whole, the Assyrians gained a steady advantage. But the Assyrian empire also had its varying fortunes before it assumed, in the 12th century, a position of decided superiority over the south. The chief adversaries of the Assyarian rulers were the Hittite groups, who continued to maintain a strong kingdom in north-western Mesopotamia. In addition, there were other groups farther north in the mountain recesses of Asia Minor, which from time to time made serious inroads on Assyria, abetted no doubt by the Hittites or by the Mitanni elements in Assyria, which had probably not been entirely absorbed as yet by the Semitic Assyrians.

As a counterpart to Sargon in the south, we have

Tiglathpileser I. in the north (*ca.* 1130–1100 B.C.). He succeeded in quelling the opposition of the Hittites, carried his triumphant arms to the Mediterranean coast, entered into relations with Egypt, as some of the Cassite rulers had done centuries before, and for a time held in check Babylonia, now again ruled by native kings. Like Sargon's conquests, the glory of the new empire of Tiglath-pileser was of short duration. Even before his death there were indications of threatened trouble. For about two centuries Assyria was partially eclipsed, after which the kings of Assyria, supported by large standing armies,[1] bear, without interruption till the fall of Nineveh in 606 B.C., the proud title of "King of Universal Rule," which, as we have seen,[2] took the place of the Babylonian "King of the Four Regions." Though "Aramæan" hordes (perhaps identical with Amorites, or a special branch of the latter) continue to give Assyrian rulers, from time to time, considerable trouble, they are, however, held in check until in the reign of Ashurnasirpal (884–860 B.C.) their power is effectually broken. This energetic ruler and his successors push on to the north and north-west into the indefinite district known as Nairi, as well as to the west and south-west. Once

---

[1] See on the organisation of the Assyrian army, Walther Manitius in *Zeitschrift für Assyriologie*, vol. xxiv. (two articles).

[2] See p. 24, note 2.

more the Mediterranean coast is reached, and at a pass on the Nahr-el-Kelb (the "Dog" river) outside of Beirut, Ashurnasirpal and his son Shalmaneser II. (860–824 B.C.) set up images of themselves with records of their achievements.[1]

We are reaching the period when Assyria begins to interfere with the internal affairs of the Hebrew kingdoms in Palestine. Another century, and the northern kingdom (722 B.C.) falls a prey to Assyria's insatiable greed of empire. Babylonia, reduced to playing the ignoble part of fomenting trouble for Assyria, succeeds in keeping Assyrian armies well occupied, and so wards off the time of her own humiliation. Compelled to acknowledge the superiority of her northern rival in various ways, Babylonia exhausts the patience of Assyrian rulers, to whose credit it must be said that they endeavoured to make their yoke as light as was consistent with their dignity. The consideration that rulers like Sargon of Assyria (721–705 B.C.) showed for the time-honoured prestige of the south was repaid by frequent attempts to throw off the hated yoke, light though it was. Sennacherib (705–681 B.C.) determines upon a more aggressive policy, and at last in 689 B.C., Babylon is taken and mercilessly destroyed. Sen-

[1] See the valuable monograph of Winckler, *Das Vorgebilde am Nahr-el-Kalb* (Leipzig, 1909), with a complete account of the records of Egyptian, Assyrian, and Babylonian rulers on this historic site.

Pl. 11. Sargon, King of Assyria (721–705 B.C.), with attendant, presumably one of his chief officers. From the king's palace at Khorsabad, and now in the Louvre. See Botta et Flandin, *Monument de Ninive*, i., Pl. 12.

Sargon, King of Assyria (721–705 B. C.) with High Official

nacherib boasts of the thoroughness with which he carried out the work of destruction. He pillaged the city of its treasures. He besieged and captured all the larger cities of the south—Sippar, Uruk, Cuthah, Kish, and Nippur—and when, a few years later, the south organised another revolt, the king, to show his power, put Babylon under water, and thus obliterated almost all vestiges of the past. The excavations at Babylon[1] carried on by the German expedition show how truthfully Sennacherib described his work of destruction; few traces of the older Babylon have been revealed by the spade of the explorer. What is found dates chiefly from the time of the Neo-Babylonian dynasty, and particularly from the days of Nebuchadnezzar, who, as the restorer of the past glory of the capital, is justified in boasting, as in the Book of Daniel, "Is not this great Babylon that I have built!"[2] Babylonia, however, had the satisfaction of surviving Assyria. By a combination of hordes from the north with Medes of the south-east,—the latter abetted no doubt by Babylonia,—Nineveh is taken in 606 B.C., and the haughty Assyrian power is crushed for ever. Shortly before the end, however, Assyria witnessed the most brilliant reign in her history—that of Ashurbanapal (668–626 B.C.)

[1] *Mitteilungen der Deutschen Orient-Gesellschaft*, especially Nos. 1–13.

[2] Dan. iv., 27 (verse 30 in the English Version).

—the Sardanapalus of Greek tradition—who was destined to realise the dreams of his predecessors, Sargon, Sennacherib, and Esarhaddon; of whom all four had been fired with the ambition to make Assyria the mistress of the world. Their reigns were spent in carrying on incessant warfare in all directions. During Ashurbanapal's long reign, Babylonia endured the humiliation of being governed by Assyrian princes. The Hittites no longer dared to organise revolt, Phœnicia and Palestine acknowledged the sway of Assyria, and the lands to the east and northeast were kept in submission. From Susa, the capital of Elam, Ashurbanapal carried back in triumph a statue of Nanâ,—the Ishtar of Uruk,—which had been captured over 1600 years before, and—greatest triumph of all—the Assyrian standards were planted on the banks of the Nile, though the control of Egypt, as was soon shown, was more nominal than real.

Thus the seed of dominating imperialism, planted by the old Sargon of Agade, had borne fruit. But the spirit of Hammurapi, too, hovered over Assyria. Ashurbanapal was more than a conqueror. Like Hammurapi, he was a promoter of culture and learning. It is to him that we owe practically all that has been preserved of the literature produced in Babylonia. Recognising that the greatness of the south lay in her intellectual prowess, in the civilisation achieved by her and transferred to Assyria, he sent

Pl. 12. Esarhaddon, King of Assyria (680–669 B.C.).

Before the king are two royal prisoners, Tirhaka, the King of Ethiopia, and Ba'alu the King of Tyre. To emphasise his greatness in contrast to the insignificance of his enemies, the king portrays himself as of commanding stature. At the head of the stone, the emblems of the great gods of Assyria, Ashur, Sin, Shamash, Ishtar, Marduk, Nebo, Ea, Ninib, and Sibitti (seven circles), with Ashur, Ishtar of Nineveh, Enlil, and Adad standing on animals. Diorite stele found at Sendschirli in Northwestern Syria. Now in the Royal Museum of Berlin. See Luschan, *Ausgrabungen in Sendschirli* (Berlin, 1893), pp. 11–43.

Esarhaddon, King of Assyria (680–
669 B.C.) with two Royal Prisoners

scribes to the archives, gathered in the temple-schools of the south, and had copies made of the extensive collections of omens, oracles, hymns, incantations, medical series, legends, myths, and religious rituals of all kinds that had accumulated in the course of many ages. Only a portion, alas! of the library has been recovered through the excavations of Layard and Rassam (1849–1854) and their successors on the site of Ashurbanapal's palace at Nineveh in which the great collection was stored.[1] About 20,000 fragments of clay bricks have found their way to the British Museum, but it is safe to say that this represents less than one half of the extent of the great library which Ashurbanapal had accumulated. His immediate purpose in doing so was to emphasise by an unmistakable act that Assyria had assumed the position of Babylonia, not only as an imperial power and as a stronghold of culture, but also as the great religious centre. The bulk, nay, practically, the whole of the literature of Babylonia was of a religious character, or touched religion and religious beliefs and customs at some point, in accord with the close

[1] In the mound Kouyunjik, opposite the modern Mosul. See, besides the account in Layard's *Babylon and Nineveh* (London, 1853), chap. xvi., and Rassam's *Asshur* (London, 1897), pp. 31 *seq.*, Menant, *La Bibliothèque du Palais de Ninive* (Paris, 1880), Bezold's *Introduction to the Catalogue of the Kouyunjik Collection*, vol. v. (London, 1899), and Hilprecht, *Explorations in Bible Lands*, pp. 121–123.

bond between religion and culture which, we have seen,
was so characteristic a feature of the Euphratean
civilisation. The old centres of religion and culture,
like Nippur, Sippar, Cuthah, Uruk, and Ur, had
retained much of their importance, despite the centralising influence of the capital of the Babylonian
empire. Hammurapi and his successors had endeavoured, as we have seen, to give to Marduk the
attributes of the other great gods, Enlil, Anu, Ea,
Shamash, Adad, and Sin, and, to emphasise it, had
placed shrines to these gods and others in the great
temples of Marduk, and of his close associate, Nebo,
in Babylon, and in the neighbouring Borsippa.[1]
Along with this policy went, also, a centralising tendency in the cult and, as a consequence, the rituals,
omens, and incantations produced in the older centres
were transferred to Babylon and combined with the
indigenous features of the Marduk cult.[2] Yet this
process of gathering in one place the literary remains
of the past had never been fully carried out. It was
left for Ashurbanapal to harvest within his palace the
silent witnesses to the glory of these older centres.
While Babylon and Borsippa constituted the chief
sources whence came the copies that he had prepared
for the royal library, internal evidence shows that he

[1] Opposite Babylon.

[2] For further details the reader is referred to a paper by the
writer, " Did the Babylonian Temples have Libraries?"
Journal of the American Oriental Society, vol. xxvii., pp. 147–182.

Pl. 13. Ashurbanapal, King of Assyria, (668–626 B.C.) with his Queen in the
Garden of the Palace at Nineveh.

Alabaster slab, found by Layard at Kouyunjik in Ashurbanapal's
palace. Now in the British Museum. See Mansell, "British
Museum Photographs," Part III. (*Assyrian Sculptures*), No. 522
B and C.

Ashurbanapal, King of Assyria (668–626 B. C.) with his Queen in the Garden
of the Palace at Nineveh

also gathered the literary treasures of other centres, such as Sippar, Nippur, Uruk. The great bulk of the religious literature in Ashurbanapal's library represents copies or editions of omen-series, incantation-rituals, myths, legends, and collections of prayers, made for the temple-schools, where the candidates for the various branches of the priesthood received their training. Hence we find supplemental to the literature proper, the pedagogical apparatus of those days—lists of signs, grammatical exercises, analyses of texts, texts with commentaries, and commentaries on texts, specimen texts, and school extracts, and pupils' exercises. The temple school appears to have been the depository in each centre of the religious texts that served a purely practical purpose, as handbooks and guides in the cult. Purely literary collections were not made in the south, not even in the temples of Babylon and Borsippa, in which the more comprehensive character of the religious texts was merely a consequence of the centralising tendency in the cult, and, therefore, likewise prompted by purely practical motives and needs. There are no temple libraries in any proper sense of the word, either in Babylonia or in Assyria. Ashurbanapal is the first genuine collector of the literature of the past, and it is significant that he places the library which he gathered, in his palace and not in a temple. Had there been temple libraries in the south, he would un-

4

doubtedly have placed the royal library in the chief temple of Ashur—as his homage to the patron deity of Assyria and the protector of her armies.

At the same time, by transferring the literature of all the important religious centres of the south to his royal residence in Nineveh, Ashurbanapal clearly intended to give an unmistakable indication of his desire to make Nineveh the intellectual and religious as well as the political capital. His dream was not that of the Hebrew prophets who hoped for the day when from Zion would proceed the law and light for the entire world, when all nations would come to Jerusalem to pay homage to Jahweh, but his ambition partook somewhat of this character, limited only by his narrower religious horizon which shut him in. For Ashurbanapal, Nineveh was to be a gathering place of all the gods and goddesses of the world grouped around Ashur, just as courtiers surround a monarch whose sway all acknowledge. To gather in his capital the texts that had grown up around the homage paid in the past to these gods and goddesses in their respective centres, was his method of giving expression to his hope of centralising the worship of these deities around the great figure of Ashur. Ashurbanapal's policy, thus, illustrates again the continued strength of the bond between culture and religion, despite the fact that in its external form the bond appeared political rather than intellectual.

The king's ambition, however, had its idealistic
side which must not be overlooked. The god Ashur
was in some respects well adapted to become the emblem of centralised divine power, as well as of political
centralisation. The symbol of the god was not, as
was the case with other deities, an image in human
shape, but a disc from which rays or wings proceed, a
reminder, to be sure, that Ashur was in his origin
a solar deity,[1] yet sufficiently abstract and imper-
sonal to lead men's thoughts away from the purely
naturalistic or animistic conceptions connected with
Ashur. This symbol[2] appears above the images of the
kings on the monuments which they erected to themselves. It hovers over the pictures of the Assyrian
armies on their march against their enemies. It was
carried into the battle as a sacred *palladium*—a
symbol of the presence of the gods as an irresistible
ally of the royal armies; and the kings never fail to
ascribe to the support of Ashur the victories that
crowned their efforts.

Professor Sayce[3] has properly emphasised the influence of this imageless worship of the chief deity on
the development of religious ideas in Assyria. Dependent as Assyria was to a large extent upon Babylonia for her culture, her art, and her religion, she

---

[1] See p. 121.   [2] See Plate 18.
[3] *The Religions of Ancient Egypt and Babylonia* (Gifford Lectures), pp. 369-372.

made at least one important contribution to what she adopted from the south, in giving to Ashur a more spiritual type, as it were, than Enlil, Ninib, Shamash, Nergal, Anu, Ea, Marduk, or Nebo could ever claim. On the other hand, the limitation in the development of this more spiritual conception of divine power is marked by the disfiguring addition, to the winged disc, of the picture of a man with a bow and arrow within the circle.[1] It was the emblem of the military genius of Assyria. The old solar deity as the protector of the Assyrian armies had become essentially a god of war, and the royal warriors could not resist the temptation to emphasise by a direct appeal to the eyes the perfect accord between the god and his subjects. This despiritualisation of the winged disc no doubt acted as a check on a conceivable growth of Ashur, which might have tended under more favourable circumstances towards a purer monotheistic conception of the divine government of the universe; for in his case the transference of the attributes of all the other great gods was more fully carried out than in the case of Marduk.[2] In his capacity as a solar deity, Ashur absorbs the character of all other localised sun-gods. Myths in which

[1] Frequently on the Assyrian monuments; see Mansell, British Museum Photographs (Assyria), Nos. 391, 394, 398, etc. Also on seal cylinders, e.g., Ward, *Seal Cylinders of Western Asia*, pp. 224, 227, etc.

[2] See above, p. 40.

Ninib, Enlil, Ea, and Marduk appear as heroes are remodelled under Assyrian influence and transferred to Ashur. We have traces of an Assyrian myth of creation in which the sphere of creator is given to Ashur.[1] Ishtar, the great goddess of fertility, the mother-goddess presiding over births, becomes Ashur's consort. The cult of the other great gods, of Shamash, Ninib, Nergal, Sin, Ea, Marduk, and even Enlil, is maintained in full vigour in the city of Ashur, and in the subsequent capital Nineveh,[2] but these as well as other gods take on, as it were, the colour of Ashur. They give the impression of little Ashurs by the side of the great one, so entirely does the older solar deity, as the guardian of mighty Assyrian armies, and as the embodiment of Assyria's martial spirit, overshadow all other manifestations of divine power. This aspect of Ashur receives its most perfect expression during the reign of the four rulers—Sargon, Sennacherib, Esarhaddon, and Ashurbanapal—when Assyrian power reached its highest point. The success of the Assyrian armies, and consequent political aggrandisement served to increase the glory of Ashur, to whose protection and aid everything was ascribed—but it is Ashur the war-god, the warrior

---

[1] Jastrow, *Religion of Babylonia and Assyria*, p. 197 *seq.*

[2] Until the end of the 8th century B.C., with some interruptions during which Calah was the official residence, Ashur remained the capital.

with bow and arrow within the solar circle, who gains in prestige thereby, while the spiritual phase of the deity as symbolised by the winged disc sinks into the background.

For all this, culture and religion go hand in hand with political and material growth, and the Euphratean civilisation with its Assyrian upper layer reaches its zenith in the reign and achievements of Ashurbanapal. From the remains of his edifices with their pictorial embellishment of elaborate sculptures on the soft limestone slabs that lined the walls of palaces and temples, we can reconstruct the architecture and art of the entire historical period from the remote past to his own days; and through the contents of the library of clay tablets we can trace the unfolding of culture from the days of Sargon, Gudea, and Hammurapi, through the sway of the Cassites, and the later native dynasties down to the time when the leadership passes for ever into the hands of the cruder but more energetic and fearless Assyrians. The figure of Ashurbanapal rises before us as the heir of all the ages—the embodiment of the genius of the Babylonian-Assyrian civilisation, with its strength and its weaknesses, its spiritual force and its materialistic form.

After the death of Ashurbanapal in 626 B.C., the decline sets in and proceeds so rapidly as to suggest that the brilliancy of his reign was merely the last flicker of a flame whose power was spent—an artificial effort to gather the remaining strength in the hopeless endeavour to stimulate the vitality of the empire, exhausted by the incessant wars of the past centuries. Babylonia survived her northern rival for two reasons. Forced by the superior military power of Assyria to a policy of political inaction or of fomenting trouble for Assyria among the nations that were compelled to submit to her control, Babylonia did not engage in expeditions for conquest, which eventually weaken the conqueror more than the conquered. Instead of war, commerce became the main occupation of the inhabitants of the south. Through the spread of its products and wares, its culture, art, and religious influence were extended in all directions. The more substantial character of the southern civilisation, the result of an uninterrupted development for many centuries, and not, as in the case of Assyria, a somewhat artificial albeit successful graft, lent to Babylonia a certain stability, and provided her with a reserve force, which enabled her to withstand the loss of a great share of her political independence. After the fall of Assyria, there came to the fore a district of the Euphrates Valley in the extreme south—known as Chaldea—which had always maintained a certain measure of its independence, even during the period of strongest union among the Euphratean states, and not infrequently had given the rulers of Babylon considerable trouble. The Babylonian empire was also shaken by the blow which brought Assyria to the ground. The Assyrian yoke, to be sure, was thrown off; but in the confusion which ensued, a Chaldean general, Nabopolassar, took advantage of it to make himself the political master of the Euphrates Valley. [1] By means of a treaty of alliance with Elam to the east, Nabopolassar maintained himself on the throne for twenty years, and on his death in 604 B.C., his crown descended to his son—the famous Nebuchadnezzar. Having won his spurs as a general during a military expedition against Egypt, which took place before his father's death, Nebuchadnezzar was seized with the ambition to found a world-wide empire—a dream which had proved fatal to Assyria. Palestine and Syria were conquered by him, and Egypt humbled, but the last years of his reign were devoted chiefly to building up Babylon, Borsippa, and Sippar in the hope of restoring the ancient grandeur of those political and religious centres.

On Babylon his chief efforts were concentrated; the marvellous constructions to which it owes its eminence in tradition and legend were his achievement. It was he who erected the famous "Hanging Gardens,"

[1] Because this neo-Babylonian dynasty was of Chaldean origin, the term Chaldea became the designation of the Euphrates Valley in Greek and Roman writers. The term is obviously a misnomer, and is now generally replaced by Babylonia, which, as we have seen, is itself a later substitute for Sumer and Akkad.

a series of raised terraces covered with various kinds of foliage, and enumerated among the "Seven Wonders of the World." A sacred street for processions was built by him leading from the temple of Marduk through the city and across the river to Borsippa— the seat of the cult of Nebo, whose close association with Marduk is symbolised by their relationship of son and father. This street, along which on solemn occasions the gods were carried in procession, was lined with magnificent glazed coloured tiles, the designs on which were lions of almost life size, as the symbol of Marduk.[1] The workmanship belongs to the best era of Euphratean art. The high towers known as Zikkurats,[2] attached to the chief temples at Babylon and Borsippa, were rebuilt by him and carried to a height greater than ever. By erecting and beautifying shrines to all the chief deities within the precincts of Marduk's temple, and thus enlarging the sacred area once more to the dimensions of a precinct of the city, he wished to emphasise the commanding position of Marduk in the pantheon. In this way, he gave a final illustration of how indissolubly religious interests were bound up with political aggrandisement.

[1] See Plate 30, Fig. 1; and also Bezold, *Kulturwelt des Alten Orients* (Leipzig, 1910), p. 48, and the writer's article, "The Palace and Temple of Nebuchadnezzar," in *Harper's Magazine* for April, 1902.

[2] See p. 282 *seq.*

The impression, so clearly stamped upon the earliest Euphratean civilisation,—the close bond between culture and religion,—thus marks with equal sharpness the last scene in her eventful history. In Nebuchadnezzar's days, as in those of Sargon and Hammurapi, religion lay at the basis of Babylonia's intellectual achievements. The priests attached to the service of the gods continued to be the teachers and guides of the people. The system of education that grew up around the temples was maintained till the end of the neo-Babylonian empire, and even for a time survived its fall. The temple-schools as integral parts of the priestly organisation had given rise to such sciences as were then cultivated—astronomy, medicine, and jurisprudence. All were either attached directly to religious beliefs, as medicine to incantations, astronomy to astrology, jurisprudence to divine oracles, or were so harmoniously bound up with the beliefs as almost to obscure the more purely secular aspects of these mental disciplines. The priests continued to be the physicians, judges, and scribes. Medicinal remedies were prescribed with incantations and ritualistic accompaniments. The study of the heavens, despite considerable advance in the knowledge of the movements of the sun, moon, and planets, continued to be cultivated for the purpose of securing, by means of observations, omens that might furnish a clue to the intention and temper of the gods.

On the death of Nebuchadnezzar, in 561 B.C., the decline of the neo-Babylonian empire sets in and proceeds rapidly, as in Assyria the decline began after the death of her *grand monarque*. Internal dissensions and rivalries among the priests of Babylon and Sippar divided the land. The glory of the Chaldean revival was of short duration, and in the year 539 B.C., Nabonnedos, the last native king of Babylon, was forced to yield to the new power coming from Elam. It was the same old enemy of the Euphrates Valley, only in a new garb, that appeared when Cyrus stood before the gates of Babylon. Nabonnedos gave the weight of his influence to the priestly party of Sippar. In revenge, the priests of Babylon abetted the advance of Cyrus who was hailed by them as the deliverer of Marduk. With scarcely an attempt at resistance, the capital yielded, and Cyrus marched in triumph to the temple of Marduk. The great change had come so nearly imperceptibly that men hardly realised that with Cyrus on the throne of Babylon a new era was ushered in. In the wake of Cyrus came a new force in culture, accompanied by a religious faith that, in contrast to the Babylonian-Assyrian polytheism with its elaborate cult and ritual, appeared rationalistic—almost coldly rationalistic. Far more important than the change of government from Chaldean to Persian control of the Euphrates Valley and of its dependencies was the conquest of the old Babylonian religion by Mazdeism or Zoroastrianism, which, though it did not become the official cult, deprived the worship of Marduk, Nebo, Shamash, and the other gods of much of its vitality.

With its assertion of a single great power for good as the monarch of the universe, Zoroastrianism approached closely the system of Hebrew monotheism, as unfolded under the inspiration of the Hebrew prophets. There was only one attribute which the god of Zoroastrianism, known as Ahura-Mazda, did not possess. He was all-wise, all-good, but not all-powerful, or rather not yet all-powerful. Opposing the power of light there was the power of darkness and evil which could only after the lapse of æons be overcome by Ahura-Mazda. But this personification of evil as a god, Ahriman, was merely the Zoroastrian form of the solution of a problem which has been a stumbling-block to all advanced and spiritualised religions:—the undeniable existence of evil in the world. The chief power of the universe conceived of as beneficent could not also be the cause of evil. It is the problem that underlies the discussions in the Book of Job, the philosophical author of which could not content himself with the conventional view that evil is in all cases a punishment for sins, since suffering so frequently was inflicted on the innocent, while the guilty escaped. The Book of Job leaves the question open, and intimates that it is an insoluble mystery. Zoroastrianism admits that the good cannot be the cause of the evil, but the aim of the good is to overcome evil and eventually it will be able to do so. The dualism of Zoroastrianism is merely a temporary compromise, and, essentially, it is monotheistic.[1]

Zoroastrianism recognised the reign of inexorable though inscrutable law in the world, and when it began to exercise its influence on Babylonia, the belief in gods acting according to caprice was bound to be seriously affected. So it happened that although the culture of Babylonia and Assyria survived the fall of Nineveh and Babylon, and for many centuries continued to exercise its sway far beyond its natural boundaries, the religion, while formally maintained in the old centres, gradually decayed. The new spiritual force that had entered the country effectually dissolved the long-existing bond between culture and religion. The profound change of spirit brought about through the advent of Zoroastrianism is illustrated by the rise of a genuine science of astron-

---

[1] Though lying beyond the scope of our immediate subject, it may not be out of place to emphasise the influence of Zoroastrianism in leading to the establishment of the monotheism of the Jewish prophets. The sympathy of Cyrus for the Jews was due, in part at least, to the similarity of the conceptions of divine government in Zoroastrianism and post-exilic Judaism; the attitude of such prophets as the second Isaiah towards Cyrus was not prompted solely by the favour shown the Jews by Cyrus, but arose in part from the bond of sympathy between Zoroastrianism and monotheistic Judaism.

omy, based on the recognition of law in the heavens, in place of astrology, which, in its Babylonian form at least, had a meaning only as long as it was assumed that the gods, personified by the heavenly bodies, stood above law.[1] The era was approaching when the sciences one by one would cut loose from the leading strings of religious beliefs and religious doctrines. When, two centuries later, another wave of culture coming from the Occident swept over the entire Orient, it gave a further impetus to the divorce of culture from religion in the Euphrates Valley. Hellenic culture, brought to Babylonia by Alexander the Great[2] and his successors, meant the definite introduction of scientific thought; and thereby a fatal blow was given to what was left of the foundations of the beliefs that had been current in Babylonia for several millenniums. Traces of the worship of some of the old gods of Babylonia are to be found almost up to the threshold of our era, but it was merely the shell of the once dominant religion that was left. The culture of the country had become thoroughly saturated with Greek elements, and what Zoroastrianism had left of the religion that once reflected the culture of the Euphrates Valley was all but obliterated by the introduction of Greek modes of thought and life, and of Greek views of the universe.

[1] See p. 253 *seq*.
[2] Alexander conquered Babylonia in 331 B.C.

LECTURE II

THE PANTHEON

I

THE religion of Babylonia and Assyria passes, in the course of its long development, through the various stages of the animistic conception of nature towards a concentration of the divine Powers in a few supernatural Beings. Naturally, when our knowledge of the history of the Euphrates Valley begins, we are long past the period when practically all religion possessed by the people was summed up in the personification of the powers of nature, and in some simple ceremonies revolving largely around two ideas, Taboo and Totemism. The organisation of even the simplest form of government, involving the division of the community into little groups or clans, with authority vested in certain favoured individuals, carries with it as a necessary corollary a selection from the various personified powers who make themselves felt in the incidents and accidents of daily life. This selection leads ultimately to the formation of the pantheon. The gods that are prominent in the cult of a religion, in both its official and its popular forms, may be defined as the remainder of the large and indefinite number of Powers recognised everywhere by primitive man. While in the early animistic stage of religion the Power or spirit that manifests itself in the life of the tree is put on the same plane with the spirit supposed to reside in a flowing stream, or with the Power that manifests itself in the heat of the sun or in the severity of a storm, repeated experience gradually teaches man to differentiate between such Powers as markedly and almost continuously affect his life, and such as only incidentally force themselves on his notice. The process of selection receives, as has been already intimated, a strong impetus by the creation of little groups, arising from the extension of the family into a community. These two factors, repeated experience and social evolution, while perhaps not the only ones involved, constitute the chief elements in the unfolding of the religious life of a people.

In the case of the religion of Babylonia and Assyria we find the process of selection leading in the main to the cult of the sun and the moon, of the Power that manifests itself in vegetation, and of the Power that is seen in storms and in bodies of water. Sun, moon, vegetation, storms, and water constitute the forces with which man is brought into frequent, if not constant, contact. Agriculture and commerce being two leading pursuits in the civilisation that developed in the Euphrates Valley, it is natural to find the chief deities worshipped in the various political centres of the earliest period of Babylonian history to be personifications of one or the other of these five Powers. The reasons for the selection of the sun and moon are obvious. The two great luminaries of the heavens would appeal to a people even before a stage of settled habitation, coincident with the beginnings of agriculture, would be reached. Even to the homeless nomad the moon would form a guide in his wanderings, and as a measure of time would be singled out among the Powers that permanently and continuously enter into the life of the group and of the individual. With an advance from the lower to the higher nomadic stage, marked by the domestication of animals, with its accompanying pastoral life, the natural vegetation of the meadows would assume a larger importance, while, when the stage is reached when man is no longer dependent upon what nature produces of her own accord but when he, himself, becomes an active partner in the work of nature, his dependency upon the Power that he recognises in the sun would be more emphatically brought home to him. Long experience will teach him how much his success or failure in the tilling of the soil must depend upon the favour of the sun, and of the rains in the storms of the winter season. Distinguishing between the various factors involved in bringing about his welfare, he would reach the conception of a great triad—the sun, the power of vegetation and fertility residing in the earth, and the power that manifests itself in storms and rains.

All this applies with peculiar force to the climate of the Euphrates Valley, with its two seasons, the rainy and the dry, dividing the year. The welfare of the country depended upon the abundant rains, which, beginning in the late fall, continued uninterruptedly for several months, frequently accompanied by thunder, lightning, and strong winds. In the earliest period to which we can trace back the history of the Euphrates Valley we find entire districts covered with a network of canals, serving the double purpose of avoiding the destructive floods occasioned by the overflow of the Euphrates and the Tigris, and of securing a more direct irrigation of the fields. To the sun, earth, and storms there would thus be added, as a fourth survival from the animistic stage, the Power residing in the two great streams, and in the Persian Gulf, which to the Babylonians was the "Father of Waters." Commerce, following in the wake of agriculture, would lend an additional importance to the watery element as a means of transportation, and the sense of this importance would find a natural expression in the cult of water deities. While the chief gods of the pantheon thus evolved are identical with the Powers or spirits that belong to the animistic stage of religion, we may properly limit the designation "deities" to that period in the development of the religious life with which we are here concerned and which represents, to emphasise the point once more, a natural selection of a relatively small number out of a promiscuous and almost unlimited group of Powers.

It is perhaps more or less a matter of accident that we find in one of the centres of ancient Babylonia the chief deity worshipped as a sun-god, in another as a personification of the moon, and in a third as the goddess of the earth. We have, however, no means of tracing the association of ideas that led to the choice of Shamash, the sun-god, as the patron deity of Larsa and Sippar, the moon-god Sin as patron of Ur and Harran, and Ishtar, the great mother-goddess, the personification of the power of vegetation in the earth and of fertility among animals and mankind, as the centre of the cult in Uruk. On the other hand, we can follow the association of ideas that led the ancient people of the city of Eridu, lying at one time at or near the mouth of the Persian Gulf, to select a water deity known as Ea as the patron deity of the place. In the case of the most important of the storm deities, Enlil or Ellil[1], associated with the

---

[1] The *n* of Enlil is assimilated to the following *l* as is shown by the form Ellinos given to this deity in Damascius' *de primis*

city of Nippur, we can also follow the process that resulted in this association; but this process is of so special and peculiar a character that it merits to be set forth in ampler detail.

We have seen[1] that the city of Nippur occupied a special place among the older centres of the Euphrates Valley, marked not by any special political predominance—though this may once have been the case—but by a striking religious significance. Corresponding to this position of the city, we find the chief deity of the place, even in the oldest period, occupying a commanding place in the pantheon and retaining a theoretical leadership even after Enlil was forced to yield his prerogatives to Marduk. The name Enlil is composed of two Sumerian elements and signifies the "lord of the storm." His character as a storm-god, thus revealed in his name, is further illustrated by traits ascribed to him. The storm constitutes his weapon. He is frequently described and addressed as the "Great Mountain." His temple at Nippur is known as E-Kur, "Mountain House," which term, because of the supreme importance of this

Principiis (ed. Kopp, 1826), cap. 125, and by Aramaic endorsements to business documents of the Persian period. See the article, "Ellil, the god of Nippur" (*American Journal of Semitic Lang.*, xxiii., pp. 269–279), by Professor Clay, who showed that the name of this deity was at all times Enlil or Ellil, and never Bel as had hitherto been assumed.

[1] Above, p. 18.

Pl. 14. Types of Enlil the Chief God of Nippur, and his Consort Ninlil. Terra-cotta figures found by Peters at Nippur, and now in the Museum of Archæology of the University of Pennsylvania. The figure to the left is Enlil, the other two Ninlil. See Peters, *Nippur*, i., p. 128, and Hilprecht, *Excavations in Assyria and Babylonia*, p. 342.

Types of Enlil, the Chief God of Nippur, and of
his Consort Ninlil

Temple, became, as we have seen,[1] the general name
for a sanctuary. Since, moreover, his consort Ninlil is designated as Nin-Kharsag, "Lady of the Mountain," there are substantial reasons for assuming that
his original seat was on the top of some mountain, as
is so generally the case with storm-deities like Jahweh,
the god of the Hebrews, the Hittite god Teshup,
Zeus, and others. There being no mountains in the
Euphrates Valley, the further conclusion is war-
ranted that Enlil was the god of a people whose home
was in a mountainous region, and who brought their
god with them when they came to the Euphrates
Valley, just as the Hebrews carried the cult of Jahweh
with them when they passed from Mt. Sinai into
Palestine. Nippur is so essentially a Sumerian settlement that we must perforce associate the earliest
cult of Enlil with the non-Semitic element in the
population. Almost the only region from which
the Sumerians could have come was the east or
the north-east—the district which in a general way
we may designate by the name Elam, though the Sumerians, like the Cassites in later days, might have
originated in a region considerably to the north of
Elam. While, as has been pointed out,[2] it is not
ordinarily possible to separate the Sumero-Akkadian
civilisation into its component parts—Semitic and
non-Semitic—and more particularly in reference to

[1] Above, p. 18, note 2. [2] Above, p. 11 *seq.*

gods, beliefs, and rites is any detailed attempt to exactly differentiate between the additions made by one group or another destined to failure, yet in some instances it is possible to do so. The god Enlil is an example of a deity whose Sumerian origin may be set down as certain. His mountainous origin is indicated in an ancient lamentation-hymn in which he is addressed as the "offspring of the mountain,"[1] while the seven chief names given to him clearly demonstrate his Sumerian origin. Many of these Sumerian hymns, forming part of a ritual of lamentation, give an enumeration of these names:[2]

> O lord of the lands!
> O lord of the living command!
> O divine Enlil, father of Sumer!
> O shepherd of the dark-headed people![3]
> O hero who seest by thine own power!
> Strong lord, directing mankind!
> Hero, who causest multitudes to repose in peace!

The terms in which he is addressed, however, reflect also the broader and more general character

[1] *Cuneiform Texts, etc., in the British Museum*, Part xv., pl. 11, 3.

[2] *E.g.*, Reisner, *Sumerisch - Babylonische Hymnen*, No. 13, 1–7; *Cuneif. Texts*, xv., pl. 10, 3–8 (six names), pl. 13, 3–9, etc. Frequently, in the adaptation of this old ritual to the Marduk cult, direct references to Marduk and the gods grouped around Marduk are added, as well as mention of cities like Sippar, Babylon, and Borsippa—likewise with a view to adapting the Nippur ritual to other centres and to later conditions. See Lecture V.

[3] A frequent designation of the Sumerians, which later becomes synonymous with mankind in general.

given to him, pointing to a deity who has far outgrown the original proportions of a local god with
limited sway. The great antiquity of the Enlil cult
at Nippur was probably the most important factor
in giving to this deity and his temple such significance in the eyes of the inhabitants of the Euphrates
Valley. As he pertained to a great religious centre
the control whereof stirred the ambition of the various rulers of Euphratean states, it was a natural
tendency to assign to Enlil attributes and qualities
belonging of right to personifications of natural powers
other than the one which he originally represented.
Transferred from his original mountain home to a
valley dependent for its support on the cultivation of
the soil, Enlil assumes the traits of the Power that
fosters vegetation. This association becomes all the
more likely in view of the climate of the Euphrates
Valley, where fertility is dependent upon the storms
and rains of winter which Enlil so distinctly personified. In these same ancient compositions he is,
therefore, addressed also as the "lord of vegetation,"
as well as the "lord of storms." The storm, sweep-
ing over the land, is personified as his "word" or
"command" and described as bringing on devastation and ruin, overwhelming the meadows in their
beauty, flooding the crops, and laying waste the
habitations of men. The god is pictured as a rushing
deluge that brings woe to mankind, a torrent sweep-

ing away buttresses and dikes, an onrushing storm which none can oppose.[1]

> The word that causes the heavens on high to tremble,
> The word that makes the earth below to quake,
> The word that brings destruction to the Annunaki.
> His word is beyond the diviner, beyond the seer,
> His word is a tempest without a rival.

The power residing in his word is well summed up in a refrain:[2]

> The word of the lord the heavens cannot endure,
> The word of Enlil the earth cannot endure.
> The heavens cannot endure the stretching forth of his hand,
> The earth cannot endure the setting forth of his foot.

But it is this same word which elsewhere[3] is described as having created the world, as having laid the foundations of the earth, and called the upper world into existence. His character as a god of vegetation is directly indicated in another hymn which opens as follows:[4]

> O Enlil, Councillor, who can grasp thy power?
> Endowed with strength, lord of the harvest lands!
> Created in the mountains, lord of the grain fields!
> Ruler of great strength, father Enlil!
> The powerful chief of the gods art thou,
> The great creator and sustainer of life!

Among the ancient Hebrews we have a parallel development; where Jahweh, originally a god of

[1] *E.g.*, Reisner, *op. cit.*, No. 1.

[2] *E.g.*, Reisner, *op. cit.*, No. 13, rev. 15–24.

[3] Reisner, *op. cit.*, No. 22, rev. 13–22. See Langdon, *Sumerian and Babylonian Psalms*, p. 129.

[4] *Cuneiform Texts*, xv., pl. 11. See Langdon, *op. cit.*, p. 198.

storms, perhaps also of earthquakes, who manifests himself in the lightning, and whose voice is heard in the thunder, is magnified into the creator of the universe, the producer of vegetation, and the protector of harvests and of crops. Like Enlil, Jahweh comes from the mountains. His seat is on the top of Mt. Sinai, or, as it is said in the Song of Deborah,[1] on Mt. Seir in Edom. Traces of this early conception of Jahweh as a storm-god still linger in the metaphors of late Psalms[2] where the power of the god of the universe is described:

> The voice of Jahweh[3] is upon the waters,
> The god of glory thundereth,
> Jahweh is upon the great waters.
> The voice of Jahweh is full of power,
> The voice of Jahweh is full of might,
> The voice of Jahweh breaketh cedars,
> Jahweh breaks the cedars of Lebanon
> and makes them skip like a calf,
> Lebanon and Sirion like a young mountain-bull.
> The voice of Jahweh hews flames of fire,
> The voice of Jahweh shakes the wilderness,
> Jahweh shakes the wilderness of Kadesh.

A vivid description, indeed, of a storm-god rushing onward in furious haste, uprooting mighty cedars and driving them before him like a flock of cattle! The voice of Jahweh is the thunder in the storm, and the flame of fire is the lightning, but what

---

[1] Judges, v., 4.   [2] *E. g.*, Ps.. xxix.
[3] The Hebrew word for "voice" might with equal propriety be rendered "word."

is set down as a metaphor in this late composition is really the survival in language of the conceptions that once were held as literal.

Like Enlil, however, Jahweh assumes also the attributes of the Canaanitish deities of vegetation —the Baals—when the Hebrews, dispossessing the older inhabitants, definitely entered on the agricultural stage. Jahweh himself becomes a Baal to whom the first fruits of the field are offered as a tribute to his power in making the grass to grow and the fields to be covered with verdure (Ps. civ., 14). A further analogy between Enlil and Jahweh is suggested by the description of the former as a mighty ox or bull, which recalls the fact that Jahweh was worshipped in the northern Hebrew kingdom under the symbol of a calf.[1] An entire series of hymns and lamentations is recognised as addressed to Enlil from the opening words "the Bull to his sanctuary," where the bull designates Enlil.[2] In a fragment of a hymn, Enlil is described as [3]

[1] Jeroboam (1 Kings, xii., 28) makes two golden calves, and places one at Bethel, and the other at the northern frontier at Dan, and tells his people, "Behold thy god, Israel, who brought thee out of Egypt." The story of the worship of the golden calf in Exodus, chap. xxxii., is based on this incident.

[2] See Langdon, *op. cit.*, No. x. Enlil is addressed as a "bull" in this composition (*e.g.*, Langdon, p. 113, line 3. See also pp. 85, 127, 277, etc.).

[3] Rawlinson, *Cuneiform Inscriptions of Western Asia*, iv., 2d ed., pl. 27, No. 2. See Langdon, No. xviii.

Crouching in the lands like a sturdy mountain bull,
Whose horns shine like the brilliance of the sun,
Full of splendour like Venus of the heavens.

In another composition the refrain reads, "A sturdy bull art thou." When we see votive offerings with the figure of a bull, or representations of a crouching bull with a human face,[1] we are tempted to assert that they are symbols of Enlil; and if this be so, further traces of the association between the god and the animal may be seen both in the colossal bulls which form a feature of Assyrian art and were placed at the entrance to temples and palaces, and in the bull as the decoration of columns in the architecture of the Persian period.[2]

The bull is so commonly in ancient religions a symbol of the power residing in the sun that the association of this animal with Enlil and Jahweh presumably belongs to the period when the original traits of these deities as storm-gods were overlaid by the extended conception of them as gods of vegetation, presiding, therefore, like the solar deities over agricultural life. The Baals of the Canaanites, we know, were personifications of the sun; and in the case of Nippur we can with reasonable certainty

[1] See Plate 22, and Heuzey, *Catalogue des Antiquités Chaldéennes*, p. 269.

[2] Perrot et Chipiez, *History of Art in Persia*, p. 93, and facing pp. 294, 298, etc.

name the solar deity, whose attributes were transferred to Enlil.

By the side of Enlil we find a god whose name is provisionally read Ninib prominently worshipped in Nippur in the earliest days to which we can trace back the history of that city. Indeed, Ninib belongs to Nippur quite as much as does Enlil, and there are reasons for believing that he is the original chief protecting deity of the region who was replaced by Enlil. Was he worshipped there before the Sumerians brought their mountain god to the Euphrates Valley? Prof. Clay, who has shown that the real form of the god's name was En-Mashtu, is of the opinion[1] that he is of Amoritish origin. Without entering into a discussion of this intricate problem, which would carry us too far, it would indeed appear that non-Sumerian influences were at work in evolving the figure of Ninib or En-Mashtu. If it could be definitely shown, as Clay assumes, that Mashtu is a variant form of Martu,—the common designation of Amurru as the "land of the west,"—En-Mashtu, "the lord of Mashtu," would be the "Sumerian" designation of this non-Sumerian deity.

In the systematised pantheon of the old Babylonian period Ninib is viewed as the son of Enlil, a relationship that expresses the superior position which Enlil acquired, and which is revealed in the common desig-

[1] *Amurru*, p. 121 *seq.*

nation of Nippur as the "place of Enlil," though we find Nippur described also as "the beloved city of Ninib."[1]

The two gods in combination, the storm and the sun, stand for the two chief forces of nature that control the prosperity and welfare of the Euphrates Valley; and this combination was viewed in terms of human relationship, with the natural consequence of an harmonious exchange of their attributes. It is from Ninib that Enlil receives the traits of a god of vegetation, and, in return, the father transfers to the son, as in another religious centre Ea does to Marduk, some of his own attributes. Like Enlil, Ninib is addressed as the "honoured one." He is the exalted hero of the universe and it is said of him, as it is said of Enlil, that "no one can grasp the power of his word."[2] A warrior, he rides forth to carry out his father's command. So close is this association with Enlil that Ninib even assumes some of the traits belonging to the father as the storm-god. In a composition that appears to be older than the days of Hammurapi, Ninib is portrayed as an onrushing storm:[3]

> In the thunderous rolling of thy chariot
> Heaven and earth quake as thou advancest.

Most significant, however, as illustrating the ex-

[1] See, *e.g.*, Jastrow, *Religion* (German ed.), i., p. 459.

[2] Reisner, No. 18; Langdon, p. 226.

[3] Rawlinson, ii., pl. 19, No. 1, obv. 16, 17; Jastrow, *Religion* (German ed.), i., p. 455.

change of traits between Enlil and Ninib, is the form assumed in an ancient myth symbolising the conquest of chaos—pictured as a great monster—by the Power that brings order into the universe. The obvious interpretation of the myth is the triumph of the sun in the spring over the storms and torrents of the winter. The character of conqueror belongs, therefore, of right to a solar deity like Ninib, just as it fits the god of Babylon, the later Marduk, who is likewise the sun personified; but in a composition[1] describing the powerful weapons wielded in this conflict by Ninib, we find among the names of the weapons such expressions as "storm-god with fifty mouths," "miraculous storm," "destroyer of mountains," "invincible mountain," which point unmistakably to a personification of the storm, like Enlil. These designations appear by the side of others, such as the "weapon whose sheen overpowers the land," "the one made of gold and lapis-lazuli," "burning like fire," that clearly belong to Ninib as the personification of the fiery sun. The conclusion has generally been drawn that the myth was originally told of Enlil and transferred to Ninib; but Enlil, as a god of the storms and rains of winter, would more naturally be identified with the conquered monster. The more reasonable assumption is that the myth dates from the period when Ninib still held a commanding postion in the "Nippur" circle

[1] See Jastrow, *Religion* (German ed.), i., p. 451.

of deities, and that, with the advance of Enlil to the headship of the pantheon, he was given a share in the conquest of chaos as a necessary condition of the creation of the universe of law and order. Enlil was, accordingly, represented as the power behind the throne who hands over his attributes—symbolised by the storm weapons—to his beloved son, who at the command of his father proceeds to conquer the monster.

We see the same process repeated, though under somewhat different circumstances, at a subsequent period when, in consequence of the political ascendency of Babylon, Marduk is advanced to the head of the systematised pantheon.[1] The time-honoured nature myth, somewhat modified in form, is transferred to him, but by this time the Ninib cult had receded into the background, and Enlil alone is introduced as transferring his powers and attributes to Marduk. Marduk is represented as replacing Enlil, from which one might conclude that, as a further compromise between Enlil and Ninib, the myth was actually told of both, despite the incongruity involved in making a storm-god the conqueror of chaotic confusion. This is not only possible but probable, since, with the expansion of Enlil into a god presiding over vegetation, thus taking on the traits of a sun-god, his original character would naturally

[1] See above, p. 40.

be obscured. As he was the head of the pantheon, possessing all the powers attributed to other gods, the tendency would arise to make him the central figure of all myths—the pre-eminent hero and conqueror. At the same time Ninib, as the old-time solar deity of Nippur, also absorbs the duties of other solar gods worshipped in other centres. He is identified with a god Ningirsu, "the lord of Girsu,"—a section of Lagash—who became the chief god of the district controlled by Gudea and his predecessors, of whose solar character there can be no doubt. In a certain hymn Ninib,[1] is associated not only with Girsu, which here as elsewhere stands for Lagash and the district of which it was the centre, but also with Kish whose patron deity was known as Zamama. In this same composition[2] he is identified also with Nergal, the solar deity of Uruk, with Lugal-Marada, "King of Marada," the designation of the solar god localised in Marada, and with the sun-god of Isin. The god Ninib appears to have become in fact a general designation for the sun and the sun-god, though subsequently replaced by Babbar, "the shining one," the solar deity of Sippar. This title in its Semitic form, Shamash, eventually became the general designation for the "sun" because of the prominence which Sippar, through the close association between

[1] Reisner, No. 18. See Langdon, p. 226.
[2] See also Langdon, pp. 146, 164–166, 208.

Sippar and Babylon, acquired as a centre of the sun cult.

II

Back of Enlil and Ninib, however, there lies still another deity who in an ancient inscription is called the "beloved father" of Enlil. This deity is Anu, whose cult was specially associated with the city of Uruk. While in the active cults of Babylonia and Assyria Anu is comparatively inconspicuous, the position assigned to him in the systematised pantheon is most significant. As early as the days of Lugal-zaggisi[1] we find the endeavour made to group the great gods recognised in connection with the important political centres into a kind of theological system— an endeavour that reveals the intellectual activity of the priests at this early period. In this grouping Anu is given the first place, and Enlil the second. Anu and Enlil, together with Ea, form a triad summarising, as we shall presently see, the three divisions of the universe—the heavens, the earth (together with the region immediately above it), and the waters flowing around and under the earth. But a god of the heavens is an abstraction, and it is difficult to suppose that this should have been the original view taken of Anu. Popular fancy deals with realities and

[1] See Thureau-Dangin, *Sumerisch-Akkadische Königsin-schriften*, p. 154.

with personified powers whose workings are seen and felt. It would hardly, therefore, have evolved the view that there was a power to be identified with the heavens as a whole, of which the azure sky is a symbol, as little as it would personify the earth as a whole or the bodies of waters as a whole. It is only necessary to state the implications involved to recognise that the conception of a triad of gods corresponding to three theoretical divisions of the universe is a bit of learned speculation. It smacks of the school. The conception of a god of heaven fits in, moreover, with the comparatively advanced period when the seats of the gods were placed in the skies, and the gods identified with the stars. Such an astral theology, however, is not a part of the earlier religious beliefs of the Babylonians; it reflects the later conditions produced under the influence of the religious system devised in the temple schools of one or another centre.[1] The deities popularly recognised, particularly in the earlier period, are personifications, each of some definite power, of the sun, of the moon, of the water, of the storms, or of the fields, as the case may be. Analogy, therefore, taken in connection with the great antiquity of Uruk, the seat of Anu worship, justifies the assumption that Anu was originally the personification of some definite power of nature; and everything points to this

[1] See p. 209, *seq.*

power having been the sun in the heavens. Starting
from this point of view, we can understand how the
great luminary of heaven should have been identified
with the heavens in an artificially devised theological
system, just as Enlil became in this system the designation of the earth and of the region above the earth
viewed as a whole.

Anu and Enlil—sun-god and storm-god—would
thus represent the same combination as was in
later times represented by Shamash and Adad—likewise sun-god and storm-god respectively,—who are
so constantly associated together.[1]   The two would
stand again for the two great forces of nature which
control the well-being of the Euphrates Valley.   In
this respect they present a parallel to the pair, Ninib
and Enlil, with this difference, however, that whereas in
the latter combination Ninib, the sun-god, is the son,
and Enlil, the storm-god, is the father, in the case of
Anu and Enlil the relationship is reversed, Anu being
the father and Enlil the son.   When, therefore, Hammurapi calls himself "the proclaimer of Anu and
Enlil,"[2]   and derives his royal authority from these
two, he is using a form of invocation that is co-exten-
sive with the powers practically controlling the uni-

[1] See Jastrow, *Religion* (German ed.), i., p. 137.
[2] King, *Inscriptions and Letters of Hammurabi*, iii., pp. 182,
187, 190.   Gudea also sets up this duality as embracing the two
chief Powers of nature (Thureau-Dangin, *Sumerisch-Akkadische
Königsinschriften*, p. 140).

verse as it presented itself to the inhabitants of the Euphrates Valley. That Anu should become the father of Enlil accords also with the physical conditions, for to an agricultural people, as has been pointed out, the sun would naturally be the supreme Power; and we have seen that the pre-eminence accorded in the practical cult to Enlil of Nippur was due to the special circumstances attendant upon the introduction of the worship of the Sumerian storm-god in Nippur. Enlil replaces Ninib at Nippur, whereas the absence of any rivalry between the Anu centre and the Enlil centre led to a more natural combination in which the old sun-god retained his place at the head of the systematised pantheon.

The beginning of an ancient myth [1] in which Ninib is again the chief character, illustrates the relation in which these three figures—Anu, Enlil, and Ninib—were pictured as standing to one another. Ninib is addressed:

> Like Anu thou art formed,
> Like Enlil thou art formed!

The evident purpose of this apostrophe is to show that Ninib has been given the qualities of both Anu and Enlil. As a sun-god, Ninib could be addressed as Anu, while, as we have seen, he derives his qualities as a storm-god direct from Enlil.

[1] Jastrow, *Religion* (German ed.), i., p. 454.

The material at our disposal does not permit us as
yet to penetrate to the earliest history of such ancient
centres as Nippur and Uruk, but the indications in
myths and hymns point unmistakably to the cur-
rency of stories, attributing to both Anu and Enlil the
creation of the universe. It was natural that each
centre should claim the privilege for its patron deity;
and we shall see that other centres did the same. In
the national epic of the Babylonians, recounting the
adventures of Gilgamesh, and which is a composite
production, dating from various periods, the first
scene is laid in Uruk, and the goddess Aruru is portrayed as forming man in the image of Anu.[1] This
clearly points to Anu as the source of all being. In
an ancient version of a creation myth, which however is modified in the process of adaptation to later
conditions,[2] the first two cities to be founded are
Nippur and Uruk, while the third city is Eridu, the
seat of the Ea cult. The myth, therefore, reflects
the constitution of the triad, Anu, Enlil, and Ea.
In another form of the myth to which attention was
above directed,[3] Ninib appears as the hero; but even
in this version, which became the favourite one, the
story retained traces of the assignment of the part
of conqueror of primæval chaos to Anu. The same

[1] Tablet I., col. ii., 33 (Jensen, *Keilinschriftliche Bibliothek*,
vi., 1, p. 120).

[2] Jastrow, *Religion of Babylonia and Assyria*, p. 444 *seq.*

[3] See p. 78.

story was evidently told of different solar gods in the various centres. In Uruk the conqueror was the sun-god Anu, in Nippur the sun-god Ninib; but with the definite establishment of Enlil as the head of the pantheon, Ninib becomes merely the agent acting at the command of Enlil, and invested with some of Enlil's attributes in return for the extension of the sphere of Enlil to include the qualities of his son Ninib.

It was inevitable that with several distinctive factors contributing to the culture and religion of Babylonia and Assyria, the endeavour should be made to adapt the conceptions of the gods and their relationships to one another, and to modify the ancient folk-tales and the cult to meet changed conditions. The evolution of a religion that at each stage reflects a different combination of the political and social kaleidoscope is necessarily complicated.

III

We have already had occasion[1] to touch upon still more momentous changes introduced into all three elements of the religion,—the pantheon, the myths, and the cult,—by the rise of the predominating influence of Babylon, which was coincident, as we have seen, with the period of Hammurapi, *ca.* 2000 B.C. The patron deity of the city, whose foundation takes us beyond the time of Sargon,[2]

[1] See above, p. 36 *seq.*   [2] See above, p. 22.

was again a solar deity, Marduk, who, however, belongs to a different group than Anu, Enlil, and Ninib.
He is so constantly termed the "son of Ea" that there
can be no doubt of his having originated in the region of the Persian Gulf at the head of which lay
Eridu, the seat of the worship of Ea. Ea and Marduk
thus bear the same relation to each other as do Enlil
and Ninib on the one hand, and Anu and Enlil on the
other. Of the character of Ea there is fortunately no
doubt. He is the god of the waters, and the position
of Eridu, at (or near) the point where the Euphrates
and Tigris empty into the Persian Gulf, suggests that
he is more particularly the guardian spirit of these
two streams. Pictured as half-man, half-fish, he is
the *shar Apsi*, "King of the Watery Deep." The
"Deep," however, is not the salt ocean but the sweet
waters flowing under the earth, which feed the streams,
and through streams and canals irrigate the fields.
This *Apsu* was personified, and presented a contrast
and opposition to Tiamat, the personification of the
salt ocean. The creation myth of Eridu, therefore,
pictures a conflict at the beginning of time between
Apsu and Tiamat, in which the former, under the
direction of Ea, triumphs and holds in check the
forces accompanying the monster Tiamat.[1] As in
the case of Enlil, Ea's strength rests in his word, but

[1] See Jastrow, "On the Composite Character of the Babylonian
Creation Story" (*Nöldeke Festschrift*, pp. 969-982).

the word of Ea is of a character more spiritual than that of Enlil—not the roar of the ocean but the gentle flow of streams. He commands, and what he plans comes into existence. A wholly beneficent power, he blesses the fields and heals mankind. His most striking trait is his love of humanity; in conflicts between the gods and mankind, he is invariably on the side of the latter. When the gods at the instance of Enlil as the god of storms decide to bring on a deluge to sweep away mankind,[1] it is Ea who reveals the secret to his favourite Utnapishtim, who saves himself, his family, and his belongings on a ship that he is instructed to build. At Eridu it is Ea who is regarded as the creator of the universe, including mankind, but he is an artificer who produces by the cunning of his hand. The world is made by him as an architect builds a house. This character he retains

---

[1] In the present version of the nature myth (see Jensen, *Keilinschriftliche Bibliothek*, vi., 1, p. 230 *seq.*), Anu and Ennugi (= Nusku) are associated with Enlil; but the older form is still to be seen at the close of the story, where it is Enlil alone who discovers that Utnapishtim has escaped, and Ea is obliged to conciliate the angry god. Hommel's supposition (*Expository Times*, 1910, p. 369) that in the new fragment of this deluge tradition, Enlil (whose name does not even appear on the few lines preserved) is the one who saves Utnapishtim, misses the point of the myth, which rests on a *conflict* between Enlil and Ea. There is not the slightest reason to assume that this new fragment, which adds nothing to our knowledge of the subject, represents a "Nippur" version. It is not even certain that the fragment was found at Nippur.

throughout all periods. It is to him that the origin of
the Arts is attributed: he is the patron of smiths and
of all workers in metals. Down through the Greek
period[1] the tradition is preserved which makes him
the teacher of mankind to whom all knowledge and
science are due—the knowledge of effective incantations, the purification from disease, the art of writing,
and the wisdom of the heavens.

The waters thus personified by Ea present a striking contrast both to the angry billows of the turbulent
and treacherous ocean, and to the waters that on the
command of Enlil come from on high, causing the
rivers to overstep their banks, bursting the dams and
canals, flooding the fields, and working general havoc
among the habitations of mankind. The deluge story
just referred to not only illustrates this contrast between Ea and Enlil but suggests the rivalry that must
at one time have existed between the two centres,
Eridu and Nippur. Ea is represented as thwarting
the purpose of Enlil, and on discovering what Ea has
done, Enlil is enraged with his rival. At the same
time, the reconciliation described at the close of the
tale indicates the process of combination and assimilation of the two cults under the influence of the
priests in their endeavour to systematise the rela-

[1] The Oannes in Berosus' account of primæval days is
evidently Ea, however the name is to be explained. See Zimmern, *Keilinschrifte und das Alte Testament*, ii., p. 535.

tionship between the deities worshipped in the important centres. Ea eloquently implores Enlil as the god of storms not to bring on a deluge again. Let mankind be punished by sending lions and jackals, by famine or pestilence, but not by a deluge. Enlil is touched with pity, and, after blessing Utnapishtim and his wife, consents to their being carried to the confluence of the streams, there to live a life like that of the gods. Just as in the association of Anu with Enlil we have the endeavour to bring the cults of Uruk and Nippur into relationship with each other, so in the reconciliation of Enlil with Ea there is foreshadowed, or rather reflected, the addition of the Eridu group of deities to those worshipped in Nippur and Uruk. To the duality of gods represented by Anu and Enlil, the priests in their systematising efforts were thus led to add a third member, Ea. All three were delocalised, as it were, and converted into symbolisations of the three divisions of the universe—heavens, earth, and water.[1] To be sure, the division was not always made with the desirable precision. The earth was in a measure common ground on which Enlil and Ea met. Of the numerous designations for Ea, a very common one was En-ki which

---

[1] A direct allusion to this Babylonian system is to be seen in the Biblical prohibition (Ex. xx., 4; Deut. v., 8) against making any image of anything in the heavens above, on the earth beneath, or in the waters under the earth.

describes him as "lord of the earth." As a water deity
it was natural that he should be associated with the
earth, also the scene of his beneficent activity. Earth
and water represent a close partnership, more particularly in a low country like the Euphrates Valley where
one does not have to dig far before coming to the
domain of Ea. Enlil thus controls the surface of the
earth and the region of storms just above it, while to
Ea belongs the control of the waters and the interior
of the earth, fed by the streams over which he presides.

IV

There are thus chiefly two factors at work in leading to the formation of a definite and theoretically
constructed pantheon: (1) the gradual rise of a
limited number of important religious and political
centres, and (2) the endeavour of the priests to bring
the cults in these centres into relationship with one
another. The delocalisation involved in the position
of Ea as the third member of the triad could proceed
without any loss of prestige on his part, since Ea was
represented as voluntarily transferring to his son,
Marduk, his chief share in the practical cult—that of
securing through purification-rites and incantation-
formulas release from sickness and physical suffering,
brought on by demons or through the machinations
of witches and sorcerers. Marduk is the complement
to Enlil. Ea and Marduk, personifying the watery

element and the sun, thus sum up the two chief Powers of nature, precisely as Enlil and Ninib represent this combination, only from another and more austere point of view.

The solar character of Marduk appears in the two signs with which his name—in its most common form —is written, which designate him as "child of day."[1] The terms in which he is addressed in hymns[2] further illustrate this character. He is "the shining one" whose course is across "the resplendent heavens." His appearance is pictured as a flaming fire. He illuminates the universe, and he is directly associated with Shamash, the chief sun-god of the later pantheon:

Thou art like Shamash, illuminator of darkness.[3]

On the other hand, his association with Ea is equally marked, and as a consequence of this association he assumes the attributes of the god of waters. In incantation-texts a dialogue is frequently introduced in which Ea, when appealed to by the exorcising priests, is represented as calling upon his son to perform the healing act[4]:

[1] The first element might more literally be taken in the sense of "heifer," but the force would be about the same, since the "heifer" suggests a young offspring.

[2] See Jastrow, *Religion* (German ed.), i., pp. 495-519.

[3] *Ib.*, p. 500.

[4] Jastrow, *Religion* (English ed.), p. 289; German ed., i., p. 142 *seq.*; and Thompson, *Devils and Evil Spirits*, ii., pp. 17, 33, 41, 47 *seq.*, 57 *seq.*, 67, 71, 75, 81, 93 *seq.*, 101, etc.

Pl. 15.   Types of Gods.

Fig. 1.   Marduk and Tiamat,—representing the conflict of a storm
god against a monster symbolical of primæval chaos. The god
armed with the lightning fork in each hand is clearly a storm
god such as Enlil, the chief god of Nippur (see p. 68), originally
was. It was he to whom, as the head of the older pantheon,
the conquest of Tiamat and the subsequent creation of the world
were ascribed. With the transfer of the headship of the pantheon
to Marduk, this solar deity takes on the attributes of Enlil. The
subjection of the winged monster is ascribed to Marduk, and is
represented in a large variety of forms on seal cylinders of the
earlier and later periods. See Ward *op. cit.*, Chaps. VIII. and
XXXVI. The horned dragon (see Pl. 30), from being the symbol
of Enlil, by the same process of transfer becomes the animal of
Marduk, and subsequently of Ashur as the head of the Assyrian
pantheon (see Pl. 17, Fig. 3). Alabaster slab found in the palace
of Ashurnasirpal at Nimroud (site of Calah—N. W. Palace). See
Layard, *Monuments of Nineveh*, ii., Pl. 5; Mansell's "British
Museum Photographs," Part III. (*Assyrian Sculptures*), No. 361.

Fig. 2.   Marduk, chief god of Babylon and head of the later Babylonian pantheon. Found at Babylon. Lapis-lazuli cylinder, with
dedicatory inscription to Marduk by Marduk-nadinshum, king
of Babylonia (*c.* 850 B.C), and deposited in the temple E-Sagila
at Babylon. See *Mitteilungen der Deutschen Orient-Gesellschaft*,
No. 5, pp. 14–15.

Fig. 3.   The storm-god Adad (or Ramman). Found at Babylon.
Lapis-lazuli cylinder, with dedicatory inscription to Marduk by
Esarhaddon, King of Assyria (680–669 B.C.), but nevertheless
expressly designated as "the seal of Adad of the temple E-Sagila,"
forming part of the treasury of Marduk. See *Mitteilungen der
Deutschen Orient-Gesellschaft*, No. 5, pp. 13–14.

Fig. 1. Conflict of Marduk with the Monster Tiamat

Fig. 2. Marduk, the
Chief God of
Babylon

Fig. 3. Adad
(or Ramman)
the God of
Storms, Thun-
d e r, a n d
Lightning

What dost thou not know that I could tell thee?
What I know, thou also knowest.
Go! My son Marduk! To the house of purification bring him
    [*i.e.*, the sick person]!
Break the ban! Release him from the curse!

Marduk, like Ea, is often addressed as the god of canals, and the opener of subterranean fountains[1]:

Lord of mountain streams and of waters,
Opener of sources and cisterns, controller of streams.

Like Ea, again, he is addressed as the source of the wisdom of mankind:

Wise one, first-born of Ea, creator of all humanity.

In representations of the god he stands above the watery deep, with a horned creature at his feet that is also the symbol of Ea.[2] Lastly, Marduk's temple at Babylon bears the same name, Esagila, "the lofty house," as Ea's sanctuary at Eridu, though this, or perhaps another sanctuary of Ea at Eridu, was also known as E-Apsu, "house of the watery deep."

This agreement in the name of the sanctuaries of the two gods confirms the evidence from other sources, which enables us actually to trace the cult of Marduk back to Eridu. If we find, therefore, the Marduk cult, from a certain period on, centred in a northern city like Babylon, we have every reason to believe that the settlement of this place was due to a move-

[1] Jastrow, *Religion* (German ed.), i., p. 498 *seq.*
[1] See Plate 15, Fig. 3.

ment from the south—and more particularly from the district of which Eridu was the centre—in accord, therefore, with the general course of civilisation in Babylonia from south to north. Babylon thus turns out to be an offshoot of Eridu. Its foundation antedates Sargon, for he finds the city already in existence and enlarges it; but it is possible that it was he who gave to it the name of Babylon.

Opposite Babylon lies the famous town of Borsippa, designated in the inscriptions as "the city of the Euphrates," which, as may be concluded from the name and from other indications, appears to be an older settlement than Babylon itself, and to have assumed earlier a position of importance as an intellectual and religious centre. When, however, Hammurapi raised Babylon to be the capital of his empire, Borsippa was obliged to yield its prerogatives, and gradually sank to the rank of a mere dependency upon Babylon—a kind of suburb to the capital city. The patron deity of Borsippa was a god known as Nebo, whose cult appears at one time to have been carried over into Babylon—perhaps before Marduk became the patron deity of the place. Marduk, however, replaces Nebo as Enlil replaced Ninib; but, just as at Nippur the older sun cult does not disappear, and Ninib becomes the son of Enlil, so the Nebo cult at Babylon is maintained, and Nebo is viewed as the son of Marduk. In both places, therefore, the "father" god appears to be the intruder who sets aside an older chief deity. The combination of Marduk and Nebo, expressed in these terms of relationship, continues to the end of the Babylonian empire. Nebo has a sanctuary within the temple area of Esagila at Babylon which bears the same name, Ezida, "the true house," as the one given to Nebo's temple at Borsippa. In return, Marduk has an Esagila, a "lofty house," in Borsippa. In the Assyrian and later Babylonian periods the two names, Esagila and Ezida, are generally found in combination, as though inseparable in the minds of the Babylonians. Similarly, the two gods, Marduk and Nebo, are quite commonly invoked together, *e.g.*, in the formula of greeting at the beginning of official letters, which, even in the case of the correspondence of the Assyrian monarchs, begin:

May Nebo and Marduk bless the king my lord! [1]

V

Who was this god Nebo? The question is not easy to answer, though the most satisfactory view is to regard him as a counterpart of Ea. Like Ea, he is the embodiment and source of wisdom. The art of writing—and therefore of all literature—is more particularly associated with him. A common form of his name designates him as the "god of the stylus,"

[1] So *passim* in Harpers, *Assyrian ond Babylonian Letters.*

and his symbol on Boundary Stones is likewise the stylus of the scribes. He was regarded by the Assyrians also as the god of writing and wisdom, and Ashurbanapal, in the colophons to the tablets of his library, names Nebo and his consort Tashmit as the pair who instructed the king to preserve and collect the literary remains of the past.[1] The study of the heavens formed part of the wisdom which is traced back to Nebo; and the temple school at Borsippa became one of the chief centres for the astrological and, subsequently, for the astronomical lore of Babylonia. The archives of that school in fact formed one of the chief resources for the scribes of Ashurbanapal, though the archives at Babylon were also largely drawn upon. In the Persian and Greek periods the school of Borsippa is frequently mentioned in colophons attached to school texts of various kinds, and it is not improbable that the school survived the one at Babylon.

Like Ea, Nebo is also associated with the irrigation of the fields and with their consequent fertility. A hymn praises him as the one who fills the canals and the dikes, who protects the fields and brings the crops to maturity. From such phrases the conclusion has been drawn by some scholars that Nebo was originally

[1] In the "omen" section of the library, Shamash and Adad as "the gods of divination," take the place of Nebo and Tashmit.

a solar deity, like Marduk, but his traits as a god of vegetation can be accounted for on the supposition that he was a water-deity, like Ea, whose favour was essential to rich harvests. We may, however, also assume that the close partnership between him and Marduk had as a consequence a transfer of some of the father Marduk's attributes as a solar deity to Nebo, his son, just as Ea passed his traits on to his son, Marduk. Although he is called upon to heal, Nebo plays no part in the incantation-ritual, which revolves, as we shall see,[1] around two ideas—water, represented by Ea, and fire, represented by the fire-god Gibil or Nusku. The predominance of the Ea ritual in incantations left no room for a second water-deity— there was place only for Marduk as an intermediary between Ea and suffering mankind. We may, therefore, rest content with the conclusion that Nebo, like Marduk, belongs to the Eridu group of deities, that, as a counterpart to Ea, his duty was always of a secondary character, and that, with the growing importance of the Marduk cult, he becomes an adjunct to Marduk. This relationship is expressed by making Nebo the son of Marduk. The two pass down through the ages as an inseparable pair—representing a duality, and forming a parallel to that constituted by Ea and Marduk. Marduk and Nebo sum up, again, the two chief Powers of nature conditioning the welfare

[1] See p. 312.

7

of the country—the sun and the watery element—precisely as do Ea and Marduk; with these latter, however, for reasons that have been given, the order is reversed, just as we have the double order, Anu and Enlil—sun and storm—by the side of Enlil and Ninib—storm and sun. The name Nebo designates the god as a "proclaimer," while another sign with which his name is commonly written describes him as an artificer or creator. No doubt in his seat of worship, Borsippa, Nebo was at one time looked upon as the creator of the universe, just as Ea, Enlil, Ninib, and Marduk were so regarded in their respective centres. He is portrayed as holding the "tablets of fate" on which the destinies of individuals are inscribed. As "writer" or "scribe" among the gods, he records their decisions, as proclaimer or herald, he announces these decisions. Such functions point to his having occupied from an early period the position of an intermediary, and we are probably not wrong in supposing that the god whose orders he carries out was originally Ea, who was later replaced in this capacity by Marduk. Nebo could, however, retain his attributes as the god of writing without injury to the dignity and superiority of Marduk, for in the ancient Orient, as in the Orient of to-day, the *kâtib* or scribe is not a person of superior rank. Authorship was at no time in the ancient Orient a basis for social or political prestige. A writer

was essentially a secretary who acted as an intermediary.[1]

The rank that Nebo holds in the systematised
pantheon is due, therefore, almost entirely to his
partnership with Marduk, and it is interesting to note
that the Assyrian kings avail themselves of this association occasionally to play off Nebo, as it were,
against Marduk. Some of them appear to pay
their homage to Nebo rather than to Marduk, because the latter was in a measure a rival to the head
of the Assyrian pantheon. Adad-nirari IV. (810–782
B.C.) goes so far in his adoration of Nebo as to inscribe
on a statue of this god (or is it his own statue?):

> Trust in Nebo! Trust in no other god![2]

The Nebo cult, which, like that of other gods, had its
ebb and flow, must have enjoyed a special popularity
in Assyria in the 9th century.

No such rivalry between the Marduk and Nebo
cults appears ever to have existed in Babylonia,
though it is perhaps not without significance that in
the days of the neo-Babylonian empire no less than
three of the rulers[3] bear names in which Nebo

[1] It is significant that there is no word for "author" in Biblical
Hebrew (or in Babylonian), but merely one for "scribe," the
term being indifferently used for one who composes something,
or for one who merely copies what others have written.

[2] Schrader, *Keilinschriftliche Bibliothek*, i., p. 193.

[3] Nabopolassar, Nebuchadnezzar, and Nabonnedos.

enters as one of the elements. The position of Marduk was, however, at all times too strong to be seriously affected by fashions in names or changes in the cult. He not only remains during all periods after Hammurapi the head of the pantheon, but as the ages rolled on he absorbed, as has already been pointed out, the attributes of all the great gods of the pantheon. He becomes the favourite of the gods as well as of men. Starting out at Babylon with the absorption of the character of Ea, combining in his person the two Powers, water and the sun, which comprise so large a share of divine government and control of the universe, he ends by taking over also the duties of Enlil of Nippur. This is of the greatest significance. It argues for the boldness of the Marduk priests and for the security of Marduk's position that they gave to Marduk the title that was so long the prerogative of Enlil, to wit, *bêl*, "the lord" paramount. The old nature-myths are once more adopted by the priests of Marduk and transformed so as to give to Marduk the central position. It is he who seizes the tablets of fate from the Zu bird—the personification of some solar deity,—and henceforth holds the destiny of mankind in his hands. The creation-myth is transformed into a pæon celebrating the deeds of Marduk. What in one version was ascribed to Anu, in another to Ninib, in a third to Enlil, and in a fourth to Ea, is in the Babylon version ascribed to Marduk. Two series of creation-stories are combined; one embodying an account of a conflict with a monster, the symbol of primæval chaos, the other a story of rebellion against Ea which is successfully quelled. In the first group we can distinguish three versions, one originating at Uruk in which the solar god Anu becomes the conqueror of Tiamat, the other two originating at Nippur, an earlier one in which the solar god Ninib takes the part assigned, in the Uruk version, to Anu, and a later one in which Enlil replaces Ninib. The character of the myth is thereby changed. Instead of symbolising the triumph of the sun of the springtime over the storms of winter, it becomes an illustration of the subjugation of chaos by the rise of law and order in the universe. In the Babylon or Marduk version, Anu is at first dispatched by the gods against the monster but is frightened at the sight of her. All the other gods, too, are in mortal terror of Tiamat but Marduk offers to proceed against her on condition that in case of his triumph the entire assemblage of the gods shall pay him homage and acknowledge his sway. The compact is accepted, and Marduk arms himself for the fray. The weapons that he takes— the four winds and the various storms, the tempest, the hurricane, and tornado—symbolise his absorption of the part of Enlil, the god of storms. Marduk meets Tiamat, and dispatches her by inflating her with an evil wind, and then bursting her open with his lance. The gods rejoice and give him their names, a procedure which, according to the views of antiquity, is equivalent to bestowing upon him their essence and their attributes. After all the gods have thus done, Enlil advances and hails Marduk as *bêl mâtâti*, "lord of lands," which was one of Enlil's special names, and finally Ea solemnly declares that Marduk's name shall also be Ea[1]:

> He who has been glorified by his fathers,
> He shall be as I am—Ea be his name!

The purpose of the story is evident. All the religious centres pay homage to Babylon—the seat of the Marduk cult; Marduk absorbs the attributes and powers of all the other gods.

In the schools this prominence of Marduk as a reflection of the political supremacy of Babylon is still further developed, and finds a striking expression in a fragment of composition preserved for us by a fortunate chance[2]:

> Ea (?) is the Marduk of canals;
> Ninib is the Marduk of strength;
> Nergal is the Marduk of war;

---

[1] King, *Seven Tablets of Creation*, Tablet VII., 119, 120.

[2] *Cun. Texts, etc.*, Part xxiv., Plate 50 (No. 47, 406, obverse). The reverse, badly preserved, gives a list of images of gods. The tablet is a neo-Babylonian copy of an older "Babylonian" text. See King's discussion of the tablet, *ib.*, p. 9 and Pinches in the *Expository Times* for February, 1911.

Zamama is the Marduk of battle;
Enlil is the Marduk of sovereignty and control;
Nebo is the Marduk of possession;
Sin is the Marduk of illumination of the night;
Shamash is the Marduk of judgments;
Adad is the Marduk of rain;
Tishpak[1] is the Marduk of the host;
Gal[2] is the Marduk of strength;
Shukamunu[3] is the Marduk of the harvest.

From this text, scholars have drawn the conclusion that the Babylonian religion resulted in a monotheistic conception of the universe. Is this justified? In so far as Marduk absorbs the characters of all the other gods, there is no escape from this much of the conclusion:—there was a *tendency* towards monotheism in the Euphrates Valley, as there was at one time in Egypt.[4] On the other hand, it must be borne in mind that similar lists were drawn up by priests. They reveal the speculations of the temple-schools rather than popular beliefs, but even when thus viewed, their aim was probably to go no farther than to illustrate in a striking manner the universality of the god's nature so as to justify his position at the head of the pantheon. This position was em-

---

[1] A foreign deity—perhaps a designation of the chief Elamite deity.

[2] *I.e.*, "great god"—also intended as a designation of a foreign god.

[3] A Cassite deity.

[4] See Steindorff, *Religion of the Ancient Egyptians*, p. 58 *seq.*

phasised in an equally striking manner by the ceremonies of New Year's day, when a formal assembly
of the gods was held in a special shrine in Babylon,
close by the temple area, with all the chief gods
grouped about Marduk, (just as the princes, governors, and generals stand about the king), paying
homage to him as their chief, and deciding in
solemn state the fate of the country and of individuals for the coming year. The Babylonian
priest could re-echo the ecstatic cry of the Psalmist
(Ps. lxxxvi., 8):

> There is none like thee among the gods, O Lord,
> And there is nothing like thy works;

with this important difference, however, that, in the
mind of the Hebrew poet, Jahweh was the only
power that had a *real* existence, whereas to the
Babylonian priest Marduk was merely the first and
highest in the divine realm. Still, that the other
gods are merely manifestations of Marduk (a fair
implication of the list) is a thought which not im-
probably presented itself to some of the choicer minds
among the priests, though it remained without practical consequences. A certain tendency toward a
monotheistic conception of the universe is after all no
unusual phenomenon, nor is monotheism in itself
necessarily, the outcome of a deep religious spirit—
it may sometimes be the product of rationalistic

speculation. In many a Babylonian composition the term *ilu*, "god," is used in a manner to convey the impression that there was only one god to be appealed to. Greek and Roman writers often speak of θεός and *deus* in much the same way as we ourselves do; and even among people on a low level of culture we are constantly surprised by indications that, albeit in a faint and imperfect manner, the thought occurs that all nature is the manifestation of a single Power, though generally not a Power to be directly approached. The distinctive feature of Hebrew monotheism is its *consistent* adherence to the principle of a transcendent deity, and of the reorganisation of the cult in obedience to this principle. No attempt was made at any time in Babylonia and Assyria to set aside the cult of other gods in favour of Marduk. On the contrary, side by side with the Marduk cult in Babylonia and with the cult of Ashur in Assyria, we find down to the latest period all— Sin, Shamash, Nebo, Ninib, Nergal, Adad, Ishtar —receiving in their special shrines the homage which tradition and long established ritual had prescribed.

VI

After having thus sketched in some detail the character and development of Anu, Enlil, Ea, Ninib, Nebo, and Marduk, we can be briefer in our consideration of the remaining chief figures in the Babylonian-Assyrian pantheon.

The importance of solar cults in an agricultural community explains the circumstance that we encounter so many centres in which the chief deity is a sun-god. It has been already pointed out that the god who was probably the original patron deity of Nippur—Ninib—was a solar deity, that Anu of Uruk was such a deity and Marduk likewise, and that Ninib, becoming in consequence of the pre-eminent religious position of Nippur the chiefest sun-god, absorbs other sun-gods such as Ningirsu of Lagash and Zamama of Kish. In addition, there are three other important centres in ancient Babylonia in which the patron deity represents some phase of the sun—Cuthah, Larsa, and Sippar. In Cuthah he was known as Nergal, in Larsa and Sippar as Ut, "day," or Babbar "shining one," for which the Semitic form is Shamash. Cuthah appears to have been a very early Sumerian settlement, though it never rose to any striking political importance, and the same is the case with Larsa, while Sippar, not far from Babylon, seems to have been one of the earliest strongholds of the Semites. Too much stress must not be laid, however, on such distinctions, for, as we have seen, the mixture of Sumerians and Semites was so pronounced, even in the oldest period revealed by the documents at our command, that a differentiation

between Semitic and non-Semitic elements in the
conceptions formed of the gods is not generally possible. Climatic and sociological conditions are more
effective factors in such conceptions than racial
traits. More important for our purposes is it to
recognise that there are two phases presented by the
sun in a climate like that of Babylonia and Assyria.
On the one hand, he is the great beneficent power who
triumphs over the storms and rains of winter, who re-
pairs the havoc wrought by the flooding of the land
and by the destruction through violent winds, and
clothes nature in a garment of verdant glory. But he
is also a destructive force. The fierce heat of the
summer evokes distress and sickness. The sun may
become a fire that burns up the crops. For reasons
that are not as clear as one might wish, Nergal becomes, in Babylonian theology, the type of the sun's
destructive power. He is associated with pestilence,
famine, and the grave; and we shall see, in a subsequent lecture, that, as a gloomy and morose god, he is
assigned to a position at the head of a special pantheon
of the lower world where the dead dwell. His city,
Cuthah, becomes a poetical designation for the great
gathering-place of the dead, and his name is explained,
perhaps fancifully, as "the lord of the great dwelling," that is, the grave. It is quite within the range
of possibility that Cuthah may have been a place
that acquired special sanctity as a burial-place, as

Kerbela, in the same region, is still regarded as such by the Shiite sect of Islam.[1] The animal associated with Nergal, as a symbol, is a fierce lion, and he is pictured as greedy for human victims. The various names assigned to him, almost without exception, emphasise this forbidding phase of his nature, and the myths associated with him deal with destruction, pestilence, and death. Naturally, Nergal is also pictured as a god of war, bringing about just the results for which he would be held responsible. In Babylonian-Assyrian astrology, he is identified with the planet Mars, and the omen-literature shows that Mars in ancient days, as still at the present time, was regarded as the planet unlucky above all others.

Whatever the reasons that led to this concentration of all the unfavourable phases of the sun-god on Nergal, the prominence that the cult of Babbar (or Shamash) at Sippar acquired was certainly one of the factors involved. This cult cannot be separated from that at Larsa. The designation of the god at both places is the same, and the name of the chief sanctuary of the sun-god at both Larsa and Sippar is E-Babbar (or E-Barra), "the shining house." The cult of Babbar was transferred from the one place to the other, precisely as Marduk's worship was carried

[1] See Peters, *Nippur*, i., p. 322 *seq.* The tradition which places here the death of the sons of Ali is merely due to a desire to invest an ancient centre of burial with a significance for Islamism.

Pl. 16.   Fig. 1.   The Sun-god Shamash in his Shrine.

Stone tablet of Nebopaliddin, King of Babylonia (*c.* 880 B.C.), representing Shamash, the sun-god of Sippar, seated in his shrine with the king (second figure) led into the god's presence by a priest, and followed by Â, the consort of Shamash—the goddess interceding, as it were, on behalf of the king.   Found by Rassam at Sippar.   See Rassam, *Asshur and the Land of Nimrod*, p. 402.

Fig. 2.   Clay Model representing the Cult of the Sun-god.

In all probabilities it illustrates a ceremony of sun worship—perhaps the greeting of the sun-god at sunrise.   Found at Susa and now in the Louvre.   See J. E. Gautier, *Recueil de Travaux*, vol. xxxi., pp. 41–49.

Fig. 1.　The Sun-god Shamash
sitting in his Shrine

Fig. 2.　Cult of the Sun-god (Susa)

from Eridu to Babylon. While Larsa appears to be
the older of the two centres, Sippar, from the days of
Sargon onward, begins to distance its rival, and, in
the days of Hammurapi, it assumes the character of a
second capital, ranking immediately after Babylon,
and often in close association with that city. Even
the cult of Marduk could not dim the lustre of Shamash at Sippar. During the closing days of the neo-
Babylonian empire, the impression is imparted that
there was, in fact, some rivalry between the priests
of Sippar and those of Babylon. Nabonnedos, the
last king of Babylonia, [1] is described as having offended Marduk by casting his lot in with the adher-
ents of Shamash, so that when Cyrus enters the city
he is hailed as the saviour of Marduk's prestige and
received with open arms by the priests of Babylon.
The original solar character of Marduk, we have seen,
was obscured by his assuming the attributes of other
deities that were practically absorbed by him, but
in the case of Shamash at Sippar no such transformation of his character took place. [2] He remains throughout all periods the personification of the beneficent
power residing in the sun. The only change to be
noted as a consequence of the pre-eminence of the cult
at Sippar is that the sun-god of this place, absorbing

[1] See above, p. 59 and Rogers, *History of Babylonia and Assyria*,
ii., p. 362 *seq.*

[2] See Plate 16, Fig. 1.   Shamash in his shrine at Sippar.

in a measure many of the minor localised sun-cults, becomes the paramount sun-god, taking the place occupied in the older Babylonian pantheon by Ninib of Nippur. The Semitic name of the god—Shamash—becomes the specific term for the sun, not only in Babylonia but throughout the domain of the Semites and of Semitic influence.

A place had, however, to be found for sun-cults at centres so important that they could not be absorbed even by Shamash of Sippar. Nippur retained its religious prestige throughout all vicissitudes, and its solar patron was regarded in the theological system as typifying more particularly the sun of the springtime; while at Cuthah Nergal was pictured as the sun of midsummer with all the associations connected with that trying season. The differentiation had to a large extent a purely theoretical import. The practical cult was not affected by such speculations and no doubt, at Cuthah itself, Nergal was also worshipped as a beneficent power. On the other hand, Ninib, as a survival of the period when he was the "Shamash" of the entire Euphrates Valley, is also regarded, like Nergal, as a god of war and of destruction along with his beneficent manifestations. In ancient myths dealing with his exploits his common title is "warrior,"[1] and

[1] Hrozny, *Sumerisch-Babylonische Mythen von dem Gotte Ninrag* (Ninib). See also Radau, *Ninib, the Determiner of Fates* (Phila., 1910), whose view of Ninib, however (p. 23), is entirely erroneous.

the planet Saturn, with which he is identified in astrology, shares many of the traits of Mars-Nergal. Shamash of Sippar also illustrates these two phases. Like Ninib, he is a "warrior," and often shows himself enraged against his subjects.

The most, significant feature, however, of the sun-cult in Babylonia, which applies more particularly to Shamash of Sippar, is the association of justice and righteousness with the god.   Shamash, as the judge of mankind, is he who brings hidden crimes to light, punishing the wrongdoers and righting those who have been unjustly condemned.   It is he who pronounces the judgments in the courts of justice.   The priests in their capacity of judges speak in his name. Laws are promulgated as the decrees of Shamash; it is significant that even so ardent a worshipper of Marduk as Hammurapi places the figure of Shamash at the head of the monument on which he inscribes the regulations of the famous code compiled by him, thereby designating Shamash as the source and inspiration of law and justice.   The hymns to Shamash, almost without exception, voice this ascription.   He is thus addressed[1]:

The progeny of those who deal unjustly will not prosper.
What their mouth utters in thy presence
Thou wilt destroy, what issues from their mouth thou wilt
    dissipate.

---

[1] Jastrow, *Religion* (German ed.), i., p. 435.

Thou knowest their transgressions, the plan of the wicked thou
    rejectest.
All, whoever they be, are in thy care;
Thou directest their suit, those imprisoned thou dost release;
Thou hearest, O Shamash, petition, prayer, and imploration.

Another passage of the hymn declares that

> He who takes no bribe, who cares for the oppressed
> Is favoured by Shamash,—his life shall be prolonged.

VII

The moon-cult of Babylon is associated chiefly
with two centres, Ur and Harran, of which Ur is the
older and the more important, and the centre of a
Sumerian dynasty which represents almost the last
effort of the non-Semitic population to control the
Euphrates Valley.[1] Harran, to the north, falls within the domain where the Semites developed their greatest strength, but despite this fact the moon-cult at
that place may represent a transfer from Ur, as that of
the sun-god was transferred from Larsa to Sippar.
The god, Sin, appears under various designations;
prominent among them is that of En-Zu, "the lord of
knowledge," of which the name Sin may be a derivative.[2] As the god of wisdom, he reminds us of
Nebo, but his knowledge lies more particularly in
reading the signs in the heavens. It is in astrological

[1] See above, p. 30, *seq.*

[2] Sin may be a contraction of Si-in and this in turn equivalent
to En-Zu inverted. See Combe, *Histoire du Culte de Sin,* pp.
1–16, for other names and designations of the moon-god.

P.. 17. Types of Gods.

Fig. 1. Seal Cylinder (hematite), showing Sin, the Moon-god.

Before Sin stands a worshipper, with the goddess Ningal, the consort of Sin, acting as interceder. The three circles behind the god symbolise the moon-god. See Menant, *Collection de Clercq*, Catalogue No. 125.

Fig. 2. Seal Cylinder (green porphyry), showing the god Ea.

Into Ea's presence, the goddess Damkina, the consort of Ea is leading a worshipper. The goat fish or capricorn under the seat of the god is the symbol of Ea. See Menant, *Collection de Clercq*, Catalogue No. 106.

Fig. 3. Procession of gods.

Rock-relief at Malatia in the Anti-Taurus range, showing seven deities mounted on animals that represent their symbols. The head of the procession is formed by Ashur on two animals one of which is the Dragon—transferred to him from Enlil and Marduk, (see comment to Pl. 30, Fig. 2)—followed by his consort Ishtar of Nineveh on the lion, Sin the moon-god on the winged bull, Enlil (or Marduk) on the Dragon, the horn of which is worn away, Shamash on a horse with trappings, Adad on a winged bull and holding the lightning fork in his hand, and lastly another Ishtar on a lion—presumably the Ishtar of Arbela, though the Ishtar of Babylon is also possible. See Place, *Ninive et l'Assyrie*, Pl. 45, from which it would appear that the design was repeated three times on the monument. See also Luschan, *Ausgrabungen in Sendschirli*, p. 23 *seq.* For another procession of gods (on an alabaster slab found at Nimroud) see Layard, *Monuments of Nineveh*, i., Pl. 65.

Fig. 1.   Sin, the Moon-god

Fig. 2.   Ea, the God of Water

Fig. 3.   Procession of Gods

lore and through the widespread influence of astrology in Babylonia and Assyria that Sin appears in the full exuberance of his powers. The moon as the great luminary of the night, with its constantly changing phases, forms, in fact, the basis of divination through the phenomena observed in the heavens. This form of divination, as we shall see in a subsequent lecture, is the direct outcome of speculation in the temple-schools—not an outgrowth of popular beliefs,—but such was the importance that astrology (which may be traced back to the days of Sargon) acquired in the course of time that in an enumeration of the gods, even in texts other than astrological compilations, Sin invariably takes precedence over Shamash. The Semitic form of his name is Nannar, which means "illumination"[1] or "luminary," and this appears to be a designation more particularly connected with the cult at Harran. It is by virtue of being the great luminary of the night also that he becomes the "father of the gods," as he is frequently called in hymns. He is depicted on seal cylinders[2] as an old man with a flowing beard, said in poetical compositions to be of a lapis-lazuli colour. His headgear consists of a cap on which the horns of the moon are

[1] See Lehmann-Haupt in *Zeits. für Assyriologie*, vol. xvi., p. 405.
[2] See Plate 17, Fig. 1, and Ward, *Seal Cylinders of Western Asia*, p. 21 *seq.*

8

generally indicated; and it is interesting to note, as pointing to the influence acquired by the moon-cult, that the horns became a general symbol of divinity which, *e.g.*, Naram-Sin attaches to his head on the famous monument on which he depicts himself as a ruler with the attribute of divinity.[1]

The antiquity of the moon-cult is attested by very ancient Sumerian hymns that have come down to us, in which he is frequently described as sailing along the heavens in a ship.[2] It is a reasonable supposition that the moon's crescent suggested this picture of a sailing bark. The association between Sin and the city of Ur is particularly close, as is seen in the common designation of this centre as the "city of Nannar." No doubt the political importance of the place had much to do with maintaining the high rank accorded to Sin in the systematised pantheon. And yet outside of his sphere in Babylonian-Assyrian astrology, the moon-cult, apart from special centres like Ur and Harran, is not a prominent feature in the actual worship. The agricultural life is too closely dependent on the sun to permit of any large share being taken by the moon. He is not among the Powers whose presence is directly felt in communities whose chief occupation is the tilling of the soil; and, as has

[1] See illustration above, p. 22.

[2] *Cuneiform Texts*, etc., Part xv., pl. 17. See Langdon, *Sumerian and Babylonian Psalms*, p. 296.

already been suggested, his position in astrological
divination determines the relationship in which he
stands to both gods and mankind. The goddess
Ishtar is often spoken of as the daughter of the moon,
but this is due to the identification of Ishtar in the
astrological system with Venus; it is natural that
Venus should be regarded as the offspring of the
luminary of night, just as the other planets, and the
stars in general, would be so regarded. This did not
hinder Ishtar from being viewed also as the daughter
of Anu. The most common sign with which the
name of the moon is written is the number "thirty"
—taken evidently from the average period of her
course.[1] Ishtar, as the daughter of the moon, is,
therefore, written with the number fifteen, while the
sun appears as twenty. So at every turn we encounter,
as regards the moon, some association with astrology
or with the calendar, which was naturally regulated
among the Babylonians, as among all other nations,
by the course and phases of the moon. There was no
possibility of rivalry between the moon and the sun.
Each had its function; and the harmonious division
of the direction of the heavens between the two was
the form in which the relationship between them was
viewed by both Babylonians and Assyrians. The

[1] In astrological compositions and reports all months are
assumed to have 30 days. It is only in the late astronomical
texts that, through the more accurate regulation of the calendar,
months of 29 and 30 days are distinguished.

moon, to be sure, was popularly viewed as having been captured when at the end of the month it disappeared for three days, but its discomfiture was not supposed to be due to any conflict between the moon and the sun. Hostile powers of the night had temporarily gained the supremacy in the heavens, and the same explanation was offered in the case of an eclipse, whether of the moon or of the sun.

As a consequence of this harmonious relationship, it was not felt to be an inconsistency that, on the one hand, Sin should be the "father" of the gods, while on the other hand, Anu as the first member of the "theological" triad should be also thus regarded and that, therefore, Ishtar should be at once the daughter of Sin and of Anu. As a solar deity Anu directs the heavens by day; and the local sun-god of Uruk becoming in the pantheon devised by the priests the god of the heavens viewed as a whole, it was natural that under the added influence of the astrological system which placed the seats of all the gods in heaven, Anu should become the progenitor of the entire pantheon. A further outcome of this double current of theological speculation is that we obtain by the side of the triad Anu, Enlil, and Ea (representing, it will be recalled, the three great divisions of the universe) a second triad of a more restricted character, betraying the influence of the astrological system, which assigns to Sin the first place, followed by Shamash, with Ishtar, as the planet Venus, as the third member. From another point of view these three deities summed up again the chief manifestations of divine Power in the universe: Sin as the leader of the hosts of the mighty heavens, Shamash, the benefi- cent power of the sun, and Ishtar, by virtue of her original attribute, as the goddess of the earth, the mother of life and the source of fertility.[1]

VIII

To this triad, a fourth figure is frequently added— the god Adad, who is also known as Ramman, and who in several respects occupies a peculiar position in the Babylonian-Assyrian pantheon. He is es- sentially a god of storms and rains, as Enlil originally was. His symbol is the thunderbolt or the forked lightning which he holds in his hand.[2] Though often referred to in myths of a high antiquity, and not in- frequently mentioned in votive inscriptions of the earlier rulers of Babylonia, he does not appear to have had any special centre of worship in Babylonia proper. There is no city specifically associated with the Adad cult. This fact, together with the circumstance that a common designation of the god describes him as a deity of the west or Amurru,[3] points to his being an

---

[1] See below, p. 126 *seq.*   [2] See Plate 15, Fig. 3.

[3] Mar-Tu, which is the ideographic form of Amurru as the land of the west. See on this whole subject, Clay, *Amurru*, p. 77 *seq.*

importation into the Euphrates Valley, brought there by an Amoritish wave of migration, and, though assimilated by the Babylonian pantheon, he retains traces of his foreign origin. Moreover, at the time that Adad, or Ramman, was carried into the Euphrates Valley, the chief political and religious centres must have been already definitely constituted, so that Adad appears in the character of an interloper. He bears this character also in Assyria for, although the oldest temple in Assyria is dedicated to him, it is in association with Anu. The double temple of this pair of gods at Ashur has been recently thoroughly excavated,[1] and can now be traced back to the very beginnings of Assyrian history—to about 2400 B.C. The temple is always spoken of as that of Anu and Adad; and this unusual combination of two gods, associated in the name of the temple, suggests that the one or the other represents an afterthought. Since the name of Anu always appears first, there can be no doubt that he is the original deity in whose honour the sanctuary at Ashur was erected.

Anu, as we have seen, was a solar deity and his association with Adad is, accordingly, of the same nature as the partnership of Anu and Enlil, of Ninib and Enlil, and of Shamash and Adad, the sun-god and

[1] See Andrae, *Anu-Adad Tempel* (Leipzig, 1909). The excavations reveal two sanctuaries with a common entrance. See p. 281 *seq.* and the plan on Plate 24, Fig. 2.

the storm-god in all these cases forming a duality which symbolises and sums up the two chief Powers of nature determining the welfare of the country. The addition of Adad to Anu thus reveals the introduction of the worship of the former in the old capital of Assyria, and the importance of the western influence represented by Adad may be gauged by the position accorded him at the side of Anu. Since Prof. Clay has made it probable that traces of this influence are to be seen in some of the conceptions connected with the other chief deities of Babylonia—Ninib, Shamash, Marduk, and even Ea—we may assume this influence to have first manifested itself in Assyria, and then to have spread to the south. We should thus have a counter-current to that northern extension of the Euphratean culture that would account for the presence of the Anu cult in the old city of Ashur. That Anu, and not Ninib or Shamash should have been the solar deity to be thus carried to the north is an indication of the great antiquity of the settlement of Ashur, since the transfer must have taken place at a time when Uruk—the seat of the Anu cult in the south—was one of the chief centres of sun-worship, just as the influence of Uruk is to be seen again in the choice of Anu as the first member of the triad. We thus have indicated the probable order in the predominance of the centres of sun-worship, Anu, Ninib, Shamash, and Marduk, corresponding to the centres, Uruk, Nippur, Sippar, and Babylon.

Adad is also designated as the "great mountain," precisely as is Enlil, and, indeed, he is so completely a counterpart of Enlil that this was perhaps a reason why Adad was never assigned to any special cult centre. It is significant, however, that in the collection of astrological omens it is Adad and not Enlil who appears as the representative of atmospheric disturbances such as thunder, lightning, tempests, tornadoes, inundations, and hail-storms—an indication, therefore, that the astrological system was not yet worked out at a time when Enlil held supreme sway. Correspondingly, in the "liver" omens—the other great division of Babylonian-Assyrian divination—the deities invoked are Shamash and Adad. The home of the Amorites being in the mountainous regions of northern Palestine and Syria, their chief deity would naturally be a mountain god, associated with storms and thunder and lightning. Like Enlil and Jahweh, however, Adad at least in his old home, Syria, under the form of Hadad takes on the traits also of a solar deity. There are some indications that in Babylonia and Assyria this transformation, through a partial assimilation of Adad with Enlil, likewise took place, though never to the extent of obscuring the original character of the god as the one presiding over the violent phenomena of nature.

Pl. 18.   Fig. 1.   Symbols of Ashur, the Chief God of Assyria.

The three smaller symbols are frequently found on seal cylinders and on Assyrian monuments—the symbol being generally placed above the head of the king.   The central one of the three is the purer and more genuine symbol of Ashur as a solar deity—a sun disc with protruding rays.   To this symbol, the warrior with the bow and arrow was added—a despiritualisation that reflects the martial spirit of the Assyrian empire.   The larger figure which appears to be the top of an Assyrian standard, carried along on the military expeditions and borne into the midst of the fray to symbolise the presence of Ashur as the protector of the Assyrian army, shows the sun's rays, and bulls as symbols of the sun-god, while the circle within which these symbols and the full-length picture of the warrior are placed takes the place of the disc.   Found at Khorsabad.   See Botta et Flandin, *Monument de Ninive*, ii., Pl. 158.

Fig. 2.   Votive Statuettes (Copper) Found at Telloh.

Now in the Louvre.   They represent female figures with hands folded across the breast, and terminating in a point which would indicate that they were to be stuck into the ground, or possibly into the walls.   See De Sarzec, *Découvertes*, Pl. I. *bis*, and p. 239 *seq.; Heuzey, Catalogue*, pp. 294–298.

Fig. 1.   Symbols of the God Ashur

Fig. 2.   Votive Statuettes

IX

In Assyria Anu is replaced by a god, bearing the same name as the ancient capital, Ashur. The Assyrian theologians themselves explained Ashur as a contraction of An-shar, which would convey the idea of "Anu of the universe." An older form of Ashur appears to be Ashir, which may have the general sense of "leader."[1] Linguistically, the change of Ashir to Ashur can be accounted for, but not the transformation of An-shar to Ashur or Ashir; so that we must assume the "etymology" of Ashur, proposed by some learned scribe, to be in the nature of a play upon the name. The correct instinct underlying this play is, however, the reminiscence that the chief god of Ashur was originally Anu, whose cult was transferred from Uruk, or some other seat in the south, following in the wake of the northward extension of the culture, just as the cult of Marduk moved from Eridu to Babylon. This presiding deity of Ashur was so generally termed the god of Ashur that in time both god and place became identical. This identification may have been assisted by the addition of the title *shar* to Anu, conveying the idea of large sway, and added, perhaps, in order to distinguish this later Anu from his southern prototype. Be this as it may, the solar character of Ashur is beyond doubt. He is

[1] See a paper by the writer on "The God Ashur" in the *Journal of the Amer. Oriental Society*, vol. xxiv., pp. 288–301.

the counterpart of Anu, as well as of Ninib and Sha-mash. His symbol is the sun-disc with wavy rays extending to the circumference of the disc[1]; and though this impressive symbol was materialised, so to speak, by the addition of a warrior with an arrow within the disc, as an expression of the warlike attributes associated by the Assyrians with their patron deity, still the influence of the symbol was not lost, in lending to the conception of the deity a more spiritual character than is possible when gods are portrayed in human or in animal shape; and, as has been pointed out,[2] it was the Assyrians who thus made a contribution, of no small import, to the stock of religious ideas which they owed to the Babylonians.

The cult of Ashur was essentially a worship devoid of images. This did not, however, prevent the god from absorbing the traits of other gods to whom he stood in no direct relationship. To the Assyrians Ashur, naturally, assumed the same rank as Enlil acquired in the older Babylonian pantheon, and as in later periods Marduk assumed. He becomes in fact the Marduk of the north, and like Marduk is regarded as the great *bêl*—the lord paramount. Other members of the pantheon affect his colour,—little Ashurs by the side of the great one. In a manner, therefore, somewhat different from the case of Marduk, he becomes the dominating figure that over-

[1] See Plate 18, Fig. 1.   [2] See above, p. 51 *seq.*

shadows all others. He is the Great God, the God of Gods beside whom all others pale into insignificance. He is the embodiment of the genius of Assyria and, with the definite establishment of Assyria as a great war power whose watchword is conquest and the aim of whose rulers is universal sway, Ashur becomes first and foremost a war-lord, the protector of Assyrian armies, and whose symbol is carried into camp and battle as an assurance of the direct presence of their god in the midst of the fray. The victories of the Assyrian armies were triumphs for Ashur, and the booty of war was his property. The standing phrase in the annals of the Assyrian kings is that "by the help of Ashur" the enemy was overthrown.

But while the kings of Assyria never fail to give to Ashur the homage due him, and invariably begin the enumeration of the pantheon with his name, the gods of Babylonia by the force of tradition retain their influence also in the north. The greatest among these kings, Tiglathpileser I., Shalmaneser III., Sargon, Sennacherib, Esarhaddon, and Ashurbanapal, manifest the greatest anxiety to associate with Ashur all the great gods of the pantheon,—Marduk, Nebo, Ea, Sin, Shamash, Adad, Ninib, Nergal, and Nusku. They apparently take every opportunity of enumerating the long list in order to emphasise their attachment to these associates of their patron deity and, by implication, the devotion of all the great gods to the service of themselves as kings. To the title "King of Assyria," they were on every occasion ambitious to add that of "King of Sumer and Akkad," and "King of the Four Regions." To these titles that had come down to them from hoary antiquity, they even added "lieutenant of Bêl," to indicate their control of the south, and "King of Universal Rule," to symbolise the policy, consistently maintained, of their conquest of the world. To the array of gods, with Ashur at the head, whom they invoke as the protectors of their realm and allies of their ambitions, they never failed to add the powerful goddess Ishtar.

This brings us in a general survey to the last of the important deities of Babylonia and Assyria, the great mother-goddess, worshipped in a threefold capacity as the goddess of fertility and vegetation, as the goddess of war, and as the goddess of love. In many respects she is the most interesting figure in the Babylonian-Assyrian pantheon.

X

While every male god of the pantheon had a consort, these goddesses had but a comparatively insignificant share in the cult. In many cases, they have not even distinctive names but are merely the counterpart of their consorts, as Nin-lil, "lady of the storm," by the side of En-lil, "lord of the storm,"[1]

[1] See above, p. 69.

or still more indefinitely as Nin-gal, "the great lady,"
the consort of the moon-god Sin, or as Dam-kina,
"the faithful spouse," the female associate of Ea, or as
Shala, "*the* lady" paramount, the consort of Adad.
In other cases they are specified by titles that furnish
attributes reflecting the traits of their consorts, as
Sarpanit, "the brilliantly shining one," the common
designation of the consort of Marduk—clearly an allusion to the solar quality of Marduk himself,—or as
Tashmit, "obedience," the consort of Nebo—plausibly
to be explained as reflecting the service which Nebo,
as son, owes to his father and superior, Marduk. In
the case of Anu we find his consort designated by
the addition of a feminine ending to his name. As
Antum, this goddess is merely a pale reflection of her
lord and master. Somewhat more distinctive is the
name of the consort of Ninib, Gula, meaning "great
one." This, at least, emphasises the power of the
goddess, though in reality it is Ninib to whom
"greatness" attaches, while Gula, or Bau,[1] as she is
also termed, shines by reflected glory.

In all these instances it is evident that the association of a female counterpart with the god is merely an
extension to the circle of the gods of the social customs prevalent in human society; and the inferior
rank accorded to these goddesses is, similarly, due to
the social position assigned in the ancient Orient to

[1] The meaning of Bau is quite uncertain.

woman, who, while enjoying more rights than is ordinarily supposed, is yet, as wife, under the complete control of her husband—an adjunct and helpmate, a junior if not always a silent partner, her husband's second self, moving and having her being in him.

But by the side of these more or less shadowy consorts there is one goddess who occupies an exceptional position, and even in the oldest historical period has a rank equal to that of the great gods. Appearing under manifold designations, she is the goddess associated with the earth, the great mother-goddess who gives birth to everything that has life—animate and inanimate. The conception of such a power clearly rests on the analogy suggested by the process of procreation, which may be briefly defined as the commingling of the male and female principles. All nature, constantly engaged in the endeavour to reproduce itself, was thus viewed as a result of the combination of these two principles. On the largest scale sun and earth represent such a combination. The earth bringing forth its infinite vegetation was regarded as the female principle, rendered fruitful by the beneficent rays of the sun. "Dust thou art and unto dust shalt thou return" illustrates the extension of this analogy to human life, which in ancient myths is likewise represented as springing into existence from mother-earth.[1] It is, therefore, in

[1] On the wide extension of this view, and the numerous folk-

centres of sun-worship, like that of Uruk, where we find the earliest traces of the distinctive personality of a mother-goddess. To this ancient centre we can trace the distinctive name, Ishtar, as the designation of this goddess, though even at Uruk, she is more commonly indicated by a vaguer title, Nanâ, which conveys merely the general idea of "lady." The opening scene of the great national epic of Babylonia, known as the adventures of Gilgamesh, is laid in Uruk, which thus appears as the place in which the oldest portion of the composite tale originated.[1] In various parts of this epic, the goddess, Ishtar is brought forward, accompanied by her maidens, who, symbolising various phases of the feminine principle, compose a court of love and passion. Ishtar woos Gilgamesh, the hero of the epic, here portrayed as a solar deity; but the hero rejects the advances of the goddess and reminds her of the sad fate incurred by her lovers, who after a brief union are driven forth from her embrace, and encounter various misfortunes, that involve a loss of vitality. The tale is clearly a form of the general nature-myth

---

customs and religious or semi-religious rites to which the conception of the earth as the great mother of mankind (as of nature in general) gives rise, see Albrecht Dietrich's valuable and suggestive monograph, *Mutter Erde* (Berlin, 1905), more particularly pp. 27–35.

[1] See chap. xxiii. of the writer's *Religion of Babylon and Assyria*.

of the union of sun and earth, which, after a short time, results in the decline of the sun's force. Tammuz, an ancient personification of the sun of the springtime, is named as the first of Ishtar's lovers; he becomes her consort and is then slain by the goddess, and consigned to the nether world, the abode of the dead. The promise made by Ishtar to Gilgamesh to present him with a chariot of lapis-lazuli, and to shelter him in a palace of plenty, unmistakably points to the triumph of the sun when vegetation is at its height. Tammuz and Ishtar, like Gilgamesh and Ishtar, thus represent the combination of the two principles which bring about life; and upon their separation follow decay and death.

Thus, parallel with the dual principle of sun and storm (variously personified as Anu and Enlil, Ninib and Enlil, Shamash and Adad, representing the two chief Powers controlling the welfare of the country), we have another and more philosophical duality, representing the male and female principles; and this, likewise, is variously personified. Under its influence the consorts of the chief gods become forms of the great mother-goddess. Sarpanit, the consort of Marduk, becomes an Ishtar and is frequently so designated. In the north, Ishtar becomes the consort of Ashur, and is then still further differentiated as the Ishtar of Nineveh, the Ishtar of Arbela, and the

"Queen of Kidmurru."[1]   Though we are no longer
able to follow the process in detail which led to the
disassociation of Ishtar from the local limitations
that must originally have hemmed her in, there can be
no question that the title, Ishtar, became, in time, the
general designation of the supreme goddess herself,
who, in association with some personification of the
supreme male principle, becomes virtually the only
distinctive female figure in the pantheon.

The name, Ishtar, becomes, in fact, the generic
designation of "goddess," from which a plural
ishtarâti is formed to convey the idea of "goddesses,"
or consorts of male deities, independent of the specific character of the latter.   In the astrological system developed in Babylonia, Ishtar is identified with
the planet Venus, and as such becomes known as the
"queen of heaven," furnishing guidance for mankind
through the omens connected with her double character of evening and morning star.   It is due to this
more purely speculative phase of the conceptions
connected with Ishtar that she is represented in the
Gilgamesh epic as the daughter of Anu, and not, as we
might have expected, his consort.   The epic reflects
herein, as in other particulars, the results of the theological and astrological elaboration of popular beliefs, which, as we have seen, led to Anu becoming the

---

[1] Originally a designation of some local goddess. See Jastrow, *Religion* (German ed.), i., p. 243, note.

personification of the heavens as a whole. All the planets, including Ishtar, become therefore Anu's children, just as from another aspect of astrological speculation Ishtar is viewed as the daughter of the moon-god Sin.[1] Sin is the head of the hosts of heaven, and in the astrological system, as we have seen, takes precedence of the sun, thereby assuming the highest position as "the father of the gods," and forming the basis of all divination-lore derived from the observance of heavenly phenomena.

The goddess Ishtar of Uruk, though traced back to an early period and undergoing various transformations, was not, as will, I trust, have become evident by this time, peculiar to that place. A similar deity, symbolising the earth as the source of vegetation—a womb wherein seed is laid,—must have been worshipped in other centres, where the sun-cult prevailed. So, as has already been intimated, the consort of the old solar deity Ninib represents this great female principle. Their union finds a striking expression in a myth which represents the pair, Ninib and Gula (or Bau), celebrating a formal marriage ceremony on the New Year's day (coincident with the vernal equinox), receiving wedding presents, and ushered into the bridal chamber with all the formalities incident to the marriage rite, as observed to this day in

[1] She is represented by the number 15—the half of 30, the symbol of the moon. See above, p. 115.

the modern Orient. When, therefore, the Psalmist
describes the sun[1] as

Coming like a bridegroom from his bridal chamber,

he is using a metaphor derived from the old myth of
the marriage of the sun with the earth in the happy
springtime of nature's awakening.

This conception of a great mother-goddess was not
limited to the Euphrates Valley. It is found where-
ever Semites settled[2] and, apparently through their
influence, spread to other nations. The Ashtart of
the Phœnicians (Greek Astarte) and the Ashtoreth—
an intentional corruption of Ashtart[3]—of the Canaanites, all represent the same goddess and the same
idea of the combination of the two principles, male
and female, designated by the Phœnicians and Canaanites as *Baal*. On Hittite monuments representa-

[1] Psalms xix., 5.

[2] See Barton, "The Semitic Ishtar Cult" (*American Journal of
Semitic Languages*, vols. ix. and x.).

[3] The form *Ashtoreth* which comes to us from the Old Testament was given the vowels of a word *bosheth*, "shame," in order to
avoid the sound of the objectionable name. Ashtart is Ishtar
plus a feminine ending, which suggests that the name itself was
once a general designation—meaning perhaps "leader" like
Ashur,—applicable to either a male or a female deity. As a
means of differentiation, a feminine ending was, therefore, attached to it by some branches of the Semites. In South-Arabic
inscriptions, the equivalent form Athtar appears as a male deity.
See Barton, *A Sketch of Semitic Origins*, p. 87 *seq.*, who finds in
this double aspect of Ishtar a support for his theory of a transformation of female deities to male deities.

tions of the mother-goddess are found, and classical writers record the tradition that the worship of Aphrodite among the Greeks originated in Cyprus, where traces of the Ashtart cult have been discovered. Ishtar is, therefore, distinctively a Semitic idealisation, as the name is certainly Semitic. Both the conception and name must therefore have been carried to the Euphrates by the earliest Semitic settlers.

As the one great goddess and as the consort of the chief god of the pantheon, Ishtar, in addition to her specific character, naturally takes the traits of her consort. A close association of two deities, as we have seen, always brings about a certain interchange of attributes, just as two persons living together are very apt to acquire each other's peculiarities, and even come to look alike. Enlil becomes like Ninib, and Ninib like Enlil, and so the association of Ishtar— under whatsoever name—with the sun-god leads to her being described in terms which might with equal propriety be addressed to Ninib, Nergal, Marduk, or Shamash. She is called "the light of heaven and earth," "the shining torch of heaven," "light of all dwellings." Her sheen is compared to a fire that illumines the land. In part, no doubt, such descriptions arise from the astrological identification of the goddess with the planet Venus, but they occur also in compositions which are free from any allusions to the planetary orb; and when we find her also apostrophised

as the one who "directs mankind," "judging the cause
of man with justice and righteousness," and "as punishing the bad and the wicked," there can be no doubt
that such traits, which, we have seen,[1] form the special
prerogatives of the sun-god, are the reflections of her
association with that deity. Again, the association
with Enlil, the storm-god, whose consort Ninlil, as
has been pointed out, becomes an Ishtar, must be regarded as the factor which leads to Ishtar's being described as "a controller of the clouds," "a raging storm
devastating heaven and earth,"[2] whose voice "thun-
ders over all parts of the universe." The association
with the water-god Ea is to be seen again in the figure
of the goddess presiding over streams and canals.[3]

More significant still is the development of the
mother goddess into the Ishtar of battles, pictured as
armed with bow and quiver, and encouraging the
army to the fray. This transformation is evidently
due to the reflection of the warlike attributes of her
consort—the patron deity of a great centre or the
chief god of the entire pantheon, who naturally becomes the protector of the ruler and of his army, either
for defence or offence.[4] A storm-god like Enlil was

---

[1] Above, p. 111.

[2] Jastrow, *Religion* (German ed.), i., p. 535.   [3] *Ib.*

[4] See the titles of Ishtar in the list, *Cuneiform Texts*, Part
xxiv., Plate 41, emphasising her martial character, followed by
others that belong to her as the mother-goddess, and the goddess of vegetation.

especially adapted to become a god of war,—but so, also, was a deity like Nergal, personified as the destructive power of the fierce rays of the sun of midsummer. We have seen how Ninib, the sun-god of the spring, also takes on the traits of the warrior Enlil, his father. Shamash, likewise, is not merely the "judge of heaven and earth" but also the "warrior," and is very frequently so termed; and when Marduk, as the head of the later pantheon, receives the qualities of all the great gods, he too becomes a god of battles and passes on those qualities to his consort Sarpanit, identified with Ishtar. In an ancient hymn, attached to a song of praise in honour of Hammurapi[1] (probably an adaptation of a composition much earlier than the time of the great conqueror), Ishtar is described as the deity who furnishes aid "in war and battle." In many of the religious compositions prepared for her cult, both of the earlier and of the later periods, the goddess is called "the warlike Ishtar," "the powerful one among the goddesses," the martial "lady of victory," "girded for the fray," and invoked to secure the stability of the throne and of the kingdom.[2]

More particularly in Assyria, in association with the war-lord Ashur—reflecting the martial genius of king and people,—is she celebrated in high-sounding

[1] See Schrader, *Keilinschriftliche Bibliothek*, iii., 1, p. 112.
[2] Jastrow, *Religion* (German ed.), i., p. 539 *seq.*

terms as the lady of war and battles. In an impressive passage in one of Ashurbanapal's inscriptions the king describes how, on the eve of an encounter with the Elamites, Ishtar with the quiver on her shoulder, armed with bow and sword, appears to him in a vision of the night and proclaims, "I walk before Ashurbanapal, the King, created by my hands."[1] It is Ishtar who on another occasion appears clothed in flames of fire and rains destruction on the Arabian host.[2] Ashurbanapal appears to have been particularly devoted to the cult of Ishtar, though he merely followed, therein, the example of his father Esarhaddon, who restored her temple at Uruk. When he takes Susa, the capital of Elam, his first step is to restore to its resting-place, in the temple E-Anna at Uruk, the statue of the goddess which 1635 years before (*i.e.*, 2300 B.C.) had been captured by the Elamites.[3] He almost invariably associates the name of Ishtar with Ashur. At the command of these two deities he enters on his campaigns. Ashur and Ishtar, representing once more the combination of sun and earth—the male and female principles,— send the king encouraging signs, and stand by him in the thick of the fight.

The contrast to this conception of the warlike

---

[1] Rawlinson, v., Plate 5, 100 (Schrader, *Keilinschriftliche Bibliothek*, ii., p. 201). See Plate 19, Fig. 1.

[2] Plate 9, 79–81.   [3] Plate 6, 107–124.

Ishtar is the goddess who, as the symbol of creation, becomes the goddess of human love. Ishtar as the mother-goddess is not only the protector of flocks, and filled with love for the animal world, but the merciful progenitor of mankind; and when a destructive deluge sweeps away her offspring, she is the first among the gods to manifest her grief. In the Babylonian account of the deluge—incorporated in the Gilgamesh epic—she is described as weeping for her offspring, which she complains "fill the sea like so many fish,"[1] and her sorrow arouses the sympathy of the other gods, who pity the sad fate of mankind, brought about at the instigation of Enlil and his divine consort. In a more real sense than is true of such gods as Enlil, Anu, Marduk, Ashur, or even Ea, she is the creator of mankind, "directing all births," as it is said of her. She is described as the mother-goddess (in a text[2] which sets forth the way in which the gods are represented by images,) "with exposed breasts, carrying a child on her left arm, sucking her breast." Votive figurines have been found in Babylonia answering to this description, and it is a plausible conjecture that they were deposited in the temple or shrines of Ishtar by women who wished to secure the aid of the goddess in the

[1] Tablet xi., 117–126. See Jastrow, *Religion* (English ed.), p. 501.

[2] *Cuneiform Texts, etc.*, Part xvii., Plate. 42, col. ii, 6–7. See Plate 19, Fig. 2.

Pl. 19.   Types of the Goddess Ishtar.

Fig. 1.   Ishtar as the goddess of war.   Stele of Anu-banini, King of Lulubu representing himself in front of the goddess Inninna (or Ishtar) and erected in commemoration of his victories in the mountain of Batir (Zagros range).   It is carved on a rock in the district of Zohab between Hassanabad and Ser-i-Pul.   See De Morgan, *Mission Scientifique en Perse*, vol. iv., Pl. X., and p. 161 *seq.;* De Morgan and Scheil, *Recueil de Travaux*, vol. xii., pp. 100–106.

Fig. 2.   Ishtar, the Mother-goddess.

Terra-cotta figurine found at Telloh and now in the Louvre, representing the naked goddess with a child in her arms.   A similar figure was found at Babylon.   See Heuzey, *Figurines Antiques*, Pl. 2, Fig. 3; and *Catalogue*, p. 356; De Sarzec, *Découvertes*, p. 254.

Fig. 3.   Ishtar, the Goddess of Love.

Naked figure with accentuation of the female parts.   Terra-cotta figurine.   Exact provenance in Mesopotamia unknown.   Now in the Louvre.   See Heuzey, *Catalogue*, pp. 357–358.   The naked goddess appears frequently on seal cylinders.   See Heuzey, *Origines Orientales de l'Art*, p. 11; Ward, *Seal Cylinders of Western Asia*, Chap. XXVI.

Fig. 3.
Ishtar, the
Goddess of Love

Fig. 1. Ishtar as the Goddess of War

2

Fig. 2.
Ishtar, the
Mother-goddess

hour of childbirth. A hymn, embodying addresses of the god Nebo to Ashurbanapal,[1] reminds the king of the protection that was granted him when he "lay in the lap of the queen of Nineveh," *i.e.*, Ishtar, and was suckled by her breasts. The picture is evidently suggested by figurines portraying Ishtar as the nurse of mankind.

This phase of the goddess is emphasised in the incident in the Gilgamesh epic, on which we have already touched,[2] when she becomes enamoured of the hero Gilgamesh. Despite the veiled language of mythological metaphor, one recognises that there is another and perfectly natural side to this goddess of love. She is the goddess of the human instinct, or passion which accompanies human love. Gilgamesh, it will be recalled, reproaches her with abandoning the objects of her passion after a brief period of union. This is brought out even more strikingly in another part of the epic where Uruk is described as the dwelling of Anu and Ishtar, and as the city where public maidens accept temporary partners, assigned to them by Ishtar. The enticements of these maidens, who win men by their charms, are described in so frank and naïf a manner as to shock the sensibilities of the modern mind. In such descriptions, found elsewhere in Babylonian-Assyrian literature, we must

[1] Jastrow, *Religion* (German ed.), i., p. 444.
[2] Above, p. 127 *seq*.

recognise the reverse of the medallion. Ishtar, as the mother of mankind, is also she who awakens passion. She is attended by maidens who appear to be her priestesses; these may well be the prototypes of the Houris with whom Mohammed peopled the paradise reserved for true believers. Ishtar, herself, is called by a term, *kadishtu*, that acquires the sense of "sacred prostitute"; and while the famous passage in Herodotus,[1] wherein is described the "shameful custom" of the enforced yet willing defilement of every woman in Babylon in the temple, before being eligible for marriage, rests in part on an exaggeration, in part on a misunderstanding of a religious rite, yet it has a basis of truth in the aforesaid religious custom in connection with the worship of Ishtar, which became an outward expression of the spiritual idea of the goddess as the mother of parturition, and as an instigator of the passion underlying the sexual mystery.

The pages of the Old Testament illumine the character of some of these rites connected with the worship of the divine mother, whose priestesses in various guises represented symbolically the marriage union. The Hebrew prophets, to whom all these rites were obscene, tell us something of the customs which the Hebrews themselves, in common with the nations

[1] Herod., i., 199. See E. S. Hartland in *Anthropological Essays presented to E. B. Tylor*, pp. 189–202.

around, at one time practised.[1] Their language is
generally veiled, for they abhorred even any allusion
to the practices which they condemned so uncompromisingly; but when these stern moralists, in de-
nouncing the people for falling away from the true
worship of Jahweh, make frequent use of the metaphor of a faithless wife, berating Israel and Judah for
having polluted the land with their wickedness,
"playing the harlot," as they term it, "on every high
mountain and under every green tree" (Jeremiah
iii., 6), they refer to some of those rites which were
intended, both in Babylonia and in Canaan as elsewhere, as a sacred homage to the great goddess of
love and of passion. The metaphor, we may be
certain, was not chosen at random, but suggested by
actual practices that formed part of the cult of Ashtart.
The Deuteronomic code[2] finds it necessary to insert
an express clause that there shall be no *kedesha*, *i.e.*,
no sacred defilement, among the daughters of Israel,
and that the "harlot's gift"—clearly again some religious rite—shall not be brought into the house of
Jahweh. Are we to see in such rites among the Semites the evidence of foreign influence? It is not impossible, especially since Dr. W. Hayes Ward has

[1] The incident related in Numbers xxv., 6–9, rests upon some
rite of sacred prostitution, no longer understood by the later
compilers.

[2] Deut. xxiii., 18.

recently shown [1] that the portrayal on seal cylinders of the naked goddess with what is distinctively female emphasised, is due to the Hittites, who as we now know, early came into contact with the Semites both in the Euphrates Valley and in Canaan and elsewhere. On the other hand, the transition from the conception of the mother-goddess to that of the goddess of human love is so easy and natural, that it is not surprising to find that after the thought had once been suggested through extraneous channels, expressive rites should have made their way into the cult. As often happens when a period of degeneracy sets in, it is these rites lending themselves to a mystic symbolism that retain their hold and survive other phases of the Ishtar cult.

Be this as it may, the two orders of ideas, the one represented by the duality of sun-gods and storm-gods, the other by the combination of the sun with the earth, were harmoniously blended in the speculative system devised in the schools of the priests. We find, by the side of the supreme triad Anu, Enlil, and Ea, the tendency to form other groups of three, whereof Ishtar was invariably one, [2] such as Shamash, Adad, and Ishtar, or, under the influence of the astrological system, Sin, Shamash, and Ishtar, or even combinations of four Powers, Sin, Shamash, Adad, and Ishtar,

---

[1] *Seal Cylinders of Western Asia* (Washington, 1910), p. 161 *seq.* See also Plate 19, Fig. 3.   [2] See above, p. 117.

introduced to symbolise and sum up the chief forces
of nature determining the prosperity of the land and
the welfare of its inhabitants. It is significant that
of the Powers involved in such combinations, Ishtar
alone passed beyond the confines of Semite settlements and continued to exercise a profound influence
after all memory of the other gods had been lost.

There is surely something impressive in the persistence of the cult of the mother-goddess; for when faith
in the gods of Greece and Rome began to wane,
people turned to the East and, giving to this cult a
mystic interpretation, found their lost faith in the
homage to the *Mater magna* of Asia Minor, who,[1] was
merely a slightly disguised Semitic Ishtar. Several
centuries after almost all traces of the Babylonian-
Assyrian religion had vanished, the Romans brought
to Rome from distant Phrygia the sacred statue of
Kybele—as the mother-goddess was there called,—
in the hope that she might save the empire from impending disaster. During the most critical period of
the struggle between Rome and Carthage, the *Mater
magna*, or *Mater dea*, made her formal entry into the
capital, a temple was built in her honour, and a
festival instituted. It was the ancient Semitic goddess Ishtar, merely in a different garb, who thus
celebrated a new triumph and an apotheosis—Ishtar

[1] See Cumont, *Les Religions Orientales parmi les Peuples
Romains* (Paris, 1908), chap. iii.

of Babylonia with an admixture of Hittite influences, transformed to meet changed conditions, but showing all the essential traits of the original Semitic Ishtar, the great female principle in nature in its various phases as mother-earth, as the source of all fertility, presiding over vegetation and the animal world, at once the loving mother of mankind and of the gods.

LECTURE III

DIVINATION

I

THE longing to penetrate the future is one of the active, impelling motives in all religions, ancient and modern. The hourly needs of daily life, combined with an instinctive dread of the unknown, lead man to turn to the Powers, on which he knows himself dependent, for some signs which may indicate what these Powers have in mind to do. Divination at one end of the chain, and uplifting invocation at the other, are prompted by the longing to break the fetters, and tear the veil from the mysterious future. The chief function of the priest is to act as mediator or interpreter between the deity and the worshippers in order that the latter may obtain guidance in the affairs of daily life. Success in any undertaking being dependent upon the co-operation of the gods, it was all important to ascertain whether or not that co-operation be forthcoming. The constant, unforeseen changes in nature, in the varying appearance of the heavens, in the unstable phenomena on earth, thus found expression in man's associating caprice and changeability with the arbiters of human destinies. One could never be sure of the mood of the higher Powers. They smiled one day only to frown the next. It was, therefore, a matter of in-calculable practical importance to learn if possible their disposition at any given moment. The cult of Babylonia and Assyria, accordingly, revolves to a large extent around methods for divining the fut-ure, and we now proceed to inquire what these methods were.

In any general survey of the vast, almost boundless, field of divination, we may distinguish two divisions; one we may somewhat vaguely designate as voluntary divination, the other as involuntary divination. By voluntary divination is meant an act of deliberately seeking out some object through which it is hoped to secure a sign indicative of future events. So, *e.g.*, the common practice among ancient Arabs of mark-ing arrows, and then throwing them before an image or symbol of some deity, and according to where they lodged or the side on which they fell, to draw a conclusion as to what the deity had in mind to do or what he desired of his worshippers; this would fall within the category of voluntary divination. All methods of deciding upon any course of action by lot belong to the same class, since the decision delib-erately sought would be supposed to be an indication of the divine will. Sending forth birds and observing their flight, as the Etruscans were accustomed to do, would represent another means of voluntary divination, the conclusions drawn from the direction and character of the flight being based upon a system more or less artifically devised. When the ancient Hebrews consulted the *Teraphim*, which were probably images or symbols of Jahweh (or some other god), they were engaged in an act of voluntary divination, though the details of its method have escaped us. Similarly, the incident related in the Book of Samuel, (I., chap. xx.,) where Jonathan is portrayed as shooting arrows and announcing the result to his companion David, was in reality a species of voluntary divination, though no longer so interpreted by the later compilers.

The field of involuntary divination, wherein signs indicating the purpose of the gods are not sought but forced upon our notice in spite of ourselves, is still larger. The phenomena in the heavens constitute the most conspicuous example of involuntary divination. The changes in the skies from night to night were supposed to correspond to variations in the dispositions of the gods, who were identified or associated with the planets and constellations. The signs were there and cried out, as it were, for an interpretation. All unusual incidents, whether in nature, such as sudden, unexpected storms, thunder out of a cloudless sky, cloud-bursts, unusually severe inundations, destructive tornadoes, swarms of locusts; or incidents in life that for one reason or another rivetted attention, such as dreams, snakes in the path, strange dogs of various colours, deformities or monstrosities in the young of animals, malformations of human offspring, the birth of twins and triplets, or a litter of pigs unusually large or unusually small—in short, anything which, whether really unusual or not, had any feature which gave it prominence, might be a sign sent by some god, and in any event demanded an interpretation by those who were supposed to possess the capacity to read in these signs the will and intention of the higher Powers.

Both voluntary and involuntary divination have a large share in the practical religion of Babylonia and Assyria. As examples of the former class we find the pouring of drops of oil in a bowl or goblet of water, and according to the number of bubbles, the side on which the bubbles were formed, the behaviour of the bubbles, as they first sank and then rose to the surface, and their line of formation, etc.,—from all these, conclusions were drawn as to their portents. In involuntary divination we find dreams, behaviour of animals, peculiar signs in or on new-born infants, or on the young of animals, strange phenomena in daily life, all carefully noted by the priests. These were interpreted according to a system, based in part upon

observation of what in the past had actually followed
any striking occurrence, with the assumption, resting
on the illogical principle of *post hoc, propter hoc*, that
the same circumstances would bring about a like result.

There are, however, two methods of divination
among the Babylonians and Assyrians which take so
prominent a part in their religion and enter so closely
into it, as to overshadow all others. One of these
methods, involving the inspection of the liver of the
sacrificial animal, falls within the category of voluntary divination, the other, based on the observation
and study of the phenomena of the heavens,—including clouds and storms as well as the stars,—
belongs to the category of involuntary divination.
Of the two, the former is a direct outcome of popular
beliefs, while the latter is the result of speculation in
the temple schools. The two methods therefore illustrate the two phases to be noted in the religion, the
beliefs and practice evolved among the people, though
under the guidance of the priests as the mediators
between the gods and their worshippers, and the more
or less theoretical amplifications of these beliefs
along lines of thought that represent early attempts
at systems of theology.

II

So deeply rooted is the belief that through a sacrificial animal a sign indicative of the divine purpose

can be obtained, that the idea of tribute involved in offering an animal appears, so far as the Babylonian religion is concerned, to have been of a secondary character, if not indeed a later addition to the divinatory aim. The theory upon which divination by the means of the liver rested is both curious and interesting. It was believed that the god to whom an animal was offered identified himself for the nonce with the proffered gift. The god in accepting the animal became, as it were, united to it, in much the same way as those who actually eat it. It lies beyond our scope to explain the origin of animal sacrifice, but in ancient religions the frequent association and identification of gods with animals suggest that the animal is sanctified by the sacrifice, acquiring the very attributes which were associated with the god to whom it is offered. Be this, however, as it may, it seems certain that in animal sacrifice an essential feature is the belief that the soul or spirit of the god becomes identical with the soul of the sacrificial animal. The two souls become attuned to one another, like two watches regulated to keep the same time. Through the soul of the animal, therefore, a visible means was obtained for studying the soul of the god, thus enabling mortals to peer, as it were, into the mental workshop of the gods and to surprise them at work, planning future events on earth—which were due, according to the current belief, to their direct initiative.

But where was the soul of the god? Using the term soul in the popularly accepted sense, it is not surprising to find mankind, while in a state of primitive culture, making the attempt to localise what it conceived to be the soul or vital essence of an animate being. Nations, even in an advanced state of culture, speak in figurative language of the heart or brain as comprising the essence or soul of being; and even after that stage of mental development is passed, where the soul is sought for in any specific human organ, human speech still retains traces of the material views once commonly associated with the soul. A goodly part of mankind's mental and physical efforts may be said to be engrossed with this search for the human soul.[1]

In most of the Aryan and Semitic languages, the word for soul means "breath," and rests upon the notion that the actual breath, emitted through the mouth, represents the real soul. This is still a widespread popular belief. Antecedent to this stage we find three organs of the human body—liver, heart, and brain—receiving in turn the honour of being the seat of the soul. This order of enumeration represents the successive stages in these simple-

[1] The search has lasted to our own days. Only a few years ago, the newspapers printed long and serious accounts of experiments made to weigh the human soul by some eccentric scientist.

minded endeavours. Among people of to-day still living in a state of primitive culture, we find traces of the belief which places the soul in the liver. The natives of Borneo before entering on a war are still in the habit of killing a pig, and of inspecting the liver as a means of ascertaining whether or not the moment chosen for the attack is propitious; and, similarly, when a chieftain is taken ill, it is believed that, through the liver of a pig offered to a deity, the intention of the god, as to whether the victim of the disease shall recover or succumb, will be revealed.[1]

The reason why the liver should have been selected as the seat of life is not hard to discover. Blood was, naturally, and indeed by all peoples, identified with life; and the liver, being a noticeably bloody organ, containing about one sixth of the blood in the human body, and in the case of some animals even more than one sixth, was not unnaturally regarded as the source of the blood whence it was distributed throughout the body. The transfer of the locality of the soul from the liver to the heart, and later to the brain, follows, in fact, the course of progress in anatomical knowledge.[2] In the history of medicine among the ancients we find the functions of the liver recognised earlier

[1] Other examples in Jastrow, *Religion* (German ed.), ii., p. 214.

[2] See a forthcoming paper of the writer, "The Liver as the Seat of the Soul."

than those of the heart. When it is borne in mind that only a few centuries have passed since Harvey definitely established the circulation of the blood, it will not be surprising that for a long time the liver was held to be the seat of the blood and, therefore, of life. The Babylonians of a later period seem to have attained to a knowledge of the important part exerted by the heart in the human organism, as did also the Hebrews, who advanced to the stage of regarding the heart as the seat of the intellect. The Babylonian language retains traces, however, of the earlier view. We find the word "liver" used in hymns and other compositions, precisely as we use the word "heart," though when both terms are employed, the heart generally precedes the liver. There are traces of this usage in Hebrew poetry, *e.g.*, in the Book of Lamentations (ii., 11), where, to express the grief of Jerusalem, personified as a mother robbed of her children, the poet makes her exclaim, "My liver is poured out on the ground," to convey the view that her very life is crushed. In Proverbs vii., 23, the foolish, young man is described as caught in the net, spread by the worthless woman, "like a bird in trap," and when he is struck by her arrows does not know that it is "his liver" which is in the hazard. In order to explain the meaning, the text adds as a synonym to "liver" the word "soul"—a further illustration of the synonymity of the two terms.

The Arabic language also furnishes traces of this early conception of the liver as comprising the entire range of soul-life—the emotions and the intellectual functions. A tradition, recording Mohammed's grief on hearing of the suspicion against the fidelity of his favourite wife, makes the prophet exclaim, "I cried for two days and one night until I thought that my liver would crack"[1]—precisely as we should say, "I thought my heart would break." Similarly, in Greek poetry (which reveals archaic usage as does poetry everywhere,) the word "liver" is employed where prose would use "heart," when indicating the essence of life. Theocritus, in describing the lover fatally wounded by the arrows of love, speaks of his being "hit in the liver," where we should say that he was "struck to the heart"; and if, in the myth of Prometheus, the benefactor of mankind is punished by having his liver perpetually renewed and eaten by a vulture, it shows that the myth originated in the early period when the liver was still commonly regarded as the seat of life. The renewal of the liver is the renewal of life, and the tragic character of the punishment consists in enduring the tortures of death continually, and yet being condemned to live for ever. All this points unmistakably to the once generally prevailing view which assigned to the liver the pre-eminent place among the organs as the seat of the in-

[1] Bokhari (ed. Krehl), ii., p. 156.

tellect, of all the emotions—both the higher and the lower,—and of the other qualities which we commonly associate with the soul.

There is no indication that the Babylonians, or for that matter any branch of the ancient Semites, reached the third stage which placed the seat of the soul in the brain. This step, however, was taken by the school of Hippocrates and corresponds to the advance made in anatomical knowledge, which led to an understanding of the important function of the brain. A Greek word for "mind," *phren*—surviving in many modern terms, such as "phrenology," etc.,—remains, however, as a witness to the earlier view, since it originally designated the part of the body below the diaphragm and takes us back, therefore, to the period when the seat of the intellect and the emotions was placed in the region of the liver. It is interesting to note that Aristotle, while recognising the important part played by the brain, still clung to the second stage of belief which placed the centre of soul-life in the heart. He presents a variety of interesting arguments for this view.[1] Plato,[2] however,

[1] See Zeller, *Philosophie der Griechen* (3d edition), ii., 2, p. 483, note 4, where the more important passages are collected, illustrative of Aristotle's view of the origin of all sensations through excitations of our sense organs, transmitted to the heart as a centre.

[2] *Timæus*, §§. 69–71. See Jowett's analysis, *Dialogues of Plato*, vol. ii., p. 503 *seq.*

in the generation before Aristotle, adopts a compromise in order to recognise all three organs. He assigns one soul which is immortal to the brain, which together with the heart, the seat of the higher mortal soul, controls the intellect and gives rise to the higher emotions, stimulating men to courage, to virtue, and to noble deeds, but he locates a third or appetitive soul below the diaphragm, with the liver as the controlling organ, which is the seat of the passions and of the sensual appetites. Plato's view is interesting as illustrative of the gradual decline which the liver was forced to endure in popular estimation. From being the seat of life, the centre of all intellectual functions and of all emotions, it is at first obliged to share this distinction with the heart, is then relegated to a still lower stage when the brain is accorded the first place, and finally sinks to the grade of an inferior organ, and is made the seat of anger, of the passions, of jealousy, and even of cowardice. To call a man "white-livered" became in Shakespearian usage an arrant coward, whereas in Babylonian speech it would designate the loftiest praise:—a man with a "white" soul. The modern popular usage still associating the chief qualities of man with the three organs—brain, heart, and liver—is well expressed in the advertisement of an English newspaper which commends itself to its readers by announcing that it is "all brain and heart, but no liver."

We must go all the way back to Babylonian divination to find the liver enthroned in all its pristine glory.
In truth to the Babylonian and Assyrian the liver
spelled life.[1] Though even popular thought moved
to some extent away from the primitive view which
saw in the liver the entire soul, still the system of divination, perfected at a time when the primitive view
was the prevailing one, retained its hold upon the
popular imagination down to the latest period of
Babylonian-Assyrian history; and accordingly, the
inspection of the liver of the sacrificed animal, and
of the liver alone, lies at the foundation of Babylonian-Assyrian divination and may be designated as
the method of all others for determining what the
gods had in mind.

To recapitulate the factors in the theory underlying
Babylonian-Assyrian hepatoscopy—or liver divination,—the animal selected for sacrifice is identified
with the god to whom it is offered. The soul of the
animal is attuned to the soul of the god, becomes one
with it. Therefore, if the signs on the liver of the
sacrificial animal can be read, the mind of the god
becomes clear. To read the deity's mind is to know
the future. Through the liver, therefore, we enter
the workshop of the gods, can see them at work, forg-

[1] It is not, as a matter of fact, impossible that the words life
and liver are ultimately connected (as German *leib* and *leber*
certainly are), though there are breaks in the chain of etymologi-
cal evidence for the hypothesis.

ing future events and weaving the fabric of human fortunes. Strange as such reasoning may seem to us, let us remember that it still appealed to the learned and profound Plato, who in a significant passage[1] declares the liver to be a mirror in which the power of thought is reflected.

III

But how is the liver to be read? No one who has ever looked at a sheep's liver—and it was invariably a sheep that was used in Babylonian-Assyrian divination—can fail to have been struck by its complicated appearance. In contrast with the heart, *e.g.*, which is not only smaller but consists merely of a series of loops having no special marks to attract attention, the liver has many striking features. There is, first of all, the gall-bladder which lies on it and terminates in a long duct, known as the cystic duct. This duct connects in turn with a second duct, lying across the liver and known as the hepatic duct. From this duct smaller ducts pass out in various directions. Through these subsidiary ducts, gall is collected from various parts of the liver. Passing into the hepatic duct, and then through the cystic duct into the gall-bladder, it is there purified and prepared for further absorption. The lobes of the liver are also of striking appearance. The two lower ones—one on the right and one on the

[1] *Timæus*, §. 71.

left—are sharply divided from one another, and the right lobe is further separated into two sections by the groove in which the gall-bladder lies.[1] The third and upper lobe, known as *lobus pyramidalis*,[2] is separated from the lower lobes by a narrow depression, still designated in modern anatomical nomenclature by a fanciful name, "the gate of the liver" (*porta hepatis*).[3] Attached to this upper lobe are two appendices, a smaller one on the left, known as the *processus papillaris*, and a larger one on the right, having the shape of a finger and known as the *processus pyramidalis*. At the upper terminus of the liver, there protrudes the large hepatic vein (*vena cava*) through which the blood from the liver is carried to the heart. To these features must be added the fissures on the surface and the markings which appear on the livers of freshly slaughtered sheep—as well as of other animals. Varying with each specimen, they present, especially in the lower lobes, the appearance of a map with cross lines and curves. These markings are, in fact,

[1] The Babylonians, however, recognised only two lobes, the *lobus dexter*, called by them the "right wing of the liver," and the *lobus sinister*, "the left wing of the liver." The third lobe is called in modern nomenclature the *lobus quadratus*.

[2] I follow the nomenclature proposed by Stieda in his article, "Ueber die aeltesten bildlichen Darstellungen der Leber," in Bonnet und Merkel, *Anatomische Hefte*, Bd. xv., 695 *seq*.

[3] In the earlier anatomical nomenclature, the other divisions of the liver also have fanciful names. See Theophilus Protospatharius, *de Corporis humani Fabrica*, ii., 13 (ed. Greenhill), p. 81.

merely the traces on the liver surface of the subsidiary ducts above referred to. They gradually fade out, but when the liver is in a fresh state they are striking in appearance. Not only do these markings differ in each specimen, but the other features—the gall-bladder, the various ducts, the lobes and appendices —are never exactly alike in any two livers; they are as little alike as are the leaves of a tree.

The field thus offered for observation and careful inspection of the liver of the sacrificial animal was an extensive one; and it was this field that was thoroughly explored and cultivated by the priests whose special office it was to divine the future by means of the liver. The gall-bladder might in one instance be reduced in size, in another abnormally swollen, or it might be swollen on one side and not on the other. Again, it might be firmly attached to the liver surface, or hang loosely on it, or protrude beyond the liver, or not. The cystic duct might be long in some instances, and short in others; and the same possible variations would apply to the hepatic duct. The latter has a wavy appearance and the number and character of these waves differ considerably in different cases. So also the shapes and sizes of the lobes are subject to all kinds of variations; and even more significant would be the varying character of the two appendices attached to the upper lobes—the *processus pyramidalis* and the *processus papillaris*. Finally, as has been suggested, the fissures and markings extend the scope of the signs to be noted almost indefinitely. To all these variations in the case of healthy livers must be added the phenomena due to pathological conditions. The diseases most common to men and animals in marshy districts like the Euphrates Valley primarily affect the liver. Liver diseases are said to be particularly common among sheep; the result is that the livers of freshly slaughtered specimens exhibit all manner of peculiarities, swellings, and contractions in the ducts and lobes as well as perforations on the liver surface known as "liver flukes," due apparently to bacteriological action. It will be seen, therefore, that the opportunity offered to the Babylonian diviners for developing an elaborate system of interpretations of the signs to be observed was a generous one. Hundreds, nay thousands, of fragments in Ashurbanapal's library bear witness to the activity displayed by the priests in embracing this opportunity.

We have large collections of tablets more or less systematically arranged and grouped together into series,[1] in which all the possible variations in connection with each part of the liver are noted and the interpretations given. Thus, in the case of the gall-bladder, among the many signs enumerated we find such as

[1] See below, p. 179 *seq.*, and Jastrow, *Religion* (German ed.), ii., p. 210, note 1, and p. 211, note 1, for indications as to the extent of the liver divination series.

whether the right or left side was sunk, whether the gall-bladder was full of gall, whether there was a fissure in the gall-bladder running from right to left or from left to right, whether the fissure was long or short. The shade of the colour of the gall was also taken into consideration, whether greenish or whitish or bluish. For the cystic duct entries are made in case it is long, reaching up to the hepatic duct, or appears to be short. The gall-bladder and the cystic and hepatic ducts—as also the lobes—were divided into sections—basis, middle, and head—and according as peculiar phenomena were observed in the one division or the other, the interpretation would vary. Thus, the basis, middle, or top of the cystic duct might be choked up or sunk in, or choked up and also sunk in, or choked up and exhibiting one or more fissures. In the case of the hepatic duct we find entries noting whether it is divided into two or more parts, whether between the divisions there are fissures or markings, whether it contains a gall-stone at the top, whether the duct appears raised or sunken, whether it is swollen, whether it contains white or dark fluid, and so *ad infinitum*. Included in the collections are long series of observations on the character of the depression between the upper lobe and the lower lobes, whether it appears narrow on the left or on the right side or on both sides, whether it is ruptured on the right side or left side, whether it is bent back "like a goat's horn," whether it is hard and firm on the left or the right side, whether it is defective on the one side or the other, whether it contains fissures "like the teeth of a saw," and so on again through an almost endless and very monotonous list of signs.

The great vein of the liver (*vena cava*) is similarly treated, and here much depends upon the varying shape of the vein, whether it is separated from the liver, or partly separated, whether there is a marking above it or below it or whether it is surrounded by markings, whether its colour is black or green, whether it contains fissures, the colour of the fissures, and the like. The lower surface of the large finger-shaped appendix was fantastically designated as its "palace," and note was taken whether the top, middle, or basis was torn away and whether the rent was on the right or the left side, or again whether the hind part of the appendix was torn, and in what section,—at the top, middle, or at the base. The relationship of one part of the liver to other parts also furnished a large number of variations which were entered in the collections of signs, and, lastly, the markings on the liver were subjected to a careful scrutiny and all kinds of variations registered. According to their shape, they were known as "weapons," "paths," or "feet." Those resembling weapons were further fantastically compared to the weapons that formed symbols of the gods, while "paths" and "feet," as

will be evident, suggested all manner of associations
of ideas that entered into the interpretation of the
signs noted.[1]

The field of observation being almost boundless,
it is evident that no collection of signs, however
large, could exhaust the variations to be noted and the
peculiarities that every specimen afforded. It was,
however, the aim of the priests in making these collections to bring together in the case of each part of
the liver as large a number of signs as possible so
that, with the interpretations added, these collections might serve as handbooks to be consulted by
priests, entrusted with this branch of priestly service.
It is from these collections of signs with their interpretations, that we are able to reconstruct the system
of liver divination devised by the uninterrupted activity of many successive generations of priests.

IV

The name given to the class of priests whose
special function it was to divine the future was *bârû*,
which means literally "inspector." It corresponds to

[1] The markings of the liver surface suggest a comparison with
the lines on the hand, and the question may be raised whether
palmistry, still flourishing in our days, may not be due to a direct
transfer to the hand of the significance attached in liver divination to the lines and cross lines in the liver. It is interesting to
observe that one of the lines of the hand is still called in palmistry
the "liver" line.

"seer," but in the literal sense, as one who "looks" at something. That is, also, the original force of our term "seer," which is a translation of a Hebrew term,[1] the equivalent of the Babylonian term *bârû*, denoting, like the latter, the power of divining through an "inspection" of some kind. The *bârû*, as the diviner through the liver—the "inspector" of the signs on the liver,—is therefore the prototype of the modern meat inspector, and, in passing, it may be noted that midway between the ancient and the modern *bârû* we find among the officials of Talmudical or Rabbinical Judaism an official inspector of the organs of the animal killed for food, whose duty is to determine whether the animal is ritualistically "clean"; upon this examination depended whether or not the meat could be eaten. There can be no doubt that this ritualistic inspection is merely a modification of the ancient examination for purposes of divination, just as the hygienic or semi-hygienic aspects of the dietary laws in the Pentateuchal codes represent the superstructures erected on the foundations of primitive "taboos."

The high antiquity to which divination through the liver can be traced back in the Euphrates Valley justifies the conclusion that the application of the

---

[1] See an article by the writer, "Ro'eh and Hozeh in the Old Testament," in the *Journal of Biblical Literature*, vol. xxviii., pp. 42–56.

term *bârû* to the "inspector" of the signs on the liver represents the oldest usage, and that the term was subsequently employed to designate other forms of divination, all of which, however, involved the scrutiny and interpretation of signs. So he who gazed at the heavens and read the signs to be noted there was also called a *bârû* and, similarly, the name was given to the priest who divined the future through noting the action of drops of oil poured in a basin of water, or through observing clouds or the flight of birds or the actions of animals, or who could interpret any other phenomenon which because of its unusual or striking character aroused attention. The term *bârû* in this way became the general term for "diviner," whose function it was to interpret omens of all kinds.

In the days of Gudea the phrase "liver inspection" had acquired the technical sense of divining the future whereby that ruler determined the favourable moment for laying the foundations of a sacred edifice to his god Ningursu. Still earlier than Gudea, we find Sargon and Naram-Sin consulting a sheep's liver before starting on a military expedition, before giving battle, on the occasion of an internal revolt, and before undertaking building operations. The evidence of the continuous employment of this method of divination is almost uninterrupted down to the end of the neo-Babylonian monarchy. We have tablets from the period of the first dynasty of Babylon and from the Cassite period, giving the results of examinations of the liver undertaken by the priests in connection with some important enterprise.[1] These were forwarded to the rulers as official reports, accompanied not infrequently by illustrative drawings. A large number of such reports have come down to us from the Assyrian period[2] which show that livers were consulted at the instance of the kings before treaties were made, before dispatching emissaries, before appointing officials to important posts, as well as in cases of illness of the king, of the king's mother, or of any member of the royal household.

In the course of time there grew up also in connection with the inspection of livers an elaborate ceremonial. The officiating *bârû* had to wash and anoint himself in order to be ritually "pure" before approaching the gods. Special garments were donned for the ceremony. A prayer was offered to Shamash, or to Shamash and Adad, who were addressed as "lords of divination," and in their names the inspection was invariably made. The question to which an answer was desired was specifically stated,— whether, or not, within the next one hundred days the

[1] See examples in Jastrow, *Religion* (German ed.), ii., pp. 297 *seq.*

[2] See Jastrow, *Religion* (German ed.), ii., pp. 285 *seq.*, for many specimens.

enemy would advance to an attack; whether or not the sick person would recover; whether or not a treaty should be made; whether or not an official would be faithful to his charge, and the like. The sacrificial sheep had to be acceptable to the gods of the divination. It must be without blemish, and care had to be taken that in slaughtering it and in the examination of the liver no smallest misstep or error whatever should be made, else the entire rite would be vitiated. Prayers were offered for divine assistance to avoid all such errors. Then the examination was made, the signs all noted, and the conclusion drawn. A single inspection, it would appear, was regarded as conclusive if all the signs or a majority of them at least were favourable. If all the signs were unfavourable or so considerable a number as to leave doubtful the purpose and will of the gods, a second sheep was offered and the entire ceremony repeated, and if this, too, proved unfavourable, a third and final attempt would be made.

The last king of Babylonia, Nabonnedos (555–539 B.C.), whose religious scrupulosity is one of his significant traits, shows how down to the advent of Cyrus, the method of ascertaining the will of the gods employed by Sargon and Gudea was still commonly resorted to. The king wishes to restore a temple to the moon-god at Harran and to carry back the images of the gods to their proper seats. In order to ascertain whether this is agreeable to Marduk, the chief deity, he consults the liver of a sheep and gives us the result of the examination, which proved to be favourable. On another occasion he proposes to make a certain symbol[1] of the sun-god and is anxious that it should be made in accordance with an ancient pattern. He has a model of the symbol made, places it before Shamash, and consults a liver in order to ascertain whether the god approves of the pious offering. To his surprise three times the signs turn out to be unfavourable. The king is dismayed and concludes that the model was not a correct reproduction of the ancient symbol. He has another prepared and again calls upon the *bârû* to make an examination of a liver. This time the signs, which he furnishes in detail,[2] are favourable. In order, however, to make assurance doubly sure, possibly suspecting his priests of manipulating the observations, he tells us that he sought among the archives for the result of a liver inspection on a former occasion when the subsequent events proved the correctness of the favourable decision; then placing the two series of omens side by side, he convinced himself that it was safe to proceed with the making of the symbol. The evident sincerity and conscientiousness of the king should make

[1] Of exactly what nature we do not know, since the term used to describe it, *zarinu*, is an otherwise unknown word.

[2] See below, p. 188 *seq.*

us charitably inclined to his superstitious regard for the primitive rite, which, as the official cult, had all the authority of a time-honoured faith and custom.

Another indication of the vast importance attached to liver inspection is to be discovered in the care with which ancient records thereof were preserved and handed down as guides for later generations of priests. In the foregoing enumeration of liver omens, there are frequent references to the fact that a particular sign had been observed in the consultation of a liver, undertaken on behalf of some important personage. Thus, we are told that a certain sign was the one noted at a time when a ruler of Kish, known as Urumush, was killed by his courtiers in an uprising.[1] Another sign is entered as having been observed at a liver inspection made on behalf of Ibe-Sin, the last king of the Ur dynasty (*ca.*, 2200 B.C.).[2] A number of omens are associated with Gilgamesh,[3] the semi-mythical hero of the Babylonian epic, indicating that underlying the myth there is a basis of historical tradition. In these associations Gilgamesh is termed a "mighty king." Such references lead to the con-

---

[1] The reference in the text reads: "If the head of the gall-bladder encloses the lymphatic gland and is surrounded by 'weapons' [*i.e.*, markings on the liver]—the omen of Urumush, the king, whom the men of his palace killed."—Jastrow, *op. cit.*, p. 333, and below, p. 184.

[2] See Jastrow, *op. cit.*, p. 226, note 3.

[3] *Ib.*, p. 226, note 3.

clusion that, because of the importance which the traditions concerning significant personages assumed, the
omens which accompanied certain events in their
careers were embodied in the collections, and it may
well be that special collections of such historical
omens were made by the priests.

We know in fact of one such collection of omens
referring to Sargon and Naram-Sin, extracted from
chronicles of their reigns,[1] in which the results of the
liver investigations made at important epochs in
their career were recorded. These extracts, whereof
we are fortunate enough to possess fragments, were
compiled, not from any historical motives but to
serve as guides for the *bârû* priests and also as school
exercises in training the young aspirants to the priesthood for their future task. The collection, furthermore, illustrates an important principle in the method
adopted for interpreting the signs; it was argued,
that if on a certain occasion, let us say before an
attack on the ancient enemy, Elam, the gall-bladder,
the various ducts and lobes, and markings showed
certain features, and the result of the battle was a
victory for Sargon, the proof was furnished *de facto*
that these were favourable signs. On the natural

[1] We have fragments of these omens in a text of Ashurbanapal's library, and also a duplicate embodied in a neo-
Babylonian copy of a chronicle of the reigns of Sargon and
Naram-Sin. See King, *Chronicles of Early Babylonian Kings*,
vol. ii., pp. 40–45.

though illogical principle, "once favourable, always favourable," it served also in case of a recurrence of the signs to prognosticate a favourable disposition on the part of the gods invoked. The significant point was not so much the *particular* favourable event that ensued, but the fact that it was *favourable*. On this same principle we have as a second fundamental canon in liver divination, "favourable for one purpose, favourable for any other." The signs noted being favourable, the application depended solely upon the nature of the inquiry and the conditions suggested by the inquiry.

But while actual experience thus constituted an important element in the system of interpretation, one can detect other factors at work in leading to favourable or unfavourable interpretations of a sign, or group of signs. Among these factors the association of ideas stands, perhaps, in the forefront. In common with all nations of antiquity, the Babylonians regarded the right side as lucky, and the left as unlucky. Applying this to the liver, a particular sign on the right side of the gall-bladder, or of one of the ducts, or lobes, or on one of the appendices to the upper lobe, was interpreted as referring to Babylonia or Assyria, to the king, or to his army, or to his household, or to the country in general; while the same sign on the left side referred to the enemy. A good sign on the right side was, therefore, favourable to the inquirer; as was also a bad sign on the left, because what is unfavourable to an enemy is favourable to one's self. On the other hand, a good sign on the left side or a bad sign on the right side was just as distinctly unfavourable.

But the question may here be properly asked—what constituted good or bad signs? The natural association of ideas in many cases suggested an answer. Thus, *e.g.*, the enlargement of any part of the liver was, by this association, regarded as pointing to an expansion of power, whereas contraction would mean a diminution thereof. A large gall-bladder would thus be a favourable symptom, but a distinction was made: if the enlargement was on the left side, the sign would be favourable to the enemy, if on the right side, favourable to the inquirer. Again, in the case of the gall-bladder, the left side is sometimes firmly attached to the liver while the right side hangs loose, or *vice versa*. The tight hold on the liver indicated a firm grasp of the enemy. Hence, if the left side was firmly attached, it indicated that the enemy would be in your grasp; whereas if it was the right side, the enemy would hold you in his grasp, and the sign would thus be unfavourable. This principle was applied to other parts of the liver, where firmness would be associated with strength, and with a tight grasp on the enemy, while a flabby character or loose adhesion would mean the reverse:—weakness and disaster. Here again, should the firmness or flabbiness be limited to one side, the right or the left would be applied to yourself or to the enemy respectively.

Considerable attention was paid to the shape and appearance of the peculiar finger-shaped appendix[1] which hangs from the upper lobe, and which was in fact called by the Babylonians the "finger of the liver."[2] It has two sides, an inner, broad surface which, as we have seen, was called the "palace," and an outer side, designated by the Babylonian *bârû*

---

[1] *Processus pyramidalis.* See above, p. 157.

[2] It is interesting to note in connection with this "finger of the liver" that reference is made to it no less than ten times in the regulations of the Biblical codes for sacrifice (Exodus xxix., 13, 22; Leviticus ii., 4, 10, 15; vii., 4; viii., 16, 25; ix., 10, 19) under the designation of "that which hangs over the liver,"—erroneously translated in our Bible as the "caul above the liver." The regulations provide that this appendix is to be burned in all kinds of sacrifice, though the rest of the liver of the sacrificial animal may be eaten by the priests. Inasmuch as the Pentateuchal codes abound in protests against customs and rites prevailing among the nations around, the ordinance to burn this part of the liver was clearly intended as a protest against using the sacrificial animal for purposes of divination, the *pars pro toto* being regarded as a sufficient reminder. See Jastrow, *Religion* (German ed.), ii., p. 231, note 10. In Rabbinical literature this appendix is likewise termed the "finger of the liver"—an interesting trace of Babylonian influence. The Greek translators of the Pentateuch correctly rendered the Hebrew phrase "that which hangs over the liver" as "the lobe of the liver," for in Greek hepatoscopy this *processus pyramidalis* is actually thus designated, as being the chief lobe. Among the Romans it was called "the head of the liver" (*caput jecoris*)—reflecting likewise the significance attached to this part of the liver in the divination system.

priests as the "rear" side. By the same association
of ideas which we have already noted, a marking on
the right side of the "palace" indicated that the
enemy would invade the land; a marking on the left
side that the king's army would invade the enemy's
land. The appendix, like the gall-bladder, lobes, and
ducts, being divided into three sections, a marking at
the base was regarded as favourable to the ques-
tioner, because the base represented the enemy. A
marking at the top was unfavourable because, again
by the association of ideas, the top represented the
king or one's own country. The relationship of the
larger appendix to the smaller[1] was also regarded as
important. In the event of the larger being abnormally small and the smaller abnormally large, the
sign was interpreted as a reversal of normal
conditions, so that the small would be great and
the weak would be strong, while the large would
become small and the strong become weak. Specific interpretations of such signs in given instances are stated to be, that the son will be more
powerful than the father, that the servant will be
superior to the master, or that the maid will become the mistress—possibly hints that domestic
troubles are not a modern invention, but that they
vexed the souls of even Babylonian housewives,
and that the servant-girl question ascends to an

[1] The *processus papillaris*.

antiquity so remote as to be time-honoured and respectable.

This same association of ideas was extended in other directions, and applied to the terms long and short. A long cystic or hepatic duct pointed to long life or to a long reign, a short duct to a short life or to a short reign. It has already been pointed out that the markings on the liver were frequently compared to weapons. Indeed this comparison was of all the most frequent, and, according to the shapes of the weapons, they were associated with Ishtar, Enlil, Ninib, Sin, and other deities.[1] By a further extension of this association, an Ishtar "weapon" or marking was interpreted as indicating the protection or the hostility of this goddess, a Ninib "weapon" was associated with its namesake, and so on, through the list. Thus the system developed; and it can be easily seen how a few basic phases of association of ideas can be extended to endless ramifications. This may be best illustrated by a few examples.

v

The collection of omens illustrative of events

---

[1] Each of the gods had his weapons; and on Boundary Stones such weapons are pictured as appropriate symbols of the gods, as, *e.g.*, a spearhead for Marduk, a mace with a lion head for Nergal, and the like. See Hinke, *A New Boundary Stone of Nebuchadrezzar I. from Nippur*, pp. 78–87.

in the reigns of Sargon and Naram-Sin begins as follows[1]:

> If the gall-bladder spreads over the liver surface—an omen of Sargon, who on the basis of this omen proceeded against Elam, subjugated the Elamites, made an enclosure around them, and cut off their supplies.

We must of course assume that these details represent extracts from a chronicle of what actually happened in the campaign against Elam, but arguing backwards from the event to the sign, it is reasonable to suppose that the priests saw in the extension of the gall-bladder the grounds for the favourable character of the sign. The picture of the gall-bladder encompassing the liver surface would further suggest the enclosure around the enemy, shutting him in.

Another sign in this collection reads:

> If the liver surface, exclusive of the gall-bladder and the "finger of the liver,"[2] is shaped like the lid of a pot,[3] on the right side of the liver a "weapon" is interposed, and on the left side and in front there are seven fissures—an omen of Sargon. On the basis of this omen the inhabitants of the whole land rebelled against him, encompassed him in Agade, but Sargon went forth, defeated them, accomplished their overthrow, humbled their great host, captured them together with their possessions, and devoted [the booty] to Ishtar.

---

[1] Rawlinson (2d ed.), iv., Pl. 34, Nr. 1. For a complete translation see Jastrow, *Religion* (German ed.), ii., pp. 227–244.

[2] *I.e.*, excluding these from consideration.

[3] *I.e.*, curved and smooth.

In this case it is evident that the seven fissures—seven being a large round number—suggested a general disruption of the empire; but a marking associated with a weapon being interposed on the right side would naturally be regarded as pointing to a successful check of the uprising, while the circumstance of the liver being otherwise well-rounded and smooth was regarded as a sign of the ultimate disappearance of the difficulties with which Sargon found himself encumbered. The chief import, however, of the omen, it must be borne in mind, is that the subsequent events *proved* the signs in question to have been favourable; but at the same time it was the purpose of the priests, as is suggested above, in compiling, from the official chronicles, a series of omens dating from the reigns of Sargon and Naram-Sin, to preserve them as a guide for the future. The great name of King Sargon, whose fame as a successful conqueror gave rise to legends of his birth and origin, was assuredly one to conjure with. If on any occasion the examination of a liver revealed a "Sargon" sign, there could be no mistaking its import. Events showed what it meant and signs given to the great king—the favourite of the gods—would, necessarily, be trustworthy guides.

These two factors, records,—or recollections of events following upon signs observed on specific occasions, and a natural, or artificial, association of ideas,—control the large collections of "liver" omens,

which in the course of time were stored in the temples
through the activity of priests. With the help of
these collections, as guides and reference-books, all
that was necessary was to observe every possible
sign on the liver; note them down; refer them to the
collection which would furnish the favourable or unfavourable interpretation; register these interpretations; and then, from a complete survey, draw a
conclusion, if haply one could be formed.

The interpretations themselves in these collections relate, almost exclusively, to the general welfare and not to individual needs or desires. They
refer to warfare; to victory or defeat; to uprisings
and devastations, pestilence and crops. Individuals
are not infrequently referred to, but the reference is
limited to the ruler or to members of his household,
under the ancient view taken of royalty,[1] that
what happens to the king and his household affects
the fortunes of the country for good or evil.
This, of itself, does not exclude the possibility that
private individuals consulted the *bârû* priests, and
had liver examinations made on their own behalf.
It must be remembered that our material consists of
official records; but it may be said in general that the
gods were supposed to concern themselves with public
affairs only, and not with the needs of individuals.

[1] See Frazer, *Lectures on the Early History of Kingship*—
especially Lecture IV.

This is in keeping with what we know generally of Babylonian-Assyrian culture, which reveals the weakness of the factor of individualism. The country and the community were all in all; the individual counted for little, in striking contrast, *e.g.*, to Greek culture, where the individual almost overshadows the community. The circumstance that, in the large collections of omens, the interpretations deal with affairs of public and general import, thus turns out to be significant; and while, as we have seen, the important feature for those who resorted to divination was merely to ascertain whether the interpretation was favourable or unfavourable, the interpretations themselves in the collections are always explicit in referring to a specific prognostication as favourable, or unfavourable.

The attempt to follow in detail the association of ideas which led to each specific interpretation would be a hopeless and also a futile task. We may well content ourselves with a recognition of the main factors involved in this association of ideas as above outlined. Thus, we can understand that a fissure on the right side of the gall-bladder should point to some disaster for the army, and a fissure on the left to disaster for the enemy's army; or that a fissure on both right and left should prognosticate general defection; but why, where there are two ruptures at the point of the gall-bladder, a short one on the right side should indicate that the enemy will destroy the produce of the land, but if the left one is short the enemy's produce will be destroyed, is not apparent, except on the basis of a most artificial association of ideas. We can understand why a double-waved hepatic duct, with the upper part defective, should point to a destruction of the king (the upper part representing, like the right side, the king and his army), and why, if the lower part is defective, the enemy's army will be destroyed (the lower part, like the left side, representing the enemy); but any ordinary association of ideas fails to account for the prediction that a rupture between the two waves of the duct means specifically that a pestilence will rage, or that there will be an inundation and universal devastation. It seems reasonable to assume that many of these specific deductions rest, as in the case of the genuinely historical omens, upon *actual* experience, that on a certain occasion, when the sign in question was observed at a liver inspection, a pestilence followed, or an inundation, accompanied by great destruction, took place. The priests would naturally take note of all events of an unusual character which followed upon any examination, and record them in connection with the sign or signs; and it is easy to see how, in the course of time, an extensive series of such specific interpretations would have been gathered, resting not upon any association of ideas between a sign and a prognostication, but upon the rule of *post hoc, proper hoc.* In such cases, the guidance for the priests would be restricted, just as in the case of historical omens, to an indication whether the interpretation was favourable or unfavourable. If favourable, the repetition of the sign would likewise be favourable and could apply to any situation or to any inquiry, quite irrespective of the specific interpretation entered in the collections. The scope would be still further enlarged by logical deductions made from an actual record of what happened after the appearance of a certain sign or series of signs observed on a single former occasion. Thus, if a specific sign on the right side of a part of the liver was, as a favourable symptom, followed by good crops, it was possible to add an entry that if the same sign occurred on the left side, it would point to bad crops.

In all these various ways, and in others that need not be indicated, the collections would, in the course of ages, grow to colossal proportions. Each important temple would collect its own series, and the ambition of the priests would be to make these series as complete as possible, so as to provide for every possible contingency. A table of contents which we fortunately possess,[1] of two such series of omen collections, enables us to estimate their size. The tables furnish the opening lines of each of the fourteen and seven-

[1] *Cuneiform Texts, etc.*, Part XX.,   Plate I.

Pl. 20. Fig. 1. Drawing of Sheep's Liver, giving the Latin terms of the chief parts of the liver, with their Babylonian equivalents, so far as determined, together with the Babylonian terms for the various markings on the liver.

Fig. 2. Omen school Tablet from Ashurbanapal's Library, showing the finger-shaped appendix (*processus pyramidalis*) attached to the upper lobe of the liver. See Boissier, *Documents Assyriens relatifs aux Présages*, pp. 36–40 and Illustration facing p. 188.

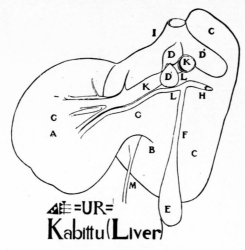

◀Ⅲ =UR= Kabittu (Liver)

◀◀◀=BA= Pântû (Liver surface)

(A) *lobus sinister* ◀Ⅲ 𒀭 𒀭 ▽ 𒈾
 kappu kabitti sa sumeli

(B) *lobus quadratus*

(C) *lobus dexter* ◀Ⅲ 𒀭 𒀭 ▽ ◁𒈾
 kappu kabitti sa imni

(D) *lobus caudatus* 𒀭𒈨 𒂍𒐊 · UR·MURUB

(D') *processus papillaris* ◁ 𒀭 MAŠ

(D") *processus pyramidalis* 𒀭 ◁𒈨 ·SU·SI *ubânu*

(E) *vesicæ fellæ* 𒂍𒈨 𒆬 ·SI·TUN·NU

(F) *ductus cysticus* 𒈾𒐊 ·NA

(G) *ductus hepaticus* 𒈾𒐊 ·GIR=NPR

(H) *dens choledochus* 𒈨 𒅗 ME·NI

(I) *vena cava caudalis*

(K) *vena portæ* 𒂍𒐊·RALAG · *danânu*
 porta hepatis ▽ 𒂍 ·CAR·TAB · *naptartu*

(L) *lympho glandulæ* ◁𒂍𒐊 ·DA· *siânu*

(M) *fossa venæ umbilicalis*

MARKINGS

𒐊 𒈨 · *eriku=eriku ikti* ◁ · BURU· *ikbi kbi*' ◁𒈨 · GIR· *padânu imid*
 𒅗 𒐊 𒂍◁ 𒐊𒈨 · NAR·ZAG·GA· *kaskasu seer filado (kboerigel)*

Fig. 1. Drawing of Sheep's Liver
with Latin and Babylonian
Terms for Chief Parts

Fig. 2. Omen School—Tablet
from Ashurbanapal's Library,
showing Finger-shaped Ap-
pendix to Upper Lobe of Liver

teen tablets of which the series respectively consisted. In one case the number of lines on each tablet is also indicated, from which we may gather that the series consisted of about fifteen hundred lines, and, since each line contained some sign noted together with the interpretation, it follows that we have not less than fifteen hundred different signs in this one series. Considering that we have remains, or references, to over a dozen series of these liver omens in the preserved portions of Ashurbanapal's library, it is safe to say that the recorded signs and interpretations mount high into the thousands. A few specimens from these collections will suffice to illustrate their character[1]:

If the cystic duct is long, the days of the ruler will be long.

If the cystic duct is long, and in the middle there is an extended subsidiary duct, the days of the ruler will soon end.

If the base of cystic duct is long, and there is a fissure on the right side, the enemy will maintain his demand against the ruler, or the enemy will bring glory from out of the land.[2]

If the base of the cystic duct is long, and there is a fissure on the left side, the ruler will maintain his demand against the enemy, or my army will bring glory out of the enemy's land.

If the base of the cystic duct is long, lying to the right of the hepatic duct, the gods will come to the aid of the enemy's army, the enemy will kill me in warfare.

If the base of the cystic duct is long, lying to the left of the hepatic duct, the gods will come to the aid of my army, and I shall kill the enemy in warfare.

---

[1] Boissier, *Choix des Textes relatifs à la Divination*, p. 40. See Jastrow, *Religion* (German ed.), ii., p. 329.

[2] *I.e.*, out of Babylonia and Assyria.

In the same way we have a long series of omens detailing the various possibilities in connection with fissures in the gall-bladder[1]:

If the gall-bladder is split from right to left, and the split portion hangs loose, thy power will vanquish the approaching enemy.

If the gall-bladder is split from left to right, and the split portion hangs loose, the weapon of the enemy will prevail.

If the gall-bladder is split from right to left, and the split portion is firm, thine army will not prevail in spite of its power.

If the gall-bladder is split from left to right, and the split portion is firm, the enemy's army will not prevail, in spite of its power.

If the gall-bladder is split from right to left, and there is a gallstone at the top of the fissure, thy general will capture the enemy.

If the gall-bladder is split from left to right, and there is a gallstone at the top of the fissure, the general of the enemy will capture thee.

Among the many signs noted in the case of the hepatic duct in the collection, we find the following[2]:

If the hepatic duct is twofold[3], and between the two parts there is a marking,[4] Nergal[5] will rage, Adad[6] will cause overflow, Enlil's word will cause general destruction.

If the hepatic duct is twofold, and between the two parts there is

---

[1] See Jastrow, *Religion* (German ed.), ii., p. 335.

[2] *Cuneiform Texts, etc.*, Part XX., Plate 3. See for a complete translation of this text, Jastrow, *Religion* (German ed.), ii., p. 341 *seq.*

[3] *I.e.*, consists of two waves or two layers.

[4] *I.e.*, trace on the surface of a subsidiary duct.

[5] God of pestilence. See above p. 107.

[6] God of storms. See above p. 117.

a "weapon"[1], visible above,[2] the enemy will advance and destroy my army.

If the hepatic duct is twofold, and between the two parts there is a "weapon," visible below,[3] my army will advance and destroy the enemy.

If the hepatic duct is twofold, and between the two parts there is a "weapon," visible on the right side,[4] march of the enemy's army against the land.

If the hepatic duct is doubled, and between the two parts there is a "weapon," visible on the left side, march of my army against the enemy's land.

Out of an even larger number of symptoms[5] associated with the depression between the upper and the lower lobes, known as "the liver-gate," a few extracts will suffice:

If the liver-gate is long on the right side and short on the left, joy of my army.

If the liver-gate is long on the left side and short on the right, joy of the enemy's army.

If the liver-gate is crushed on the right side and torn away,[6] the ruler's army will be in terror.

If the liver-gate is crushed on the left side and torn away, the enemy's army will be in terror.

If the liver-gate is torn away on the right side, thine army will go into captivity.

If the liver-gate is torn away on the left side, the enemy's army will go into captivity.

---

[1] A marking compared to a weapon. See above p. 174.

[2] Upper part=Babylonia and Assyria.

[3] Lower part=enemy.

[4] Right side=Babylonia and Assyria.

[5] *Cuneiform Texts, etc.*, Part XX., Plate 31–35. No less than one hundred and fourteen different signs are registered.

[6] *I.e.*, defective.

If, in the curvature[1] of the liver-gate, there are fissures to the right of the hepatic duct, the enemy will advance to my dwelling-place.

If, in the curvature of the liver-gate, there are fissures to the left of the hepatic duct, I will advance against the enemy's army.

If, in the curvature of the liver-gate, there is one fissure to the right of the hepatic duct, thine army will not prevail, despite its power.

If, in the curvature of the liver-gate, there is one fissure to the left of the hepatic duct, the enemy's army will not prevail, despite its power.

Similarly, two fissures mean "captivity," three fissures "enclosure," and four fissures "devastation" —applying to the enemy or to the king's side according to the appearance of the fissures to the right or to the left of the hepatic duct. Lastly, a brief extract from a text dealing with symptoms connected with the finger shaped appendix[2]:

If the finger is shaped like a crescent, the omen of Urumush, the king whom his servants put to death in his palace.[3]

If the finger is shaped like a lion's head, the servants of the ruler will oppose him.

If the finger is shaped like a lion's ear, the ruler will be without a rival.

If the finger is shaped like a lion's ear, and split at the top, the gods will desert thy army at the boundary.[4]

---

[1] *I.e.*, the deep part of the depression.

[2] See Jastrow, *Religion* (German ed.), ii., p. 392 *seq.*

[3] A specimen of an historical omen. See above p. 168. Urumush was one of the early rulers of the district of which Kish was the centre and capital.

[4] *I.e.*, the gods will not march with the army into foreign territory.

If the finger is shaped like an ox's tongue, the generals of the ruler will be rebellious.

If the finger is shaped like a sheep's head, the ruler will exercise power.

If half of the finger is formed like a goat's horn, the ruler will be enraged against his land.

If half of the finger is formed like a goat's horn, and the top of it[1] is split, a man's protecting spirit will leave him.

If the finger is shaped like a dog's tongue, a god[2] will destroy.

If the finger is shaped like a serpent's head, the ruler will be without a rival.

In the official reports of liver examinations forwarded to the rulers, and at times embodied in their annals, all the signs, as observed, were recorded, and the interpretations added as quotations from these omen collections. It thus happened that, in many cases, these interpretations had no direct bearing on the character of the inquiry, but the interpretation showed whether or not the sign was favourable, which was the chief concern of both priests and applicants. On the basis of the extracts, therefore, a decision was rendered, and often a summary given at the end of the reports, indicating the number of favourable and unfavourable signs.

The number of signs recorded on the liver varied considerably. Every part of the liver was scrutinised, but frequently no special marks were found

---

[1] *I.e.*, of the "finger."

[2] Throughout the omen texts, "god" without further qualification means Nergal, the god of destruction, warfare, pestilence, and death.

on one part or the other. The minimum, however, of signs recorded, in any known instance, appears to have been ten, and from this number upward we have as many as fifteen and even twenty variations. To give an example from the days of the Assyrian empire, we find, in response to a question put to a *bârû* priest whether or not an uprising that had taken place would be successful, the following report of the results of the examination of the liver of a sacrificial sheep[1]:

The cystic duct is normal; the hepatic duct double, and if the left part of the hepatic duct lies over the right part of the hepatic duct, the weapons of the enemy will prevail over the weapons of the ruler.

The hepatic vein is not normal—this means siege.

There is a depression to the right of the cystic duct[2]—overthrow of my army.

The left side of the gall-bladder is firm, through thee,[3]—conquest of the enemy. The "finger" and the papillary appendix[4] are normal.

The lower part of the liver[5] to the right is crushed—the leader will be crushed, or there will be confusion in my army.[6]

The upper part is loose.

The curvature over the lower point[7] is swollen, and the basis of the upper lobe is loose.

---

[1] Jastrow, *Religion* (German ed.), ii., pp. 288–290.

[2] An explanatory note adds "The hepatic duct is choked up and closed."

[3] The address is to the king or to the inquirer.

[4] The small *processus* at the other end of the upper lobe. See above, p. 157.

[5] *I.e.*, the lower part of the "finger."

[6] An alternative interpretation of the "finger."

[7] Of the "finger" likewise.

The liver "fluke"[1] is destroyed, the network of the markings consists of fourteen [meshes], the inner parts of the sheep are otherwise normal.

The "inspector" then adds as a summary that five of the signs are unfavourable, specifying the five he has in mind, and closes with the decision "it is unfavourable." The examination thus showed that the gods were not favourable to the king's natural desire to quell the rebellion, and that more trouble was to be expected.

As a second example of the recorded result of a liver examination let us take a report incorporated by king Nabonnedos in his annals, on the occasion of his consulting the priests in order to ascertain whether or not the deities approved of the king's purpose to make a symbol of the sun-god as a pious offering.[2] The first result, though favourable, did not quite satisfy the king; it showed the following signs, together with the interpretations as furnished by the omen collections[3]:

The cystic duct is long—the days of the ruler will be long.

The compass of the hepatic duct is short—the path of man will be protected by his god;[4] god will furnish nourishment to man, or waters will be increased.[5]

---

[1] See above, p. 159.   [2] See above, p. 167, note 1.

[3] Jastrow, *Religion* (German ed.), ii., p. 252 *seq.*

[4] *I.e.*, by the protecting demon which, according to Babylonian views, accompanies the individual, unless driven off by a more powerful evil demon.

[5] Alternative interpretation.

The lymphatic gland is normal—good luck.

The lower part of the gall-bladder is firm on the right side, torn off on the left—the position of my army will be strong, the position of the enemy's army endangered. The gall-bladder is crushed on the left side—the army of the enemy will be annihilated, the army of the ruler will gain in power.

The "finger" is well preserved—things will go well for the sacrificer[1], and he will enjoy a long life.

The papillary appendix is broad—happiness.

The upper surface[2] wobbles[3]—subjection, the man will prevail in court against his opponent.

The lower part of the "finger" is loose—my army will gain in power.

The network of markings consists of fourteen well developed meshes—my hands will prevail in the midst of my powerful army.

Although, for reasons indicated, the interpretations have no bearing whatsoever on the inquiry, they are all favourable, and the king might have been satisfied with the result. In order, however, to remove all possible doubt as to the correctness of the conclusions, he selected from the archives a series of signs, noted on a former occasion, when the subsequent events *proved* that the signs were favourable, and compared the two lists. This second series reads as follows:

The cystic duct is long,—the days of the ruler will be long.

The hepatic duct is double on the right,—the gods will assist.

The lymphatic gland is well formed, the lower part firm—peaceful habitations.

The hepatic duct is bent to the right of the gall-bladder, the

---

[1] *I.e.*, the king or the inquirer in general.

[2] *Sc.* of the "finger."

[3] Moves freely to and fro.

gall-bladder itself normal—the army will be successful and return in safety.

The gall-bladder is long,—the days of the ruler will be long.

The left side of the gall-bladder is firm,—through thee, destruction of the enemy.

There is a "weapon" in the middle of the back surface of the "finger" with downward curve,[1]—the weapon of Ishtar will grant me security, the attack of the enemy will be repulsed.[2]

The upper part of the hind surface of the liver[3] protrudes to the right, and a liver fluke has bored its way into the middle,— the protector of my lord will overthrow the army of the enemy by his power. The lower point[4] rides over the ditch[5],—the protection of (his) god[6] will be over the man. The angry god will become reconciled with man.

The signs recorded in the two series are not the same throughout, but there are enough points of agreement to reassure the king that the decision of the priests in the case of the first series was correct; and, what is equally to the point, there are no signs and interpretations in the second series that contra-

---

[1] *I.e.*, the marking, compared to a weapon, curves as it runs along. The shape suggests a comparison with the weapon of the goddess Ishtar (above p. 174). Hence the interpretation.

[2] An explanatory note adds that the name of the weapon is "conqueror"—a designation actually given to one of the weapons of Marduk, the consort of Ishtar. See Jastrow, *Religion* (German ed.), ii., p. 261, note 10.

[3] Though the term "liver" is used, it is the "finger" of the liver that is meant.

[4] Of the "finger."

[5] The depression separating the *processus pyramidalis* from the lower right lobe is meant—which is pictured as a ditch. The "finger" of the liver is often curved, and lies across this depression.

[6] *I.e.*, the protecting demon as above, p. 187, note 4.

dict the first. The king, no doubt, was anxious to have the judgment of his "inspector" confirmed, and rested content, therefore, with a proof that might possibly not have appealed to a spirit more critically disposed.

VI

Childish as all these superstitious rites may appear to us, hepatoscopy had at least one important result in Babylonia. It led to a genuine study of the anatomy of the liver; and in view of the antiquity to which the observation and nomenclature of the various parts of the liver may be traced, there can be small doubt that to the *bârû* priests belongs the credit of having originated the study of anatomy[1]; just as their associates, the astrologers of Babylonia, also known as *bârû*, *i.e.*, "inspectors," of the heavens, laid the elementary foundations of astronomy, though, as we shall see, astronomy worthy of the name did not develop in the Euphrates Valley until a very late period.

In another respect the study of the liver divination in Babylonia and Assyria is fraught with significance. Through it, a definite link is established between the ancient civilisations of the East and those of the West.

[1] See a paper by the present writer, "The Liver in Antiquity and the Beginnings of Anatomy," in the *Transactions of the College of Physicians of Philadelphia*, vol. xxix., pp. 117-138.

Pl. 21.   Fig. 1.   Clay Model of Sheep's Liver.

Now in the British Museum. Purchased in 1889 by Mr. Budge at Bagdad, and emanating probably from the temple of Marduk at Babylon. See *Cuneiform Texts from Babylonian Tablets, etc., in the British Museum*, Part VI., Pl. 1–2, and Boissier, *Note sur un Monument Babylonien se rapportant a l'Extispicine* (Geneva, 1899), who was the first to recognise its real character as a model of a sheep's liver, used as an object of instruction in hepatoscopy in some temple school. The chief parts of the liver are shown. The object is covered with inscriptions which give the prognostications derived from signs on the liver, each prognostication referring to some sign near the part of the liver where the words stand. The characters point to the time of Hammurapi (*c.* 2000 B.C) as the date of the model.

Fig. 2.   Bronze Model of Liver found near Piacenza in 1877—showing chief parts of the liver, very much conventionalised and covered with Etruscan characters, which furnish for the most part names of deities. The model was evidently used for purposes of instruction in the Etruscan system of hepatoscopy—just like the Babylonian model. See Körte, "Die Bronzeleber von Piacenza" (*Mitteilungen des Kais. Deutsch. Archaeologischen Institute* [Römische Abt.] XX., pp. 348–379) and the literature given in the course of the article. It dates from about the 3rd century B.C.

Fig. 1.   Clay Model of Sheep's Liver
(Babylonian, *c.* 2000 B. C.)

Fig. 2.   Bronze Model of Liver (Etruscan, *c.* 3d century B. C.)

This primitive process of divining the future, gradually elaborated into a complicated system, spread far and wide through the influence shed on the ancient world by the Euphratean culture. For centuries, it must be borne in mind, the study of hepatoscopy was carried on in the schools attached to the temples of Babylonia and Assyria, the collections made by the priests serving the double purpose of handbooks for practical use, and text-books for instructing pupils in training for the priesthood. From the remote days of Hammurapi there has come down to us an eloquent witness to the prominence occupied by hepatoscopy in the religious life of Babylonia, in the form of a clay model of a sheep's liver[1] whereon the various divisions are carefully indicated, and in addition is covered with interpretations, applicable to signs noted in every portion of the organ. This model was unquestionably an object-lesson employed in a Babylonian temple school—probably in the very one attached to Marduk's temple in Babylon itself[2]—to illustrate the method of divination and to explain the principles underlying the interpretation of the signs.

Similar models have quite recently been found in one of the centres of Hittite settlements at Boghaz-Kevi, and in view of the close relationship between

---

[1] First published in *Cuneiform Texts, etc.*, VI., Plate 1. See Plate 21, Fig. 1.

[2] See below, p. 273 *seq.*

the Hittites and the Babylonians, which can now be traced to the threshold of the third millennium before our era, there can be no doubt that the Babylonian system of hepatoscopy was carried far into the interior of Asia Minor. Babylonian-Assyrian hepatoscopy also furnishes a strong support for the hypothesis—probable on other grounds—which connects the Etruscan culture with that of the Euphrates Valley. Among the Etruscans we likewise find liver divination not only occupying an important position in the official cult, but becoming a part of it. As a companion piece to the Babylonian model of a sheep's liver, we have a bronze model,[1] found about thirty years ago near Piacenza in Italy, which, covered with Etruscan characters, shows almost the same general design as the Babylonian model. This Etruscan

[1] See Körte, "Die Bronzeleber von Piacenza," in the *Mitteilungen des kais. Deutsch. Archaeolog. Instituts* (Römische Abteilung), vol. xx., pp. 348–379. The Etruscan characters have been identified as the names of deities, and the sixteen divisions marked along the edge of the model connected with the sixteen regions into which the heavens were divided. Körte, therefore, correctly designates this model as a microcosm reflecting the macrocosm. This combination of hepatoscopy and astrology has suggested to Wanda von Bartels the theory that the Etruscans developed an elaborate cosmological symbolism in connection with the liver. See her monograph, *Die Etruskische Bronzeleber von Piacenza in ihrer symbolischen Bedeutung* (Berlin, 1910). While I cannot accept all of the ingenious and industrious author's deductions, I consider Frau von Bartels's main hypothesis to be one eminently deserving the careful consideration of scholars. See Plate 21, Fig. 2.

model, dating probably from the third century
B.C., but taking us back to a prototype that may
be considerably older, served precisely the same
purpose as its Babylonian counterpart: namely,
to explain liver divination to the young haruspices
of Etruria. The importance of this form of divination is illustrated by other Etruscan antiquities,
such as the tomb of an haruspex, who holds
in his left hand a liver as the sign-manual of his
profession.[1]

Through the Etruscans hepatoscopy came to the
Romans, and it is significant that down through the
days of the Roman Republic the official augurs were
generally Etruscans, as Cicero[2] and other writers expressly tell us. The references to liver divination
are numerous in Latin writers, and although the term
used by them is a more general one, *exta*,—usually
rendered "entrails,"—when we come to examine the
passages,[3] we find, in almost all cases, the omen
specified is a sign noted on the liver of a sacrificial
animal. So Livy, Valerius Maximus, Pliny, and
Plutarch unite in recording that when the omens were
taken shortly before the death of Marcellus, during the
war against Hannibal, the liver of the sacrificial ani-

[1] Reproduced in Kōrte's article, and also by Blecher, *De Extispicio* (Giessen, 1905), together with other objects in which the
liver as the symbol of divination is pictured.

[2] *De Divinatione*, i., 2.

[3] Collected by Blecher, *op. cit.*, pp. 11–22.

mal had no *processus pyramidalis*,[1] which was regarded as an unfavourable sign, presaging the death of the Roman general. Pliny[2] specifies a large number of historical occasions when forecasts were made by the augurs, and almost all his illustrations are concerned with signs observed on the liver.

The same is the case with the numerous references to divination through sacrificial animals found in Greek writers; for the Greeks and Romans alike resorted to this form of divination on all occasions. In Greek, too, the term applied to such divination is a general one, *hiera* or *hiereia*, the "sacred parts," but the specific examples in every instance deal with signs on the liver.[3] Thus, *e.g.*, in the *Electra* of Euripides,[4] Ægisthos, when surprised by Orestes, is represented in the act of examining the liver of an ox sacrificed on a festive occasion. Holding the liver in his hand, Ægisthos observes that "there was no lobe,[5] and that the gate[6] and the gall-bladder portended evil." While Ægisthos is thus occupied, Orestes steals upon him from behind and deals the fatal blow. Æschylus, in the eloquent passage in

[1] Called in Latin hepatoscopy *caput jecoris*. See above, p. 172, note 2.

[2] *Hist. Nat.*, Book XI., 189–191.

[3] See the passages collected by Blecher, *De Extispicio*, pp. 3–11.

[4] Ll. 826–29.

[5] *I.e.*, again the *processus pyramidalis* which the Greeks called "the lobe" *par excellence;* see above, p. 172, note 2.

[6] The depression between the upper and the lower lobes.

which the Chorus describes the many benefits con-
ferred on mankind by the unhappy Prometheus, ascribes to the Titan the art also of divination, but while
using the general term, the liver is specified:

The smoothness of the entrails, and what the colour is, whether
portending good fortune, and the multi-coloured well-formed gall-
bladder.[1]

Whether or not the Greeks adopted this system of
hepatoscopy through the influence likewise of the
Etruscans, or whether or not it was due to more direct
contact with Babylonian-Assyrian culture is an open
question. The eastern origin of the Etruscans is
now generally admitted, and it may well be that
in the course of their migration westward they came
in contact with settlements in Greece; but on the
other hand, the close affiliation between Greece and
Asia Minor[2] furnishes a stronger presumption in
favour of the more direct contact with the Babylonian system through its spread among Hittite
settlements.

VII

Liver divination, however, in thus passing to the
Greeks and Romans, underwent an important modification which was destined eventually to bring the
practice into disrepute. It will be recalled that the

[1] *Prom.*, lines 495–97.
[2] See D. G. Hogarth, *Ionia and the Far East*, p. 27 *seq*; 67 *seq*.

entire system of hepatoscopy rested on the belief that the liver was the seat of the soul, and that this theoretical basis was consistently maintained in Babylonia and Assyria throughout all periods of the history of these two states. Although there are indications in phrases used in the penitential hymns and lamentations of Babylonia and Assyria that the heart was associated with the liver,[1] just as the Hebrews combined the liver and heart in their later religious poetry to cover the emotions and the intellect,[2] the pre-eminent position accorded to the liver as the seat of all soul life, the source of intellectual activity and of all emotions—good and bad—was not seriously affected by any advance in knowledge that may have led to a better recognition of the functions of the heart. The existence of an elaborate system of divination, based upon primitive theory, acted, with the Babylonians, as a firm bulwark against the introduction of any rival theory. Not so, however, among the Romans, whose augurs took what seemed an innocent and logical step, in order to bring the system of divination into accord with more advanced anat-

[1] A phrase frequently appearing as a refrain in these poetical compositions reads "may thy heart be at rest, thy liver be appeased." See Jastrow, *Religion* (English), p. 324. See above, p. 151.

[2] In the Psalms, heart and liver are used in this way; *e.g.*, Ps. xvi., 9, and also Ps. lvii., 9, cviii., 2, where the text is to be changed to *kābēd*, "liver," instead of *kābôd*, "glory," which gives no sense.

omy, by adding to the examination of the liver that
of the heart, as being likewise an organ through which
an insight could be obtained into the soul of the
animal, and hence into that of the god to whom it
was sacrificed. Pliny has an interesting passage in
his *Natural History* in which he specifies the occasion
when, for the first time, the heart in addition to
the liver of the sacrificial animal was inspected to
secure an omen.[1] The implication in the passage of
Pliny is that prior to this date, which corresponds
to *c.* 274 B.C., the liver alone was used.

Liver and heart continued to be, from this time on,
the chief organs inspected, but occasionally the lungs
also were examined, and even the spleen and the
kidneys. Owing to the growing habit of inspecting
other organs beside the liver, it became customary to
speak of consulting the *exta*—a term which included
all these organs. Similarly, we may conclude from
the use of the terms *splangchna* ("entrails") and
hiera ("sacred parts") in Greek writers, when referring
to divination through the sacrificial animal, that
among the Greeks also, who as little as the Romans
were restrained by any force of ancient tradition,
the basis on which hepatoscopy rested was shifted,
in deference to a more scientific theory of anatomy
which dethroned the liver from its position in primitive and non-scientific beliefs. This step, though ap-

[1] Book XI., 186; at the time when Pyrrhus left Italy.

parently progressive, was fatal to the rite, for in abandoning the belief that the liver was sole seat of the soul, the necessity for inspecting it in order to divine the future was lost. There could be but one claimant as the legitimate organ of divination. If the soul were not in the liver but in the heart, then the heart should have been inspected, but to take both the liver and the heart, and to add to these even the lungs and other organs was to convert the entire rite into a groundless superstition—a survival in practice, based on an outgrown belief.

It is significant that this step was not taken by the Babylonians or Assyrians nor, so far as we know, by the ancient Etruscans, but only by the Romans and the Greeks. That they did so may be taken as an additional indication that hepatoscopy among them was an importation, and not an indigenous growth. As a borrowed practice, the Greeks and Romans felt no pressure of tradition which in Babylonia kept the system of liver interpretation intact down to the latest days. A borrowed rite is always more liable to modification than one that is indigenous, as it were, and attached to the very soil; thus it happens that, under foreign influences, divination through the liver, resting upon deductions from a primitive belief persistently maintained, degenerates into a foolish superstition without reason. It is also an observation that has many parallels in the history of religion:—a

borrowed rite is always more liable to abuse. It is not,
therefore, surprising to find that the "inspection" of
an animal for purposes of divination degenerated still
further among Greeks and Romans into wilful deceit
and trickery. Frontinus[1] and Polyænus[2] tell us of the
way in which the "inspectors" of later days had recourse to base tricks to deceive the masses. They
tell, for instance, of a certain augur, who, desirous
of obtaining an omen that would encourage the army
in a battle near at hand, wrote the words, "victory of
the king," backwards on the palm of his hand, and
then, having pressed the smooth surface of the sacrificial liver against his palm, held aloft to the aston-
ished gaze of the multitude the organ bearing the
miraculous omen.[3] The augur's name is given as
Soudinos "the Chaldean," but this epithet had become at this time, for reasons to be set forth in the
next lecture, generic for soothsayers and tricksters,
indiscriminately, without any implied reference to
nationality. Hence *Soudinos*, who may very well
have been a Greek, is called "the Chaldean."

Whatever the deficiencies of the Babylonian-As-

[1] *Strategematon*, i., 11–14.

[2] *Strategematon*, iv., 20. See also Hippolytus, *de Errore Re-
ligionum*, i., 40, who speaks of it as a common trick.

[3] Frontinus tells the story in connection both with a campaign of Alexander the Great and with a war waged by Eumenos,
the son of Attalos I., of Pergamos. Polyænus places the incident in the days of Philip of Macedon.

syrian "inspectors" may have been, it must be allowed, from the knowledge transmitted to us, that down to the end of the neo-Babylonian empire they acted fairly, honestly, and conscientiously. The collections of omens and the official reports show that they by no means flattered their royal masters by favourable omens. It would have been, indeed, hazardous to do so; but whatever their motives, the fact remains that in the recorded liver examinations we find unfavourable conclusions quite as frequently as favourable. In a large number of reports delivered by the priests there seems nothing, so long as the religion itself held sway, to warrant a suspicion of trickery or fraud of any kind. At most, we may possibly here and there detect a not unnatural eagerness on the part of a diviner to justify his conclusion, or to tone down a highly inauspicious prognostication.

With the decline of faith in the ancient gods and goddesses, which sets in after the advent of Cyrus (539 B.C.), leaving in its wake, as we have seen,[1] a new and much more advanced and more spiritual religion, a different spirit is spread abroad. Contact with Greek culture also proved another serious blow to the time-honoured religious system. An era of degeneration followed in the Euphrates Valley, which is responsible for the disrepute into which the term " Chaldean" now

[1] See above, p. 59 *seq*.

fell.[1] The old *bârû* priests, the "inspectors" of livers and the "inspectors" of the heavens, became the tools of rulers whose interest was to keep alive the superstitions of the past. An end, sad indeed for a religious rite which had been so carefully cherished and developed into an elaborate system by generations of priests, who also took, it must be remembered, a large and honourable share in rearing the imposing structure of Euphratean civilisation.

VIII

In addition to divination through the liver there were various other methods of divination practised by Babylonians and Assyrians. Prominent among them is the pouring of oil into a basin of water, or of pouring water on oil, and then observing the bubbles and rings formed by the oil. References to this method are frequently found in ritualist texts, with allusions that point to its great antiquity.[2] Besides an interesting allusion to the use of this method by a ruler of the Cassite period (*c.* 1700 B.C.), before undertaking an expedition to a distant land to bring back the statues of Marduk and his consort, which had been carried off by an enemy,[3] we have two elaborate

[1] See further p. 262 *seq.* .

[2] In one of these texts (Zimmern, *Beiträge zur Kenntniss der Babylonischen Religion*, Nr. 24), the method is traced back to the legendary founder of the *bârû* priesthood.

[3] Rawlinson, V., Plate 33, col. ii., 8.

texts, dating from the Hammurapi period,[1] forming a handbook for the guidance of the *bârû* priests, which expound a large number of signs to be observed in the mingling of oil and water, together with the interpretations thereof. From these examples we can reconstruct the system devised by the priests, which, as in the case of hepatoscopy, rested largely upon an association of ideas, but in part also upon the record of subsequent events. Divination by oil is, however, entirely overshadowed by the pre-eminence obtained by hepatoscopy, and does not appear to have formed, at least in the later periods, an integral part of the cult.

The field of divination was still further enlarged by the inclusion of all unusual happenings in the life of man, or of animals or in nature, which, in any way, aroused attention. The suspense and anxiety created by such happenings could be relieved only through a *bârû* priest if happily he could ascertain, by virtue of his closer relations to the gods, what the latter intended by these ominous signs. Extensive collections of all kinds of these everyday omens were made by the priests (just like the liver divinations), the aim whereof is to set forth, in a systematic manner everything of an unusual character that followed the omen. The scope is boundless, embracing as it does strange

[1] *Cuneiform Texts, etc.,* Part III., Plates 2–5. See Hunger, *Becherwahrsagung bei den Babyloniern* (Leipzig, 1903).

movements among animals, such as the mysterious appearance and disappearance of serpents, which impart to them a peculiar position among all ancient nations; or the actions of dogs who to this day, in the Orient, enjoy some of the privileges accorded only to sacred animals. The flight of birds was regarded as fraught with significance; swarms of locusts were a momentous warning in every sense of the word; with ravens also the Babylonians, in common with many another nation, associated forebodings, though not always of a gloomy character.

Monstrosities among men and brutes, and all manner of peculiarities among infants or the young of animals, or among those giving birth to them, form another large division in the extensive series of omens compiled by the Babylonian and Assyrian priests. The mystery of life, giving rise everywhere to certain customs observed at birth and death, would naturally fix attention on the conditions under which a new life was ushered into the world; yet many of the contingencies recorded in this division, as well as in others, are so remote and indeed so improbable as to leave on us the impression that, to some extent, at least, these collections may be purely academic exercises, devised to illustrate the application of the underlying principles of the whole system of interpretation. There can be no doubt, however, of the practical purpose also served by these collections, after making due allowance for their partially theoretical character. Their special interest for us lies in their representing a phase of divination wherein the private individual had a larger share. While the priests are in all cases the interpreters of omens and incidents, there is no reason to suppose that the consultation of them was limited to the rulers. Many of the interpretations of the signs in the miscellaneous omen collections bear directly on the private life of the individual and not, as we have seen in the case of hepatoscopy, on public events. The priests, when consulted by "the man in the street," merely take the place of the magic workers of more primitive ages, of the medicine-men, of the rain-makers, or the wizards. No doubt, these priests were also paid for their services to individuals; and we may safely assume that the fees for answering questions furnished a considerable proportion of the income of the temple.

Midway between an official and an unofficial phase of divination, is the interpretation of dreams; this was, likewise, a perquisite of the *bârû* priests. Almost as deep as the mystery of life and of death is the mystery of sleep. The visions during sleep have therefore a special significance. It is in a dream that Gudea receives the command to build a sanctuary to Ningirsu,[1] and in the later period of Babylonian-

[1] Thureau-Dangin, *Sumerisch-Akkadisch Königsinschriften*, p. 90 *seq.*

Assyrian history, the great conqueror, Ashurbanapal,
is, in a dream, bade to be of good cheer by Ishtar, who
appears to him in flames of fire and armed with
bow and arrow.[1] Such direct and vivid dreams
need no priest to interpret; but the signs ordinarily conveyed by dreams are of a character so
indirect and mysterious that the average man fails
to unravel them. The *bârû* priests here come to
the aid of their fellow-men, of both noble and
commoner. Armed with their exhaustless collections, which were not so very greatly above the
level of modern "dream books" that still make their
appeal to a large and willing public, the Babylonian and Assyrian dream interpreters were fortified
for all emergencies.

But all these phases of divination are found abun-
dantly throughout antiquity and are not confined to
Babylonia and Assyria. They may be dismissed,
therefore, with a brief mention, nor would more
examples, that might be furnished, add aught
to what may be paralleled in almost any part
of the ancient world. There is, however, one
branch of divination, falling within the category
of what we have designated as involuntary divination, which, like hepatoscopy, bears an exclusively official character, and in its bearing on the

[1] Rawlinson, V., Plate 5, 97–104. See *Assyrian and Babylonian
Literature* (ed. R. F. Harper), p. 114.

general welfare ranks in importance with divination through the liver. That branch is the observation of the phenomena of the heavens, to which we now turn.

LECTURE IV

I

A N attempt to read the future in the stars is hardly
to be found in the earliest stirrings of civilisation. The ability to grasp even the thought of it
transcends the mental reach of man in the lower stages
of civilisation. Astrology, does not, therefore, emerge
until we come to the higher phases of culture. It appears at the start rather as an expression of the science
of the day, as attained by the select few, than as an
outcome of the beliefs held by the many. In this respect, astrology presents a contrast to liver divination, which, as we have seen, is based on the beliefs
that are distinctly primitive and popular in character,
though it was finally developed into an accurate system, through the agency of the priests of Babylonia
and Assyria.

The fundamental factor in astrology is the identification of the heavenly bodies with the chief gods of
the pantheon. The personification of the sun and
moon as gods—using the term god in its widest sense

as the belief in a superior Power, supposed to exercise a direct influence upon man—comes within the scope of popular beliefs; but the further step involved in astrology, to wit, the identification of the planets and fixed stars with the gods themselves, is beyond and above this scope, though this identification represents a logical extension of the thought which led to the personification of sun and moon as gods. It is precisely this extension of the logical process that stamps astrology from its rise as a reflection of the science, or, possibly, the pseudo-science of the day. A moment's thought will make this clear. The influence of sun and moon as active powers, affecting the fortunes and welfare of mankind, is manifest even to people living in a primitive state. The sun is an all-important element, not only as furnishing light and heat, but because of its co-operation in producing fertility of the soil; and, naturally, when the agricultural stage is reached the sun becomes indispensable to the life of the individual as well as to the community. The moon, though its utility is less obvious, is serviceable as a guide at night; its regular phases constitute an important factor in the measurement of the seasons. While the thought, however, that the stars, too, are gods might occur to man in his earlier stages, it would not be likely to make any deep impression, because of the absence of any *direct* link between his own existence and theirs. Winds and

storms would be personified because they directly
affect man's well-being. This includes a personification of thunder and lightning. But even assuming that
the stars too had been personified, the symbolism
involved in making them the equals of gods, and in
identifying them with the powers whose real functions
belong to the earth, could only have arisen in connection with a more profound theory regarding the relation
of the starry universe to occurrences on this globe.

The theory upon which astrology rests—for it did
not originate in mere fancy or caprice—is the assumption of a co-ordination between occurrences on earth
and phenomena observed in the heavens. One needs
only to state this theory in order to recognise its abstract character—relatively abstract, of course. It
smacks of the school, and is just the kind of theory
that would emanate from minds intent on finding explanations of the mysteries of the universe, more
satisfactory than those deduced from the crude animistic conceptions inherent in primitive culture. To
be sure, even on the assumption of a co-ordinate relation between heaven and earth, there is still room
for a considerable measure of arbitrary speculation,
but the theory itself marks an important advance toward the recognition of law and order in the universe.
The gods, whose manifestations are to be seen in the
heavens, still act according to their own fancy, yet
they at least act in concert. Each separate deity is no

longer an unrestrained law unto himself; and, more-over, what the gods decide is certain to happen. Astrology makes no attempt to turn the gods away from their purpose, but merely to determine a little in advance what they propose, so as to be prepared for coming events.

Through the theory upon which astrology rested an explanation was found for the constant changes of the heavenly bodies. These changes, involving not only alterations in the appearance and position of the moon but also in the position of certain stars, were inter-preted as representing the activity of the gods in pre-paring the events to take place on earth. Changes in the heavens, therefore, portended changes on earth. The Biblical expression "hosts of heaven" for the starry universe admirably reflects the conception held by the Babylonian astrologers. Moon, planets, and stars constituted an army in constant activity, executing military manœuvres which were the result of deliberation and which had in view a fixed purpose. It was the function of the priest—the *bârû*, or "in-spector," as the astrologer as well as the "inspector" of the liver[1] was called — to discover this purpose. In order to do so, a system of interpretation was evolved, less logical and less elaborate than the system of hepatoscopy, which was analysed in the preceding chapter, but nevertheless meriting attention both as

[1] See above, p. 162 *seq.*

an example of the pathetic yearning of men to peer into the minds of the gods, and of the influence that Babylonian-Assyrian astrology exerted throughout the ancient world. This astrology, adopted by the Greeks, and welded to Greek modes of thought and Greek views of life, was handed on from generation to generation through the Middle Ages down to the very threshold of modern science. Before, however, discussing this theory and its interpretation, we must consider the heavenly bodies specially recognised by Babylonian and Assyrian astrologers.

II

Inasmuch as astrology deals primarily, as a system of divination, with the phenomena observed only at night, the foremost place is naturally occupied by the great orb of night, the moon, which, when a personified power, was designated as En-Zu, "the lord of wisdom," and had the general name Sin.[1] While the designation of Sin, as the "lord of wisdom," is perhaps older than the mature astrological system, the name well illustrates the views associated with the moon-god in astrology. The "wisdom" meant is, primarily, that which he, the moon-god, derives from his pre-eminent position among the forces or hosts of heaven.

[1] I am inclined to see in En-Zu or Zu-En an artificial combination based on a "punning" etymology of Sin, and intended to set forth a chief attribute of the moon-god. See above, p. 112, note 2.

He is there the wisest of the gods, the chief councillor in directing the affairs of mankind and of the universe. The title, so frequently assigned to him, of the "father" of the gods, to be found in "Sumerian" compositions of an early period,[1] is likewise particularly applicable to a system of astral theology; it is as the chief luminary of the night that he becomes the "father" of the planets and stars, particularly when we bear in mind that in ancient as well as in modern Oriental speech, "father" is a synonym of chief and leader.

In astrological texts, Sin always takes precedence over Shamash, the sun-god, and as a direct consequence of the influence exerted by astrology upon the development of the Babylonian-Assyrian religion, Sin is placed before Shamash in the enumeration of the members of the pantheon in all kinds of texts, after a certain period.[2] In the case of the moon, the chief phenomena to which attention was directed were the appearance of the new-moon or conjunction with the sun; the period of full-moon or opposition to the sun; the disappearance of the moon at the end of the month; halos—large and small—appearing around the moon; unusual phenomena, such as obscurations

[1] So, e.g., in the old Babylonian compositions for the Sin cult published in Cuneiform Texts, etc., Part XV., Plate 17. See Langdon, Sumerian and Babylonian Psalms, pp. 296–99.

[2] For examples, see Jastrow, Religion (German ed.), ii., p. 457, notes 2 and 3.

of the moon's surface due to atmospheric causes, and, lastly, eclipses.

Astrology in Babylonia is many centuries older than the regulation of the calendar by adjusting the movements of the moon to the annual revolution of the sun. Indeed, it is not until after the conquest of the Euphrates Valley by the Persians that we come upon calculations regarding the movements of the new-moon, while a lunar cycle of nineteen years was not introduced until about the third century B.C. Prior, therefore, to this advance in genuine astronomical knowledge, actual observation was the sole method employed to determine each month the time of the appearance of the new-moon, whether it would be on the evening of the 29th or on the evening of the 30th day. In case the heavens were obscured by clouds on the night when the new-moon was expected to appear, it was considered a bad omen; and an astrologer was obliged to wait for a clear night, before it could be determined by the position and appearance of the moon, whether or not the expected day had been the first day of the month.

This uncertainty in regard to the new-moon involved an even greater uncertainty each month in regard to the time of full-moon. The astrological texts offer a margin of no less than five days, as a possible time of full-moon, from a premature appearance on the 12th and 13th day to a belated appearance on the 15th or 16th day, with the 14th regarded as the normal period. Both the too early and the too late appearance were regarded as unfavourable omens, because of the element of abnormality, but the exact nature of the unfavourable omen varied with the months of the year. It prognosticated bad crops if it occurred in one month; pestilence, if in another; internal disturbances of the country, if in a third. Thus, also, a premature disappearance of the moon at the end of the month, or an absence of the moon for more than the normal three days, was viewed with dismay, and, indeed, even its disappearance at the normal time occasioned anxiety—a survival of earlier beliefs which regarded this disappearance as the capture of the moon by hostile powers in the heavens.[1] This day of disappearance was called a "day of sorrow."[2] Solemn expiatory rites were prescribed, primarily, for the ruler, who had to exercise special precautions not to provoke the gods to anger during those anxious days. The Arabs of our days still hail the appearance of the new moon with exclamations of joy and clapping of hands, calling it by a term, *hilâl*,[3]

[1] See the myth of the capture of the moon, embodied in an incantation ritual, Jastrow, *Religion* (German ed.), i., p. 362 *seq.*

[2] *Um bubbuli*—literally "the day of snatching away" (*sc.* of the moon), also applied to the heliacal setting of the planets.

[3] Hilâl belongs to the class of onomatopoetic words ("sound-imitation words") like our English "Hail" and "Hello." "Hallelujah" is a verbal form of the same "sound imitation" stem with the addition of the divine name, signifying, therefore, "Hail to Jah!" or "Hail to Jahweh!" See below, p. 336, note 2.

which, like its derivative "Hallelujah," emphasises in its very sound the relief felt at the release of the moon from captivity.

Greater terror was proportionately aroused by an eclipse or by any unexpected obscuration of the moon's surface. It does not appear that the Babylonians and Assyrians, even in the latest period, suspected the real cause of an eclipse of the moon or of the sun; though it is not impossible that at a late date they noted the regular recurrences of eclipses. In the astrological texts the term for eclipse—*atalû*, signifying "shadow"—is used for any kind of obscuration of the moon or the sun, including the greyish or yellowish appearance due to purely atmospheric effects. The astrologers, therefore, speak of an "eclipse" occurring on any day of the month,[1] without realising that an eclipse of the moon can take place only in the middle of the month, and a solar eclipse at the end of the month. No better illustration can be desired of their deficiency in any genuine astronomical knowledge, until, at a comparatively late period, the spell of astrological divination was broken by the recognition

[1] See examples in Jastrow, *Religion* (German ed.), ii., pp. 553–566, for the moon (especially p. 563 *seq.*) and 585–599 for the sun —all of them extracts from the official collection of astrological omens. See below, p. 246 *seq.* and 251 *seq.* In the astrological reports and letters of later Assyrian days, furnishing the interpretations for *actual* occurrences, eclipses of the moon are of course correctly entered for the middle of the month. See examples in Jastrow, *Religion* (German ed.), ii., pp. 514–530.

of the regularity of the movements of the heavenly bodies.

In the case of the sun, obscurations and eclipses constitute the most striking features. As in the case of the monthly disappearance of the moon, popular fancy imagined an eclipse of the moon or sun to be due to a temporary discomfiture of these two great luminaries in a conflict with the hosts of heaven. Among a primitive people the terror aroused by an eclipse thus became the origin for the general unfavourable character of the omens associated with such disturbances in the heavens. To this extent, therefore, there is a connecting link between popular beliefs and the developed system of astral theology, but we pass beyond popular beliefs when we come to other phenomena connected with the sun, such as mock-suns appearing around the sun, which are due to atmospheric conditions, or horizontal rays occasionally seen extending from either side or from both sides of the sun. Such phenomena appear to have excited attention among a primitive people in no greater degree than the halos around the moon, which the Babylonian-Assyrian astrologers designated as courts or stalls according to their size. These phenomena, as well as the changes in the position of the wandering stars or planets, fall within the observation of a restricted circle of more scientific observers, who scanned the heavens for

signs of the activity of the gods to whom seats had
been there assigned.

III

In regard to the planets, there are reasons for believing that Jupiter and Venus were the first to be
clearly differentiated, Jupiter by virtue of its brilliant
light, Venus through the striking fact that it appeared
as an evening star during one part of the year, and as
morning star during another. In the astrological
system Jupiter was identified with Marduk, who, we
have seen, became the chief god of the pantheon after
the Hammurapi period; and Venus with the chief
goddess Ishtar. As was pointed out in a previous
lecture,[1] Marduk appears to have been, originally, a
solar deity. This identification with Jupiter is,
therefore, artificial and entirely arbitrary; and shows
that in this combination of planets with the chief gods
and goddesses of the pantheon, the original character
of the latter was entirely set aside. The same is
true in the identification of Venus with Ishtar, for
Ishtar is distinctly an earth goddess, the personification of mother-earth, viewed as the source of vegetation and of fertility in general. The twofold aspect
of Venus as evening star and morning star was no
doubt a factor in suggesting the analogy with the goddess Ishtar, who likewise presents two aspects—one

[1] See above, p. 92.

during the season of vegetation, and quite another during the rainy and wintry season, when she appears to have been withdrawn from the scene of her labours, or, as the popular fancy supposed, when she was imprisoned in the bowels of the earth by her hostile sister—the goddess of the lower regions.

The identification of Jupiter with Marduk furnishes us with a valuable clue for determining the period when the system, to be noted in the astrological texts, was perfected. As a direct consequence of the high position assumed by Babylon after the union of the Euphratean states under Hammurapi, the patron deity of that city is advanced to the position of head of the pantheon. Had the astrological system been devised at an earlier period, Enlil, the chief god of Nippur and the head of the earlier pantheon, would have been associated with Jupiter, and Ninlil (or, possibly, Nanâ of Uruk) with Venus, while, had the priests of Eridu been the first to make each planet a personification of one of the great gods, they would have assigned the most important place among the planets to Ea, as the chief deity of Eridu. In fact, we find few allusions to astrology in inscriptions before the first dynasty of Babylon, though it is quite certain that the beginnings of Babylonian astrology belong to the days of Sargon. Still, it is significant that the only omens about Sargon and his son Naram-Sin that have come down to us are explanations of signs derived from the inspection of the liver of sacrificial animals.[1]

In like manner, other allusions to the early heroes and rulers of Babylonia—to Urumush, Ibe-Sin, and Gilgamesh—occur chiefly in the liver divination texts,[2] and only rarely in collections of astrological omens.[3] We may, therefore, trace the perfected system of astrology (as revealed in what texts we have) back to *ca.* 2000 B.C. As to Jupiter, attention was paid to the time of its heliacal rise and disappearance, and to its lustre—whether, to use the astrological terms, it was "strong" or "weak." Certain months were assigned to certain countries:—the first, fifth, and ninth to Akkad; the second, sixth, and tenth to Elam (to the east); the third, seventh, and eleventh to Amurru (to the west); the fourth, eighth, and twelfth to Subartu or Guti (to the north); and, according to the month when Jupiter appeared or disappeared, the omen was applied to the corresponding country. The "strong" appearance of the planet was a favourable omen; its "weak" appearance, by association of ideas, pointed to loss of power; but whether the loss was for the king and his land or his forces, or for the enemy's land would depend on such factors as the month, or

[1] See above, p. 175 *seq.*

[2] See Jastrow, *Religion* (German ed.), ii., p. 226, note 3.

[3] Examples will be found in the citation referred to in the preceding note.

even the day of the month when the phenomenon was observed.

For Venus we have, at the outset, the distinction between her appearance as an evening star and as a morning star. Elaborate tables were prepared, based on observation, or drawn up after a conventional pattern, noting the time of her heliacal rise as morning star, the duration of visibility, the time of her setting, the length of time during which she remained "hidden in the heavens," as runs the astrological phrase, and the day and month of her reappearance as evening star. To each entry the interpretation was attached, and this varied according to the length of time that Venus was visible, and the character of the month wherein she reappeared. These long lists, worked out in great detail, again illustrate the purely empirical character of such astronomical knowledge as the Babylonians and Assyrians possessed, down at least to the sixth century B.C. For instance, the period, according to scientific investigation, between the heliacal setting of Venus and her heliacal rise is seventy-two days; but in the Babylonian-Assyrian astrological texts, the period varies from one month to five months—too short on the one hand, and too long on the other. In order to account for such discrepancies, we must, perforce, assume that the observations were defective—for which there is indeed abundant evidence—and that the lists, being composite productions of various periods, embody the errors of earlier ages incorporated in the more accurate records of later periods, though even these too were based upon merely empirical knowledge. But whatever be the explanation, the ignorance of the Babylonian and Assyrian astrologers is patent; and the infantile fancies which frequently crop out in these astrological texts keep pace with the ignorance. Thus, the peculiar scintillations of Venus, when particularly bright, give to her outline the appearance of rays. When these rays were observed, Venus was said to "have a beard,"[1] and when the sparkling edges faded in lustre, Venus was said to have "removed her beard." Venus with a "beard" was in general favourable, while Venus without a beard was in general unfavourable, though here, too, the interpretation varied according to the month in which the "beard" was put on, or taken off. When the rays appeared over Venus, she was recorded as "having a crown," and a distinction was made between a "sun" crown and a smaller one, a "moon" crown, or crescent,—all of which illustrates the *naïveté* of their astronomical explanations even while revealing their anxiously close observations.

The remaining three planets—Saturn, Mercury, and Mars—were at first combined in the designation Lu-Bat, which became the general term for "planet."

[1] See Jastrow, *Religion* (German ed.), ii., p. 633.

The term[1] conveys the idea that the movements of these planets were observed for the purpose of securing omens, but, originally, either Saturn, or Mercury, or Mars was meant when the movement or the position of a Lu-Bat was referred to. This circumstance carries with it the plausible conclusion that, before the three planets were more sharply differentiated from one another, the interpretation given to phenomena connected with any one of them was the same as that given to the others. The reason, no doubt, for thus grouping the three into one class was the difficulty involved in observing their separate courses. They bore no specially striking features, such as Jupiter or Venus possessed, and this was, also, no doubt, a cause which led to their being at first put upon the same plane. Of the three, Saturn appears to have been the first to be more definitely differentiated from the others. At all events, in the completed system Saturn was placed above Mercury and Mars. It received the designation of the "steady" Lu-Bat[2]

[1] It is composed of two elements, Lu, which means "sheep," and Bat, which means "dead," and since in hepatoscopy the sacrificial animal employed was invariably the sheep, the combination "dead sheep" acquired the force of "omen." The term thus incidentally points to the dependence of astrology upon hepatoscopy. See a paper by the writer, "Hepatoscopy and Astrology in Babylonia and Assyria" (*Proc. Am. Philos. Society*, vol. xlvii., pp. 663 *seq.*).

[2] Sag-Ush = *kaimânu*, "steady," identified with the *kêwân* of the Old Testament (Amos v., 26).

because of the slowness and regularity of its movements. Requiring about twenty-nine and a half years
for the revolution in its orbit, Saturn is visible for a
longer continuous period than Mercury or Mars.
Possibly by an association of ideas that might occur
to them but not to us, Saturn was also looked upon
as a kind of second sun—a smaller Shamash by the
side of the great Shamash of the day.[1] Was there,
perchance, a "learned theory" among the astrologers
that the illumination of the night was due to this
inferior sun of the night, which, because of its pro-
longed presence, seemed more likely to be the cause
thereof than the moon, which nightly changed its
phase, and even totally disappeared for a few days
each month?[2] It would verily seem so; but, at all
events, the fact that Saturn was also called the "sun"
is vouched for, both by explanatory notes attached
to astrological collections, and by notices in classical
writers to that effect. As one of these writers[3] has
it, "Saturn is the star of the sun"—its satellite, so to
speak, and *alter ego.*

[1] See an article by the writer, "Sun and Saturn," in the
Revue d'Assyriologie, vol. vii., pp. 164–178.

[2] The southern skies, it must be remembered, are much
brighter at night than are our northern heavens, and appear
to be illuminated even when the moon is a faint crescent or is entirely absent. It was natural, therefore, for astrologers in their
fondness for speculation to hit upon the idea, that the light of the
night was due to a body like that of the sun of the day.

[3] Diodorus Siculus, *Biblioth. Histor.*, ii., §. 30, 3, 4.

This association of Saturn with the sun may have been a reason for identifying Saturn with a solar deity, Ninib, who, it will be recalled, was the sun-god of Nippur, and only second in rank to Enlil after this "intruder" displaced Ninib[1] from the actual leadership of the pantheon which he once occupied. Ninib, accordingly, is well fitted to be the associate and "lieutenant" of Shamash, the paramount sun-god from a certain period onward.

Next in importance to Saturn comes Mars, which, in contrast to Saturn exerting, on the whole, a most beneficent influence, was the unlucky planet. This unlucky and downright hostile character of Mars is indicated by his many names: such as the "dark" Lu-Bat; "pestilence"; the "hostile" one; the "rebellious" one; and the like. He was appropriately identified with Nergal, the sun-god of Cuthah, who, in the process of differentiation among the chief solar deities of Babylonia, became the sun of midsummer, bringing pestilence, suffering, and death in its wake;[2] in contrast with Ninib who was viewed more particularly as the sun-god of the spring, restoring life and bringing joy and gladness. In the systematised pantheon, it will be recalled, Nergal was regarded as the grim god of war, and also as the deity presiding over the nether world—the Pluto of Babylonia, who, with his consort Ereshkigal, keeps the dead imprisoned

[1] See above, p. 76 *seq.*   [2] See above, p. 78.

in hi⌐ gloomy kingdom. The association of ideas between Nergal, the lord of the "dark" region, and the dark-red colour of Mars may be regarded as an element of the identification of Mars with Nergal, just as the ideas associated with the colour red—suggesting blood and fire—furnished the further reason for connecting ill-boding omens with the appearance of Mars, and with his position relative to other planets and stars. As an unlucky planet, the "stronger" Mars appeared to be in the heavens, the more baneful his influence. Hence the brilliant sheen of the planet —in contrast to what we have seen to have been the case with Jupiter-Marduk—augured coming misfortune, while the "faint" lustre, indicating the weakness of the planet, was regarded as a favourable sign.

The least important of the planets in Babylonian-Assyrian astrology is Mercury. Because of its nearness to the sun, it is less conspicuous than the others, and the most difficult to observe, and was, therefore, termed the "faint" planet.[1] It is also visible for the shortest period. It can be seen with the unaided eye for only a little while, either shortly after sunset or before sunrise, and only during a part of the year. In northern climes even these restricted glimpses are not always accorded, and Copernicus is said to have regretted on his death-bed that he had

[1] Gu-ud, which I read *shakhtu*, and now take in the sense of "weak, handicapped," and the like.

never actually seen Mercury. As the least significant of the planets, there was not the same reason to
distinguish Mercury by a specific designation, and
hence, instead of being always referred to as the
"faint" planet, it is just as often termed simply
Lu-Bat, not in the sense of being the one planet of all
others as was at one time supposed, but simply as a
planet having no special distinction. Mercury as
Lu-Bat is, as it were, the relict of the planets, the one
left over of the group, the Cinderella among the
planets, relegated to an inferior position of relative
unimportance and neglect. Because of its smaller
size and of its associations, Mercury is identified with
the god Nebo, who in the systematised pantheon, it
will be recalled, was the son of Marduk, and the scribe
in the assembly of the gods, the recorder of the decrees of the divine court, and also the court messenger.
This relationship of son to father wherein Nebo stands
to Marduk—Jupiter—is well brought out in an Assyrian astrological report where Mercury is called
"the star of the crown prince" with an allusion to the
frequent designation of Jupiter as the "king" star.[1]
Frequently also Mercury is described as the "star of
Marduk,"[2] the satellite and "lieutenant" of Jupiter,
much as Saturn is in the same way styled "the star of
Shamash." This varied character of the planet had,

[1] Jastrow, *Religion* (German ed.), ii., p. 652, note 13.
[2] *Ib.*, ii., p. 666, note 2.

however, curious consequences. In Greek astrology, which, as will be presently shown, is largely dependent upon the Babylonian-Assyrian system, Mercury possesses qualities belonging to all the other planets. It is both male and female, and the only one of the planets of whom this is said. The association of ideas connected with Nebo, the god of wisdom, in a very specific sense, and of the art of writing, led to Mercury's being regarded also as the planet of intelligence. The designation of Mercury as Lu-Bat indicated that Mercury summed up the essence of the powers attributed to the planets in general, so that even in the latter-day astrology, which survived the revolution of thought brought about by the natural sciences, Mercury is still associated with the soul— the seat of all vitality.[1] In Babylonian-Assyrian astrology Mercury is a planet of a favourable nature. Its appearance is in almost all cases a good omen. The interpretations fluctuate with the months in which the planet is seen, but frequently refer to abundant rains and good crops.

The scope of Babylonian-Assyrian astrology was still further extended by the inclusion of the more conspicuous stars and constellations, such as the Pleiades, Orion, Sirius, Aldebaran, the Great Bear, Regulus, Procyon, Castor and Pollux, Hydra, and others. The omens deduced, however, from constellations and

[1] See, e.g., Ellen Bennett, *Astrology* (N. Y., 1903), p. 98.

single stars were dependent, primarily, upon the position of these constellations and stars relative to the planets. According as the planets approached or moved away from them, the omen was regarded as favourable or unfavourable, and the decision was again dependent upon their own associations. Thus, if Venus passed beyond Procyon, it pointed to the carrying away of the produce of the land; if she approached Orion it prognosticated diminished crops, —a meagre yield from palms and olives.[1]

With a realisation of the fact that the sun and planets move in well-defined orbits, the need of distinguishing the exact position occupied at any given moment by any of those bodies naturally became pressing. The ecliptic, known as the "pathway of the sun," was divided into three sections, each designated for one of the deities of that theoretically accepted triad which summed up the powers and subdivisions of the universe.[2] These sections were known as the paths of Anu, Enlil, and Ea respectively. Each of these sections was assigned to a country, the Anu section to Elam, the Enlil section to Akkad, and the Ea section to Amurru. Elam lying to the east of the Euphrates Valley, and Amurru lying to the west, Akkad was in the middle between the two. According as a planet in its course stood in one division or

[1] Virolleaud, *L'Astrologie Chaldéenne*, Ishtar, No. vii., 37.
[2] See above, p. 37.

an other, the omen was supposed to have special reference to the land in question. Thus the planet Venus, when rising in the division of Ea, portended that Amurru would have superabundance, if in the division of Anu that Elam would be prosperous, and if in the division of Enlil that Akkad would be benefited. In like manner, if Venus reached her culmination in the division of Anu, Elam would enjoy the grace of the gods, if in the division of Enlil, then Akkad, and if in the division of Ea, Amurru would be so favoured.[1]

This threefold division of the ecliptic does not appear, however, to have been an indication sufficiently precise of the position of the planet; accordingly, the stars near the ecliptic were combined into groups, and designations more or less fanciful were given to them. In this way, twelve such groups were gradually distinguished, corresponding to our constellations of the zodiac, though, it should be added, there are no indications that the Babylonians or the Assyrians divided the ecliptic into twelve equal divisions of 30° each. Retaining the division of the ecliptic into three equal sections, they distributed constellations among these sections as a further means of specifying the position of a planet at any moment, and also as an enlargement of the field of astrological divination. From symbols on the so-called boundary stones, it

[1] See Jastrow, *Religion* (German ed.), ii., 626 *seq.*

appears that up to *ca.* 1000 B.C., only four or five constellations in the zodiac were distinguished, and we
must descend to the Persian period before we find the
full number twelve marked out along the ecliptic.
Undoubtedly, the enlargement of four or five to twelve
—for which there seems no special reason, unless to
bring about a correspondence with the twelve months
of the year—represents the result of continued observation, but its main purpose was to enlarge still
further the field of divination. Astrology, like every
system of divination, thrives in proportion to an increase in its signs. The more complicated the system, the greater its hold upon the masses, who had no
means of checking the element of capriciousness in
the interpretations by the *bârû* priests. The twelve
constellations, thus gradually traced along the ecliptic
by the priests of Babylonia and Assyria, correspond,
with some exceptions, to the twelve signs of the
zodiac still employed in modern astronomy. Thus
we have ram, twins, lion, crab, scorpion, archer, and
fishes in Babylonian-Assyrian astrology. In place of
the virgin we have a constellation designated as
"plant-growth," instead of the bull, a spear; the
remainder are still in doubt.[1] The dependence
of modern astronomical nomenclature on Baby-

[1] A difficulty arises, because in some cases the ancient and
modern constellations do not embrace the same combinations of
stars.

Pl. 22.   Boundary Stones, Showing Symbols of the Gods.

The one to the right is from the reign of the Cassite King Nazi-maruttash (c. 1320 B.C.)—found at Susa and now in the Louvre. The symbols shown on Face D (reproduced in the illustration) are: (a) in the uppermost row, Anu and Enlil, symbolised by shrines with tiaras, (b) in the second row—probably Ea [shrine with goat-fish and ram's head (?)], and Ninlil (shrine with symbol of the goddess); (c) third row—spear-head of Marduk, Ninib (mace with two lion heads); Zamama (mace with vulture head); Nergal (mace with lion's head); (d) fourth row, Papsukal (bird on pole), Adad (or Ramman—lightning fork on back of crouching ox); (e) running along side of stone, the serpent-god, Siru. On Face C (not shown) are the symbols of (a) Sin, the moon-god (crescent); (b) Shamash the sun-god (solar disc); (c) Ishtar (eight-pointed star); (d) goddess Gula sitting on a shrine with the dog as her animal at her feet; (e) Ishkhara (scorpion); (f) Nusku, the fire-god (lamp). The other two faces (A and B) are covered with the inscription. Nineteen gods are mentioned at the close of the inscription, where these gods are called upon to curse any one who defaces or destroys the stone, or interferes with the provisions contained in the inscription. See *Délégation en Perse Mémoires*, vol. ii., Pl. 18–19 and pp. 86–92 (also vol. i., Pl. XIV.,–XV., and pp. 170–172), and Hinke, *A New Boundary Stone of Nebuchadrezzar*, I., pp. 90–91 and p. 231.

The other boundary stone of which two faces are shown is dated in the reign of Marduk-baliddin, King of Babylonia (c. 1170 B.C.),—found at Susa and now in the Louvre. The symbols shown in the illustration are: (1) Zamama (mace with the head of a vulture); (2) Nebo (shrine with four rows of bricks on it, and horned dragon in front of it); (3) Ninib (mace with two lion heads); (4) Nusku, the god of fire (lamp); (5) Marduk (spear-head); (6) Bau (walking bird); (7) Papsukal (bird perched on pole); (8) Anu and Enlil (two shrines with tiaras); (9) Sin, the moon-god (crescent). In addition there are (not distinguishable on the illustration): (10) Ishtar (eight-pointed star), (11) Shamash (sun disc), (12) Ea (shrine with ram's head on it and goat-fish before it), (13) Gula (sitting dog), (14) goddess Ishkhara (scorpion), (15) Nergal (mace with lion head), (16) Adad (or Ramman—crouching ox with lightning fork on back), (17) Siru—the serpent god (coiled serpent on top of stone).

Pl. 22—*Continued*

All these gods, with the exception of the last named, are mentioned in the curses at the close of the inscription together with their consorts. In a number of cases, (*e. g.*, Shamash, Nergal, and Ishtar) minor deities of the same character are added which came to be regarded as forms of these deities or as their attendants; and lastly some additional gods notably Tammuz (under the form Damu), his sister Geshtin-Anna (or *belit şeri*), and the two Cassite deities Shukamuna and Shumalia. In all forty-seven gods and goddesses are enumerated which may, however, as indicated, be reduced to a comparatively small number. See *Délégation en Perse Mémoires*, vol. vi., Pl. 9–10 and pp. 31–39; Hinke, *op. cit.*, pp. 25 and 233–234.

Boundary Stones, showing Symbols of the Gods

lonian astrology—through the mediation of the Grecian—is thus recognised beyond reasonable doubt,[1] but the significant feature of this dependence lies in the circumstance that what, under the moulding of the Greek scientific spirit, became astronomical in character was adopted by the Greeks as a purely fanciful combination of stars into groups, introduced as a means of fixing more accurately the stations of the sun and planets in their course along the ecliptic, and for the sole purpose of enlarging the field of divinatory lore.

IV

It now behooves us to turn to a description of the system devised by the *bârû* priests in their endeavour to read in the movements of the heavenly bodies and in the general phenomena of the heavens, the purpose and designs of the gods.

Although not belonging to astrology proper, yet, from the Babylonian point of view, storms, winds, rains, clouds, thunder, and lightning constitute an

[1] The detailed proof for the origin of our signs of the zodiac from Babylonian astrology was first furnished by the German Assyriologist Peter Jensen in his elaborate work, *Kosmologie der Babylonier* (Strassburg, 1890), but the advance of the last two decades, due chiefly to the researches of Epping, Strassmaier, and Kugler, has made portions of Jensen's work antiquated. The standard work for Babylonian astronomy and cognate fields is Kugler, *Sternkunde und Sterndienst in Babel*—now in course of publication.

integral part of divination based upon the phenomena of the heavens; and we have seen that this phase of divination,[1] like divination from the movements and position of the sun and moon, represents an outcome of the popular beliefs that naturally connected these phenomena with beings that had their seats on high. We cannot, in fact, separate the interpretations of winds, clouds, rain, hail, thunder, lightning, and even earthquakes from astrology proper, for, in the astrological texts, Adad, who, as the god of storms, presides over all the violent manifestations in the heavens that show their effect on earth, is accorded a place by the side of Sin, Shamash, and the gods identified with the five planets, Marduk, Ishtar, Ninib, Nebo, and Nergal. These eight deities in fact constitute the chief gods of the perfected pantheon, to which the ancient triad Anu, Enlil, and Ea should be added, together with Ashur in Assyria[2] as the additional member of a conventionalised group of twelve deities.

Naturally, the phenomena ascribed to Adad furnished a particularly wide scope for the astrologer. The character and ever-changing shapes of clouds were observed, whether massed together or floating in thin fleecy strips. Their colour was noted, whether dark, yellow, green, or white. The number of thunderclaps, the place in the heavens whence the sound proceeded, the month or day or special circumstances

[1] See above, p. 209.   [2] See above, p. 123.

when heard, were all carefully noted, as was also the quarter whence the lightning came, and the direction it took, the course of winds and rain, and so on, without end.

In studying the system devised for the interpretation of omens, we may take as a point of departure the subdivision dealing with the activity of the god Adad. As in liver divination, the general principles were deduced from the observation of events actually following upon certain noteworthy phenomena in the heavens. If, for example, a battle was fought during a thunderstorm and ended in the discomfiture of the enemy, the precise conditions under which the battle took place, the day of the month, the direction of the wind, and the number of thunderclaps were noted. The conclusion was then drawn that, given a repetition of the circumstances, the same result or at least some favourable outcome would follow. This same principle was applied to the position of the sun, moon, or any of the planets at any given moment. As a necessary outcome of the theory that whatever occurred in the heavens represented the activity and co-operation of the gods in events on earth, the *post hoc* was equated with the *propter hoc* in the case of all important or striking occurrences, directly affecting the general welfare. The conclusion was inevitable that the phenomenon itself portended the events. Hence, the scrupulously careful observation of heavenly phenomena yielded an infallible guide for the most confident prediction —always provided that the records confirmed an occurrence in the past when preceded by similar phenomena, or provided that in any other way a correct reading of the sign could be given. How was this possible when records or tradition were lacking? The answer is the same that was suggested in regard to the system of liver divination,—it was by certain more or less logical deductions, and also by more or less fanciful association of ideas.[1]

V

It does not appear that the Babylonians and Assyrians advanced so far as the mapping out of the heavens to correspond with the distribution of lands, mountains, rivers, and seas on earth; though this would have been a perfectly logical extension of the theory of a preordained correspondence between heaven and earth. It was actually carried out, however, by the later Greek astrologers.[2] We have already seen that the divisions of the ecliptic were associated with certain countries; certain divisions of the moon, the left and right sides, the upper and

[1] See above, p. 173 seq.

[2] See Cumont, La plusancienne Geographie Astrologique (Klio, vol. ix., pp. 263–73).

lower portions, were parcelled out in the same way.[1]
The world was divided for purposes of astrology into
four chief lands with which the Babylonians had come
into contact. Elam was the general designation of
the east, Amurru, or the land of the Amorites, meant
the west, Akkad, or Babylonia, stood for the south,
and Subartu, alternating with Guti, for the north.
The omission of the later name, Ashur, for Assyria
is important; it points to the development of the
astrological system prior to the rise of the Assyrian
empire, which, in fact, is not prominent until sometime
after the period of Hammurapi. Subartu stands in
the conventional enumeration for the later Assyria,
and the astrologers of that country are careful enough
expressly to note this fact.[2] These four divisions,
Elam, Amurru, Akkad, and Subartu (with Guti as an
alternative[3]) constituted the "four regions" of the

[1] The right side of the moon was Akkad, the left Elam, the
upper portion Amurru, the lower portion Subartu. See
further below, p. 239.

[2] In an astrological report in the days of Esarhaddon (681–
668 B.C.), there appears the significant note attached to an omen
about Subartu: "We [*i.e.*, the Assyrians] are Subartu." See
Thompson's *Reports of the Magicians and Astrologers of Nineveh
and Babylon*, No. 64, obv. 4.

[3] Guti—a land in the distant north; it comes into contact at
an early period with the Euphrates Valley, and, centuries later,
also with Assyria. The name is therefore frequently introduced as an alternative to Subartu and, indeed, for the later
periods, Subartu, which, we have seen, was originally Assyria, is
conventionally used for the north and, therefore, also for lands

earth. Rulers, like Naram-Sin, who claimed control of these sections, therefore gave themselves the title of "King of the Four Regions,"—with the implication that their empire was of universal sway. It was not necessary to map out the heavens to correspond to these four divisions. Indeed, a larger margin was allowed to the astrologers by not doing so; the divisions could then be applied to any of the five planets, to the constellations, and single stars, as well as to the sun and moon and to the divisions of the ecliptic. Jupiter, quite independently of his position in the heavens at any given time, was regarded as the planet of Akkad or Babylonia, while Mars, as the hostile and unlucky planet, was assigned to the two unfriendly lands, Amurru and Elam. Thus, too, the constellations and prominent single stars were apportioned among the same four countries. We are fortunate enough to possess lists wherein the planets, constellations, and stars, arranged in groups of twelve to correspond to the twelve months of the year, are thus divided among Elam, Akkad, Amurru, and Subartu. [1] We have already seen that the months were in the

---

to the north of Assyria (as well as of Babylonia), including Guti proper. The varying terminology in the astrological texts is a further indication of the different periods from which the official Anu-Enlil series is put together.

[1] *Cuneiform Texts, etc.*, Part XXVI., Plates 41 and 44, col. v., 8–11. The list can be almost completed from indications and references in the Anu-Enlil series.

same way distributed among these four countries, and the system was even extended to days, so that each day of the month was referred to one country or another.[1] It was thus possible to connect almost every phenomenon in the heavens with some country. This was more particularly important in the case of unfavourable omens, like eclipses, or obscurations of the sun or moon from atmospheric causes, where the application of the interpretation would thus vary according to the month and the day on which the phenomenon was observed. The scope thus given to the prognostications of the *bârû* priests was extended still further by connecting the months with the gods as well as with countries, and, according to the character and nature of each deity, an appropriate interpretation was proposed for the many cases in which no record existed of any event of special significance following upon some sign in the heavens. Thus, the first month was assigned to Anu and Enlil, the second to Ea, the third to Sin, the fourth to Ninib, the fifth to Ningishzida (also a solar deity and a god of vegetation), the sixth to Ishtar, the seventh to Shamash, the eighth to Marduk, the ninth to Nergal, the tenth to the messenger of Anu and Ishtar—pre-

---

[1] The 1st, 5th, 9th, 13th days, etc., to Akkad, the 2d, 6th, 10th, 14th days, etc., to Elam, the 3d, 7th, 11th, 15th, etc., to Amurru, the 4th, 8th, 12th, 16th, etc., to Subartu. See above, p. 219, for the apportionment of the months.

sumably Nebo,—the eleventh to Adad, the twelfth to Sibitti, the intercalated, so-called second Adar to Ashur, the head of the Assyrian pantheon.[1]

The factors involved in such associations are various. To discuss them in detail would take us too far afield; it is sufficient to call attention to the "mythological" considerations involved. The sixth month—marking the division of the year into two halves—is connected with the goddess Ishtar, who spends half of the year on earth and half in the nether world. Climatic conditions underlie the association of the eleventh month—the height of the wintry and stormy season—with the god of storms and rains, Adad. Similar associations are to be found in the famous Babylonian epic known as the adventures of Gilgamesh, which was recounted on twelve tablets, each tablet being made to correspond to a certain month of the year. The sixth tablet narrates the descent of Ishtar to the lower world—symbolising the end of the summer season of growth and of vegetation; the story of the great Deluge that swept away mankind is recounted in the eleventh tablet—corresponding, therefore, to the month associated with Adad. Besides the division of the four sides of the

---

[1] Rawlinson, iv., (2d ed.), Pl. 32. The addition of Ashur points to the late redaction of the list by Assyrian scribes, but the other associations, no doubt, rest upon older Babylonian traditions.

moon—right and left, upper and lower—among the
four regions of the world, as above pointed out, we
find a special distribution when the moon was crescent, the right horn being assigned to Amurru or the
west land and the left horn to Elam or the east.
In this case, orientation, which in Babylonia was from
the south, is clearly the controlling factor. Facing
the south, the west is to the right and the east to the
left, whereas when the full moon is divided among the
four countries, the assigning of Akkad to the right
side and of Elam to the left is due to the natural association of ideas between right and lucky, on the one
hand, and left and unlucky on the other, which, we
have seen, played so important a part in liver divination. Facing Akkad, as the land of the south, the
lower portion of the moon would again be the left
and therefore unlucky side, and the upper portion the
right or lucky side, which leads to the former being
associated with the land of the enemy, Amurru,
and the latter with Assyria—replaced, whenever it
suited the purpose of the astrologers, by Subartu. In
this and in divers other ways the association of ideas
becomes perhaps the most important factor in the
development of the system of interpretation, by the
side, or in default, of the direct observation of events
following upon certain phenomena in the heavens.
This latter phase must, never, of course, be lost sight
of, and especially when extraordinary phenomena

appeared in the skies, such as a thunderclap out of a clear sky, rain during the dry season (in the 4th, 5th, and 6th months), an apparently belated new-moon or full-moon, and, above all, eclipses of the sun or moon, or obscurations of either of these heavenly lamps. All such occurrences would make a deep impression, and special care would be taken to note every event that followed, in the belief that all the signs here instanced being unfavourable, whatever misfortune or unlucky occurrence happened, it was a direct consequence of the unfavourable sign in the heavens, or was at all events prognosticated by the sign.

VI

The events would naturally be of general public import. These may be chiefly enumerated as the result of a military expedition, condition of the crops, pestilence, invasion of the enemy, disturbances within the country, a revolt, an uprising in the royal household, or any untoward event at court, such as the sickness or death of the monarch, or of a member of his house—always indicative of the anger of the gods, —a miscarriage of the queen, a mishap to the crown-prince, and the like.

Thus as in the case of hepatoscopy, the point of view was always directed to the general welfare. Private affairs hardly entered into consideration; not

for such were the stars to be read. The *bârû*
priests did not painfully search the heavens to find out
under what special conjunction of planets a humble
subject was born, or try to determine the fate in store
for him. This aspect of astrology is conspicuous by
its absence. And when astronomy devoted itself
to the service of the king or to a member of his household—for the interpretations in the astrological texts
often bear upon events in the palace or at the court,—
it is due[1] to the peculiar position held by the king
throughout antiquity. He was regarded either as the
direct representative of the deity on earth, or as
standing in a peculiarly close relationship to the gods;
wherefore should he act in any way to provoke the
gods to anger, his punishment would affect the entire
population. On the other hand, the favour of the
gods toward the king ensures victory in arms, the
repulse of an enemy, abundant crops, and the blessings of health and happiness. In return, the kings
had to exercise special precautions in all their acts—
official and otherwise. A misstep, a failure to observe
certain rites, a neglect of any prescribed ceremonial, or a distinctly ethical misdemeanour, an act of
injustice or cruelty, might be fraught with the most
dire results. If a catastrophe or misfortune affecting the general welfare occurred, it was taken as a
sign of divine displeasure. In such cases, expiatory

[1] See above, p. 177

16

rites were prescribed for the king, and often for the members of his household also, for fear that the anger had been evoked by some misdeed of theirs, albeit an unintentional one.

This trait of solidarity of king and people and gods, as opposed to individualism, marks the Babylonian-Assyrian religion in all its phases. It is by no accident that the hymns and prayers and penitential appeals and ritualistic directions are almost universally engrossed with the relation of the rulers to the gods. The prayers to Enlil, Marduk, Sin, Shamash, Nebo, Ninib, or Ishtar are generally royal appeals; the hymns voice the aspirations of the kings, while the penitents, whose humiliation before the divine throne is portrayed in such effective manner, in the penitential outpourings,[1] are in almost all instances the rulers themselves. To be sure, this condition is in a measure due to the official character of the religious material in the library of Ashurbanapal, and yet this material taken directly from the archives of the temples fairly reflects the general features of the religion. Even in the incantations, the formulas and observances prescribed for exorcising mischievous demons (the causes of all the ills of existence, and of the unpleasant accidents of every day life), we receive the impression that the collections were largely formed to relieve the kings of their troubles; though, no doubt, in this

[1] See p. 320 *seq.*

branch of the religious literature, the needs of the individual received a more considerable share of attention. Thus also, signs that directly affected the individual, such as dreams, a serpent in one's path, peculiar actions of dogs in a man's house, birth of monstrosities among domestic animals[1]—all illustrate the "lay" features of the cult, but with these exceptions, the cult of Babylonia and Assyria as a whole, partook of a character official rather than individual.

What is thus true of other fields, is true of astrology. An explanation is thus found for the fundamental fact that the reading of stars by the Babylonians and Assyrians had no concern with the individual. What to us would seem to be the essence of astrology,— the determination of the conditions under which the individual was born, and the prediction from these conditions of the traits that would be his, and of the fate in store for him,—is not in Babylonian-Assyrian astrology. This aspect represents the contribution of Greek astrologers, when they carried Babylonian astrology into their own lives. To the Greeks, and afterwards to the Romans, genethlialogy,—as the science, dealing with the conditions under which a man is born, was called,—became the alpha and omega of astrology. The reason why it was left to the Greeks

[1] Examples will be found in Jastrow, *Religion* (German ed.), Parts 16–18.

to add this important modification to the borrowed product is not far to seek. In the religion as in the culture of the Greeks, the individual was more than merely an infinitesimal part of the whole. The entire spirit of Greek civilisation was individualism, and the spirit of its institutions correspondingly democratic. The city, to be sure, was regarded as an ideal unity, but the very emphasis laid upon citizenship as a condition to participation in Greek life is an indication that the individual was not lost sight of in the welfare of the whole. The individual in Greece was also, a part of the whole, but an *integral* part, and one that had an existence also apart from the whole. The relation between the individual and the gods was of a personal nature. The Greek gods concern themselves with individuals; whereas among the Babylonians and Assyrians the welfare of the community and of the country as a whole was primarily the function ascribed to the gods. The latter stood aloof from the petty concerns of individuals and relegated these to the inferior Powers, to the demons and spirits, and to the sorcerers and witches in whom some evil spirit was supposed to have taken up his abode.

VII

Returning to the astrological system of the Babylonians and Assyrians, it still remains for us to indicate the final form given to this system. The notes and entries made by the priests of significant events following upon noteworthy phenomena in the heavens, grew in the course of time to large proportions. Further enlarged by the settling of certain criteria for reading the stars on the basis of a logical or arbitrary association of ideas, and by the introduction of other factors, these memoranda became an extensive series in which the signs were entered in a more or less systematic manner and the interpretations added. It did not follow that, because a certain event occurred subsequent to some phenomenon in the moon, sun, or in one of the planets or in some constellation, the *same* conditions would always produce the *same* result. As was stated above, the important feature of the interpretation given to a sign was its general character as favourable or unfavourable. The essential point was whether the sign was a good or a bad omen. Hence, in many instances we find alternative interpretations given in the astrological collections—either good crops or recovery from disease, long reign of the king or success in war, uprising in the land or low prices in the markets,—always regarded as an ill omen,—peace, and grace of the gods or abundant rains, diminution of the land or insufficient flooding of the canals during the rainy season, invasion of locusts or disastrous floods. The number of such alternative interpretations was not limited to two. Often we find three or four and as many as six contingencies. In such cases it seems simplest to suppose that these alternatives represent interpretations taken from various sources, and combined by the priests in their collections, whereof the value and trustworthiness would be increased by embodying as far as possible the *entire* experience and wisdom of the past for guidance in the present.

As in the case of "liver" divination, there are indications that various collections of astrological omens were compiled in the temples of the south and north, through the steady growth of the observations and deductions of the *bârû* priests; there was also one extensive series covering the entire field of astrology, which became, as it were, the official Handbook and main source. From the opening words it was known as the *Enuma Anu-Enlil* series (*i.e.*, "When Anu, Enlil,*" etc.), and probably comprised as many as one hundred tablets, of which, however, only a portion has been recovered from the great royal library at Nineveh; the tablets and fragments of tablets already preserved represent different editions or recensions of the text. Fortunately, the beginning of the series is extant, both in the original "Sumerian," and in a somewhat free translation into Semitic Babylonian. It expounds a piece of cosmological tradition as follows:

When Anu, Enlil, and Ea, the great gods, in their council entrusted the great laws of heaven and earth to the shining [?]

moon, they caused the new-moon crescent to be renewed [*sc.* every month], created the month, fixed the signs of heaven and earth so that it [*i.e.*, the moon] might shine brilliantly in heaven [and] be bright in heaven.[1]

Anu, Enlil, and Ea, it will be recalled, represent in theory the triad of divine powers, who precede the creation of the active gods. They stand, as it were, above and behind "the great gods," and, just as the latter entrust the smaller affairs of the world—the fate of individuals—to the lower order of Powers, to the demons and spirits, so Anu, Enlil, and Ea delegate to the great gods the general affairs of mankind as a whole. The opening lines of the series are evidently quoted from a poetical composition, setting forth the order of creation. In the Sumerian original, which belongs to a very high antiquity, the moon is significantly the first and most important of the "great gods." A reference to the sun—which is only in the Semitic translation—is presumably a later addition. The precedence hereby accorded to the moon reveals the pre-eminent position occupied by the moon in Babylonian-Assyrian astrology, and the quotation from the old cosmological poem was probably chosen as a befitting introduction to the exposition of omens, derived from observations of the moon. The system

[1] The free "Babylonian" translation renders the closing phrases as follows: "That men may see the sun within the gate of heaven and earth regularly shine forth."

of the *bârû* priests was thus justified by the doctrine that the ancient triad in council deputed the
government of the universe primarily to the moon,
through which the signs to be observed in the heavens
and on earth were interpreted.

There are distinct indications, throughout the recovered portions of the series, of the existence of a
very old Sumerian text, which, at a period subsequent to Hammurapi, was given a Semitic form, and,
in the course of this process, modified and enlarged.
Equally strong is the evidence for the composite
character of the series, whereof the component parts,
as has already been indicated, belong to different
periods and, as it would appear, embody other astrological collections that were taken over in whole
or in part to form the great official guide for the
priests. In short, the series is a compilation, just as
are the Pentateuch and the historical books of the
Old Testament. The Gilgamesh epic as well as the
incantation rituals and other specimens of Babylonian Assyrian literature reveal this same practice of
compilation, which is, in fact, a characteristic trait of
literary composition among the Semites at all times.
The great Arabic historians of the four centuries
after Mohammed are, in the same way, essentially
compilers and furnish a proof of the continuance of the
same literary process, notwithstanding the profound
changes wrought by the two millenniums between the

old Babylonian literature and the intellectual activity
of Mohammedan writers.

Our fragments of the Anu-Enlil series enable us to
divide it into five groups; the first deals with omens
derived from the moon; the second with such as deal
with phenomena of the sun; the third with those of
the remaining five planets; the fourth with constellations, stars, and comets, and the fifth with the various
manifestations of the activity of Adad, including
storms, winds, rains, thunderbolts, and lightning. In
making this division it is not claimed that the tablets
of the series were actually divided in this way. The
Babylonian scribes and compilers were, probably, not
quite so systematic; but there is sufficient internal
evidence that the phenomena connected with the moon
were for convenient reference grouped together. In
the same way, the phenomena of the sun and those
of each of the planets were dealt with in a series of
tablets that aimed to exhaust all possible contingencies
in connection with the movements and position of the
heavenly bodies. The period of the final redaction
of the series can be only approximately determined.
Historical references in connection with the omens
justify the conclusion that portions of the Sumerian
original may be as old as the days of Sargon (*circa*
2500 B.C.), but the greater portion is certainly much
later, while for the final redaction we must pass far
below the period of Hammurapi. Additions to it

were constantly being made, and no doubt every scribe
tried to improve upon his predecessors by adding
more omens with their interpretations. Even the
Assyrian scribes, in copying the "Babylonian"
originals, did not hesitate to make additions of this
kind; in a very general way we may say, however,
that about 1500 B.C., the Anu-Enlil series was already
in existence as the official astrological handbook.
We are also safe in fixing upon the city of Babylon
and its neighbour Borsippa—the two representative
centres of the Marduk and Nebo cults—as the district
in which the series was compiled and first recognised
as the official authority.

The proof that the Anu-Enlil series was official, and
consulted by the priests of Marduk and Nebo on all
occasions, and that through the influence of the Marduk cult it had become the standard authority
throughout Babylonia and Assyria, is furnished by
the official reports and letters of the astrologers at the
Assyrian court. These reports, of which we have
several hundred, consist of two sections, one containing the description of the phenomena, the other
supplying the interpretations in the form of quotations from a collection of astrological omens. We now
have the source of many of these quotations from the
Anu-Enlil series. In like manner, in letters of Assyrian officials to their royal masters, astrological
omens are not infrequently embodied, and these,

too, we can trace back to the Anu-Enlil series.[1]
Moreover, the series itself is directly referred to both
in the reports and in the letters, being either quoted
by its title or designated simply as "the Series." It
appears, therefore, that when an inquiry was put to
the astrologers as to the meaning of a particular sign
in the heavens, the Anu-Enlil series was forthwith consulted, the sign in question hunted up, and copied
verbatim, together with the interpretation or the alternative interpretations, and forwarded to the kings
with any needful explanations.

VIII

Despite the elaborate system, however, developed
by the Babylonian priests, the decline of astrology
sets in toward the close of the Assyrian period. It is
significant that in the inscriptions of the rulers of the
neo-Babylonian dynasty,—Nabopolassar to Nabonnedos, 625 to 539 B.C.,—we find no direct references
to astrological omens. The gods reveal themselves
in dreams and by the liver of sacrificial animals, but
there are no omens derived from phenomena in the
heavens. This may be, of course, accidental, and
yet, considering that this period marks the beginning
of a noteworthy advance in astronomy, it would
rather seem that the rise of genuine astronomical

[1] See numerous examples in Jastrow, *Religion* (German ed.),
ii., pp. 458–692.

science gave the death-blow to the belief in the re-
velations of stars. The advent of the Persians, who
put an end to the neo-Babylonian empire in 539 B.C.,
was followed, as so frequently happens with the
coming of a great conqueror, by an intellectual impulse. In contrast with the Babylonian religion and
cult, (so full of survivals from the animistic stage),
Zoroastrianism or Mazdeism, brought into Babylonia by the Persian rulers, was rationalistic in the extreme. Instead of a multiplicity of divine Powers,
we have one great spirit presiding over the universe,
the creator of everything, whose power was held to be
limited only by the existence at his side of a great
power of evil, Ahriman, who thwarted the efforts of
Ahura-Mazda until, after the completion of certain
cycles, the good spirit would finally triumph over
Ahriman and reign supreme. We may be permitted
to suppose also that contact with the Hebrews, who
under the influence of their prophets had advanced
to a monotheistic conception of the universe, was a
factor in leading the choicer spirits of the Babylonians
to a clearer recognition of a universal divine law. A
third factor destined to work still more profound
changes throughout the ancient Orient was the contact with Greek culture and Greek modes of thought.
Greek philosophy rested even more firmly than Hebrew monotheism on the theory of the sway of inexorable law in nature.

Thus, Persian, Hebrew, and Greek influences acted as disintegrating factors in Babylonia and Assyria, leading to a general decline in time-honoured beliefs, and, more particularly, to a diminution of faith in the gods. Astrology, along with other superstitions, was doomed the moment it was recognised that whatsoever occurred in the heavens, even including all unusual phenomena, was the result of law—eternal and unchanging law. In place of astrology, we see, therefore, a genuine science coming to the fore, which, starting from the axiom of regularity in the universe, set out to find the laws underlying the phenomena of the heavens. In the three centuries following the Persian occupation of the land we find the Babylonian priests exchanging their former profession as diviners for that of astronomers. They engage in elaborate calculations of the movements of moon and sun. They prepare tables of the movements of the planets in their orbits, with exact calendars for extensive periods of the heliacal rise and setting of the same; they calculate the duration of their forward movement, the hour of culmination, and the beginning of the retrograde movement. The yearly calendar is regulated with more scientific precision; and even though the recognition of the fact that eclipses of the sun and moon were, in common with all other heavenly phenomena, subject to law did not lead in Babylonia to the discovery of a true theory of eclipses, still the blasting of the belief that eclipses were symptomatic of the anger of the gods shook the very foundations of astrology. If the signs in the heavens were due to immutable laws, then the study of these signs could no longer serve to determine what the gods were purposing to do on earth. The immediate result of this progress toward a genuine astronomical science was not to bring about an era of skepticism in regard to the existence of the gods, but only to overthrow the basis on which astrology rested. If the heavens merely revealed the workings of regular laws, brooking no exceptions and proceeding independently of what happened on earth, then the function of the astrologer ceased. The connecting link between heaven and earth was snapped through the recognition of law in the universe, over which even the gods had no control.

Astronomy *versus* Astrology marks the beginning of the conflict between Science and Religion in Babylonia and Assyria, which, as in all subsequent phases of that conflict elsewhere, could have only one outcome,—the triumph of Science. Astrology, we have seen, started out as an expression of the science of the day. Dethroned from that position, it became, in the literal sense of the word, a superstition, a survival of an intellectual phase that had been outgrown.

Strange to say, however, the rise of astronomy and the decline of astrology in Babylonia were coincident with the introduction of astrology into the lands swayed by Greek culture. The two movements are connected. Whereas astronomy began among the Greeks long before their contact with the East, it yet received a strong impulse, as did other sciences, through the new era inaugurated by Alexander the Great, and marked by the meeting of Orient and Occident. Several centuries, however, before the days of Alexander the Greeks had begun to cultivate the study of the heavens, not for purposes of divination but prompted by a scientific spirit as an intellectual discipline that might help them to solve the mysteries of the universe. The tradition recorded by Herodotus[1] that Thales discovered the law of eclipses rests on an uncertain foundation; but, on the other hand, it is certain that by the middle of the fourth century B.C., the Greek astronomers had made great advances in the study of heavenly movements. Nor is there any reason to question that, in return for the impulse that contact with the Orient gave to the Greek mind, the Greeks imparted their scientific view of the universe to the East. They became the teachers of the East in astronomy as in medicine and other sciences, and the credit of having discovered the law of the precession of the equinoxes belongs to Hipparchus, the Greek astronomer, who announced this important theory about the year 130 B.C. On the other hand,

[1] Book I., § 74.

and in return for improved methods of astronomical calculation, which, it may be assumed, contact with Greek science also gave to the Babylonian astronomers, the Greeks accepted from the Babylonians the names of the constellations of the ecliptic; but in the case of the planets, they substituted for the Babylonian gods the corresponding deities of their own pantheon. More than this, they actually adopted from the Babylonians the system of astrology and grafted it on their own astronomical science. We have the evidence of Vitruvius,[1] and others, to the effect that Berosus the "Chaldean" priest, a contemporary of Alexander the Great, settled in the island of Cos (the home of Hippocrates), and taught astrology to a large number of students who were attracted by the novelty of the subject. Whereas in Babylonia and Assyria we have astrology first and astronomy afterwards, in Greece we have the sequence reversed—astronomy first and astrology afterwards.

How was it possible for the Greek scientific spirit to affix a pseudo-science to a genuine one? The answer to this obvious question is near at hand. It has been already[2] pointed out that the casting of an individual horoscope was the important modification introduced by the Greeks in adopting the Babylonian astrology. By this step an entirely different aspect was given to astrology, and above all, a much more

[1] Vitruvius, *de Architectura*, ix., 6.   [2] See above, p. 243.

scientific appearance. It was not merely the individualist spirit of Greek civilisation that led the Greeks to make an attempt to read in the stars the fate of the individual, but the current doctrine of preordained fate, which takes so large a share in the Greek religion, and was therein an important factor. Thanks to this doctrine, the harmonious combination of Greek astronomy and Babylonian astrology was rendered possible. A connecting link between the individual and the movements in the heavens was found in an element which they shared in common. Both man and stars moved in obedience to forces from which there was no escape. An inexorable law controlling the planets corresponded to an equally inexorable fate ordained for every individual from his birth. Man was a part of nature and subject to its laws. The thought could therefore arise that, if the conditions in the heavens were studied under which a man was born, that man's future could be determined in accord with the beliefs associated with the position of the planets rising or visible at the time of birth or, according to other views, at the time of conception.[1] These views take us back directly to the system of astrology developed by Babylonian *bârû* priests. The basis on which the modified Greek system rests is likewise the same that we have observed in Babylonia —a correspondence between heaven and earth, but

[1] Bouché-Leclercq, *L'Astrologie Grecque*, p. 373 *seq.*

17

with this important difference, that instead of the caprice of gods we have unalterable fate controlling the entire universe—the movements of the heavens and the life of the individual alike.

The recognition of law in the heavens, which eventually put an end to astrology in Babylonia, was the very factor that gave to the transplanted system a new hold among the Greeks. Hence the harmonious combination of astronomy and astrology which has been maintained from the days of Greek civilisation, through the Middle Ages, and down to the threshold of modern science. Wherever Greek philosophy wandered, Greek astronomy, like Greek medicine, also went, and with Greek astronomy went a modified astrological system of Babylonia. Astronomy and astrology became inseparable twin sciences. The two became blended—presenting merely two aspects of one and the same object. The study of the heavens was designated "natural astrology"; the application of the study in casting the horoscopes was called "judicial astrology." If all the great astronomers of Europe during the Middle Ages—men like Copernicus and Galileo—were also astrologers, it was due to this harmonious combination between astronomy and astrology.

But by the side of this plausible though erroneous alliance between a science and a pseudo-science, we must not fail to observe that there existed a con-

tinued influence of the old Babylonian astrology, less
honourable in its character and less agreeable to con-
template. We have already taken note of the fact
that when a religious custom is transplanted to a
foreign soil, its degeneration sets in.[1] This happened
when the divination methods of Babylonia made
their way to the West. Not only was the Babylonian
astrology transferred to Greece but the *bârû* priests
went with it. During the three centuries after Alexander we frequently read in Greek and Roman authors
of "Chaldeans" following the armies as diviners,
and plying a profitable trade in furnishing omens on
all occasions. These "Chaldeans" emerge not only as
astrologers, but as diviners by the liver. Their repu-
tation was none of the best. Greek and Latin writers
rehearse the tricks with which they plied their trade,[2]
until in time "Chaldean" became synonymous with
"imposter." But, on the other hand, it is also
significant of the influence which Babylonian practices continued to exert three centuries before our
era, that the term "Chaldean" became synonymous
with diviner and more particularly with one who read
the future in the stars. It does not follow, therefore,
that all diviners who are spoken of as "Chaldeans"
necessarily come from Mesopotamia. They appear
frequently to have been natives of Egypt, where
—no doubt under influences coming from the

[1] See above, p. 198.   [2] See above, p. 199.

East—divination flourished during these three centuries as it never did in the pre-Grecian period of Egyptian history. In fact, with the wave of mysticism that swept over Asia Minor, over Greece, and over the lands around the Mediterranean, and as the simple faith in the old order declined, the superstitions of the past acquired fresh vigour. Divination of various kinds became the "fad" of cultured circles as well as of the ignorant masses, and the prominence assumed by astrology among these practices led to the application of the term "Chaldean wisdom" to the observation of the stars. We must, however, bear in mind that the term as used by Greek and Roman writers means primarily astrology, and not astronomy. The Babylonian *bârû* priests, who left their native soil in search of a more profitable market elsewhere, found plenty of imitators who were too anxious to be known also as "Chaldeans," though no doubt, for a time at least, the main supply of diviners in Greece, Rome, Asia Minor, and Egypt came from the Euphrates Valley.

IX

The movement which took place in Babylonia and Assyria when, through Persian, Greek, and other influences, the basis of the astrological system was weakened by the increasing importance of a genuine science growing out of the study of the phenomena of the heavens, reminds us of what happened in Judea. There, through the concentration of the legitimate Jahweh cult in the sanctuary at Jerusalem, the priests of the numerous local sanctuaries scattered throughout Palestine were deprived of their prestige, and to a large extent of their means of livelihood. These priests, known as Levites [1] "lost their job," if the expressive colloquial phrase be permitted. The local sanctuaries were abandoned, but fortunately provision was made for the Levites in the priestly code. They were assigned to the lower menial duties at the temple in Jerusalem, and to act as attendants to the Jahweh priests—the *kôhanîm*,—to be their "hewers of wood and drawers of water." In Babylonia no Priestly Code was evolved to provide for the new order of things, and so when the *bârû* priests were replaced by the astronomers, the former left their homes, and, attracted by the prospect of successful careers in foreign lands, became the strolling magicians and soothsayers of antiquity.

The old, as almost invariably happens, partially survived by the side of the new; with the new alliance between astrology and astronomy, brought about by the accommodation of Babylonian methods to the Greek spirit, the old-time astrology continued in force

[1] The term seems to mean "followers"—"attachés," as it were—to a god, the guardians of his shrine.

and is represented by these "Chaldean" mountebanks. The pseudo-scientists adopted in time the phraseology and a superficial smattering of astronomical lore from the more genuine devotees of the study of the heavens, but their method remained essentially that of the old Babylonian astrologers. We have, thus, on the one hand, the serious cultivation of the newer astrology under the guise of genethlialogy, and, on the other, the continuation of the older form resting on a pseudo-scientific basis, but degraded to the rank of a dishonest profession through the "Chaldean" priests, who no longer found recognition in their native land.

With the entire collapse of astrology even in the form given to it by the Greek astronomers, through the newer scientific spirit of our own days which has destroyed the bond between the individual and the phenomena of the heavens, the divorce between astronomy and astrology became absolute and complete; but the "Chaldeans" of Greek and Roman times have their successors in the modern "astrologers" who, indifferent to the postulates of modern science, have adopted the jargon of scientific nomenclature, and still carry on a flourishing trade in the cities and country districts of Europe and America, and seem to justify the harsh dictum ascribed to Pope Paul IV.: *mundus vult decipi ergo decipiatur.*[1] Perhaps it is just as well that those who do not wish to be convinced

[1] "The world wishes to be deceived—let it be deceived."

should be deceived; and, after all, astrology is possibly the most innocent form of charlatanism in our modern life. We must, however, beware of the error of confusing these modern "astrologers" with the astrologer-astronomers of the Middle Ages with whom they naturally strive to claim relationship. This honourable guild of scientists was limited merely by the intellectual and scientific horizon of their day. The astronomers of the Middle Ages who attached astrology to their scientific study of the heavens continued the traditions of the Greek astronomers, who adopted the astrology of the Babylonians and Assyrians as a practical application of the scientific astronomy long cultivated by them. The alliance was misguided but was not unholy. The modern "astrologers" who, through the law of demand and supply, pose as casters of individual horoscopes, may be thus directly traced back to the old *bârû* priests. Unscientific or pseudo-scientific, like their more immediate ancestors,—the "Chaldean" charlatans,—the astrologers of our days continue to ply a profession for which the tools are simple and the tricks complicated.

The question may arise, while following this story of the birth and growth of astrology, why exhume the superstitions and follies of the past? Of what use is it? Various are the answers. The path of mankind in its progress toward an unknown goal is devious, leading over wastes of error and falsehood. History is as full of failures as of achievements, and we must study the one as fully as the other. But perhaps the most satisfactory answer is suggested by the distinguished Bouché-Leclercq, who, raising this very question at the close of the introduction to his standard work on Greek astrology,[1] heroically declares— and what heart will not respond?—that it is not a waste of time to find out how other people have wasted theirs.

[1] *L'Astrologie Grecque*, p. ix.

LECTURE V

THE TEMPLES AND THE CULTS

I

THE modern and occidental view of a temple as a place of worship gives only a part of the picture when we come to regard the sanctuaries of the gods in Babylonia and Assyria. Throughout antiquity, the sanctuary represents, first and foremost, the dwelling of a god. Among the Semites it grows up around the sacred stone, which, originally the god himself, becomes either, in the form of an altar, a symbol of his presence, or is given the outlines of an animal or human figure (or a combination of the two), and becomes a representative of the deity—his counterfeit. Stone, altar, and image are merely phases of the primitive animistic conception. Without differentiating sharply between the various manifestations of life in the universe, primitive man sought to localise the unseen Powers; and, through an instinct, forming part of his meagre equipment at the outset of his strange and miraculous career, he dimly felt that they should be propitiated, since at times he clearly perceived that they controlled his welfare, and apparently intervened at critical moments in his own life, or in that of the group to which he belonged.

The charming legend of Jacob's dream,[1] devised to account for the sanctity of an ancient centre of worship—Luz,—illustrates this development of the temple, from an ancient and more particularly from a Semitic point of view. The "place"[2] to which Jacob comes is a sacred enclosure formed by stones. His stone pillow is the symbol of the deity, and originally the very deity himself. The god in the stone "reveals" himself, because Jacob by direct contact with the stone becomes, as it were, one with the god, precisely as a sacred relic—an image, or any sacred symbol—communicates a degree of sanctity to him who touches it, whether by kissing it or by pressing against it.[3] When Jacob awakes he realises that Jahweh is the

---

[1] Genesis, chap. xxviii., 11–22. The story in its present form represents the combination of two versions.

[2] The Hebrew term *mākôm* corresponds to the Arabic *makâm*, which is still used to designate a shrine or a chapel.

[3] The Hebrew term *māshah*, "to anoint" (from which we obtain the term Messiah), means to "press," and to this day the Mohammedan pilgrims at Mecca press against the Caaba— the sanctuary at that place—in order to gain for themselves the sanctity attaching to it. See Wellhausen, *Reste Arabischen Heidentums*, p. 105 *seq.* The same motive appears to underlie the custom of the orthodox Jews of Palestine who in praying press against the wall at Jerusalem that is traditionally regarded as part of Solomon's temple.

god of the sacred enclosure, which he designates as "the house of the Lord" (Elohim) and "gate of heaven." He sets up the stone as an altar, anoints it (thus doing homage to the deity represented by the stone,) precisely as one anoints a king or a priest. He changes the name of the sacred place to Bethel, *i.e.*, "house of God," and declares his intention on his return to his father's house to convert the stone into a "house of the Lord." The stone becomes the house, and the sanctuary is the home of the god represented by the stone.

When later on the temple at Jerusalem was built, the name given to it was the "holy house," and it is commonly spoken of as the "house of Jahweh" in which he was supposed to dwell. "I have built a lofty house for Thee," says Solomon, "a place for Thy dwelling for all times."[1] To this day the central sanctuary of Islamism, the Caaba at Mecca, is known as the "house of Allah"; and such is the intimate character of the relation between Allah and his worshippers that the latter regard the mosque not merely as a place for prayer, but as a paternal mansion into which they can wander at any time of the day for rest and recreation. It is not uncommon in the Orient to see a worshipper taking a *siesta* in a mosque, and even performing his toilet there. The temple thus becomes a home for the worshipper as well as for the

[1] 1 Kings viii., 13.

deity. In a recent address,[1] Prof. Flinders Petrie has shown that the interior arrangement of an Egyptian temple was planned after the mansions of the nobles, and that the cult in its general features followed the daily routine observed in large households. The room containing the image of the deity was swept and prepared for the day's duties. A fire was lit, the god washed, anointed, and food was placed before him; thereafter the god was ready to receive his worshippers, just as the *grand seigneur* receives in the morning the homage of his clients and the visits of the members of his household.

In like manner, the "house" *motif* prevails in the Babylonian and the Assyrian sanctuaries. Temple and palace adjoin one another in the great centres of the north and south. The temple is the palace of the deity, and the royal palace is the temple of the god's representative on earth—who as king retains throughout all periods of Babylonian and Assyrian history traces of his original position as the "lieutenant," or even the embodiment of god—a kind of *alter ego* of god, the god's vicegerent on earth.[2] The term which in Babylonian designates more specifically the palace, *êkallu*, *i.e.*, "great-house," becomes in Hebrew, under the form *hēkhāl*, one of the designations of Jahweh's

---

[1] Presidential address before the Egyptian Section of the Third International Congress for the History of Religions. *Transactions*, vol. i., pp. 186 *seq.*

[2] See above, p. 241.

sanctuary in Jerusalem. Temple and palace are almost interchangeable terms. Both are essentially
houses, and every temple in Babylonia and Assyria
bore a name which contained as one of its elements
the word "house."[1] The ruler, embodying, originally, what we should designate as both civil and religious functions, was god, priest, and king in one.
We have seen that the kings were in the earlier period
often designated as divine beings: they regarded
themselves as either directly descended from gods or
as "named" by them, *i.e.*, created by them for the
office of king. To the latest days they could perform
sacrifices—the distinct prerogative of the priests—
and among their titles both in ancient and in later
days, "priest" is frequently included.[2] With the
differentiation of functions consequent upon political
growth and religious advance the service of the god
was committed to a special class of persons. Priests

[1] Thus we have E-Zida, "legitimate house," the name of
Nebo's temple in Borsippa, E-Anna, "heavenly house," the
name of Ishtar's temple in Uruk, E-Sagila, "the lofty house,"
the name of Ea's temple in Eridu and of Marduk's sanctuary
in Babylon, E-Barra, "the shining house," the name of the
temple of Shamash in Sippar, and Larsa, "house of joy,"
the name of Sin's temple in Ur, etc.

[2] So, *e.g.*, Lugalzaggisi calls himself "priest of Anu," "great
servant of Sin," etc. (Thureau-Dangin, *Sumerisch-Akkadische
Königsinschriften*, p. 154 lines 7 and 12), and at the close of
Babylonian history, we find Nebuchadnezzar II. designating
himself as the "lofty Patesi," *i.e.*, "priestly ruler" (Rawlinson, I.,
Plate 59, col. i., 5).

from being the attendants of the kings, became part of the religious household of the god. The two households, the civil and the religious, supplemented each other. Over the one presided the ruler, surrounded by a large and constantly growing retinue for whom quarters and provisions had to be found in the palace; at the head of the temple organisation stood the god or goddess, whose sanctuary grew in equal proportion, to accommodate those who were chosen to be servitors. Even the little shrines scattered throughout the Islamic Orient of to-day—commonly fitted up as tombs of saints, but often replacing the site of the dwelling-place of some ancient deity—have a place set aside for the servitor of the god,—the guardian of the sanctuary,—just as a private household has its quarters for the servants. As the temple organisation became enlarged, the apartments for the priests correspondingly increased. Supplementary edifices became necessary to accommodate the stores required for the priests and the cult. The temple grew into a temple-area, which, in the large religious centres, in time assumed the dimensions of an entire sacred quarter.

There is still another aspect of the temples of Babylonia and Assyria. We have already taken note[1] of the tendency to group the chief gods and goddesses and many of the minor ones also around the

[1] Above, pp. 18 *seq.*; 104, 122 *seq.*

main deity, in a large centre. A god like Enlil at
Nippur, Shamash at Sippar, Ningirsu at Lagash, Sin
at Ur, and Marduk at Babylon, is not only served by
a large body of priests, but, again, as in the case of the
great ruler who gathers around his court the members
of his official family, smaller sanctuaries were erected
within the temple area at Nippur to Ninlil, Enlil's consort, to Ninib, Nusku, Nergal, Ea, Sin, Shamash, Marduk, and others, all in order to emphasise the dominant position of Enlil.[1]   It is safe to state that in the
zenith of Nippur's glory all the important gods of the
pantheon were represented in the cult at that place.
We have a list of no less than thirteen sanctuaries at
Lagash,[2] and we may feel certain that they all stood
within the sacred area around E-Ninnu, "house of
fifty," which was the name given to Ningirsu's dwelling at that place. At the close of Babylonian history we find Nebuchadnezzar II. enumerating, among
his numerous inscriptions, the shrines and sanctuaries
grouped around E-Sagila, "the lofty house," as Marduk's temple at Babylon was called.   His consort Sarpanit, his son Nebo, his father Ea, were represented,
as were Sin, Shamash, Adad, Ishtar, Ninib and his
consort Gula, Nergal and his consort Laz, and so on

---

[1] See, *e.g.*, the list of temples in a Nippur text from the Cassite period, published by Clay, *Dated Cassite Archives* (Babylonian Expedition, vol. xiv.), No. 148,

[2] Scheil, *Recueil de Travaux*, vol. xvii., 39.

through a long list. There was no attempt made to assimilate the cult of these deities to that of Marduk, despite the tendency to heap upon the latter the attributes of all the gods. The shrines of these gods, bearing the same names as those of their sanctuaries in their own centres of worship,[1] served to maintain the identity of the gods, while as a group around Marduk they illustrated and emphasised the subsidiary position which they occupied. In a measure, this extension of the "house" of a deity into a sacred quarter with dwellings for gods whose actual seat was elsewhere, displaced the original idea connected with a sanctuary, but kings also erected palaces for themselves in various places without endangering either the prestige or the conception of a *central* dwelling in the capital of the kingdom. The shrines of the gods within the sacred area of E-Sagila represented temporary abodes, or "embassies" as it were, and so it happened that even Marduk had a foreign sanctuary, *e.g.*, at Borsippa to symbolise the close relationship between him and Nebo.

The rulers of Assyria vied with those of the south in beautifying and enlarging the temples of their gods, and in constantly adding new structures; or re-

[1] Thus Nebo's temple in Babylon was known as E-Zida, "the legitimate house," which was the name also of his temple in the central place of his worship at Borsippa. Shamash's temple at Babylon was E-Barra, "the shining house," as at Sippar, etc·

building the old which had fallen into decay. The
sacred quarter in the old capital at Ashur, and in the
later capital at Nineveh, was studded with edifices,
and the priests have left us lists[1] of the many gods and
goddesses "whose names were invoked," as the phrase
ran, in the temples of the capital.

II

With the growth of the temple organisation, its
administration also assumed large proportions. The
functions of the priests were differentiated, and assigned to several classes—diviners, exorcisers, astrologers, physicians, scribes, and judges of the court,
to name only the more important; and as early as the
days of Hammurapi, we learn of priestesses attached
to the service of Shamash and of other gods. The
importance of these priestesses, however, appears to
have grown less, as the religion developed. An institution like that of the vestal virgins also existed
at an early period, though the material at our disposal is as yet too meagre to enable us to specify the
nature of the institution, or the share in the cult allotted to these virgins.

The temple was also the centre of intellectual life.
Within the sacred precinct was the temple school in
which the aspirants to the priesthood were prepared

[1] Rawlinson, III. Plate 66.

18

for their future careers—just as to this day the instruction of the young in Islamism, as well as the discussions of the learned, takes place within the precincts of the mosques. Learning remained under the control of the priests throughout all periods of Babylonian and Assyrian history. In a certain very definite sense all learning was religious in character, or touched religion at some vital point. In the oldest legal code of the Pentateuch, the so-called "Book of the Covenant," the term used for the exercise of legal functions is "to draw nigh to the Lord" (Elohim), *i.e.*, to appear before God,[1] and this admirably reflects the legal procedure in Babylonia and Assyria. The laws of the country represented the decrees of the gods. Legal decisions were accordingly given through the representatives and servitors of the gods—the kings, in the earlier ages, and later the priests. At the close of his famous code, Hammurapi, whose proudest title is that of "king of righteousness," endowed with justice by Shamash—the paramount god of justice and righteousness,—states that one of the aims of his life was to restrain the strong from oppressing the weak, and to procure justice for the orphan and the widow. He appropriately deposits in E-Sagila, the temple of Marduk in Babylon, the stone on which he had inscribed the laws of the country "for rendering decisions, for decreeing judgments in the land,

[1] Exodus xxi., 6.

for the righting of wrongs." The ultimate source of all law being the deity himself, the original legal tribunal was the place where the image or symbol of the god stood. A legal decision was an oracle or omen, indicative of the will of the god. The Hebrew word for law, *tôrah*, has its equivalent in the Babylonian *têrtu*, which is the common term for "omen."[1] This indissoluble bond between law and religion was symbolised by retaining the tribunal, at all times, within the temple area and by placing the dispensing of justice in the hands of the priests—a condition that is also characteristic of legal procedure in all the Pentateuchal codes, including the latest, the so-called Priestly Code.

The power thus lodged in the priests of Babylonia and Assyria was enormous. They virtually held in their hands the life and death of the people, and while the respect for authority, the foundation of all government, was profoundly increased by committing the functions of the judges to the servitors of the gods, yet the theory upon which the dispensation of justice rested, though a logical outcome of the prevailing religious beliefs, was fraught with grave dan-

[1] The Hebrew tradition, or rather dogma, of the divine origin of the Pentateuch is merely another way of saying that legal decrees represent the oracles furnished by the gods. Moses, to whom tradition ascribes the Pentateuch, is merely the instrument through which the laws are transmitted by Jahweh, just as Hammurapi is the mouthpiece of Shamash.

gers. A single unjust decision was sufficient to shake the confidence not merely in the judge but in the god whose mouthpiece he was supposed to be. An error on the part of a judge demonstrated, at all events, that the god no longer cherished him; he had forfeited the god's assistance. Accordingly, one of the first provisions in the Hammurapi code[1] ordains that a judge who renders a false decision is to be removed from office. There was no court of appeal in those days; nor any need of one, under the prevailing acceptance of legal decisions. The existence of this provision may be taken as an indication that the incident was not infrequent. On the other hand, the thousands of legal documents that we now have from almost all periods of Babylonian-Assyrian history furnish eloquent testimony to the scrupulous care with which the priests, as judges, sifted the evidence brought before them, and rendered their decisions in accordance with this evidence.

The temples were the natural depositories of the legal archives, which in the course of centuries grew to veritably enormous proportions. Records were made of all decisions; the facts were set forth, and duly attested by witnesses. Business and marriage contracts, loans and deeds of sale were in like manner drawn up in the presence of official scribes, who were also priests. In this way all commercial transactions re-

[1] § 5 (col. vi., 6–30, ed. R. F. Harper).

ceived the written sanction of the religious organisation. The temples themselves—at least in the large
centres—entered into business relations with the populace. In order to maintain the large household represented by such an organisation as that of the temple
of Enlil at Nippur, that of Ningirsu at Lagash, that
of Marduk at Babylon, or that of Shamash at Sippar,
large holdings of land were required which, cultivated
by agents for the priests, or farmed out with stipula-
tions for a goodly share of the produce, secured an income for the maintenance of the temple officials. The
enterprise of the temples was expanded to the furnishing of loans at interest—in later periods, at 20%—
to barter in slaves, to dealings in lands, besides engaging labour for work of all kinds directly needed for
the temples. A large quantity of the business documents found in the temple archives are concerned with
the business affairs of the temple, and we are justified
in including the temples in the large centres as among
the most important business institutions of the
country.[1] In financial or monetary transactions the
position of the temples was not unlike that of national
banks; they carried on their business with all the
added weight of official authority. The legal and business functions thus attached to the temple organ-

[1] For further details see Peiser's Introduction to his *Keilinschriftliche Aktenstücke;* Kohler-Peiser-Ungnad, *Aus dem Babylonischen Rechtsleben* (4 parts); and *Hammurabis Gesetz* (4 vols.).

isations enlarged also the scope of the training given in the temple-schools. To instruction in methods of divination, in the rituals connected with exorcising demons and in other forms of incantations, in sacrificial and atonement rituals, in astrology, and in the treatment of diseases as supplementary to incantation rites, there was added training in the drawing up of legal documents, in the study of the laws, and in accounting, including calculations of interest and the like.[1]

It is to the temple-schools that we owe the intellectual activity of Babylonia and Assyria. The incentive to gather collections of omens, of incantations, and, of medical compilations, came from these schools. Though the motive was purely practical, viz., to furnish handbooks for the priests and to train young candidates for the priesthood, nevertheless the incentive was intellectual both in character and scope, and necessarily resulted in raising the standard of the priesthood and in stimulating the literary spirit. The popular myths and legends were given a literary form, and preserved in the archives of the temple-

[1] Whether instruction in clay modelling and in drawing on clay was included in the temple curriculum, as Hilprecht claimed, in a passage of his *Explorations in Bible Lands*, p. 527, may be questioned. The example that he gives of a supposed drawing of a bird on clay turns out to be a fragment of a stone vase, and the other "bird" on clay which he claims was discovered in the temple at Nippur appears to have flown away.

schools. An interest in fables was aroused, and the wisdom of the past preserved for future generations. Texts of various kinds were prepared for the schools. Hymns, rituals, incantations, omens, and medical treatises were edited and provided with commentaries or with glasses, and explanatory amplifications, to serve as text-books for the pupils and as guides for the teachers. For the study of the language, lists of signs with their values as phonetic symbols, and their meanings when used as ideographs were prepared. Lists of all kinds of objects were drawn up, names of countries and rivers, tables of verbal forms, with all kinds of practical exercises in combining nouns and verbs, and in forming little sentences. The practical purpose served by many of these exercises is shown by the character of the words and phrases chosen—they are such as occur in legal documents, or in omens, or in other species of religious texts used in the cult. Many of these school texts, including the collections of omens and incantations as well as hymns and rituals, were originally written in a "Sumerian" version, though emanating from priests who spoke Babylonian. It was found necessary to translate, or to "transliterate," them into the Semitic Babylonian. We thus obtain many bilingual texts furnishing both the Semitic and the Sumerian versions. A large proportion of the literary texts in Ashurbanapal's library thus turn out to be school texts, and since we know that the scribes of Ashurbanapal prepared their copies from originals produced in Babylonia,—though Assyria also contributed her share towards literary productions,—the conclusion seems justified that it was through the temple-schools and for the temple-schools that the literature, which is almost wholly religious in character, or touches religion at some point, was produced.

It will be apparent, therefore, that the temples of Babylonia and Assyria served a variety of purposes, besides being merely places of worship. They formed —to emphasise the point once more—the large religious households of the country, harbouring large bodies of priests for whose sustenance provision had to be made, superintending all the details of the administration of large holdings, exercising the functions of legal courts, acting as the depositories of official records—legal and historical,—besides engaging in the activities of business corporations and of training institutions in all the branches of intellectual activity that centred around the religious beliefs and the cult. It was through the temples, in short, that the bond between culture and religion, which was set forth in a previous lecture, was maintained during all periods of Babylonian and Assyrian history.

III

The present ruined condition of the temples of

Babylonia and Assyria makes it difficult to obtain an
accurate idea of their construction; and a note of
warning must be sounded against reconstructions,
made on the basis of earlier excavations, which are, in
almost all respects, purely fanciful. Thanks, however, to the careful work done by the German expedition at Ashur—the old capital of Assyria[1]—our
knowledge of details has been considerably extended;
and since the religious architecture of Assyria by
the force of tradition follows Babylonian models,
except in the more liberal use of stone instead of
bricks, the results of the excavations and investigations of the temple constructions of Ashur may be
regarded as typical for Babylonian edifices as well.

The "house" *motif*, which, we have seen, domin-
ated the construction of temples, led to the setting
apart of a special room to receive the image of the
deity for whom the edifice was erected as a dwelling-
place. The private quarters of the deity constituted
the "holy of holies," and this was naturally placed in
the remotest part of the edifice. To this room, known
as "the sacred chamber," only the priests and kings

[1] See Andrae, *Der Anu-Adad Tempel* (Leipzig, 1909), and the
Mitteilungen der Deutschen Orient-Gesellschaft, especially No.
22 *seq.* Much is also to be expected from C. S. Fisher's work on
Nippur (in course of publication), devoted to a careful study
of the architecture of the walls and constructions unearthed in
the course of the Nippur excavations, conducted by Messrs.
Peters and Haynes.

had access; they alone might venture into the presence of the deity. It was separated from the rest of the building by an enclosure which marked the boundary between the "holy of holies" and the long hall or court where the worshippers assembled. Outside of this court there was a second one, in which, presumably, the business affairs of the temple were conducted. Grouped around these two courts were the apartments of the priests, the school, and the archive rooms, as well as the quarters for the temple stores. In the case of the larger centres, we must furthermore suppose many special buildings for the various needs of the religious household, stalls for the animals, workshops and booths for the manufacture of temple utensils, fabrics, and votive offerings, quarters for the tribunals, offices of the notaries, and the like.

A feature of the temple area in the large centres was a brick tower, formed by from two to seven superimposed stages, which stood near the temple proper. These towers were known as *zikkurats*—a term that has the sense of "high" places. Elaborate remains of the *zikkurats* at Nippur and at Ashur have been unearthed, and these together with the famous one at Borsippa, still towering above the mounds at that place, and currently believed among the natives to be the traditional tower of Babel, enable us to form a tolerably accurate idea of their construction. Huge and ungainly quadrangular masses of bricks, placed one above the other in stories diminishing in the square mass as they proceed upwards, these towers attained the height of about one hundred feet and at times more.[1] The character of such a sacred edifice differs so entirely from the Babylonian temple proper, that, in order to account for its presence in Nippur, Lagash, Ur, Sippar, Larsa, Babylon, Borsippa, Ashur, Nineveh, and other places, we must perforce assume a second *motif* by the side of the "house" scheme of a temple. The height of these towers, as well as the diminishing mass of the stones, with a winding balustrade, or a direct ascent from one stage to the other up to the top, at once recalls the picture of a mountain.

The semblance suggests that the *motif* must have originated with a people dwelling in a mountainous country, who placed the seats of their gods on the mountain-tops, as was so generally done by ancient peoples. The gods who are thus localised, however, are generally storm gods like Jahweh, who dwells on the top of Mt. Sinai—or according to another view on Mt. Seir,—or like Zeus on Mt. Olympus. The gods whose manifestations appear in the heavens—in the storm, in the thunder, and in the lightning—would naturally have their seats on high mountains whose

[1] Sir Henry Rawlinson estimated the one at Borsippa to have been 140 feet high. Plate 23, Fig. 1.

tops, so frequently enveloped in clouds, would be regarded as forming a part of heaven.[1] If this supposition be correct, we should furthermore be obliged to assume that the "mountain" *motif* was brought to the mountainless region of the Euphrates by a people entering the valley from some mountainous district. Since the *zikkurats* can be traced back to the Sumerian period (we find them in Gudea's times and during the Sumerian dynasties of Ur), their introduction must be credited to the Sumerians, or to an equally ancient section of the population. We have seen that it is not possible to affirm positively that non-Semitic settlers were the earliest inhabitants of the Euphrates Valley; but the circumstance that where we find *zikkurats* in Semitic settlements (such as the minarets attached to the Mohammedan mosques), they can be traced back, as we shall presently see, to Babylonian prototypes, furnishes a strong presumption in favour of ascribing the "mountain" *motif* to Sumerian influence.

It is not without significance that the temple at

[1] The general view among primitive people appears to have been that the expanse of heaven is not so very far from the earth. Hence the ambition to scale the heavens, which forms the basis of so many ancient myths. Even in the Biblical story of the building of the tower (Genesis, chap. xi.) which was to reach to heaven, the task is not viewed as an impossible one but as a wicked plan. Jahweh is afraid in fact lest the wicked plan may succeed; therefore he seeks to frustrate it by confusing the speech of the builders. See below, p. 298.

Nippur, which is certainly a Sumerian settlement, and one of the oldest, bore the name E-Kur, "mountain-house," and that Enlil, the chief deity of Nippur, bears the indications of a storm-god,[1] whose dwelling should, probably, therefore, be on a mountain. Herodotus[2] is authority for the statement that there was a small shrine at the top of the *zikkurat*, in which there was a statue of the god in whose honour the tower was built. This shrine, therefore, represented the dwelling of the god, and corresponded to the sacred chamber in the temple proper. To ascend the *zikkurat* would thus be equivalent to paying a visit to the god; and we have every reason to believe that the ascent of the *zikkurat* formed a part of the ceremonies connected with the cult, just as the Jewish pilgrims ascended Mt. Zion at Jerusalem to pay their homage to Jahweh, who was there enshrined after the people had moved away from Mt. Sinai and Mt. Seir.[3]

There is no reason to assume that these towers were ever used for astronomical purposes, as has been frequently asserted. Had this been the case, we should long ere this have found reference to the fact in

---

[1] See above, p. 68 *seq.*   [2] Book I., 181.

[3] The sanctuary on Mt. Zion is older than the settlement of the Hebrews. Jahweh dispossesses the god of Zion, just as his people dispossess the older settlers of Canaan. Jahweh wanders with his people, and though tradition continued to associate him with Mt. Sinai, to the later Hebrews Mt. Zion is Jahweh's home.

some inscription. References to an observatory for the study of the heavens, known as the *bit tamarti*, *i.e.*, "house of observation," are not infrequent, but nowhere is there any indication that the *zikkurats* were used for that purpose. They must have been regarded as too sacred to be frequently visited, even by the priests. Access to them was rather complicated, and for observations needed for astrological divination a high eminence was not required. Still more groundless, and hardly worthy of serious consideration is the supposition that it was customary to bury the dead at the base of the *zikkurat*, which in this case would be a Babylonian equivalent of the Egyptian pyramid, namely, as the tomb of monarchs and of grand personages.

On the other hand, the imitation of a mountain suggested a further symbolism in the *zikkurats*, which reveals itself in the names given to some of them. While no special stress seems, at any time, to have been laid on the number of stories or stages of which a *zikkurat* consisted, the chief aim of the builders being the construction of a high mass, seven stages seems to have become the normal number, after a certain period. There seems to be no reason to doubt that this number was chosen to correspond to the moon, sun, and five planets, which we have seen were the controlling factors in the Babylonian-Assyrian astrology. Gudea describes the *zikkurat* at Lagash known as

E-Pa as the "house of the seven divisions"[1]; and from the still fuller designation of the tower at Borsippa as the "seven divisions of heaven and earth," it would appear that in both cases there is a symbolical reference to the "seven planets," as the moon, sun, and five planets were termed by the Babylonians themselves.[2] Less probable is the interpretation of the name of the tower at Uruk as the "seven enclosures" (or possibly "groves") as applying likewise to the seven planets, though to speak of the moon, sun, and five planets as "enclosures" would be a perfectly intelligible metaphor. That the symbolism of the *zikkurats* was carried any further, however, and each stage identified with one of the planets, may well be doubted, nor is it at all likely that the bricks of each stage had a different colour, corresponding to colours symbolically associated with the planets. Even if seven different colours were used in the construction, there is no evidence thus far that these colours were connected with the planets.[3]

Moreover, a valuable hint of one of the fundamental ideas associated with the *zikkurat* is to be found in the name given to the one at Larsa: "the house of the link

[1] Thureau-Dangin, *Sumerisch-Akkadische Inschriften*, pp. 76, 84, 86, etc.

[2] Rawlinson, III. Plate 57, No. 6, 65.

[3] The only colours mentioned in astrological texts in connection with the planets are white for Jupiter or Mars, dark red for Mars, and black (or dark) for Mercury.

of heaven and earth." Attention has already been called to the fact[1] that the heavens, according to the prevailing view of antiquity, were not elevated very far above the earth. The tops of the mountains were regarded as reaching into heaven,—in fact as belonging to the heavens. The *zikkurat*, therefore, as the imitation of the mountain, might well be called the "link" uniting earth to heaven. The name is of interest because of the light which it throws on the famous tale in Genesis (chap. xi.) of the building of the tower. To the Hebrew writers, particularly those who wrote under the influence of the religious ideals of the prophets, the ambitious aims of the great powers of antiquity—conquest, riches, large armies, brilliant courts, the pomp of royalty, and indulgence in luxury—were exceedingly distasteful. Their ideal was the agricultural life in small communities governed by a group of elders, and with the populace engaged in tilling the soil and in raising flocks,— living peacefully under the shade of the fig tree. In the view of these writers, even such a work as the temple of Solomon, built by foreign hands, in imitation of the grand structures of other nations, was not pleasing in the eyes of Jahweh, whose preference was for a simple tabernacle, built of wood without the use of hewn stones and iron,—both of which represented innovations. These writers were what we should call

[1] See above, p. 284, note 1.

"old-fashioned,"—advocates of the simple life.[1]
They abominated, therefore, the large religious
households of the Babylonians and Assyrians and
particularly the high towers which were the "sky-
scrapers" of antiquity.[2] The narrative of the tower
of Babel is told as a protest against such ambitious
efforts, but the interesting feature of the narrative
for us is, that it correctly interprets the purpose of
these towers as aiming to reach up to heaven. The
name of the *zikkurat* of Larsa well illustrates this
aim—to serve as a "link," uniting heaven and earth.
To the pious Hebrew writer such an undertaking

[1] This preference for the lower form of culture over the higher
crops out in many tales of the Old Testament, which received
their present form under the influence of the prophets. So, *e.g.*,
in the Cain and Abel story, Abel the keeper of flocks is preferred
to Cain the tiller of the soil and the builder of cities. Vini-
culture—a higher form of agriculture—is condemned in the
story of Noah. The Patriarchs are keepers of flocks, representing the higher type of nomads but lower than the agriculturists.
When the Hebrews invaded Palestine and dispossessed the Canaanites, they became, as the Canaanites had been for generations,
tillers of the soil. In this stage, agriculture is preferred to the
higher form of culture represented by commerce. The Priestly
Code, by prohibiting the taking of interest, puts its stamp of
disapproval upon mercantile pursuits, which cannot be carried
on without loans of money at a reasonable rate of interest. The
Priestly Code is opposed to the establishment of a kingdom,
and the additions to the Deuteronomic Code threaten the institution of the kingdom as a punishment for the sins of the
nation.

[2] This spirit of opposition to huge structures is still prevalent
among the natives of the Tigris and Euphrates districts, who
look upon such endeavours as due to the instigation of Satan.

19

seemed ungodly. He does not regard the task as impossible, but impious,—a wanton insult to Providence. He, therefore, represents Jahweh as intervening to prevent the plan from being carried out. The simple-hearted story, in picturing Jahweh as coming down to see what his creatures were doing, reveals its origin as a genuine folk-tale, and probably an old one, which a later writer, in sympathy with the opposition of primitive folk to the bolder ambitions of an advanced culture, adopts to emphasise the ungodliness of Babylonia, which represented just the things which the prophets opposed with such vehemence.

The "ladder" which Jacob saw in his dream reaching from earth to heaven was likewise suggested by the *zikkurat*. The "ladder" is pictured as a link uniting earth to heaven, and the term used in the narrative might just as well be rendered "tower."[1]

IV

Tower and temple remain, through all periods of Babylonian-Assyrian history, the types of religious

[1] The word *sullām* occurs only in this place (Genesis xxviii, 12) in the Old Testament; and the translation "ladder" is merely a guess. A more legitimate rendering would be "roadway," and since the towers had, as above pointed out, a road winding to the top, *sullām* might have been applied to describe this "road," and then the *zikkurat* itself. It should be noted that in Genesis chap. xi., two stories have been combined, one of the building of a city, the other of a tower. See the writer's article "The Tower of Babel" above (p. 3, note 1) referred to.

Pl. 23.   Fig. 1.   The two Zikkurats of the Anu-Adad Temple at Ashur.

See comment to Pl. 24, Fig. 2.   The temple being a double construction, one zikkurat or stage tower belongs to the Anu sanctuary, the other to the sanctuary of Adad.   The construction of this stage tower may be traced back to the reign of Ashurreshishi I. (*c.* 1150 B.C.).   It was rebuilt by Shalmaneser III. (858–824 B.C.). The illustration shows the restoration of the younger construction on the basis of the systematic excavations conducted chiefly by Andrae.

Fig. 2.   The Stage Tower at Samarra.

Dating from the 9th century A.D. and built of hard stone; it is still standing at Samarra, a settlement on the Tigris, and used as a minaret in connection with an adjoining mosque.   The shape is directly derived from the old Babylonian (or Sumerian) Zikkurats and may be regarded as typical of these constructions. In most mosques, the minaret is directly attached to the main building like the tower or steeple of a church, but there are some which still illustrate the originally independent character of the tower.   See Ernst Herzfeld, *Samarra* (Berlin, 1907), and Hermann Thiersch, *Pharos, Antike, Islam und Occident* (Leipzig, 1909).

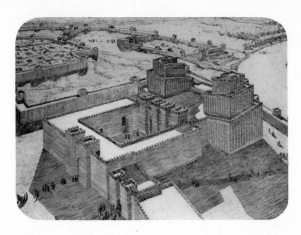

Fig. 1. Zikkurats of the Anu-Adad at Ashur

Fig. 2. Stage-tower at Samarra

architecture and survive the fall of both countries. The survival of religious traditions, despite radical changes in outward forms, is illustrated by the adoption of the *zikkurat* by Islamism. At Samarra, about sixty miles above Bagdad, there survives to this day an almost perfect type of a Babylonian *zikkurat*, as a part of a Mohammedan mosque.[1] Built about the middle of the ninth century of our era, and rising to a height of about one hundred and seventy feet, it has a winding ascent to the top, where in place of the sacred shrine for the god is the platform from which the *muezzin* calls the faithful to prayer. The god has been replaced by his servitor, and instead of the address *bêlu rabû* ("great lord") with which it was customary to approach the deities of old, *Allah akbar* ("Allah is great") is heard from the *minarets*[2]—which, as will have become evident, are merely modified *zikkurats*. Arabic writers themselves trace the custom of building a minaret at the side of a mosque, or as an integral part of the sacred structure, to the *zikkurat* at Samarra; and the chain of evidence has recently been completed to show that the steeples of our modern churches are a further step in the evolution of the *zikkurat*.[3]

[1] See Herzfeld's monograph, *Samarra* (Leipzig, 1908). and the illustration. Plate 23, Fig. 2.

[2] *Minaret* signifies literally "light-house" or "light-tower." Applied originally to the famous "light-tower" at Pharos, it was extended by analogy to the towers attached to the mosques.

[3] See Thiersch, *Pharos* (Leipzig, 1909), chap. v.

In Babylonia and Assyria, temple and tower, once entirely distinct, show a tendency to unite. In the city of Ashur, the oldest temple, or rather double temple, dedicated to Anu and Adad,[1] has a *zikkurat* on either side, each being directly attached to the respective temple or "house" of the deity. Elsewhere—as at Nippur—the *zikkurat* is close behind the temple, but even when adjacent the *zikkurat* remains an independent structure, and it is interesting to note that in the traditional forms of Christian architecture, the church tower retains this independent character. In Catholic countries where traditions are closely followed, it is provided that though the tower should be a part of the church, there must be no direct access from the one to the other.[2]

The opposition of the Hebrews to the allurements of Babylonian-Assyrian civilisation was strong enough to check the introduction of *zikkurats* into Palestine, but it could not prevent the imitation of the Assyrian temple in the days of Solomon. The type of religious edifice erected by this *grand monarque* of the Hebrews followed even in details the Assyrian model with its threefold division, the broad outer court, the oblong

[1] Andrae, *Anu-Adad-Tempel*, pp. 2 *seq.* and the illustration Plate 23, Fig. 1.

[2] The *campaniles* or bell-towers of the Italian churches (see the illustrations in Thiersch, *l.c.*, pp. 180–182), separated from them by a short distance, well illustrate the original relation of temple to tower in Babylonia and Assyria.

Pl. 24. Fig. 1. Plan of the Temple of Enlil at Nippur.

In this temple which may be regarded as typical for sacred edifices in Babylonia, B represents the outer court, and A, the inner court, the two being practically parallel in size and shape. The Zikkurat or stage tower (A1) is at the back of the inner court. The narrower section represents the sacred chamber (or the approach to it) in which the image of Enlil stood. In the outer court, B1 represents one of the smaller shrines of which there were many within the sacred area to the gods and goddesses associated with the cult of Enlil and Ninlil. See Hilprecht, *Excavations in Assyria and Babylonia*, p. 470, and the detailed plans and drawings in C. S. Fisher, *Excavations at Nippur*.

Fig. 2. Plan of the Temple of Anu and Adad at Ashur.

The temple was originally built in honour of Anu, the solar deity (who is replaced by Ashur) but at a very early date, Adad (or Ramman) was associated with him. The two temples, consistently referred to in the Assyrian inscriptions as the "Temple of Anu and Adad," have a large entrance court in common. Behind this court lie the two temples proper, each having (a) a broad outer court, (b) an oblong inner court, leading (c) to the sacred chamber where the images of Anu-Ashur and Adad, respectively, stood. This deviation from the Babylonian model, a broad outer and an oblong inner court instead of two practically parallel courts, is typical of Assyrian scared architecture. Each temple has its Zikkurat immediately adjoining it. See Andrae, *Der Anu-Adad Tempel* (Leipzig, 1909), Pl. V., and especially pp. 80–84.

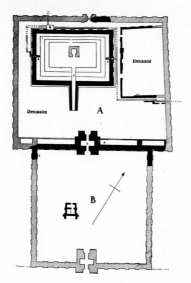

Fig. 1. Plan of Temple
of Enlil at Nippur

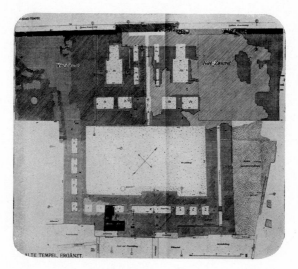

Fig. 2. Plan of Anu-Adad Temple at Ashur

narrow inner court, and the "holy of holies,"[1] where
in place of the statue of the deity was the sacred box
(or "Ark") with the Cherubim over it as the symbol
of Jahweh.

The history of the Babylonian and Assyrian temples
and their *zikkurats* furnishes an index to the religious
fervour of the rulers. The records left by rulers of
the oldest period are in the main votive inscriptions,
indicative of their activity in building or rebuilding
religious edifices. Conquerors, like Sargon and Hammurapi, are proud of the title of "builder" of this or
that temple; and their example is followed by the
war-lords of Assyria, who interrupt the narration of
their military exploits by detailed accounts of their
pious labours in connection with the great sanctuaries
of the country. Taking the temples at Nippur, Sippar, Babylon, and Ashur as typical examples, we
find a long chain of rulers leaving records of their
building activities in these centres. Kings of Kish,
Uruk, Ur, and Agade vie with the rulers of Babylon
and Nineveh in paying homage to the "mountain
house" at Nippur, repairing the decayed portions,

[1] See Andrae, *Der Anu-Adad-Tempel in Assur* (Leipzig, 1909),
pp. 82 *seq.* There was, as Andrae has shown, an important variation in the interior arrangement of the Assyrian temples from that
followed in Babylonia. Instead of an outer and an inner court
of the same width, the inner court in Assyrian temples was narrow
and long. This departure from the Babylonian type may be
due, as Andrae thinks, to Hittite or Syrian influence. See the
illustrations on Plate 24.

extending its dimensions, and adding to the mass of its *zikkurat*. They dedicate the spoils of war to Enlil and deposit votive offerings in his shrine. From Sargon of Agade to Ashurbanapal of Nineveh, E-Kur continued to be a place of pilgrimage whither the rulers went to acknowledge the authority of Enlil, and of his consort Ninlil. Long indeed after the tutelary deity of the city had been forgotten, the city retained its odour of sanctity, and the temple area became a burial-place for Jews and Christians, who bear witness to the persistence of time-worn beliefs by inscribing in Aramaic dialects on clay bowls incantations against the demons of ancient Babylonia, belief in whose power to inflict injury on the dead had not yet evaporated in the sixth and seventh centuries of our era.[1]

The last king of Babylonia, Nabonnedos (555–539 B.C.), who aroused the hostility of Marduk and the priests of Esagila by his preference for the sun-god,[2] gives us, in connection with his restoration of the temple of Shamash at Sippar, the history of that time-honoured sanctuary. As an act of piety to the memory of past builders, it became an established duty in Babylonia to unearth the old foundation stone of a temple before the work of restoration could be

---

[1] A publication of some forty clay bowls from Nippur is announced by Prof. J. A. Montgomery of the University of Pennsylvania.   [2] See above, p. 59.

begun. On that stone the name of the builder was inscribed, generally with a curse on him who removed it or substituted his name for the one there written. After many efforts the workmen of Nabonnedos succeeded in finding the stone, and the king tells us how he trembled with excitement and awe when he read on it the name of Naram-Sin. Incidentally, he gives us the date of Naram-Sin, who, he says, ruled 3200 years before him. It is one of the many great triumphs of modern investigation that we can actually correct the scribes of Naram-Sin, who made a mistake of over 1000 years.[1] Nabonnedos mentions also the names of Hammurapi and Burnaburiash as among those who, many centuries before him, repaired this ancient edifice, after, it had fallen into decay through lapse of ages. Toward the end of the Cassite dynasty (*ca.* 1200 B.C.) nomadic hordes devastated the country, and the cult suffered a long interruption, but E-Barra was restored to much of its former grandeur by Nebopaliddin in the ninth century, and from this time down to the time of Nabonnedos, it continued to be an object of great care on the part of both Assyrian and Babylonian kings. Esarhaddon, Ashurbanapal, Nabopolassar, and Nebuchadnezzar are among those who during this later

[1] See Meyer, *Geschichte des Altertums*, ii., 1 pp. 344 *seq.*, on the basis of Lehmann-Haupt, *Zwei Hauptprobleme der Altorientalischen Chronologie*, pp. 186 *seq.*

period left records of their activity at E-Barra, the
"house of splendour" at Sippar.

V

It is now incumbent on us to turn to the cult
fostered at these sanctuaries in the south and the
north. At the outset of this discussion it must be
acknowledged that many of the details are still lost.
We have, to be sure, in the library of Ashurbanapal
the material for a reconstruction of the cult at the
great centres, through the collection which this king
made of hymns and incantations, omens and rituals,
that formed part of the temple archives and of the
equipment of the temple-schools at Nippur, Ur, Sippar, Babylon, Borsippa, Cuthah, Uruk, and no doubt,
at many other places, though the bulk of the material
appears to have come from two temples, E-Sagila at
Babylon and E-Zida in Borsippa.[1] This material is,
however, in an almost bewildering state of confusion,
and many investigations of special features will have
to be made before it can be arranged in such a
manner as to give a connected picture of the general
cult. Fortunately, we have also, as supplementary
to this material, original texts, belonging to the oldest
period,—chiefly hymns, litanies, and lamentations,—

[1] See the writer's paper "*Did the Babylonian Temples Have
Libraries?*" (*Journal of the Amer. Oriental Society*, vol. xxvi.,
pp. 173 *seq.*)

which written in Sumerian, have recently been carefully studied and are now pretty well understood.[1]

The omen texts, including the omens of liver
divinations, the astrological collections, and the miscellaneous classes of omens, may be excluded from
the cult proper. Interpretations of omens, at all
events, do not form an integral part of the *official* cult
at the temples, despite the fact that they are concerned chiefly with public affairs or with those of
the royal households, which, as repeatedly emphasised,[2] have an official or semi-official rather than a
personal character. They might be designated as
religious rites, subsidiary to the official cult. In connection with the inspection of the liver of the sacrificial animal there was an invocation to Shamash,
or to Shamash and Adad, combined; we have specimens of such appeals, dating from Assyrian days, in
which the sun-god is invoked to answer questions
through the medium of trustworthy omens, and im-
plored to prevent any error in the rites about to
be performed which would naturally vitiate them.[3]

[1] Chiefly the texts published in *Cuneiform Texts*, Part XV., Plate
10–23. See Zimmern, "Tammuz Lieder" (*Berichte der Kgl. Sachs.
Akad. d. Wiss. Philol.-Histor. Classe*, vol. lix., pp. 201–252);
Langdon, *Sumerian and Babylonian Psalms* (Paris, 1909), and
the various papers by J. D. Prince and Frederick Vanderburgh in
the *Journal of the American Oriental Society* and in the *American Journal of Semitic Languages*.   [2] See above, p. 177.

[3] Knudtzon, *Assyrische Gebete an den Sonnengott*, pp. 73, 74, etc.;
and extracts also in Jastrow, *Religion* (German ed.), ii., pp. 300 *seq*.

There were, however, no *fixed* occasions for the consultations of livers. Whenever any necessity arose, as before a battle or previous to some important public undertaking, or in case of illness or some accident to the king or to a member of his immediate household, hepatoscopy was employed to determine the attitude of the gods toward the land or toward the royal household. Similarly, as we have seen, the observation of the heavenly bodies formed the perpetual concern of the *bârû* priests. Astrological reports were frequently sent to the rulers, always at new-moon and full-moon, and in the case of eclipse or obscurations of the moon's or sun's surface from any cause whatsoever. In cases where the signs of the heavens portended evil, expiatory rites were prescribed,[1] and these being conducted in the temples, no doubt formed part of the official expiatory ritual. The ritual on these occasions is, however, independent of the observation of the heavenly bodies, and follows as an attachment to the omens derived from the observation. Finally, the miscellaneous collections of omens, are merely to be regarded as handbooks to guide the *bârû* priests in answering questions that might be put to them concerning any unusual or

[1] The technical term for these rites is Nam-Bur-Bi, on which see Behrens, *Assyrisch-Babylonisch Briefe religiösen Inhalts*, pp. 95–98, and Morgenstern, *Doctrine of Sin in the Babylonian Religion*, pp. 137 *seq.*

striking appearance among men or animals, or in nature in general. Every unusual happening being regarded as a sign from some god or goddess, it became the priest's business to determine its import. Although he did this in his official capacity, the act of securing and furnishing the interpretation formed no part of the ritual; and the omens, even in these instances, frequently bore on the public welfare rather than on the fate or fortune of the individual. Such interpellations and decisions might be compared to the inquiries regarding ritualistic observances put to the Jewish Rabbis from Talmudic times down to our days in orthodox circles, which gave rise to an extensive branch of Rabbinical literature technically known as "Questions and Answers."[1]

An intermediate position between the official and the extra-official cult is held by the incantation formulas, and the observances connected therewith. In this branch of religious literature the layman received a large share of attention—larger even than in the case of the miscellaneous omens dealing with occurrences in daily life. In so far as the incantations represent the practices supplementary to medicinal treatment to release individuals from the tortures of the demons, or from the control of the sorcerers, they partake of the nature of private rites, which, although

[1] See the article "Shealôtu–Teshubôth " in the *Jewish Encyclopedia*, vol. xi, pp. 240–250.

observed under the guidance and superintendence of priests, can be regarded only in a limited sense as forming part of the official cult.

Nevertheless, we must be careful not to draw the dividing line between public and private rites too sharply. Even incantations, when performed for individuals, have their official side; for the ritual accompanying them is derived from the observances prescribed more particularly for the rulers on occasions of public misfortune. At such times the endeavour was made to appease the gods through the chanting of lamentations, through confession of guilt, and through expiatory sacrifices and atonement ceremonies. The incantations themselves abound in references to the public welfare. The technical term *shiptu* ("incantation"), by which they are known, is extended to hymns—a valuable indication that the hymnal literature is an outgrowth from incantations, and that the primary purpose of these hymns was neither praise, thanksgiving, nor tribute, but the reconciliation of the gods, who had shown their displeasure in some manner, or had sent advance signals of an impending catastrophe.

Dr. Langdon[1] believes he has found evidence that

[1] See his paper, "A Chapter from the Babylonian Books of Private Penance," in the *Transactions* of the 3d International Congress of the History of Religion (1908), vol. i., pp. 248 *seq.*, and Introduction to his *Sumerian and Babylonian Psalms* (Paris, 1909).

the incantation rites were originally performed over
afflicted persons in huts erected preferably on the
bank of a flowing stream, and that therefore at this
stage of their development they formed no part of the
official cult of the temples.   On the basis of this evidence he distinguishes between public and private
services, and assigns incantations and prayers, designated as *shiptu*, to the private service.   Without
entering into a detailed examination of this theory
here, but even accepting its full force, it would prove
only that the Babylonian religion contains survivals
of the early period when magic—in its widest sense
—formed the chief element in the religion; or (according to those scholars, who like Mr. J. G. Frazer,[1]
separate magic from religion) of that period when
magic held sway to the exclusion of religion.   At all
events, the incantation rites, whatever their original
character, were taken over into the official cult—as
Langdon also admits—and this fact carries with it,

[1] See the discussion on "Magic and Religion" in the 2d ed. of
Frazer's *Golden Bough*, vol. i., pp. 62 *seq.*, and Andrew Lang's
reply in *Magic and Religion*, which though unfair (and at
times offensive) in its tone against a scholar of such vastly
superior erudition as Mr. Frazer, nevertheless refutes (as I believe) the position that magic preceded and is a distinct stage
from religion.   Whatever our definition of religion may be, the
religious element is never lacking even in the most primitive
form of magic.   Magic is a very poor sort of a religion—but it
is religious, though for the sake of human dignity one may be
loath to admit it.

I think, the conclusion that the *âshipu*, as the "magician" or exorciser was generally called, was a member of the priestly organisation. Even the early examples of incantations at hand reveal their official character by the introduction of such terms for the various classes of incantations as "house of light," "house of washing," and "house of baptism,"[1] and show that we are long past the stage when magic was, if ever, an extra-official rite.

We are justified, however, in drawing the conclusion that the incantation rituals—including under this term both the collection of the magic formulas and the rites to be performed in connection with them — represent a link between the more primitive features of the Babylonian religion, and those elements which reflect the later period of an organised and highly specialised priesthood, with a correspondingly elaborate organisation of the cult. To dogmatise about the phases of that cult, and to declare the incantation ritual to be the oldest division is hazardous, especially in the present state of our knowledge, but, I think, it is safe to say that the beliefs and practices found in this ritual bring us close to the earliest aspects of the popular religion.

[1] These terms, referring originally to the particular place where incantation rites were employed, became the designations of the formulas recited in those places.

VI

It is difficult to suppose that the jumble of often meaningless formulas in the incantation texts, with their accompaniment of rites, originating in the lowest kind of sympathetic and imitative magic, should have been evolved by the same priests who added to these earlier elements, and frequently overshadowed them by ethical reflections, emphasising high standards of ethics; they also attached to them prayers that breathe a comparatively lofty religious spirit.

But not always. For instance, here is one where there are almost childish invocations to the evil spirits to leave the body of their victim: [1]

> Away, away, far away, far away!
> For shame, for shame, fly away, fly away!
> Round about face, away, far away!
> Out of my body away!
> Out of my body far away!
> Out of my body, for shame!
> Out of my body, fly away!
> Out of my body, face about!
> Out of my body, go away!
> Into my body do not return!
> To my body do not approach!
> My body do not oppress!
> By Shamash, the mighty, be ye exorcised!
> By Ea, the lord of all, be ye exorcised!
> By Marduk, the chief exorciser of the gods, be ye exorcised!

---

[1] *Maklû*, Incantation Ritual, Tablet V., lines 166–184. See Jastrow, *Religion*, Engl. edition, pp. 287 *seq.*, German ed., i., pp. 302–320.

> By Gish-Bar,[1] your consumer, be ye exorcised!
> Be ye restrained from my body!

But in the midst of these we find introduced prayers to various deities of which the following, addressed to the fire-god, may serve as an example:

> O Nusku,[2] great god, counsellor of the great gods,
> Guardian of the offerings of all the Igigi,[3]
> Founder of cities, renewer of sanctuaries,
> Glorious day,[4] of supreme command,
> Messenger of Anu,[5] obedient to the oracle of Enlil,
> Obedient to Enlil, the counsellor, the mountain[6] of the Igigi.
> Mighty in battle, of powerful attack,
> O, Nusku, consumer, overpowering the enemy,
> Without thee no table is spread in the temple,[7]
> Without thee the great gods do not inhale the incense,
> Without thee, Shamash, the judge executes no judgment.[8]

The hymn glides almost imperceptibly into an appeal to burn the sorcerer and sorceress:

[1] The god of fire.

[2] Also the god of fire.

[3] A collective name for the lower order of gods.

[4] An allusion to the bright light of the fire which is compared to the brilliant daylight.

[5] The god of heaven, an allusion to the sun as the heavenly fire.

[6] A frequent epithet of Enlil, the storm-god (see above, p. 68), who is the guardian of the lightning, another aspect of fire. In India, too, we find these three aspects of the fire—the earthly fire, the sun, and the lightning. See Hopkins, *Religions of India*, p. 105.

[7] Allusion to the fire as consuming the offerings on the altar.

[8] A reference to the sacrifices offered to Shamash, the sun-god, through whom just decisions are granted.

I turn to thee, I implore thee, I raise my hands to thee, I sink
    down at thy feet,
Burn the sorcerer and the witch!
Blast the life of the dreaded sorcerer and the witch!
Let me live that I may make thy heart glad, and humbly pay
    homage to thee.

Both the incantation formulas and the impressive prayers assume, as an accompanying rite, the
burning of an image, or of some symbol of the witch
or sorcerer.[1] This is done, in the firm belief that the
symbolical destruction will be followed by a genuine
release from their grasp. And yet it is evident that
the incantation texts and incantation rituals represent a composite production, receiving their final
shape as the result of the collaboration of many
hands. Primitive and popular elements were combined with doctrines and practices which, developed
in the schools of theological speculation, furnished
an outlet for the intellectual and spiritual activity of
those to whom, as the special servitors of the gods and
as the mediators between the gods and the populace,
the unfolding of the religious life of the country was
entrusted.

The influence of the religious theories elaborated by
the priests is to be seen in the prominence given to the
idea of purification throughout the incantation rituals.

---

[1] The instructions added to the formulas and prayers specify
that the image is to be of honey, wax, tallow, pitch, clay, meal,
of *binu*, or of cedar wood, or of copper, a different formula being
prescribed for each material.

The idea itself, to be sure, belongs to the primitive notion of *taboo*, which specifies an "unclean" condition, due to contact with something either too sacred or too profane to be touched, but the application of the *taboo* to all circumstances for which incantation rites are required takes us beyond the well-defined limits of primitive conceptions. Under the influence of the purification scheme, the primitive rites of sympathetic magic receive a new and higher interpretation. They become symbolical ceremonies, intended to emphasise the single aim of one who has fallen under the spell of evil spirits to cleanse himself from the sickness, or the misfortune, whatever its nature, that has been brought upon him.[1]

I have washed my hands, I have cleansed my body,[2]
With the pure spring-water which flows forth in the city of Eridu.
All that is evil, all that is not good,
Which is in my body, my flesh, and my sinews,
The evil dream at night, the evil signs and omens that are not
    good.

Instead of the common exorcisers—medicine-men and lay magic-workers,—we find the officials of the temple combining with the primitive rites an appeal to the gods, particularly Ea, Marduk, Nusku (or

[1] *Maklû*, Incantation Ritual, Tablet VII., 115–120.

[2] The same association of cleanliness and godliness passes on to modern days, as, *e.g.*, in Bishop Berkeley's panacea of tar-water for all bodily ills, which was supposed to cleanse the mind as well as the body. See Fraser, *Life and Letters of George Berkeley*, pp. 292 *seq.*

Girru), Shamash, Adad, and the 'Anunnaki.[1] Disease becomes, under this aspect of higher purification, the punishment for sins committed against the
gods, and, gradually, the entire incantation ritual
assumes the colour of an expiatory ceremony.

An occasion is thus found for the introduction of
the ethical spirit, the desire to become reconciled with
the gods by leading a pure and clean life—corresponding to the material cleanliness, which the suppliant hopes to attain by the incantation rites.
Hence, in the midst of a collection of incantation
formulas, based on the most primitive kind of sympathetic magic, we meet not merely prayers to gods
that represent a far higher grade of thought, but also
ethical considerations, embodied in the enumeration
of a long category of possible sins that the suppliant
for divine forgiveness may have committed. The
question is asked why punishment in the shape of
bodily tortures was sent, and incidental thereto the
Biblical ten commandments are paralleled.[2]

Has he estranged father from son?
Has he estranged son from father?
Has he estranged mother from daughter?
Has he estranged daughter from mother?
Has he estranged mother-in-law from daughter-in-law?
Has he estranged daughter-in-law from mother-in-law?

---

[1] For other gods playing a more or less prominent part, see
Morgenstern, *Doctrine of Sin*, chap. v.

[2] *Shurpu*, Incantation Ritual, Tablet II., 20–67.   See Jastrow,
Religion, Engl. ed., pp. 290 *seq.;*   German ed., i., pp. 325 *seq.*

Has he estranged brother from brother?

Has he estranged friend from friend?

Has he estranged companion from companion?[1]

Has he not released a prisoner, has he not loosened the bound one ?

Has he not permitted the prisoner to see the light?

Has he in the case of the captive, commanded, " take hold of him," in the case of one bound (said), " bind him!"[2]

Is it a sin against a god, a transgression against a goddess ?

Has he offended a god, neglected a goddess?

Was his sin against his god, was his wrong toward his goddess?

An offence against his ancestor,[3][?] hatred toward his elder brother?

Has he neglected father or mother, insulted the elder sister?

Given too little, refused the larger amount ?[4]

For " no " said " yes," for " yes " said " no " ?

Has he used false weights ?

Has he taken the wrong sum, not taken the correct amount?[5]

Has he disinherited the legitimate son, has he upheld an illegitimate son?

Has he drawn a false boundary, not drawn the right boundary?

Has he removed the limit, mark, or boundary?

Has he possessed himself[6] of his neighbour's house?

Has he shed his neighbour's blood?

Has he stolen his neighbour's garment?

Has he not released a freedman [?] out of his family?

Has he divided a family once united?

Has he set himself up against a superior?

Was his mouth frank, but his heart false?

Was it "yes" with his mouth, but "no" with his heart?

.   .   .   .   .   .

Has he taught what was impure, instructed in what was not proper?

---

[1] *I.e.*, Has he sown dissensions among the members of a family or among friends?

[2] *I.e.*, is he a ruler who has exercised unnecessary cruelty?

[3] The exact meaning of the word used is not known.

[4] *I.e.*, Has he cheated?   [6] Literally "entered."

[5] *I.e.*, Has he defrauded?

Pl. 25. Fig. 1. Exorcising Demons of Disease.

Bronze tablet in the de Clercq collection (Paris). The figure at the top is a typical demon. In the uppermost row are the symbols of the gods similar to those found on Boundary Stones (see comment to Pl. 22). Those here depicted are Anu (shrine with tiara), Ea (mace with ram's head), Adad (lightning fork), Marduk (spear-head), Nebo (double staff), Ishtar (eight-pointed star), Shamash (sun disc), Sin (crescent), Sibitti (seven circles). The second row shows the group of seven demons so frequently referred to in the incantation texts (p. 310 *seq.*). In the third row, the exorcising ceremonial is depicted. The afflicted sufferer lies on a bed, at either end of which stands an officiating exorciser, clad in a fish robe as the priest of Ea, the god of the waters, who with Girru or Nusku, the god of fire, plays a chief part in the incantation ritual. The demon behind the fish-priest to the right seems to be warding off the two other demons, while behind the other fish-priest is an altar with a lamp—the symbol of Nusku, the fire-god. In the third compartment are various objects: two jars, a bowl, a water bag, and articles of food—intended probably as offerings to the demons. In the centre is the demon Labartu holding a serpent in each hand, a swine at each breast, and resting with one knee on an ass—the symbol of Labartu. The ass is lying on a ship, the water being indicated by swimming fishes. Lastly, to the left of Labartu is another demon in a threatening attitude with a whip in his upraised hand—perhaps a protecting demon, driving off the cruel Labartu, who sails away in her ship. The reverse shows the back of the demon looking over the head of the tablet. Other tablets of this nature—in bronze or stone— have been found, showing more or less significant variations. Up to the present eight such specimens are known. See Frank, *Babylonische Beschwörungsreliefs* (Leipzig, 1908).

Fig. 2. Types of Demons.

Now in the British Museum. See R. C. Thompson, *The Devils, and Evil Spirits of Babylonia* (London, 1903), vol. i., Pl. II.

Fig. 1.   Exorcising Demons of Disease

Fig. 2.   Types of Demons

Did he follow the path of evil?
Did he overstep the bounds of what was just?

In contrast with this high plane, which is, however, not infrequently reached in the incantation rituals, the accompanying ceremonies remain persistently on the same level which we find in primitive religions everywhere. Nor will it escape the attention of the careful student that the possible sins enumerated pass indiscriminately from ritualistic errors to moral offences. Nevertheless, and with due regard for the obvious limitation of the ethical principles introduced, the wide departure from the starting-point of incantation formulas must be given full recognition. One cannot question that in this strikingly modified and advanced form, even though the rites themselves continued to rest on an essentially primitive basis, the incantation cult exercised an elevating influence and, at all events, acted as a moral restraint.

The evil spirits, supposed to cause sickness and other ills, were of various kinds, and each class appears to have had its special function. Some clearly represent the shades of the departed,[1] who return to earth to plague the living; others are personifications of certain diseases. The existence of special demons for consumption (or wasting disease), fever, ague, and headache forms a curious parallel

[1] Known as *etimmu*—which is the usual term for the shade of the departed—or *utukku*. For other names, see Morgenstern, *Doctrine of Sin*, p. 12.

to specialisation in the practice of modern medicine. There was even a "gynecological" demon, known as Labartu, whose special function it was to attack women in childbirth, and steal the offspring. Other demons appear to have been associated chiefly with the terrors of the storm, or with the night, while some seem to have been of a general character or, if they had a special function, it has not as yet been discovered. Their general dwelling place was in the nether world—the domain of Nergal, the god of pestilence and death. The names given to these demons, such as "pestilence," the "seizer," the "one lying in wait," "destroyer," "storm," illustrate the uncompromisingly forbidding and gloomy views held of them, which is even further emphasised by the terrifying shapes given to them—leopards, dragons, serpents, etc. Not confined solely to the nether world, their presence was also seen in the angry clouds that rolled across the heavens, their voice was heard in the storms that swept over the land. They come up from their habitation and conceal themselves in dark holes and unsuspected crannies, ready to pounce upon their victims unawares. In short, like the modern "germs" of which they are the remote prototypes, they are universal and everywhere. They move preferably in groups of seven[1]:

---

[1] *Utukku limnuti* Ritual, Tablet V., col. ii., 65—iii., 25. See Thompson, *Devils and Evil Spirits of Babylonia*, i., pp. 62 *seq.*

Destructive storms and evil winds are they,
A storm of evil, presaging the baneful storm,
A storm of evil, forerunner of the baneful storm.
Mighty children, mighty sons are they,
Messengers of Namtar are they,
Throne-bearers of Ereshkigal.[1]
The flood driving through the land are they.
Seven gods of the wide heavens,
Seven gods of the broad earth,
Seven robber gods are they.
Seven gods of universal sway,
Seven evil gods,
Seven evil demons,
Seven evil and violent demons,
Seven in heaven, seven on earth.

Another incantation thus describes them[2]:

Neither male nor female are they.
Destructive whirlwinds they,
Having neither wife nor offspring.
Compassion and mercy they do not know.
Prayer and supplication they do not hear.
Horses reared in the mountains,
     Hostile to Ea.
Throne-bearers of the gods are they.
Standing on the highway, befouling the street.
Evil are they, evil are they,
Seven they are, seven they are,
     Twice seven they are.

Or again, in illustration of their ability to penetrate everywhere[3]:

[1] The mistress of the nether world, while Namtar is the god of pestilence.

[2] Same series, Tablet V., col. v., 38–57.   Thompson, *l.c.*, p. 76 *seq.*

[3] Tablet V., col. i., 25–39.   Thompson, *l.c.*, p. 52 *seq.*

The high enclosures, the broad enclosures like a flood they pass
  through.
From house to house they dash along.
No door can shut them out,
No bolt can turn them back.
Through the door, like a snake, they glide,
Through the hinge, like the wind, they storm.
Tearing the wife from the embrace of the man,
Snatching the child from the knees of a man,[1]
Driving the freedman from his family home.

Such are the demons against whom man had continually to be on his guard.

VII

To summarise the incantation cult, it will be
sufficient to indicate that, while, as we have seen,
many gods are appealed to, the most important share
in the rites is taken by water and fire—suggesting,
therefore, that the god of water—more particularly Ea
—and the god of fire—appearing under various designations, Nusku, Girru, Gish-Bar—are the chief deities
on which the ritual itself hinges. Water and fire are
viewed as the two purifying elements above all others.
The "unclean" person was sprinkled with water,
while the priest pronounced certain sacred formulas,
having the power of "cleansing" a patient from sickness. The water was of course specially sanctified

[1] An interesting reference to a widespread custom in antiquity of having the new-born child received on the knees of
the father. See Job iii., 12.

for this purpose, drawn from springs or sacred streams, as both the Euphrates and the Tigris rivers were regarded. There was probably connected with every large temple one or more springs, and a *bît rimki* or "bath-house"[1] where the purification rites were performed, although this house was no doubt originally outside of the temple area in a field or some remote place. We are reminded of the "bath-house" to this day attached to synagogues of the rigid orthodox type, whereto the women resort monthly to cleanse themselves.[2] It is tempting to discern in this rite, now restricted to women, who represent everywhere the conservative element in religion, a survival of the old Babylonian purification ritual. Instead of water, oil of various kinds was also used. Details of the rites no doubt varied in different cities, and there are indications that the purification rites were, even in later times, occasionally performed on the banks of running streams—perhaps a survival of the period when the incantation ritual did not yet form part of the official cult.

By the side of the "bath-house," we meet frequent references to a *bît nûri*, "house of light," and it is permissible to recognise in this term the designation of a special place within the temple area, wherein the purification by fire was completed.

[1] More literally "house of washing."   See above, p. 302.
[2] *Jewish Encyclopedia*, vol. viii, p. 588.

Originally, no doubt, fire was used as a means of directly destroying the demons in human form—the sorcerers and witches—who, either of their own initiative, or at the instigation of those who had invoked their aid, had cast a spell upon the victims. A favourite method employed by the exorcisers of these demons was to make images of them, modelled in clay, pitch, tallow, dough, or other materials,[1] that could be melted or destroyed by fire, and then to throw the images into the fire to the accompaniment of formulas which generally expressed the hope that, as the images were consumed, the sorcerers and witches might feel the tortures of the flames, and either flee out of the bodies of their victims, or release their hold upon them. Parallels to this procedure, resting entirely on sympathetic magic, are to be found in abundance among peoples of primitive culture.[2]

There was, however, another aspect of fire. As the sacred god-given element, the flame was associated with purity, and it became in many religions —notably in Zoroastrianism—a symbol of life itself. Through contact with it, therefore, freedom from contamination was secured. The true meaning of the practices of the Canaanites, who, as we are

[1] See above, p. 305, note 1.

[2] The common practice of tying knots to symbolise the tying of the witch or sorcerer, and untying knots to symbolise the release of the victim is also referred to in the Babylonian-Assyrian incantations

told, caused their children to "pass through the fire"[1]
(which seemed so abhorrent to the Hebrew prophets),
was a desire thoroughly to purify the new-born child.
Among many customs, found all over the world, illustrative of this quality of fire, it is sufficient to recall
that down to a late day the custom obtained among
the peasants of Germany—and, perchance, still survives in remote corners—of driving cattle through a
fire kindled in the fields, thereby securing immunity
from the cattle plague.[2]   In the case of the sick, and of
those otherwise afflicted, the contact with the fire
was purely symbolical—vicarious, so to speak.   Besides the method just described, the incantation texts
tell us of various objects, such as certain plants, wood,
wheat, onions, dates, palm-blossoms, wool, and seeds
which were thrown into a fire, while an incantation
was recited to the effect that, as the object disappears
in the fire never to return, so the man's sins, uncleanliness, or sickness may vanish never to return.   One
of these incantations reads[3]:

> As this onion is peeled, and thrown into the fire,
> Consumed by Girru,[4] never again to be
> Planted in a bed, never again to be furrowed,
> Never again to take root,

---

[1] *E.g.*, 2 Kings xvi., 3; Ezek. xx., 31; *cf.* Lev. xviii., 21.

[2] Chantepie de la Saussaye, *Religion of the Teutons*, pp. 374
seq.

[3] *Shurpu* Incantation Ritual, Tablet V., 60–72.

[4] The fire-god.

Its stalk never to grow again, never to see the shining sun,
Never again to be seen on the table of god or king,
So may the curse, the ban, pain [?] distress [?]
Sickness, sighing, sin, transgression, injury,
Misdeed, the sickness in my body, which is in
My flesh and bowels be treated like this onion,
Be consumed this day by Girru.
May the ban be removed, may I see the light![1]

But while water and fire thus constitute the chief factors in the purification rites, the ceremonies themselves are further complicated by elaborate preparations for the final act of exorcising the demons, or of destroying the sorcerers and witches. The patient had to be prepared for the act. The exorcising priests donned special garments—often in imitation of the god in whose name they acted. Pieces of flesh and a mixture of dates, flour, honey, and butter, and other viands were offered to the demons as bribes, that they might thus be made more kindly disposed. The rites were generally performed at sunrise or shortly before—though occasionally also at night. The place where they were to be performed was to be swept clean, a table and often several tables were set, whereon the objects for the sacrifice were arranged, torches were lit, libations of wine poured out, and various other details were prescribed, some of which are not at all clear. In connection with every sep-

[1] This wish, with which every section of this part of the ritual ends, appears to be an allusion to the "house of light" in which the ceremony took place.

arate act of preparation a formula or prayer was recited, and great care was exercised that every detail
should be carried out according to established custom.
The slightest error might vitiate the entire ceremony.

We are fortunate in having several pictorial representations, on bronze, and stone tablets, of exorcising
rites[1] which help us to understand the directions in the
text.   In these representations we see the seven chief
demons, frequently mentioned in the incantation
rituals, grouped together, and revealing by the expression of their faces and their threatening attitude
their nature and purpose.   The afflicted sufferer is
lying on a bed at either end of which stands an
ashipu ("exorciser") or *mashmashu* ("purifier").[2]
The protecting deity and favourable spirits are also
portrayed as helping to ward off the evil demons.
Labartu, with the ass as her attendant, appears in the
lowest compartment, where also are seen the offerings
to appease the demons, and the ceremonial imple-
ments used in the incantation ceremonies.

It must not be supposed, however, that these purification rites were always and everywhere carried out

[1] See Plate 25, Fig. 1.   Frank, *Babylonische Beschwörungsreliefs*
(Leipzig, 1908), gave the correct interpretation of these monuments, which had hitherto been regarded as illustrations of the
abode of the dead in the nether world.

[2] The more common designation for exorciser was *ashipu*.
There were several classes, and the *mashmashu* appears to have
been of a subordinate class.   See Morgenstern, *Doctrine of Sin in
the Babylonian Religion*, pp. 39 *seq.*

in the same way. The variations and modifications seem to be endless. Instead of treating the sick man in his apartment, the ceremonies were frequently enacted on the roof of his house, and this appears to have been quite generally the case when the deity especially invoked was Ishtar. Directions are given to sweep the roof, holy water is sprinkled over it, a table is spread for the goddess with dates and a mixture of meal, honey, and butter, and a libation of wine is poured out.

Sickness itself being held as unclean, purification rites were observed on recovery; these included the purification of the house in which the patient had lain. After a king's recovery from illness, the directions are specific that in addition to the ceremonies around the king's bed, the palace was to be purified by passing through it with torches and censers. In the palace court seven tables must be spread to the seven chief deities, with offerings of various kinds of bread, dates, meal, oil, honey, butter, milk, with some sweet drink. Seven censers and seven vessels of wine were furthermore to be provided[1] and finally a lamb for sacrifice. Elsewhere, we are told that for the purification of a house that had in any way become unclean, the rooms, the threshold, the court roof, beams, and windows must be touched with asphalt, gypsum, oil, honey, butter, or holy water. Similar ceremonies

[1] See Morgenstern, *Doctrine of Sin*, pp. 120 *seq.*

Pl. 26.　Fig. 1.　King Ashurbanapal, King of Assyria (668–626 B.C.), in a lion hunt and pouring a libation over four dead lions.

This alabaster slab is one of a large series illustrative of the royal sport in Assyria—hunting lions, wild horses, gazelles, and other animals. These slabs formed the decoration of portions of the walls in the large halls of the palace of Ashurbanapal at Kouyunjik (Nineveh). They were found by Layard and are now one of the great attractions of the British Museum. See Layard, *Monuments of Nineveh*, i., Pl. 10–12 and 31–32; Place, *Ninive et l'Assyrie*, Pl. 50–57 and 62, as well as Mansell's "British Museum Photographs," Part III. (*Assyrian Sculptures*), Nos. 455–520 A. As specimens of the art of Assyria they are of deep interest, but no less as illustrations of life and manners, supplemented by the equally extensive series of slabs which illustrate the campaigns waged by this king. (Layard, *op. cit.*, i., Pl. 13–30; 40–41; 57–83; ii., Pl. 18–19; 25–31; 33–50; Place, *op. cit.*, Pl. 58–66 and Mansell Nos. 438–50). Similar martial designs in the palace of Sargon at Khorsabad illustrating his campaigns, for which see Botta et Flandin, *Monument de Ninive*, Pl. 31–40; 49–73; 86–101; 117–147; (Hunting Scenes, Pl. 108–113).

Ashurbanapal with his attendants behind him is pouring a libation over four lions killed in the hunt. An altar is in the centre, and a pole or tree such as is often seen on the seal cylinders when sacrificial scenes are portrayed. The musicians to the left precede the attendants carrying a dead lion on their backs.

Fig. 2.　Kneeling Winged Figures before the Sacred Tree.

Alabaster slab found in the North-West Palace at Nimroud. (Ashurnasirpal 883–859 B.C.). See Layard, *Monuments of Nineveh*, i., Pl. 7 A, and Mansell, "British Museum Photographs," Part III., (*Assyrian Sculptures*), No. 326.

The sacred tree or the tree of life, as it should perhaps be called, is frequently portrayed on Assyrian seal cylinders in all manner of variations. Though found also on Babylonian specimens its earliest occurrence, indeed, being on a boundary stone (c 1112 B.C.) as a decoration of the garment of a Babylonian ruler, Marduk-nadinakhê, it is a distinctive characteristic on Assyrian monuments. The tree intended is clearly the palm, though it becomes conventionalised to such a degree as to lose almost all the traits of that species. Instead of kneeling winged figures we find on other slabs of the N.-W. Palace of Nimroud as well as at Khorsabad

Pl. 26—*Continued*

and Kouyunjik (see Layard, *op. cit.*, i., Pl. 5–8; 34–39; 43–45; Botta et Flandin, *Monument de Ninive*, Pl. 24–30; 74–75, and Place, *Ninive et l'Assyrie*, Pl. 46–47): (a) standing winged figures with human faces, (b) eagle-headed figures, and (c) kings with the winged figures, further conventionalised as ornaments on robes into (d) all kinds of fantastic shapes, winged bulls, winged horses, ostriches, winged sphinxes, etc. (See Layard, *op. cit.*, i., 6–8 and 43–50).

The winged figures preferably carry a cone in one hand and a basket in the other, or a branch in one hand and a basket in the other. On the seal cylinders the variations are even more numerous. Instead of winged figures, we find bulls or lions with birds and scorpions to either side of the tree, or the winged figures stand on sphinxes, or human headed bulls take the place of the winged figures; and more the like. It is evident that the scene is in all cases an adoration of the tree. In a purer form this adoration appears on seal cylinders like No. 687 in Ward, *Cylinders of Western Asia* (p. 226), where we find two priests clad in fish robes —as attendants of Ea—with a worshipper behind one of the priests; on No. 688 with only one priest and a worshipper to either side; or No. 680, the goddess Ishtar on one side of the tree, and a god—perhaps Adad—on the other side with a worshipper behind the latter; or still simpler on No. 689 where there is only one priest and a worshipper to either side of the tree.

The winged figures in such various forms represent, as do also the sphinxes, protecting powers of a lower order than the gods, but who like Ishtar and Adad in the specimen just referred to are the guardians of the sacred tree, with which the same ideas were associated by the Babylonians and Assyrians as with the tree of life in the famous chapter of Genesis, or as with trees of life found among many other peoples. The cones which the winged figures beside the tree hold indicate the fruit of the tree, plucked for the benefit of the worshippers by these guardians who alone may do so. A trace of this view appears in the injunction to Adam and Eve (Genesis ii.) to eat of the fruit of all the trees except the one which, being the tree of knowledge, was not for mortal man to pluck—as little as the fruit of the "Tree of Life." For further details see the valuable Chapter XXXVIII. on "The Tree of Life," in Ward, *Cylinders of Western Asia.*

Fig. 1. King Ashurbanapal in Lion Hunt and pouring
Libations over Four Lions killed in the Hunt

Fig. 2. Kneeling Winged Figures before Sacred Tree

were enacted to purify the image of a god before it
could be put to use, or after it had become unclean.[1]

This purification of the dwelling reminds one of
the regulations in the Priestly Code of the Old Testament for the ritualist cleansing of the house that had
shown symptoms of infection.[2] Whether or not we
may assume that, at the comparatively late date to
which the Priestly Code belongs,—about the middle of
the fifth century B.C.,—medical science had advanced
to a knowledge that disease could lurk in the walls
and floors of houses, and that the regulations of the
Priestly Code, therefore, reflect the influence of this
advance, the basis of the Pentateuchal purification
ritual is certainly of a much more primitive character,
and identical with that which we find in the incantation ritual of Babylonia. The main emphasis in both
is on purification from ritualist uncleanliness, and
this point of view is a direct issue from the primitive
ideas associated with *taboo*.

VIII

A further development of the *taboo*, but in a much
higher direction, is represented by the public lamentation ritual, which from early days appears to have
formed a part of the official cult on occasions of public

[1] See Morgenstern, *Doctrine of Sin*, pp. 122 *seq.*
[2] Leviticus xiv., 33–53.

distress, when the gods had manifested their displeasure by sending a pestilence, by disaster in war, by atmospheric disturbances, dealing death and destruction, or by terrifying phenomena in the heavens. We have numerous examples of such lamentations whereof the antiquity is sufficiently attested by the fact that they are written in Sumerian,[1] though for a better understanding translations into Babylonian, either in whole or in part, were added in the copies made at a later date. The basis of these texts is likewise the notion of uncleanliness. The entire land was regarded as having become *taboo* through contamination of some kind, or through some offence of an especially serious character. The gods are depicted as having deserted the city and shown their anger by all manner of calamities that have been visited upon the country and its inhabitants. Atonement can be secured only by an appeal to the gods, and a feature of this atonement ritual—as we may also call this service—is abstention from food and drink. We may well suppose that on such occasions the people repaired to the temples and participated in the service, though no doubt the chief part was taken by the priests and the king. It was probably for these occasions that purification ceremonies (which appear to have been particularly elaborate) were prescribed

[1] See especially the texts, *Cuneiform Texts*, xv., Plate 10–23, and *cf.* above, p. 279, and below p. 327, note 1.

for the priests, though it should be added that for all other occasions, also, the priests had to take precautions so as to be in a state of ritualist cleanliness before undertaking any service in the temples.[1] Atonement for the priests and the king, for the former as the mediators between the gods and their worshippers, for the latter as standing nearer to the gods than the masses and in a measure, as we have seen, a god's representative on earth, was an essential preliminary to obtaining forgiveness for the people as a whole. In the public lamentation-songs it is the general condition of distress that is emphasised, and the impression is gained that the priests send forth their appeals to the gods for forgiveness on behalf of the people in general.

We have already had occasion to indicate the pre-eminent position occupied by the city of Nippur in the religious life of Babylonia.[2] It is therefore interesting to note that the atonement and lamentation ritual worked out by the priests of this centre became the pattern which was followed in other places —such as Isin, Ur, Larsa, Sippar, Babylon, and Borsippa. The proof is furnished by examples of lamentations, bearing internal evidence of their original connection with the temple E-Kur at Nippur, but in which insertions have been made to adapt them to other centres.

[1] Morgenstern, *Doctrine of Sin*, pp. 146 *seq.*   [2] Above, p. 18.

The laments themselves are rather monotonous in character, though the rhythmic chanting no doubt lessened the monotony and heightened their solemnity. They describe the devastation that has been wrought, repeating in the form of a litany the prayer that the gods may be appeased. Occasionally, the laments contain picturesque phrases. As an instance, one will perhaps be sufficient,[1] which contains the insertions referred to, adapting the Nippur composition to Ur and Larsa.

O honoured one, return, look on thy city!
O exalted and honoured one, return, look on thy city!
O lord of lands, return, look on thy city!
O lord of the faithful word, return, look on thy city!
O Enlil, father of Sumer, return, look on thy city!
O shepherd of the dark-headed people, return, look on thy city!
O thou of self-created vision, return, look on thy city!
Strong one in directing mankind, return, look on thy city!
Giving repose to multitudes, return, look on thy city!
To thy city, Nippur, return, look on thy city!
To the brick construction of E-Kur, return, look on thy city!
To Ki-Uru,[2] the large abode, return, look on thy city!
To Dul-Azag,[3] the holy place, return, look on thy city!
To the interior of the royal house,[4] return, look on thy city!
To the great gate structure, return, look on thy city!

---

[1] *Cuneiform Texts*, Part XV., Plate 12 and 13. Parallel text, Rawlinson IV. (2d ed.), 28*, No. 4, with partial Semitic translation. See Langdon, *Sumerian and Babylonian Psalms*, pp. 292–295; *Babyloniaca*, ii., pp. 275–81; and F. A. Vanderburgh, *Journal Amer. Oriental Society*, vol. xxx., pp. 61–66.

[2] A designation of a part of E-Kur—perhaps the large court.
[3] The holy chamber of the temple.
[4] Note the juxtaposition of temple and palace.

To E-Gan-Nun-Makh,[1] return, look on thy city!
To the temple storehouse, return, look on thy city!
To the palace storehouse, return, look on thy city![2]
Unto the smitten city—how long until thou returnest?
To the smitten—when wilt thou show mercy?
The city unto which grain was allotted,
Where the thirsty was satiated with drink.
Where she could say to her young husband, "my husband,"[3]
Where she could say to the young child, "my child,"
Where the maiden could say, "my brother."
In the city where the mother could say, "my child,"
Where the little girl could say, "my father."
There the little ones perish, there the great perish.
In the streets where the men went about, hastening hither and
    thither,
Now the dogs defile her booty,
Her pillage the jackal destroys,
In her banqueting hall the wind holds revel,
Her pillaged streets are desolate.[4]

In reading the closing lines of this litany, we are instinctively reminded of the prevailing note in the Biblical book of Lamentations, the five chapters of which represent independent compositions. These lamentation-songs still constitute, in orthodox Judaism, an integral part of the ritual for the day com-

---

[1] Some official structure—perhaps the temple granary.

[2] Here the insertion adapting the lamentation to Ur and Larsa is entered,

"To the brick construction of Ur return, look on thy city,

To the brick construction of Larsa return, look on thy city."

While in another version the adaptation for Sippar, etc., is made.

[3] *I.e.*, Newly-wedded couples were not separated through the husband being obliged to go to war.

[4] Additional line in Rawlinson, IV. (2d ed.), 28*, No. 4.

memorative of the double destruction of Jerusalem —the first by Nebuchadnezzar in 586 B.C., and the second in 70 A.D., by the Romans—and, precisely as in ancient Babylonia, fasting constitutes one of the features of the day. Whether or not the second destruction actually occurred on the day commemorated is more than doubtful; and it is not even certain that the first destruction occurred on the 9th day of the 5th month. It is more likely that this day had acquired a significance as a day of fasting and lamentation, long before Jerusalem fell a prey to Babylonia, and for this reason was chosen by the Jews in commemoration of the great national catastrophe.[1] Be this as it may, the resemblance between the Hebrew and the Babylonian "lamentation" rituals suggests a direct influence on the Hebrews; which becomes all the more plausible if it be recalled that another fast day, which in post-exilic times became for the Jews the most solemn day of the year, took its rise during the sojourn of the Jews in Babylonia.[2]

[1] Another Jewish fast day, the 17th of Tammuz, though associated by Jewish tradition with the capture of Jerusalem by the Romans, is likewise much older and, in all probability, the old mourning festival for the youthful Tammuz (or Adonis), the god of spring, who at the end of the summer season is slain and carried to the nether world. See Jastrow, *Religion* (English ed.), p. 682, and the references there given.

[2] Celebrated on the 10th day of the festival month Tishri, but not mentioned in the pre-exilic codes of the Pentateuch. The combination with the Atonement day of a primitive ritual

Destructions of cities are often mentioned in the dates attached to business documents of ancient Babylonia. We have also a series of texts[1] in which the distress incident to national catastrophes brought about by the incursion of enemies is set forth in diction which recalls the style of the lamentation-psalms. It is interesting to note that in the astrological omens (which formed the subject of the previous lecture) references to invasions by foreign foes are very frequent, and phrases are introduced, clearly taken from these commemorative compositions. All this points to the deep impression made upon the country by the disasters of the past, and suggests the question whether, in commemoration of these events, a certain day of fasting and lamentation may not have been yearly set aside, whereon the ancient compositions of the "Nippur" ritual were recited or sung in the temples, with an enumeration of the various occasions in the past when the gods had manifested their displeasure and wrath.

With such a supposition, one could reasonably account for the additions in the old ritual, referring to

for exorcising sin marked by the Azazel ceremony (Leviticus, chap. xvi.), suggests that it represents in part also the revival of an old nomadic festival that survives in some of the ceremonies incidental to the 10th day of the month of pilgrimage among the Arabs. See Wellhausen, *Reste Arabischen Heidentums*, p. 77.

[1] *Cuneiform Texts*, etc.. Part XIII., Plate 44–50.

catastrophes in Ur, Larsa, Sippar, Babylon, and so forth, instead of the mere substitution of these names for that of Nippur which would have sufficed if the purpose had been merely to recall some particular event. Lacking direct evidence of a day set apart as a general fast-day and day of penitence, humiliation, and prayer for favour and grace during the coming year, a certain measure of caution must be exercised; but we are fully justified in going so far at least as to assume that the lamentation ritual was performed in the great centres when there was an actual or impending catastrophe, and that on such occasions the dire events of the past were recalled in laments which, by virtue of the sanctity that everything connected with the cult at Nippur had acquired, were based on the "Nippur" ritual.

The fear of divine anger runs, as an undercurrent, throughout the entire religious literature of Babylonia and Assyria. Rulers and people are always haunted by the fear lest Enlil, Sin, Shamash, Ea, Marduk, Nebo, Nergal, Ishtar, or some other deity manifest displeasure. This minor key is struck even in hymns which celebrate the kindness and mercy of the higher powers; there was a constant fear lest their mood might suddenly change. Death and sickness stood like spectres in view of all men, ready at any moment to seize their victims. Storms and inundations, however needful for the land, brought death and woe for man and beast. Enemies were constantly pressing in on one side or the other; and thus the occasions were frequent enough when the people were forced to cringe in contrition before the gods in the hope that they might soon smile with favour, and send joy into the heart of man, or else that a threatened blow might never fall.

As a complement to the public lamentation ritual, we have numerous compositions in which woe is poured forth before a god or goddess, and emphasis is laid upon the consciousness of guilt.[1] The soul is bowed down with the consciousness of some wrong committed, and even though the particular sin for

[1] The first systematic study of this class of compositions was made by H. Zimmern, *Babylonische Busspsalmen* (Leipzig, 1885). Translations of the most important of them will be found in Jastrow, *Religion*, English ed., pp. 312–327, and of practically all known in the German edition, ii., pp. 62–134. While the age of these "personal" laments and confessions of sin cannot be determined, there is every reason to believe that they go back to an ancient period—though they are perhaps not so old as the public lamentation ritual. Many of them have come down to us in a double revision, in "Sumerian" with a "Babylonian" rendering, but it would appear that the "Sumerian" represents, in most if not in all cases, a retranslation from the Babylonian. The fact that such a retranslation was made points to the existence of penitential psalms of a personal character in *Sumerian*. The purpose of the retranslation was to provide a text in the ancient "Sumerian" that had acquired the position of a sacred tongue, and was considered the language in which the psalms should be recited, or at all events, that in which they should be couched.

which misfortune—sickness or some misadventure or trouble—has been sent is unknown to the suppliant himself, he yet feels that he must have committed some wrong to arouse such anger in the god who has struck him down. This is the significant feature in these "penitential psalms," as they have been called, and one that raises them far above the incantation ritual, even though they assume the belief also in the power of demons and sorcerers to bring to pass the ills whereto human flesh is heir. To be sure, most, if not all, of these penitential psalms assume that the penitent is the king, just as most of the other classes of hymns are royal hymns[1]; but this would appear to be due mainly to the official character of the archives from which the scribes of Ashurbanapal obtained their material. In compositions of Assyrian origin, or modified by Assyrian priests, the official character is even more pronounced, since these priests, acting directly at the command of their royal master, had him more particularly in mind. We are safe in assuming that these royal laments and confessions formed the model for those used by the priests when the lay suppliant came before them, though exactly to what extent they were used in the case of individuals, as supplementary to the incantation rites, it is impossible to say.

[1] See Jastrow, *Religion* (German ed.), ii., p. 106.

Confession and lament are the burden of these psalms:[1]

Many are my sins that I have committed,
May I escape this misfortune, may I be relieved from distress!

and again:

> My eye is filled with tears,
> On my couch I lie at night, full of sighs,
> Tears and sighing have bowed me down.[2]

The indications are distinct in these compositions that they formed part of a ritual, in which the officiating priest and the penitent each had his part. The priest, as mediator, enforces the appeal of the penitent:

He weeps, overpowered he cannot restrain himself.
Thou hearest earnest lament, turn thy countenance to him!
Thou acceptest petition, look faithfully on him!
Thou receivest prayer, turn thy countenance to him!
Lord of prayer and petition, let the prayer reach thee!
Lord of petition and prayer, let the prayer reach thee!

The appeal is here made to Enlil, Marduk, and Nebo, and closes with the refrain which is frequent in the penitential psalms:

---

[1] See Jastrow, *Religion* (German ed.) ii., pp. 85 *seq.* See also Reisner, *Sumerisch-Babylonische Hymnen*, No. 30.

[2] In another composition (Jastrow, *Religion*, ii., p. 76) we read:

> " Food I have not eaten—weeping was my nourishment
> Water I have not drunk—tears were my drink."

May thy heart be at rest, thy liver [1] be appeased!
May thy heart like the heart of the young mother,—
Like that of the mother who has borne, and of the father who
    has begotten,—return to its place!

Reference has been made to the fact that the sense
of guilt in these hymns is so strong as to prompt the
penitent to a confession, even when he does not know
for what transgression—ritualistic or moral—he has
been punished, nor what god or goddess he has offended. The penitent says in one of these psalms[2]:

O lord my transgressions are many, great are my sins.
My god, my transgressions are many, great are my sins.
O god, whoever it be,[3] my transgressions are many, great are my
    sins.
O goddess, whoever it be, my transgressions are many, great
    are my sins.
The transgressions I have committed, I know not.
The sin I have done, I know not.
The unclean that I have eaten, I know not.
The impure on which I have trodden, I know not.

    .   .   .   .   .   .

The lord in the anger of his heart has looked at me,
The god in the rage of his heart has encompassed me.
A god, whoever it be, has distressed me,
A goddess, whoever it be, has brought woe upon me.
I sought for help, but no one took my hand,
I wept, but no one hearkened to me,
I broke forth in laments, but no one listened to me.
Full of pain, I am overpowered, and dare not look up.
To my merciful god I turn, proclaiming my sorrow.

---

[1] On this use of heart and liver for the mind and emotions
see above, p. 151.

[2] Jastrow, *Religion* (English ed., pp. 321 *seq.*, German ed., ii.,
pp. 102 *seq.*).

[3] Literally "known or unknown."

To the goddess [whoever it be, I turn proclaiming my sorrow].

O lord, [turn thy countenance to me, accept my appeal].

O goddess, [look mercifully on me, accept my appeal].

O god [whoever it be, turn thy countenance to me, accept my appeal].

O goddess whoever it be, [look mercifully on me, accept my appeal].

How long yet, O my god, [before thy heart shall be pacified]?

How long yet, O my goddess, [before thy liver shall be appeased]?

O god, whoever it be, may thy angered heart return to its place!

O goddess, whoever it be, may thy angered heart return to its place!

The higher intellectual plane reached by these compositions is also illustrated by the reflections attached to them on the weakness of human nature and the limitations of the human mind, unable to fathom the ways of the gods:

Men are obtuse,—and no one has knowledge.

Among all who are,—who knows anything?

Whether they do evil or good,—no one has knowledge.

O lord, do not cast thy servant off!

In the deep watery morass he lies—take hold of his hand!

The sin that I have committed, change to grace!

The transgressions that I have committed,—let the wind carry off!

Tear asunder my many iniquities like a garment!

Even more interesting are the reflections put into the mouth of an ancient—probably legendary—king of Nippur, Tabi-utul-Enlil, in a composition[1]

---

[1] Rawlinson IV. (2d. ed.), 60.*   A complete translation and study of the text will be found in the writer's article, "A Babylonian Parallel to Job" (*Journal of Biblical Literature*, vol. xxv., pp. 135–191). See also Jastrow, *Religion* (German ed.), ii., p. 121–

which combines with an elaborate and touching lament the story of an aged royal sufferer, who like Job was known for his piety, and yet was severely punished and sorely tried by painful disease. As in the book of Job, the tone of the composition is pessimistic and skeptical—at least to the extent of questioning whether any one can understand the hidden ways of the gods:

> I attained (mature) life, to the limit of life I advanced.[1]
> Whithersoever I turned—evil upon evil!

This penitential psalm ends with the answer to the king's appeal; its most striking passage is the following—one of the finest in the whole realm of Babylonian literature, and marked by a remarkably modern undertone. The king declares that he did everything to please the gods; he prayed to them; he observed the new-moon, and the festivals, and brought the gods offerings:

> Prayer was my rule, sacrificing my law,
> The day of worship of my god, my joy,
> The day of devotion to my gods, my profit and gain.

He instructed his people in the ways of the gods

133, and Jastrow, "A Babylonian Job," in *Contemporary Review*, December, 1906; also Martin, "Le Juste Souffrant Babylonien" (*Journal Asiatique*, 10 Series, vol. xvi., pp. 75–143), who embodies an additional fragment published by R. C. Thompson; and Landersdorfer, "Eine Babylonische Quelle für das Buch Job?" (*Biblische Studien*, xvi., 2).

[1] *I. e.*, "I have grown old."

and did all in the hope of pleasing the higher powers
—but apparently in vain:

What, however, seems good to one, to a god may be displeasing.
What is spurned by oneself may find favour with a god.
Who is there that can grasp the will of the gods in heaven?
The plan of a god is full of mystery,—who can understand it?
How can mortals learn the ways of a god?
He who is still alive at evening is dead the next morning.
In an instant he is cast into grief, of a sudden he is crushed.
This moment he sings and plays,
In a twinkling he wails like a mourner.
Like opening and closing,[1] (mankind's) spirit changes.
If they hunger, they are like corpses.
Have they been satiated, they consider themselves a rival to
    their god.
If things go well, they prate of mounting to heaven.
If they are in distress, they speak of descending into Irkallu.[2]

IX

As we have seen,[3] neither the cause or the nature of
an eclipse was understood until a very late period,
and, accordingly, the term "darkening" was applied
indiscriminately to any phenomenon that temporarily
obscured the moon. At the end of each month,
therefore, the king proceeded to the sanctuary to
take part in a ritual that must have had the same
sombre character as the "lamentation" cult. In a
collection of prayers, technically known as "Prayers

---

[1] A commentary on the text puts it "like day and night."
[2] One of the names of the lower world where the dead congre-
gate. See below, p. 354.   [3] See above, p. 215.

for the Lifting Up of the Hand,"[1] *i.e.*, prayers of imploration, we have an example of a prayer recited on the disappearance of the moon at the end of the month, to which an allusion to an eclipse is added.[2] The addition illustrates the association of ideas between the disappearance of the moon and a genuine eclipse. One suggested the other, and we gain the impression that the belief prevailed that unless one succeeded in pacifying the gods at the end of the month, an eclipse would soon follow. It was a belief hard to disprove; if no eclipse took place, the conclusion followed that the gods had been pacified. The prayer reads thus:

O Sin, O Nannar, mighty one . . .
O Sin, unparalleled, illuminator of the darkness!
Granting light to the people of all lands,
Guiding aright the black-headed people.
Bright is thy light, in the heavens thou art exalted!
Brilliant is thy torch, like fire burning,
Thy brightness fills the wide earth.
The joy [?] of mankind is increased at thy appearance.
O lofty one of the heavens, whose course no one can fathom!
Supreme is thy light like Shamash, thy first-born.
Before thee the great gods prostrate themselves,
The oracle of all lands is entrusted to thee.
The great gods beseech thee to give counsel!
Assembled, they stand in submission to thee!

---

[1] See on this term, King, *Babylonian Magic and Sorcery*, p. xi. *seq.*

[2] King, *Babylonian Magic and Sorcery*, No. 1. The prayer occurs as part of a text which contains also a prayer to Ishtar, and one to Tashmit.

O Sin, glorious one of E-Kur, they beseech thee that thou mayest render a decision!

The day of disappearance is the day of the proclaiming the decision of the great gods![1]

The thirtieth day is thy holy day, a day of appeal to thy divinity.

In the evil hour of an eclipse of the moon in such and such a month and on such and such a day.[2]

Against the evil omens and the evil unfavourable signs which threaten my palace and my land.

The complement to the day of disappearance of the moon, elsewhere called "a day of distress," is the new-moon day, when, amidst exclamations of joy, the return of the moon is hailed as its release from captivity. A prayer for this occasion—to be recited at night—is attached to the above text and reads as follows:

O god of the new-moon, unrivalled in might, whose counsel no one can grasp,

I have poured for thee a pure libation of the night, I have offered to thee a pure drink.

I bow down to thee, I stand before thee, I seek thee!

Direct thoughts of favour and justice towards me!

That my god and my goddess who since many days have been angry towards me,

May be reconciled in right and justice, that my path may be fortunate, my road straight!

And that he may send Zakar,[3] the god of dreams, in the middle of the night to release my sins!

---

[1] I.e., the decision whether he will show mercy or be angry.

[2] Here the name of the month and day is to be inserted.

[3] Zakar is called the "envoy" of the moon-god.

May I hear that thou hast taken away my iniquity.
That for all times I may celebrate thy worship!

We have an interesting proof that this new-moon prayer was actually used on the occasion of the appearance of the new-moon. A tablet has been found at Sippar,[1] containing this very prayer, put into the mouth of Shamash-shumukin (the brother of King Ashurbanapal) who, by appointment of his brother, ruled over Babylonia for twenty years (648–628 B.C.). Attached to this prayer are directions for the accompanying ritual, which includes an offering of grain, dates, and meal, of *binu* wood, butter, cream, and wine.

To this day the Arabs greet the new-moon with shouts of joy,[2] and the Jewish ritual prescribes a special service for the occasion which includes the recital of psalms of "joy."[3] This joy on the reappearance of the moon is well expressed in various "Sumerian" hymns, originating with the moon-cult at Ur. They have all the marks of having been chanted by the priests when the first crescent was seen in the sky. The crescent is compared to a bark, in which

[1] Scheil, *Une Saison des Fouilles à Sippar* (Cairo, 1894), p. 104, No. 18. See also Combe, *Histoire du Culte de Sin*, pp. 124–26.

[2] Doughty, *Arabia Deserta*, vol. i., p. 366; ii., p. 305. The technical term for this rejoicing is *hilâl*—on which see above, p. 214.

[3] The so-called *Hallel* psalms (Ps. 113–118) or portions of them.

the moon-god sails through the heavens.   In one of
these chants we read:[1]

Self-created,[2] glorious one, in the resplendent bark of heaven!
Father Nannar, lord of Ur!
Father Nannar, lord of E-Kishirgal![3]
Father Nannar, lord of the new-moon!
Lord of Ur, first-born son of Enlil!
As thou sailest along, as thou sailest along!
Before thy father, before Enlil in thy sovereign glory!
Father Nannar, in thy passing on high, in thy sovereign glory!
O bark, sailing on high along the heaven in thy sovereign glory!
Father Nannar, as thou sailest along the resplendent road (?)
Father Nannar, when, like a bark on the floods, thou sailest
    along!
Thou, when thou sailest along, thou, when thou sailest along!
Thou when thou risest, thou when thou sailest along!
In thy rising at the completion of the course, as thou sailest
    along!
Father Nannar, when like a cow thou takest care of the calves![4]
Thy father looks on thee with a joyous eye—as thou takest care!
Come! glory to the king of splendour, glory to the king who
    comes forth!
Enlil has entrusted a sceptre to thy hand for all times,
When over Ur in the resplendent bark thou mountest.[5]

In this somewhat monotonous manner, and evidently arranged for responsive chanting, the hymn
continues.   The keynote is that of rejoicing at the
release of the new-moon, once more sailing along the

---

[1] *Cuneiform Texts*, etc., Part xv., Plates 16, 17.   See Langdon, *op.
cit.*, pp. 296–299, and Combe, *Histoire du Culte de Sin*, pp. 107 *seq.*

[2] In other hymns the moon is also addressed as "self-created."

[3] Temple of Sin (or Nannar) at Ur.

[4] *I.e.*, the stars.

[5] The rest of the hymn is imperfectly preserved.

heavens, which it is hoped augurs well also for relief from anxiety on earth.

Besides the beginning and end of the month, the middle of the month was fraught with significance. Experience must have taught the priests and the people that a genuine eclipse of the moon could take place only at this period, when the moon appears to be taking a "rest" for a few days—remaining apparently unchanged. The middle of the month was therefore designated as *shabbatum*,[1] conveying the idea of "resting." The term corresponds to the Hebrew *Shabbath* or *Shabbathon*,[2] which among the Hebrews was applied originally to the four phases of the moon, and then to a regular interval of seven days, without reference to the moon's phases, and thus became the technical term for the weekly "day of rest." In a previous lecture, we dwelt on the importance attached to the appearance of the full-moon. An appearance too early or somewhat belated augured a misfortune,—defeat in war, bad crops, insufficient flooding of the canals, or death. Rejoicing therefore followed the appearance of the full-moon at the expected time; and joy was multiplied when the danger of an eclipse was passed. This Babylonian "Sabbath" was, therefore, appropriately designated as "a day of pacification"

[1] See Zimmern, "Sabbath," in *Zeitschrift d. Deutsch. Morgenländ Gesellschaft*, vol. lviii., p. 200. In Lev. xxiii., 11 and 15, there is a trace of this usage in Hebrew.

[2] Both forms occur in Hebrew.

Pl. 27.   Winged Figure with Palm Branch and Spotted Deer.

See Layard, *Monuments of Nineveh*, i., Pl. 35, and Mansell, "British Museum Photographs," Part iii., (*Assyrian Sculptures*), No. 358. In Layard (and Mansell, No. 357) a second winged figure may be found carrying a branch of the palm tree and an ibex, while Pl. 34 presents as a third variation a winged figure with basket and branch; and Pl. 5 winged figure with cone and basket like on the representation of the tree of life (see comment to preceding plate). The palm branch symbolises the tree of life which has been plucked for the benefit of the king to whom the branch and therefore the blessings of life are thus offered. The deer as well as the ibex is a sacrificial animal, and symbolises the gift offered by the royal worshippers in return, and received on behalf of the god by the winged figure acting as mediator or priest. Attached to the figure (alabaster slab) is the so-called standard inscription of Ashurnasirpal, King of Assyria (883–859 B.C.) in whose palace (N.-W. Palace of Nimroud) at Calah it was found. Now in the British Museum.

Winged Figure with Palm Branch and Spotted Deer

when the gods appeared to be at peace with the world, smiling on the fields and gracious toward mankind. Among the collections of hymns to Sin there are several that bear the impress of having been composed for the celebration of the full-moon:[1]

> O Sin, resplendent god, light of the skies, son of Enlil, shining one of E-Kur!
> With universal sway thou rulest all lands! thy throne is placed in the lofty heavens!
> Clothed with a superb garment, crowned with the tiara of ruler-ship, full grown in glory!
> Sin is sovereign—his light is the guide of mankind, a glorious ruler,
> Of unchangeable command, whose mind no god can fathom.
> O Sin, at thy appearance the gods assemble, all the kings prostrate themselves.
> Nannar, Sin . . . thou comest forth as a brilliant dark-red stone,[2]
> . . . as lapis lazuli.   At the brilliancy of
> Sin the stars rejoice, the night is filled with joy.
> Sin dwells in the midst of the resplendent heavens, Sin, the faithful beloved son.
> Exalted ruler, first-born of Enlil . . .
> Light of heaven, lord of the lands . . .
> His word is merciful in Eridu . . .
> Thou hast established Ur as thy dwelling[?].

The sun, as well as the moon, was celebrated in hymns, and there can be little doubt that, in the many localities of sun-worship, both at his rising and at his setting, the priests daily chanted those hymns,

[1] Perry, *Hymns to Sin*, No. 5.
[2] An allusion to the frequently dark-red colour of the full-moon.

accompanied by offerings and by a more or less elaborate ritual.[1]

x

Festival days sacred to a deity were numerous and formed another important feature of worship. As was to be expected of an agricultural people like the ancient Babylonians, these festivals were connected originally with the seasons of the year. The most important was the spring festival, symbolised by the marriage of the young sun-god of the spring with the goddess of vegetation. At Nippur the pair was Ninib and his consort Gula; at Lagash, Ningirsu and Bau. When the attributes of all the various local solar deities were transferred to Marduk of Babylon, the consorts of Ninib and Ningirsu and other consorts were replaced by Marduk's consort Sarpanit,—the Ishtar[2] of Babylon. To an agricultural people the spring represented the birth of the year. Thereupon this spring festival naturally became the new year's celebration, known by the Sumerian name, Zag-Muk. As Babylon grew in political and religious importance, the new year's festival became the most solemn occasion of the year.

We have seen[3] that the cult of Nebo, whereof the

[1] For examples of such hymns see Jastrow, *Religion*, English ed., pp. 300–304, and German ed., i., pp. 426–436.
[2] See above, p. 125.   [3] Above, p. 95 *seq.*

Pl. 28.   Fig. 1.   Votive Tablet of Ur-Enlil, Patesi of Nippur (*c* 3000 B.C.).

Limestone tablet with brief votive inscription found by Haynes at Nippur and now in the Imperial Ottoman Museum at Constantinople. The upper scene represents a naked worshipper who is none other than Ur-Enlil himself, offering a libation to Enlil, the chief god of Nippur. In accordance with the principle of symmetry, so frequently illustrated on the seal cylinders, the scene is given in double form. The lower section shows a goat and sheep followed by two men, one with a vessel on his head the other with a stick in his hand. The animals may represent sacrifices to be offered to the god. Another limestone tablet has been found at Nippur, likewise showing a naked worshipper—perhaps the same Ur-Enlil—before Enlil and a gazelle in the lower section. See Hilprecht, *Babylonian Expedition*, i., 2 Pl. XVI. and No. 94, and the same author's *Excavations in Assyria and Babylonia*, p. 417. The naked worshipper—a custom of primitive days for which there are parallels in other religions—is also found on a limestone bas-relief from Telloh (de Sarzec, *Découvertes*, p. 209; Heuzey, *Catalogue*, pp. 117–118).

Fig. 2.   Babylonian Type of Gilgamesh, the Hero of the Babylonian Epic

Terra-cotta. Found at Telloh. Now in the Louvre. The hero who is naked holds a vase from which a jet of water streams to either side, symbolising the association of the solar hero with the sun-god (see comment to Pl. 6–7), who is frequently represented with streams. See de Sarzec, *Découvertes*, p. 251; Heuzey, *Catalogue*, p. 341. So also frequently on seal cylinders. See Ward, *Seal Cylinders of Western Asia*, Chap. XI.

Fig. 1.   Offering to Ur-Enlil, Chief God of Nippur

Fig. 2.   Babylonian Type of
Gilgamesh, the Hero
of the Babylonian
Epic

centre was in the neighbouring Borsippa, was closely
associated with that of Marduk, and that Nebo himself became, in the systematised pantheon, the son of
Marduk.   A feature of this annual festival was the
visit paid by Nebo to his father, Marduk, marked
by a procession of the images of the great gods, borne
along the *via sacra* leading to the Marduk temple in
Babylon.[1]   A heightened solemnity was imparted to
the festival by an assemblage of all the great gods in a
special chapel, known as the "chamber of fates,"[2]
in order to decree for the coming year the fate of the
country and of individuals.   Over this assembly Marduk presided with his son, Nebo, at his side, acting
as recorder.   The festival lasted for eleven days, and
on the concluding day, as it would appear, the fates
decreed by the gods were definitely sealed.

A special interest attaches to this new year's
festival, because it served as the pattern for both the
New Year and the Day of Atonement of the Jews.
The popular Jewish tradition represents God as sitting
in judgment during the first ten days of the year, surrounded by his court of angels, who inscribe in the
book of fate the names of all persons with what is to be
their destiny for the coming year.   To this day the

[1] See the monograph of Koldewey, *Die Pflastersteine von
Aibur-schabu in Babylon* (Leipzig, 1901), giving an account of
the excavation of a part of this *via sacra*, the walls of which were
lined with glazed and coloured tiles, portraying lions moving in
procession.   See Plate 30, Fig. 1.   [2] *Ubshu-kennu.*

New Year's greeting among Jews is: "May you be inscribed for a good year!" The nine days intervening between the New Year's Day and the Day of Atonement are days of probation, but at the close of the tenth day the book of fate for the year is sealed, and the wish of this day therefore is, "May you be sealed for a good year!"[1]

The first days of the new year, among the Babylonians, as well as among the Jews, after their close contact with the Babylonians during the Exilic period, thus assumed an austere character, marked by penitential and expiatory rites and offerings. The consciousness of sin and guilt was brought home at this season of the year with special force to ruler, priests, and people. The rulers, standing nearer to the gods as they did, first performed the expiatory ceremonies, the general term for which was *Nam-Bur-Bi*,[2] but we may be sure that on this occasion the priests and people participated in the solemn rites. We may further suppose that some of the penitential and lamentation hymns of a personal character, of which we have many examples in the library of Ashurbanapal, and in which the personal sense of guilt and sin is emphasised with fervent appeals for for-

[1] See articles "New Year" and "Atonement, Day of," in the Jewish *Encyclopædia*, and S. Karppe in the *Revue Sémitique*, ii., pp. 146–151.

[2] On this term, see above, p. 298, note 1.

Pl. 29. Votive Offerings (Copper) from Lagash.

Found at Telloh and now in the Louvre. The two kneeling figures represent deities—probably in both cases Ningirsu—and bearing dedicatory inscriptions of Gudea, the Patesi of Lagash (*c.* 2350 B.C.) The two bulls contain dedicatory inscriptions of Gudea to the goddess Inninna for her temple E-Anna in Girsu (a section of Lagash). The two female figures with baskets on their heads, likewise bear dedicatory inscriptions. Similar figures—male and female—have been found with inscriptions of various rulers. The basket on the head is the symbol of participation in the erection of a sacred edifice, as in the case of Ur Ninâ (see Pl. 2). See De Sarzec, *Découvertes*, Pl. 28, pp. 245–247; Heuzey, *Catalogue*, pp. 300–318.

Votive Offerings from Lagash

giveness, were recited during these penitential days of the new year's festival, even though their application was general, and they may not have been composed for this special occasion.

The Babylonians and Assyrians must have had harvest festivals, marked like those of other people by rejoicings and thanksgivings to the gods, but as yet we have not unearthed these rites and ceremonies. We are, however, fortunate enough to know a good deal about a festival that forms a complement to the new year's celebration and, because of its antiquity and wide bearings on the general religious ideas of the Semites, commands a special interest.

The sun-god of the spring was pictured as a youthful warrior triumphing over the storms of winter. The goddess of vegetation—Ishtar, under various names—unites herself to this god, and the two in unison—sun and earth—bring forth new life in the fields and meadows. But after a few months the summer season begins to wane, and rains and storms again set in. The change of seasons was depicted as due to the death of the youthful god; according to one tradition he was deserted by the goddess who had won his love; according to another, he was slain by a wild boar. An old Sumerian designation of this god was Dumu-Zi, abbreviated from a fuller designation, Dumu-Zi-Ab-zu, and interpreted as "the legitimate [or "faithful"] child of the deep."[1] The allusion is apparently to the sun rising out of the ocean, which was supposed to flow about and underneath the world. The name passed over to the Semites of Babylonia, and thence spread throughout and beyond the borders of Semitic settlements under the form Tammuz. With the name, went the myth of the youthful god, full of vigour, but who is slain, and condemned to a sojourn in the lower world, from which he is released and revivified in the following spring. The antiquity of the cult of Tammuz in Babylonia is confirmed by religious compositions in Sumerian, bewailing the loss of the god and also hailing his return. This, of itself, would not, necessarily, prove the Sumerian origin of the myth, which indeed is of so widespread a character as to justify us in regarding it as common to Sumerians and Semites; but it shows that the weeping for Tammuz, which Ezekiel (viii., 14) portrays as being practised even in his days by the women at the north gate of the temple in Jerusalem, is one of the oldest items of the Sumero-Babylonian cult. In the older Babylonian calendar the summer solstice fell in the sixth month; in the later calendar in the fourth month, which became known as the month of the festival of Tammuz, and then briefly as the month of

[1] See Zimmern, *Der Babylonische Gott Tamuz*, p. 6 (in the *Abhd. Phil. Hist. Klasse d. Königl. Sächs. Akad. d. Wiss.*, No. xx.), where all the other designations under which the god appears are enumerated and discussed.

Pl. 30. Fig. 1. Lion of Babylon.
Fig. 2. Dragon of Babylon.

Pieced together from numerous fragments of glazed tiles of the Neo-Babylonian period, found at Babylon. See *Mitteilungen der Deutschen Orient-Gesellschaft*, Nos. 2–3; 6 (pp. 13–17); 12–13; 19, etc.

This lion is one of a large number of such figures that were placed as decorations in the *Via Sacra* of Babylon, leading to E-Sagila the temple of Marduk, and along which on the New Year's festival (and no doubt on other festive occasions) the gods were carried in procession. The lions—as symbols of Marduk—faced to the north, and lined the walls of both sides of the street which, built by Nebuchadnezzar II. (604–561 B.C.), rose high above the houses of the city. The name given to the street Ai-ibur-shabu signified "may the oppressor not wax strong"; it was paved with large blocks of limestone and volcanic breccia, containing inscriptions commemorating the work of Nebuchadnezzar in honour of Marduk. See Koldewey, *Die Pflastersteine von Aiburschabu* in Babylon (Berlin, 1901).

As specimens of art, these glazed tiles, brilliantly coloured—blue and yellow predominating—are of special interest in enabling us to trace the splendid achievements of the Achæmenian Kings at Susa (see Perrot and Chipiez, *History of Art in Persia*, pp. 136–161) direct to their Babylonian and Assyrian prototypes. For similar glazed tiles on Assyrian edifices see Layard, *Monuments of Nineveh*, i., 84–87; Botta et Flandin, *Monument de Ninive*, ii., Pl. 155–156 and the restorations in Place, *Ninive et l'Assyrie*, Pl. 14–17; 27–31 (Khorsabad).

The dragon—a composite monster with a horned serpent's head, the scaled body, the front legs of a lion and the hind legs of an eagle—belongs to the same category of ideas that produced the human headed bulls and lions, the winged human figures, and the eagle-headed winged figures resting, probably, upon primitive notions of hybrid beings, as reported by Berosus (see Zimmern *Keilinschriften und das Alte Testament*, ii., p. 488 *seq.*), that were supposed to precede the more regular forms of animal creation. It was natural, therefore, that such monsters should become on the one hand the symbols of gods, and on the other hand be chosen as the representations of the inferior order of gods—the demons or

Pl. 30—*Continued*

spirits—here serving as protectors of temples and palaces and as guardians of the tree of life (see comment to Pl. 26, Fig. 2). The picture of Marduk (Pl. 15, Fig. 2) shows the dragon as the symbol of this god, though probably transferred to him from Enlil. (See comment to Pl. 15, Fig. 1.)

The dragon together with the unicorn (or wild ox) and ornamented friezes formed the exterior decoration of the walls of the magnificent gate of Ishtar, excavated by the German expedition at Babylon, and that formed the approach to the sacred area of Marduk's temple. It is estimated that these walls had no less than thirteen rows of alternating dragons and bulls superimposed one upon the other, together with ornamented friezes which were likewise glazed tiles. Repeated at regular interstices, we would thus obtain a pattern furnishing many hundreds of these animal designs. It is such designs that the prophet Ezekiel in his vision (Chap. viii., 10) sees "portrayed on the wall" of the temple at Jerusalem.

Fig. 1.   Lion of Babylon

Fig. 2.   Dragon of Babylon

Tammuz.[1] With the summer solstice the year begins
to wane, and it was appropriate, therefore, to hold
at this time a festival commemorating the gradual
waning of the god's vigour.

While we meet references to Tammuz in hymns
and other compositions, we hear little or nothing of
his cult in later days. The question may be raised,
therefore, whether or not it was officially recognised
in the temples after a certain date. There are, indeed,
good reasons for believing that the worship of Tammuz continued as a private, rather than as an official,
cult; but from this point of view, the cult becomes even
more significant, since it affords an insight into the
popular religion, apart from rites merely official.

In contrast to the lamentation hymns, which formed
part of the atonement ritual,[2] the hymns to Tammuz are remarkably free from references to national
disasters. A personal note runs through them, in
keeping with the popular character of a festival, based
on the change of seasons, and which is fraught with
such significance to an agricultural people. They are
largely composed of an enumeration of the names of
the god, accompanied by phrases expressive of grief
at his removal to the lower world—the abode of the
dead. One of them reads, in part:[3]

[1] So in the Jewish calendar up to the present day.

[2] See above, p. 321 *seq.*

[3] *Cuneiform Texts*, xv., Plates 20, 21. See Zimmern, *Sumerisch-
Babylonische Tamuzlieder*, No. 4 (*Berichte d. Phil. Hist. Klasse*

[Oh for the lord sitting in sorrow], oh for the lord sitting in sorrow!
Damu sits, oh for the lord sitting in sorrow!
Ama-Ushum-Gal sits, oh for the lord sitting in sorrow!
Alas! my hero Damu!
Alas! child, legitimate lord!
Alas! Kadi of the shining [?] eyes!
Alas! Nagar, lord of the net!
Alas! prince, lord of invocation!
Alas! my heavenly wailer!
The raging storm has brought him low,—him that has taken his
    way to the earth.
Like a reed he is broken . . .
A hero, he has forsaken his field.
A shepherd, Tammuz is cast in sorrow.
His mother[1] wails—she begins the wailing for him.
Wailing and sighing—she begins the wailing for him.
She rises—bitterly she wails!
She sits—she puts her hand on her heart[2]
She breaks out in wailing—bitter is her wailing.
She breaks out in lament—bitter is her lament!

In another lament,[3] we are specifically told:

He is gone, he is gone to the bosom of the earth,
And the dead are numerous in the land!

While Tammuz is hidden in the earth, verdure dis-

---

der Königl. Sächs. Akad. d. Wiss., vol. lix., pp. 22 *seq.*); Langdon,
pp. 312–317; Prince, "A Hymn to Tammuz" in *Amer. Journal
of Semitic Languages*, vol. xxvii., pp. 84–89. The beginning is
defective.

[1] Known as Sirdu. The sister of Tammuz, Geshtin-Anna or
in Babylonian *Belit-ṣeri*, "lady of the field," is also represented
as bewailing the fate of her brother. See Zimmern, *Der Babylonische Gott Tamuz*, p. 14.

[2] An expressive gesture of deep grief.

[3] Rawlinson IV. (2d ed.), 30, No. 2. Zimmern, *Tamuzlieder*,
No. 1; Langdon, *op. cit.*, 304 *seq.*

appears, vegetation ceases, and fertility among animals pauses:

> How long will the springing up of verdure be withheld?
> How long will vegetation be withheld?

In other compositions, Ishtar is described as herself proceeding to the nether world to seek out her
lover and spouse, Tammuz, in order to bring the
god back to earth again amidst general rejoicing
that clearly symbolises the return of vegetation.
May we see in this association of Ishtar with Tammuz the reason why in the later periods we do not
find references to the popular festival as part of the
official cult? Ishtar and Tammuz are closely related figures; both symbolise vegetation—one as the
personification of the sun, the other as the personification of mother earth. The combination of Tammuz and Ishtar, as husband and wife, is merely the
usual artificial attempt to combine two figures that
represent the same idea—induced in this instance by
the analogy of the male and female principles. There
are, in fact, indications that Tammuz was, at certain places, or at an early period, regarded as a goddess and not as a god.[1]

The story of Tammuz's annual journey to the

---

[1] Zimmern, *Der Babylonische Gott Tamuz*, pp. 7 *seq.*, from which
it appears that Tammuz is designated by various names, as Ama-
Ushumgal-Anna ("all ruling mother of heaven"), Ningishzida,
and Kadi, which represent female deities.

nether world is paralleled by Ishtar's descent into the realm of Nergal and Ereshkigal.[1] The two stories embody the same myth of the change of seasons, and it is natural, therefore, that with the later predominance of the Ishtar cult, Ishtar should gradually have displaced Tammuz in the official ritual of the temples. In place of the lament for Tammuz we have the myth of Ishtar's enforced journey to Aralû,—as the nether world was commonly termed,[2]—and of her ultimate escape, which was recited in the temples at the festival marking the waning of the summer season;[3] the lament for the goddess was tempered, however, by the certain hope of her return. Popular customs survive theoretical and official reconstructions of beliefs and practices through the speculations and the intellectual influence of priests. The testimony of Ezekiel[4] is a significant witness to the persistence in the Semitic world, as late as the sixth century B.C., of the custom of bewailing the disappearance of Tammuz. No less significant is the spread of the Tammuz myth under various forms far beyond the confines of the Semitic world. Is it, perhaps, also significant that the Hebrew prophet describes the women of Jerusalem as practising this rite? In all

[1] See p. 370 seq.   [2] See p. 354.

[3] The change from Tammuz to Ishtar is marked by the later designation of the 6th month—once sacred to Tammuz (see above, p. 344)—as "the month of the descent of Ishtar."

[4] Above, p. 344.

religious bodies, as has already been suggested,[1] women represent the conservative element, among whom religious customs continue in practice after they have been abandoned by men. The women—outside of their functions as priestesses—took no part, so far as we know, in the official cult of Babylonia and Assyria, as they took no such part among the ancient Hebrews. It may turn out, therefore, to be the case that in Babylonia, as in Palestine, the non-official or extra-official cult of Tammuz was maintained outside of the temples through the influence of the female population—as a popular rite, surviving from very ancient days, and having had at one time a significance equal to that which was afterwards assumed by the cult of Ishtar.

In another regard the mourning for Tammuz is invested with a special interest. Under the form Adôn, —a title of Tammuz signifying "lord,"—the myth passed to the Phœnicians, and thence to the Greeks, who, adapting it to their own mythology (which may also have preserved a similar myth of the change of seasons), replace Ishtar by Aphrodite.[2] The story of Adonis and Aphrodite in any case is to be traced directly to the Sumerian-Babylonian Tammuz-Ishtar myth. The weeping for the lost sun-god is the complement to the rejoicing at the return of the sun-god in the spring—the new year's festival—when

[1] Above, p. 313.   [2] See Frazer, *Adonis, Attis, and Osiris*, p. 8.

nature awakens to new life. The weeping and the rejoicing appear to have been continued up to late days. In one form or another we find among Greeks and Romans the commemoration in the spring of the death of a god, followed by a rejoicing at his return. [1] In view of this, the theory has been advanced that in its last analysis, the story of the crucifixion and resurrection of the Christ embodies a late echo of the Tammuz-Adonis myth. [2] The "son of God" is slain to reappear as the "risen Lord," just as in the Phrygian story of Attis and Cybele, and in the Egyptian tale of Osiris and Isis, we have another form of the same myth symbolising the change of seasons. [3]

[1] Frazer, *op. cit.*, 198 *seq.*

[2] To this Tammuz-Adonis myth, there have been added elements taken from the Roman Saturnalia and the Persian Sacaea festival. See Vollmer, *Jesus und das Sacaeanopfer* (Giessen, 1905), and other literature there referred to; also Frazer, *Golden Bough*, 2d ed., vol. iii., pp. 186 *seq.* It is perhaps well to add (in view of Andrew Lang's elaborate criticism, *Magic and Religion*, pp. 76–204) that all these extraneous elements affect merely the form gradually assumed by the story of the death (or disappearance) of Jesus.

[3] Frazer, *Adonis, Attis, and Osiris*, pp. 165 *seq.* and 212 *seq.*

LECTURE VI

ETHICS AND LIFE AFTER DEATH

I

THE view that life continues in some form after death has ensued is so common among people on the level of primitive culture, or who have just risen above this level, that its presence in advanced religions may be regarded as a legacy bequeathed from the earliest period in the history of mankind. To the savage and the untutored all nature is instinct with life. The changes and activity that he sees about him, in the woods and fields, in the streams and mountains and in the heavens—the boundless extent of ceaseless change—he ascribes to an element which he instinctively associates with the life of which he is conscious in himself, and he interprets this life in terms applicable to himself. Man in the earlier stages of his development is unable to conceive of life once begun as coming to an end, just as an unsophisticated child who, when it begins to ponder on the mystery of existence, is incapable of grasping the thought of death as a total extinction of life. The doubt comes at a later stage of mental development and so, in the history of mankind, the problem involved in a discussion regarding life after death is to determine the factors that led man to question the continuance of life in some form after it had fled from the body. In the Old Testament it is only in the later books, like Ecclesiastes and Job, that the question is raised or suggested whether or not there is anything for man to look forward to after the breath of life has passed out of him. We may detect in certain aspects of the problem in these frankly skeptical productions of the Hebrew mind the influence—direct or indirect—of Greek philosophical thought, which early began to concern itself with this problem. Out of this doubt there arises after an interval of some centuries, on the one hand, the Jewish and Christian doctrine of the immortality of the soul, and on the other, the belief in a resurrection of the dead in some form. In Buddhism we see the persistency of the belief that life is continuous leading to the hope of release from life, as the ideal that can be attained only by those who, after a succession of existences in which they have schooled themselves to get rid of the desire of living, have merited also by their increasing purity the rare reward of Nirvâna.[1]

[1] The idea does not appear to be limited to India, unless we are to recognise Hindu influences in such tales as that of the mediæval legend of the Wandering Jew, who is condemned to

Here and there we find in Babylonian-Assyrian literature faint suggestions of skepticism, but the prevailing view throughout all periods is that the dead continue in a conscious or semi-conscious state after this life is come to an end.   To be sure, the condition of the dead is not one to be envied.   They are condemned to inactivity, which in itself might not be regarded as an unmixed evil, but this inactivity carries with it a deprivation of all pleasures.   Deep down in the bowels of the earth there was pictured a subterranean cave in which the dead are huddled together.   The place is dark, gloomy, and damp, and in a poetic work it is described as a neglected and forlorn palace, where dust has been allowed to gather—a place of dense darkness where, to quote the fine paradox of Job (x., 22), "even light is as darkness."   It is a land from which there is no return, a prison in which the dead are confined for all time, or if the shade of some spirit[1] does rise up to earth, it is for a short interval only, and merely to trouble the living.   The horror that the dwelling-place of the dead inspired is illustrated by the belief that makes it also the gen-

---

live as a punishment for mocking Jesus while on his way to the cross, or in the story of the Flying Dutchman, who cannot die until another life is voluntarily sacrificed for his.   A somewhat similar thought enters as a factor in the myths of Prometheus and Tityos, who are condemned to the perpetual tortures of death, and yet continue to live.

[1] See above, p. 309.

23

eral abode of the demons, though we have seen that they are not limited to this abode. Again, this dwelling-place is pictured as a great city, and, curiously enough, it is at times designated like the temple of Enlil at Nippur as E-Kur-Bad, "Mountain-house [or "temple"] of the dead." The most common name for this abode, however, is *Aralû*—a term that occurs in Sumerian compositions, but may nevertheless be a good Semitic word. By the side of this term, we find other poetic names, as "the house of Tammuz," based upon the fact that the solar god of spring and vegetation is obliged to spend half of the year in the abode of the dead, or Irkallu, which is also the designation of a god of the subterranean regions, or Cuthah—the seat of the cult of Nergal,—because of the association of Nergal, the god of pestilence and death, with the lower world. The names and metaphors all emphasise the gloomy conceptions connected with the abode of the dead.

It was, however, inevitable that speculation by choicer minds should dwell on a theme so fascinating and important, and endeavour to bring the popular conceptions into harmony with the conclusions reached in the course of time in the temple-schools. Corresponding to the endeavour to connect with the personified powers of nature certain ethical qualities, reflecting a higher degree of moral development, we meet at least the faint inkling of the view that the gods, actuated by justice and mercy, could not condemn all alike to a fate so sad as eternal confinement in a dark cave. Besides Aralû, there was also an "Island of the Blest," situated at the confluence of the streams, to which those were carried who had won the favour of the gods. One of these favourites is Ut-Napishtim, who was sought out by Ea, the god of humanity, as one worthy to escape from a deluge that destroyed the rest of mankind; and with Ut-Napishtim, his wife was also carried to the island, where both of them continued to lead a life not unlike that of the immortal gods. But though the theory of this possible rescue seems to have arisen at a comparatively early period, it does not appear, for some reason, to have been developed to any extent. In this respect, Babylonia presents a parallel to Greece, where we likewise find the two views, Hades for the general mass of humanity and a blessed island for the rare exceptions—the very rare exceptions—limited to those who, like Menelaos, are closely related to the gods, or, like Tiresias, favoured because of the possession of the divine gift of prophecy in an unusual degree.

We might have supposed that, among the Babylonians, the rulers, as standing much closer to the gods than the common people, would have been singled out for the privilege of a transfer to the Island of the Blest, but this does not appear to have been the case.

Like the kings and heroes of the Greek epic, they all pass to the land of no-return, to the dark dwelling underground. An exception is not even made for kings like Sargon and Naram-Sin of Akkad, or for Dungi of the Ur dynasty and his successors, and some of the rulers of Isin and Larsa, who have the sign for deity attached to their names, and some of whom had temples dedicated in their honour, just like gods. The divinity of these Babylonian kings appears to have been, as with the Seleucid rulers, a political and not a religious prerogative, and the evidence would seem to show[1] that this political deification of kings was closely bound up with their control of Nippur as the paramount religious centre of the country. In theory, the ruler of this city was the god, Enlil, himself, and, therefore, he who had control of the city was put on a parity with the god, as his son or representative—the vicar of Enlil on earth, a kind of *pontifex maximus*, with the prerogatives of divinity as the symbol of his office.

We do not find that the speculations of the Babylonian and Assyrian priests ever led to any *radical* modification of the conceptions concerning Aralû. It remains a gloomy place,—a tragic terminus to earthly joys, and always contemplated with horror. The refrain, running through all the lessons which the

[1] See Kugler's admirable discussion of the problem in his *Sternkunde und Sterndienst in Babel*, ii., 1, pp. 144-149.

priests attached to popular myths in giving them a literary form, is that no man can hope to escape the common fate. Enkidu,[1] who is introduced into the Gilgamesh epic[2] and appears to be in some respects a counterpart to the Biblical Adam,[3] is created by Aruru, the fashioner of mankind, but when slain by the wiles of the goddess Ishtar, goes to Aralû as the rest of mankind. Even Gilgamesh himself, the hero of the epic, half-man, half-god, whose adventures represent a strange conglomeration of dimmed historical tradition and nature myths, is depicted as being seized with the fear that he too, like Enkidu, may be dragged to the world of the dead. He seeks to fathom the mystery of death and, in the hope of escaping Aralû, undertakes a long journey in quest of Ut-Napishtim, to learn from him how he had attained immortality. The latter tells Gilgamesh the story of his escape from the destructive deluge. Ut-Napishtim and his wife are filled with pity for the stranger, who has been

[1] On this reading of the name instead of Eabani, as hitherto assumed, see Ungnad in the *Orientalistische Literaturzeitung*, vol. xiii. (1910), pp. 306, 307.

[2] See, for an analysis of the epic, Jastrow, *Religion* (English ed., pp. 467–517), and for translations Jensen in *Keilinschriftliche Bibliothek*, vi., 1, pp. 116–265; the same author's *Das Gilgamesh-epos in der Weltliteratur*, and Ungnad, *Das Babylonische Gilgameshepos*, and, also, in *Altorientalische Texte und Bilder* (ed. Hugo Gressmann), ii., pp. 39–61.

[3] See Jastrow, "Adam and Eve in Babylonian Literature," in *Amer. Journal of Semitic Languages*, vol. xx., pp. 193–214.

smitten with a painful disease. They afford him relief by mystic rites, based on the incantation ritual, but they cannot cure him. Gilgamesh is told of a plant which has the power of restoring old age to youth. He seeks for it, but fails to find it, and, resigned to his fate, he returns to his home, Uruk.

The last episode in the epic furnishes a further illustration of the sad thoughts aroused in the minds of the priests and people at the contemplation of the fate in store for those who have shuffled off the mortal coil. Gilgamesh is anxious to find out at least how his friend and companion, Enkidu, fares in Aralû. In response to his appeal, the shade of Enkidu rises before him. "Tell me, my friend," Gilgamesh implores, "tell me the law of the earth which thou hast experienced." Mournfully the reply comes back, "I cannot tell thee, my friend, I cannot tell thee." Enkidu continues:

Were I to tell thee the law of the earth which I have experienced,
Thou would 'st sit down and weep the whole day.

There is only one thing that can make the fate of the dead less abhorrent. A proper burial with an affectionate care of the corpse ensures at least a quiet repose.

Such a one rests on a couch and drinks pure water,
But he whose shade has no rest in the earth, as I have seen and you will see,[1]

---

[1] *I.e.*, as Enkidu has experienced, and as Gilgamesh will experience.

His shade has no rest in the earth.
Whose shade no one cares for, as I have seen and you will see,
What is left over in the pot, remains of food
That are thrown in the street, he eats.

II

Proper burial is, therefore, all essential, even though it can do no more than secure peace for the dead in their cheerless abode, and protection for the living by preventing the dead from returning in gaunt forms to plague them. Libations are poured forth to them at the grave, and food offered by sorrowing relatives.

The greatest misfortune that can happen to the dead is to be exposed to the light of day; far down into the Assyrian period we find this exemplified in the boast of Ashurbanapal that he had destroyed the tombs of the kings of Elam, and removed their bodies from their resting-place.[1] The corpses of the Babylonians who took part in a rebellion, fomented by his treacherous brother Shamash-shumukin, Ashurbanapal scattered, so he tells us,[2] "like thorns and thistles" over the battle-field, and gave them to dogs, and swine, and to the birds of heaven. At the close of the inscriptions on monuments recording the achievements of the rulers, and also on the so-called

[1] Rawlinson V., Plate 6, col. vi., 70–73 (Schrader, *Keilinschriftliche Bibliothek*, ii., p. 207).
[2] Rawlinson V., Plate 4, col. iv., 72–86 (Schrader, *l.c.*, p. 193).

boundary stones,[1] recording grants of lands, or other privileges, curses are hurled against any one who destroys the record; and as a part of these curses is almost invariably the wish that the body of that ruthless destroyer may be cast forth unburied.

Mutilation of the corpses of foes, so frequently emphasised by Assyrian rulers,[2] is merely another phase of this curse upon the dead. On one of our oldest pictorial monuments, portraying and describing the victory of Eannatum, the *patesi* of Lagash (*ca.* 3000 B.C.), over the people of Umma, the contrast between the careful burial of the king's warriors, and the fate allotted to the enemy is shown by vultures flying off with heads in their beaks.[3] The monument is of further interest in depicting the ancient custom of burying the dead unclad, which recalls the words of Job (i., 21), "naked came I out of my mother's womb and naked shall I return thither," which may be an adumbration of this custom. To this day, among Mohammedans and orthodox Jews, the body is not buried in ordinary clothes but is merely wrapped in

[1] See Plate 22.

[2] *E.g.*, in the Annals of Ashurbanapal, Rawlinson, V., Pl. 3, col. iii., 36; Plate 4, col. iv., 135; Plate 7, col. vii., 39–47, etc. (Schrader, *l.c.*, ii., pp. 181, 213, etc.).

[3] See Plate 31; also De Sarzec, *Découvertes, en Chaldée*, Plate 3, 4; Heuzey, *Catalogue des Antiquités Chaldéennes*, p. 102, and King, *History of Sumer and Akkad*, facing p. 138. God Ningirsu is also represented as clubbing the heads of warriors gathered together in a net (King, *l.c.*, p. 131).

Pl. 31.   Stele of E-annatum, Patesi (and King) of Lagash (*c.* 2900 B.C.).

Portions of the reverse of a remarkable limestone monument carved on both sides with designs and inscriptions. Found at Telloh. See De Sarzec, *Découvertes*, Plates 3 to 4 *ter*, pp. 94–103, 174–195; Heuzey, *Catalogue*, pp. 101–117, and Heuzey and Thureau-Dangin, *Restitution Materielle de la Stéle des Vautours* (Paris 1909). The monument was found in a badly mutilated condition, but by careful study the seven pieces now recovered enable us to form a fairly accurate view of it. It represents the conquest of the people of Umma by Eannatum, and records the solemn agreement made between Eannatum and the people of Umma. The upper piece represents vultures flying off with the heads of the slain opponents—to illustrate their dreadful fate. These dead are shown in the second figure, while in the third others who have fallen in battle are carefully arranged in groups and a burial mound is being built over them by attendants who carry the earth for the burial in baskets placed on their heads. Traces of a ceremonial offering to the dead are to be seen in another fragment. The designs on the obverse are symbolical—the chief figure being the patron deity, Ningirsu with the eagle on two lions as the emblem of the god (see Pl. 5, Fig. 1) in his hand, and the net in which the deity has caught the enemies.

Stele of Eannatum, Patesi of
Lagash (*c.* 2900 B. C.)

Fig. 1.   Mutilation of the Dead   Fig. 2.   Dead arranged in Rows

Fig. 3.   Burial of Dead

a shroud; this custom is only a degree removed from
the older custom of naked burial.   Whether or not
in Babylonia and Assyria this custom was also thus
modified as a concession to growing refinement, we
do not know, but presumably in later times the dead
were covered before being consigned to the earth.
There are also some reasons for believing that, at
one time, it was customary to sew the dead in
bags, or wrap them in mats of reeds.   At all times,
however, the modes of burial retained their simplicity.
If from knowledge derived from later ages we may
draw conclusions for earlier ages, it would seem that
the general custom was to place the dead in a sitting
or half-reclining posture, on reed mats, and to cover
them with a large jar or dish, or to place them in clay
compartments having the shape of bath-tubs.[1]   The
usual place of burial seems to have been in vaults,
often beneath the houses of the living.[2]   In later
periods, we find the tubs replaced by the long slipper-
shaped clay coffins, with an opening at one end into
which the body was forced.[3]   Throughout these various customs a desire is indicated not merely to
bury the body, but to imprison it safely so as to avoid
the danger of a possible escape.   Weapons and ornaments were placed on the graves, and also various

[1] Hilprecht, *Explorations in Bible Lands*, facing p. 337.

[2] *Mitteilungen der Deutschen Orient-Gesellschaft*, Nos. 27 and 31;
for another somewhat different mode of burial, see No. 42.

[3] See Plate 32.

kinds of food, though whether or not this was a common practice at all periods has not yet been determined.

In general, it may be said, the tombs of the Babylonians and Assyrians were always exceedingly simple, and we find no indications whatever that even for monarchs elaborate structures were erected as their resting-place. Herein Babylonia and Assyria present a striking contrast to Egypt, which corresponds to the difference no less striking between the two nations in their conceptions of life after death. In Egypt, the preservation of the body was a condition essential to the well-being of the dead, whereas in Babylonia a mere burial was all-sufficient and no special care was taken to keep the body from decay. The elaborate mortuary ceremonial in Egypt[1] finds no parallel in the Euphrates Valley, where the general feeling appears to be that for the dead there was not much that could be done. Such customs as were observed were prompted, as has been said, rather by a desire to protect the living from being annoyed or tortured by the shades of the unburied or neglected dead. That this fear was genuine is indicated by the belief in a class of demons, known as *etimmu*,[2] which means the "shade" of a departed person. This conception is best explained as a

[1] See Budge, *The Mummy, Chapters on Egyptian Funeral Archæology* (London, 1893).   [2] See above, p. 309, note 1.

Pl. 32. Babylonian Coffins.

Fig. 1. Earlier Type—showing bath-tub shape.

Fig. 2. Later Type—slipper-shaped coffins, chiefly of the Persian period, which frequently have glazed covers with ornamental designs. The illustrations showing the coffins as found are from photographs taken by the University of Pennsylvania Expedition to Nippur.

The coffins may be regarded as typical of the mode of burying the dead in coffins in Babylonia and Assyria, though as indicated in the text there are various other modes. See the Illustrations and comments in Peters, *Nippur*, vol. ii., facing pp, 214–220; Hilprecht, *Excavations in Assyria and Babylonia*, pp. 337 and 422 *seq.* Recently, e. g. (*Mitteilungen der Deutschen Orient-Gesellschaft*, No. 42, p. 14 *seq.*), graves have been found in Babylon which were vaulted in by brick walls. So also at Nippur (Hilprecht, *Excavations in Assyria and Babylonia*, p. 510) and Ashur, *Mitteilungen der Deutschen Orient-Gesellschaft*, No. 27, pp. 29–32 (also Nos. 25, p. 55; 26, p. 13).

Fig. 1.   Earlier Type of Babylonian Coffins

Fig. 2.   Later Type of Slipper-
Shaped Coffins

survival of primitive beliefs found elsewhere, which among many people in a stage of primitive culture led to a widespread and complicated ancestor worship. That this worship existed in Babylonia also is highly probable, but it must have died out as part of the official cult before we reach the period for which we have documentary material; we find no references to it in the ritual texts

III

In seeking a reason why the speculations of the temple-schools, regarding the mysteries of the universe, should not have led to the doctrine of a more cheerful destiny for the dead such as in the Blessed Island (to which, as we have seen, only a few favourites of the gods were admitted), we are surprised by the almost complete absence of all ethical considerations in connection with the dead.

While much stress was at all times laid upon conduct agreeable to the gods (and one of the most sigficant members of the pantheon is Shamash, the god of justice and righteousness), the thought that good deeds will find a reward from the gods after life has ceased is absent from the religious literature of Babylonia and Assyria. There is a special pantheon for the nether world, where the dead sojourn, but there is no figure such as Osiris in the Egyptian religion, the judge of the dead, who weighs the good deeds against the bad in order to decide the destiny of the soul. To be sure, everything is done by the living to secure the favour of the gods, to appease their anger, and to regain their favour by elaborate expiatory rites, and by confession of sins, and yet all the hopes of the people are centred upon earthly happiness and present success. The gods appear to be concerned neither for the dead nor with them. Their interest, like that of their worshippers, was restricted to the living world. Even with so exceptional a mortal as Ut-Napishtim, who is carried to the Blessed Island, no motive is ascribed to Ea, who warns Ut-Napishtim of the coming destruction of mankind, and provides for his escape by bidding him build a ship. It is not even alleged of Ut-Napishtim that he was a faithful worshipper, much less that by exemplary conduct he merited the special favour bestowed on him. Of his Biblical counterpart, Noah, we are told that he was "perfect and righteous"—praises that are applied to only one other character in the whole range of Old Testament literature, to wit, Job.[1] But no such encomium is passed on Ut-Napishtim, who, in another version, is designated merely as a "very clever one."[2]

[1] Chap. xii., 4.

[2] *Atra-khasis*, the inverted form of which, *Khasis-atra*, furnishes the name Xisuthros (in Berosus' list of mythical antediluvian kings), who is the hero of the deluge. See Zimmern, *Keilinschriften und das Alte Testament*, ii., pp. 532 and 543 *seq.*

Had an ethical factor been introduced, in however faint a degree, we should have found a decided modification of the primitive views in regard to the fate of the dead. Perhaps there might have been a development not unlike that which took place among the Hebrews, who, starting from the same point as the Babylonians and Assyrians, reached the conclusion (as a natural corollary to the ethical transformation which the conception of their national deity, Jahweh, underwent) that a god of justice and mercy extended his protection to the dead as well as to the living, and that those who suffered injustice in this world would find a compensatory reward in the next.

Among the Babylonians we have, as the last word on the subject, an expression of sad resignation that man must be content with the joys of this world. Death is an unmitigated evil, and the favour of the gods is shown by their willingness to save the victims as long as possible from the cold and silent grave. A deity is occasionally addressed in hymns as "the restorer of the dead to life," but only where he saves those standing on the brink of the grave—leading them back to enjoy the warm sunlight a little longer.

The question indeed was raised in Babylonia why after a brief existence man was condemned to eternal gloom? The answer, that is given, is depressing but most characteristic of the arrest in the development of ethical conceptions concerning the gods, in spite of certain appearances to the contrary. The gods themselves are represented, in an interesting tale, based on a nature-myth, as opposed to granting mankind immortal life, and actually having recourse to a deception, in order to prevent another favourite of Ea—the god of humanity—from attaining the desired goal.

The story,[1] as is so frequently the case, is composite. A lament for the disappearance of the two gods of vegetation—Tammuz and Ningishzida[2]—is interlaced with a story of a certain Adapa, who is summoned to appear before Anu, the god of heaven, for having, while fishing, broken the wings of the south-wind, so that for seven days that wind did not blow. At the suggestion of Ea, Adapa dons a mourning garb before coming into the presence of Anu, and is told to answer, when asked why he had done so, that he is mourning for two deities who have disappeared from earth. He is further cautioned against

[1] See Jastrow, *Religion* (English ed., pp. 544–555); Ungnad in Gressmann's *Altorientalische Texte und Bilder*, ii., pp. 34–38.

[2] Tammuz and Ningishzida are "doublets," viewed in the relation of husband and wife. Each represents the sun-god of the spring that brings vegetation but is carried away from the earth with the waning of the summer season. Ningishzida, it will be recalled (above, p. 347, note 1), is one of the designations of the consort of Tammuz. The mourning garb of Adapa symbolises the lament for Tammuz (or Ningishzida), and the story is therefore part of a myth reflecting the change of seasons. With this myth, the story of Adapa, which is of an entirely different order, has been combined.

drinking the waters of death, or eating the food of death that will be offered him when he comes before the council of the gods. Adapa faithfully carries out the instructions, but Tammuz and Ningishzida, the guardians at the gate of the heavens, are moved by pity when they learn from Adapa that he is mourning for their own removal from earth, and decide to offer him food of life and water of life. Adapa, ignorant of the substitution, refuses both, and thus forfeits immortal life. The tale implies that, while Tammuz and Ningishzida are distressed at Adapa's error, Anu, the head of the pantheon, experiences a sense of relief, in the assurance that man is not destined to receive the boon of the gods—immortality. The tale belongs to the same class as the famous one in the third chapter of Genesis, where, to be sure, Adam[1] is punished for disobedience to the divine command, but there is a decided trace of the belief that the gods do not wish men to be immortal in the fear uttered (Genesis iii., 22) by Jahweh-Elohîm that man, having tasted of the tree of knowledge, "may find his way to the tree of life and live for ever."

The two tales—of Adapa and of Adam—certainly stand in some relation to each other. Both are intended as an answer to the question why man is not

---

[1] The name Adam, although it has a Hebrew etymology, may have been suggested by Adapa, which might also be read Adawa, as Prof. Sayce was the first to point out.

immortal. They issue from a common source. The Biblical tale has been stripped almost entirely of its mythical aspects, as is the case with other tales in the early chapters of Genesis which may be traced back to Babylonian prototypes,[1] but the real contrast between the two is the introduction of the ethical factor in the Hebrew version. Jahweh-Elohîm, like Anu, does not desire man to be immortal, but the Hebrew writer justifies this attitude by Adam's disobedience, whereas the Babylonian in order to answer the question is forced to have recourse to a deception practised upon man; Adapa obeys and yet is punished. That is the gist of the Babylonian tale, which so well illustrates the absence of an ethical factor in the current views regarding life after death.

IV

The gods who are placed in control of Aralû partake of the same gloomy and forbidding character as the abode over which they rule. At the head stands the god of pestilence and death, Nergal,[2] identified in astrology with the ill-omened planet Mars, whose centre of worship, Cuthah, became, as we have seen, one of the designations of the nether world. By the side of Nergal stands his consort Ereshkigal (or Allatu)—the Proserpine of Babylonian mythology,—

[1] See below, p. 415.   [2] See above, p. 224.

as forbidding in her nature as he is, and who appears to have been, originally, the presiding genius of Aralû with whom Nergal is subsequently associated.

A myth[1] describes how Nergal invaded the domain of Ereshkigal, and forced her to yield her dominion to him. The gods are depicted as holding a feast to which all come except Ereshkigal. She sends her grim messenger Namtar—that is, the "demon of plague"—to the gods, among whom there is one, Nergal, who fails to pay him a proper respect. When Ereshkigal hears of this, she is enraged and demands the death of Nergal. The latter, undaunted, proceeds to the abode of the angry goddess, encouraged to do so apparently by Enlil and the gods of the pantheon. A gang of fourteen demons, whose names indicate the tortures and misery inflicted by Nergal, accompany the latter. He stations them at the gates of Ereshkigal's domain so as to prevent her escape. A violent scene ensues when Nergal and Ereshkigal meet. Nergal drags the goddess from her throne by the hair, overpowers her, and threatens to kill her. Ereshkigal pleads for mercy, and agrees to share with him her dominion.

Do not kill me, my brother! Let me tell thee something.

Nergal desists and Ereshkigal continues:

[1] Jastrow, *Religion* (English ed.), pp. 584 *seq.*; Jensen, *Keilinschriftliche Bibliothek*, vi., 1, pp. 72–79; Ungnad, *op.cit.*, pp. 69–71.

24

Be my husband and I will be thy wife.
I will grant thee sovereignty in the wide earth, entrusting to
    thee the tablet of wisdom.
Thou shalt be master, and I the mistress.

In this way the myth endeavours to account for the existence of two rulers in Aralû, but one may doubt that a union so inauspiciously begun was very happy.

Another myth, again portraying the change of seasons,[1] describes the entrance of Ishtar, the goddess of vegetation, into the domain of Ereshkigal. The gradual decay of the summer season is symbolised by the piece of clothing, or ornament, which Ishtar is obliged to hand to the guardian at each of the seven gates leading to the presence of Ereshkigal, until, when Ishtar appears at last before her sister, she stands there entirely naked. All trace of vegetation has disappeared, and nature is bare when the wintry season appears and storms set in. In a rage Ereshkigal flies at her sister Ishtar, and orders her messenger Namtar to keep the goddess a prisoner in her palace, from which she is released, however, after some time, by an envoy of Ea. While Ishtar is in the nether world, all life and fertility cease on earth—a clear indication of the meaning of the myth. The gods mourn her departure. Shamash the sun-god laments before Sin and Ea:

[1] Jastrow, *Religion* (English ed.), pp. 565–575; Jensen, *l.c.*, pp. 80–91; Ungnad, *l.c.*, pp. 65–69.

Ishtar has descended into the earth and is not come up.
Since Ishtar is gone to the land of no-return,
The bull cares not for the cow, the ass cares not for the jenny,
The man cares not for the maid in the market[1],
> The man sleeps in his place,
> The wife sleeps alone.

Ea creates a mysterious being, Aṣushu-namir,[2] whom he dispatches to the nether world to bring the goddess back to earth. The messenger of Ea is clearly a counterpart of Tammuz, the solar god of the spring, who brings new life to mother earth. Ishtar is sprinkled with the water of life by Aṣushu-namir and, as she is led out of her prison, each piece of clothing or ornament is returned to her in passing from one gate to the other, until she emerges in all her former glory and splendour. The tale forming originally, perhaps, part of the cult of Tammuz, and recited at the season commemorating the snatching away of the youthful god, illustrates again the hopelessness of escape from the nether world for ordinary mortals. Ishtar can be released from her imprisonment when the spring comes. Tammuz, too, is revived and returns to the world; but alas for mankind, doomed to eternal imprisonment in the "land of no-return"! The tale ends with a suggestion of hope

[1] *I.e.*, does not go out to woo. See Herodotus, Book I, § 196.

[2] Signifying "his rising is brilliant"—evidently the designation of a solar deity.

that "in the days of Tammuz," that is at the lament for Tammuz (which here assumes the character of a general lament for the dead), the dead, roused by the plaints of the living, may rise and enjoy the incense offered to them—but that is all. They cannot be brought back to earth and sunlight.

The messengers and attendants of Nergal and Ereshkigal are the demons whom we have met in the incantation rituals. They are the precursors of all kinds of misery and ills to mankind, sent as messengers from the nether world to plague men, women, and children with disease, stirring up strife and rivalry in the world, separating brother from brother, defrauding the labourer of the fruits of his labour, and spreading havoc and misery on all sides; depicted as ferocious and terrifying creatures, ruthless and eternally bent on mischief and evil. The association of these demons with the world where no life is, further emphasises the view held of the fate of the dead. With such beings as their gaolers what hope was there for those who were imprisoned in the great cavern? If conscious of their state, as they appear to have been, what emotion could they have but that of perpetual terror?

The absence of the ethical factor in the conception of life after death, preventing, as we have seen, the rise of a doctrine of retribution for the wicked, and belief in a better fate for those who had lived a virtuous and godly life, had at least a compensation in not leading to any dogma of actual bodily sufferings for the dead. The dead were at all events secure from the demons who came up to plague the living, but whose duty so far as the dead were concerned seemed to be limited to keeping the departed shades in their prison. Nor did the gods of the upper world concern themselves with the dead, and while in the descriptions of Nergal and Ereshkigal and their attendants we have all the elements needed for the revelation of the tortures of hell, so vividly portrayed by Christian and Mohammedan theologians, so long as Aralû remained the abode of *all* the dead, it was free from the cries of the condemned—a gloomy but a silent habitation. A hell full of tortures is the counterpart of a heaven full of joys. The Babylonian-Assyrian religion had neither the one nor the other; and the natural consequence was the doctrine that what happiness man may desire must be secured in this world. It was now or never.

This lesson is actually drawn in a version of the Gilgamesh epic,[1] which, be it remembered, dates from the period of Hammurapi. The hero, smitten with disease and fearing death, is discouraged by the gods themselves in his quest of life, and in his desire to

[1] Meissner, "Ein altbabylonisches Fragment des Gilgamos-epos" (*Mitteilungen der Vorderasiatischen Gesellschaft*, vol. vii., No. 1).

escape the fate of his companion Enkidu.[1] Shamash, the sun-god, tells him:

> Gilgamesh, whither hurriest thou?
> The life that thou seekest thou wilt not find.

Sabitu, a maiden, dwelling on the seacoast, to whom Gilgamesh goes, tells him the same. In reply to the following greeting of the hero:

> Now, O Sabitu, that I see thy countenance,
> May I not see death which I fear!

Sabitu imparts to him a guidance for life:

> Gilgamesh, whither hurriest thou?
> The life that thou seekest thou wilt not find.
> When the gods created man,
> They fixed death for mankind.
> Life they took in their own hand.
> Thou, O Gilgamesh, let thy belly be filled!
> Day and night be merry,
> Daily celebrate a feast,
> Day and night dance and make merry!
> Clean be thy clothes,
> Thy head be washed, bathe in water!
> Look joyfully on the child that grasps thy hand,
> Be happy with the wife in thine arms!

This is the philosophy of those whom Isaiah (xxii., 13) denounces as indifferent to the future: "Let us eat and drink, for to-morrow we must die." Like an echo of the Babylonian poem the refrain of Ecclesiastes rings in our ears:[2]

[1] See above, p. 357.

[2] Chaps. ii., 24; iii., 12, 13; v., 18; viii., 15—the same thought in slightly varied forms.

Pl. 33.　Assyrian Type of Gilgamesh, the Hero of the Babylonian Epic.

Found at Khorsabad.　See Botta et Flandin, *Monument de Ninive*, Vol. I., Pl. 41; a second specimen, Pl. 47, like the one here reproduced—both portraying Gilgamesh in the act of strangling a lion.　The scene is frequently reproduced in a variety of forms on seal cylinders, and evidently represents one of his heroic deeds, though not included in the portions of the Epic that have up to the present been recovered.　See Ward, *Seal Cylinders of Western Asia*, Chapter X.　See also Pl. 28, Fig. 2.

Assyrian Type of Gilgamesh

There is nothing better for a man than that he should eat, and that his soul should enjoy his labour.

"All go to one place," says Ecclesiastes (iii., 20). "All are of the dust and all turn to dust. Vanity, vanity—all is vanity."

Almost the very words of the Babylonian poem are found in a famous passage of Ecclesiastes (ix., 7–9):

Go thy way, eat thy bread with joy and drink thy wine with a merry heart. Let thy garments be always white, and let thy head not lack ointment. Live joyfully with thy wife whom thou lovest, all the days of thy life of vanity which he has given thee under the sun—for this is thy portion.[1]

The pious Hebrew mind found the corrective to this view of life in the conception of a stern but just god, acting according to self-imposed standards of right and wrong, whose rule extends beyond the grave. This attitude finds expression in the numerous additions that were made to Ecclesiastes in order to counteract the frankly cynical teachings of the original work, and to tone down its undisguised skepticism. "Know," says one of these glossators, "that for all these things God will bring thee unto judgment" (xi., 9). "The conclusion of the whole matter," says another, "is to fear God and keep his command-

[1] It is difficult to resist the conclusion that there is a direct connection between these words and the passage from the Gilgamesh epic. The white garments, as contrasted with black, are symbols of joy, and the "pure" garments in the Babylonian poem convey the same idea. The order of enumeration, "garments," "head," "wife," is the same in both.

ments" (xii., 13). "A good name," says a third, "is better than precious ointment" (vii., 1).[1]

Ethical idealism, by which is here meant a high sense of duty and a noble view of life, is possible only—so it would seem—under two conditions, either through a strong conviction that there is a compensation elsewhere for the wrongs, the injustice, and the suffering in this world, or through an equally strong conviction that the unknown goal toward which mankind is striving can be reached only by the moral growth and ultimate perfection of the human race—whatever the future may have in store. The ethics of the Babylonians and Assyrians did not look beyond this world, and their standards were adapted to present needs and not to future possibilities. The thought of the gloomy Aralû in store for all coloured

[1] On these and other additions, made with the intent to change a skeptical book into a pious production, see Haupt, "The Book of Ecclesiastes," in *Oriental Studies of the Oriental Club of Philadelphia* (Boston, 1894), pp. 254 *seq.*, the same author's *Book of Ecclesiastes* (Baltimore, 1905), and Barton, *Critical and Exegetical Commentary on the Book of Ecclesiastes*, pp. 43–46. Despite these additions to Ecclesiastes, considerable opposition was manifested against its admittance into the Jewish canon, on which see Barton, *l.c.*, pp. 5 *seq.* A parallel to this endeavour to convert a heterodox work into an orthodox one is furnished by the treatment accorded to Hafiz by the Mohammedan theologians, who first bitterly opposed the celebrated poems but finding this opposition useless, adopted and interpreted them as symbolical expositions of the teachings of Islam. See Payne's Introduction to his translation of *The Poems of Hafiz* (London, 1901), pp. xxii. *seq.*

their view of life,—not indeed in leading them to take a pessimistic attitude towards life, or in regarding this world as a vale of tears, but in limiting their ethical ideals to what was essential to their material well-being and mundane happiness.

V

It would be an error, however, to infer that such a view of life is incompatible with relatively high standards of conduct. That is far from being the case—at least in Babylonia and Assyria. Even though the highest purpose in life was to secure as much joy and happiness as possible, the conviction was deeply ingrained, particularly in the minds of the Babylonians, that the gods demanded adherence to moral standards. We have had illustrations of these standards in the incantation texts,[1] where by the side of ritualistic errors we find the priests suggesting the possibility that misfortune has been sent in consequence of moral transgressions—such as lying, stealing, defrauding, maliciousness, adultery, coveting the possessions of others, unworthy ambitions, injurious teachings, and other misdemeanours. The gods were prone to punish misdoings quite as severely as neglect of their worship, or indifference to the niceties of ritualistic observances.

[1] See above, p. 307 *seq.*

The consciousness of sinful inclinations and of guilt, though only brought home to men when misfortunes came or were impending, was strong enough to create rules of conduct in public and private affairs that rested on sound principles. The rights of individuals were safeguarded by laws that strove to prevent the strong from taking undue advantage of the weak. Business was carried on under the protection of laws and regulations that impress one as remarkably equitable. Underhand practices were severely punished, and contracts had to be faithfully executed. All this, it may be suggested, was dictated by the necessities of the growth of a complicated social organisation. True, but what is noticeable in the thousands of business documents now at our behoof and covering almost all periods from the earliest to the latest, is the *spirit* of justice and equity that pervades the endeavour to regulate the social relations in Babylonia and Assyria.[1] This is particularly apparent in the legal decisions handed down by the judges, of which we have many

[1] For an excellent summary account with numerous illustrations of actual cases of all kinds, see C. H. W. Johns, *Babylonian and Assyrian Laws, Contracts, and Letters* (N. Y., 1904), and the work of Kohler-Peiser and Ungnad above quoted, p. 277, note 1, also Peiser, *Texte Juristischen und Geschäftlichen Inhalts* (Schrader, *Keilinschriftliche Bibliothek*, vol. iv.), and the same author's, "Skizze der Babylonischen Gesellschaft" (*Mitteilungen der Vorderasiatischen Gesellschaft*, i., No. 3).

specimens.[2] As a protection to both parties engaging in business transactions, a formal contract
wherein the details were noted was drawn up, and
sealed in the presence of witnesses. This method
was extended from loans and sales to marriage agree-
ments, to testaments, to contracts for work, to rents,
and even to such incidents as engaging teachers, and
to apprenticeship. The general principle, already
implied in the Hammurapi Code, and apparently in
force at all periods, was that no agreement of any kind
was valid without a duly attested written record.
The religious element enters into these business transactions in the oath taken in the name of the gods, with
the frequent addition of the name of the reigning king
by both parties as a guarantee of good faith. In
some cases the oath is, in fact, prescribed by law.

If a dispute arose in regard to the terms of a contract, and no agreement could be reached by the contracting parties, the case was brought before the
court, which appears to have been ordinarily composed of three judges, as among the Jews (whose
method of legal procedure was largely modelled
upon Babylonian prototypes). All the documents
in the case had to be brought into court, and each
party was obliged to bring witnesses to support any
claims lying outside the record. The impression

[1] See Johns, *l.c.*, pp. 100–115, and Harper, *Assyrian and Babylonian Literature*, pp. 276 *seq.*, for examples.

that one receives from a study of these decisions is that they were rendered after a careful and impartial consideration of the documents, and of the statements of the parties and of previous decisions. An example taken from the neo-Babylonian period[1] will illustrate the spirit by which the judges were actuated in deciding the complicated cases that were frequently brought before them. It is the case of a widow Bunanit, who brings suit to recover property, devised to her by her husband, which has been claimed by her brother-in-law. Her case is stated in detail:

Bunanit, the daughter of Kharişâ, declared before the judges of Nabonnedos, king of Babylon, as follows: "Apil-addunadin, son of Nikbadu," took me to wife, receiving three and a half manas of silver as my dowry, and one daughter I bore him. I and Apil-addunadin, my husband, carried on business[2] with the money of my dowry, and bought eight GI[3] of an estate in the Akhula-galla quarter of Borsippa,[4] for nine and two thirds manas of silver,[5] besides two and a half manas of silver which was a loan from Iddin-Marduk, son of Iķischa-aplu, son of Nur-Sin, which we added to the price of said estate and bought it in common.[6]

---

[1] Strassmaier, *Babylonische Texte, Inschriften von Nabonidus, König von Babylon*, No. 356. See Peiser, *Texte Juristischen und Geschäftlichen Inhalts*, pp. 234–237.

[2] Literally "sale and puchase."

[3] A land measure.

[4] Opposite Babylon.

[5] Through business transactions the capital of the pair had increased to this amount.

[6] *I.e.*, the total price was 12¼ manas of which 2½ represents borrowed capital.

"In the fourth year of Nabonnedos, king of Babylon, I put in a claim for my dowry against my husband Apil-addunadin, and of his own accord he sealed over to me the eight GI of said estate in Borsippa and transferred it to me for all time,[1] and declared on my tablet[2] as follows: '2½ manas of silver which Apil-addunadin and Bunanit borrowed from Iddin-Marduk and turned over to the price of said estate they held in common.[3] That tablet he sealed and wrote the curse of the gods on it.[4]

"In the fifth year of Nabonnedos, king of Babylon, I and my husband Apil-addunadin adopted Apil-adduamara as son,[5] and made out the deed of adoption,[6] stipulating two manas and ten shekels of silver and a house-outfit as the dowry of Nubta, my daughter. My husband died, and now Aḳabi-ilu, son of my father-in-law,[7] has put in a claim for said estate and all that has been sealed and transferred to me, including Nebo-nûr-ili whom we obtained[8] from Nebo-akh-iddin. Before you I bring the matter. Render a decision."

The case has been stated with great clearness. The legal point involved, because of which the brother-in-law puts in a claim on behalf of the deceased hus-

[1] *I.e.*, in consideration that it was the wife's dowry that had increased to the value of 9⅔ manas, the husband gave her the estate.

[2] *I.e.*, on the formal document of transfer.

[3] The wife thus admits her responsibility for at least one half of the debt.

[4] *I.e.*, invoked at the close the curse of the gods on any one who altered the tablet or put in a false claim—as was invariably done in the case of boundary stones, and frequently in other legal documents. See Johns, *l.c.*, pp. 93 *seq*, and below, p. 385.

[5] There being no male heir, a portion of the estate at least would pass to the husband's family. To avoid that contingency the pair adopted a son.

[6] For such formal deeds, see Johns, *l.c.*, pp. 154–160.

[7] *I.e.*, her brother-in-law who appears as the representative of the husband's family claiming the estate.

[8] *I.e.*, as a slave.

band's family, turns on the question whether the wife is entitled to the entire estate, seeing that her original dowry was only three and one half manas, or, in other words, whether the husband had a right to turn over to her the whole property on the ground that it was her dowry which, through business transactions conducted in common, had increased to nine and two thirds manas. Bunanit, in stating her case, lays great stress, it will be observed, on the circumstance that she and her husband did all things in common —bartered in common, bought in common, borrowed in common, adopted a son in common, and acquired a slave in common.

The decision rendered by the judges is remarkably just, manifesting a due regard for the ethics of the situation, and based on an examination of the various documents or tablets in the case and which in such an instance had to be produced. The document continues as follows:

The judges heard their complaints,[1] and read the tablets and contracts which Bunanit[2] had laid before them. To Akabi-

---

[1] It is assumed that Akabi-ilu has also stated his case.

[2] Akabi-ilu of course had no documents. Among the documents which Bunanit produced there must have been included (1) the marriage contract, (2) documents of the business transactions, (3) the purchase of the estate, (4) the loan of Iddin-Marduk, (5) the transfer of the estate to her, (6) the document of adoption, (7) the document of the daughter's dowry, (8) the purchase of a slave in common. Some of these are actually in existence.

ilu they grant nothing of the estate in Borsippa, which in lieu of
her dowry had been transferred to Bunanit, nor Nebo-nûr-ili,
whom she and her husband had bought, nor any of the property
of Apil-addunadin. They confirmed the documents of Bunanit
and Apil-adduamara. The sum of two and one half manas of
silver is to be returned forthwith to Iddin-Marduk who had advanced it for the sale of the house. Then Bunanit is to receive
three and one half manas of silver—her dowry—and a share of
the estate. Nebo-nûr-ili is given to Nubta in accordance with
the agreement of her father.[1]

The names of the six judges through whom the said
decision was rendered are then given, followed by the
names of two scribes and the date

Babylon, 26th of Ulul (6th month), 9th year of Nabonnedos, king
of Babylon.[2]

The balance of the estate evidently passed over
to the adopted son. Bunanit won her case against
her brother-in-law, but it looks on the surface as
though she had not won all that she had claimed.
The judges practically ignored the transfer of the
entire estate to her, for they granted her merely her
dowry and the share of her husband's property to
which as widow she was entitled. Had there not
been an adopted son, the claim of Aḳabi-ilu would
probably have been upheld for the balance of the
estate, exclusive of the slave. Bunanit is obliged to
confess that her husband transferred the property

[1] Evidently one of the documents before the court revealed
this stipulation of the deceased Apil-addunadin.

[2] Corresponding to 546 B. C.

"of his own accord," which means that it was not upon an order of the court, and therefore not legally established. It is safe to assume that the court would not have regarded such a transaction as legal, for despite the fact that the pair do not adopt a son until after the transfer, the judges allowed the widow her dowry only and her share of the estate. On the other hand, though it might appear that, as a partner, Bunanit would only have been responsible for one half of the amount borrowed from Iddin-Marduk, the judges, by ignoring the transfer, could order that Iddin-Marduk must be paid in full out of the property left by Apil-addunadin.

VI

The kings themselves, although not actuated, perhaps, by the highest motives, set the example of obedience to laws that involved the recognition of the rights of others. From a most ancient period there is come down to us a remarkable monument recording the conveyance of large tracts of land in northern Babylonia to a king of Kish, Manishtusu,[1] (*ca.* 2700 B.C.), on which hundreds of names are recorded from whom the land was purchased, with specific descriptions of the tracts belonging to each one, as well as the conditions of sale. The king here

[1] See on this ruler, King, *History of Sumer and Akkad*, pp. 206 *seq.*

appears with rights no more exclusive or predominant than those of a private citizen. Not only does he give full compensation to each owner, but undertakes to find occupation and means of support for fifteen hundred and sixty-four labourers and eighty-seven overseers, who had been affected by the transfer.

The numerous boundary stones that are come down to us (recording sales of fields or granting privileges), which were set up as memorials of transactions, are silent but eloquent witnesses to the respect for private property. The inscriptions on these stones conclude with dire curses in the names of the gods against those who should set up false claims, or who should alter the wording of the agreement, or in any way interfere with the terms thereon recorded. The symbols of the gods[1] were engraved on these boundary stones as a precaution and a protection to those whose rights and privileges the stone recorded. The Babylonians could well re-echo the denunciations of the Hebrew prophets against those who removed the boundaries of their neighbours' fields. Even those Assyrian monarchs most given to conquest and plunder boast, in their annals, of having

---

[1] On these symbols, see Hinke, *A New Boundary Stone of Nebuchadnezzar I.*, pp. 71–115, whose work is also to be recommended as the best general treatise on the *Kudurru* (or boundary stone) monuments and inscriptions. See the illustrations on Plate 22.

restored property to the rightful owners, and of having respected the privileges of their subjects and dependents. For instance, Sargon of Assyria (721–705 B.C.), while parading his conquests in vain-glorious terms, and proclaiming his unrivalled prowess, emphasises[1] the fact that he maintained the privileges of the great centres of the south, Sippar, Nippur, and Babylon, and that he protected the weak and righted their injuries. His successor Sennacherib[2] claims to be the guardian of justice and a lover of righteousness. Yet, these are the very same monarchs who treated their enemies with unspeakable cruelty, inflicting tortures on prisoners, violating women, mutilating corpses, burning and pillaging towns.

More significant still is the attitude of a monarch like Hammurapi, who, in the prologue and epilogue to his famous Code, refers to himself as a "king of righteousness," actuated by a lofty desire to protect the weak, the widow, and the orphan. In setting up copies of this Code in the important centres of his realm, his hope is that all may realise that he, Hammurapi, tried to be a "father" to his people. He calls upon all who have a just cause to bring it before the courts, and gives them the assurance that justice will

[1] Rawlinson, I., Plate 36, 4 (Schrader, *Keilinschriftliche Bibliothek*, ii., p. 41. See also p. 77).

[2] Rawlinson, I., Plate 37, col. i., 4 (Schrader *l.c.*, p. 83).

be dispensed,—all this as early as nigh four thousand years ago!

On a tablet[1] commemorative of the privileges accorded to Sippar, Nippur, and Babylon—to which, we have just seen, Sargon refers in his annals—there are grouped together, in the introduction, a series of warnings, which may be taken as general illustrations of the principles by which rulers were supposed to be guided:

If the king does not heed the law, his people will be destroyed; his power will pass away.

If he does not heed the law of his land, Ea, the king of destinies, will judge his fate and cast him to one side.

If he does not heed his *abkallu*,[2] his days will be shortened.

If he does not heed the priestess [?], his land will rebel against him.

If he gives heed to the wicked, confusion will set in.

If he gives heed to the counsels of Ea, the great gods will aid him in righteous decrees and decisions.

If he oppresses a man of Sippar and perverts justice, Shamash, the judge of heaven and earth, will annul the law in his land, so that there will be neither *abkallu* nor judge to render justice.

If the Nippurians are brought before him for judgment, and he oppresses them with a heavy hand, Enlil, the lord of lands, will cause him to be dispatched by a foe and his army to be overthrown; chief and general will be humiliated and driven off.

If he causes the treasury of the Babylonians to be entered for looting, if he annuls and reverses the suits of the Babylonians, then Marduk, the lord of heaven and earth, will bring his enemy against him, and will turn over to his enemy his property and possessions.

---

[1] *Cuneiform Texts, etc.*, Part XV., Plate 50.

[2] A high priestly dignitary who communicates the will of the gods to the people.

If he unjustly orders a man of Nippur, Sippar, or Babylon to be cast into prison, the city where the injustice has been done, will be made desolate, and a strong enemy will invade the prison into which he has been cast.

In this strain the text proceeds; and while the reference is limited to the three cities, the obligations imposed upon the rulers to respect privileges once granted may be taken as a general indication of the standards everywhere prevailing. We must not fail, however, to recognise the limitation of the ethical spirit, manifest in the threatened punishments, should the ruler fail to act according to the dictates of justice and right. For all this, whether it was from fear of punishment, or desire to secure the favour of the gods, the example of their rulers in following the paths of equity and in avoiding tyranny and oppression must have reacted on their subjects, and incited them to conform their lives to equally high standards.

There is extant a text—unfortunately preserved only in part—which, somewhat after the manner of the Biblical "Book of Proverbs," lays down certain moral precepts that were intended to be of general application. That it is a fragment, and an Assyrian copy of an older text, suggests an inference that there may have been similar and even more extensive collections; and, perhaps, some fortunate chance will bring to light more texts among the archives of

Babylonian temples, from which the texts of Ashurbanapal's library were for the most part copied.[1]
The fragment, which may be taken as a fair example
of the ethical teachings prescribed by the priests,
reads as follows:[2]

Thou shalt not slander—speak what is pure!
Thou shalt not speak evil—speak kindly!
He who slanders (and) speaks evil,
Shamash[3] will visit recompense on his head.
Let not thy mouth boast—guard thy lip!
When thou art angry, do not speak at once!
If thou speakest in anger, thou wilt repent afterwards,
And in silence sadden thy mind.
Daily approach thy god,
With offering and prayer as an excellent incense!
Before thy god (come) with a pure heart,
For that is proper towards the deity!
Prayer, petition, and prostration,
Early in the morning shalt thou render him;
And with god's help, thou wilt prosper.
In thy wisdom learn from the tablet.[4]
The fear (of god) begets favour,
Offering enriches life,
And prayer brings forgiveness of sin.
He who fears the gods, will not cry [in vain(?)].
He who fears the Anunnaki,[5] will lengthen [his days].
With friend and companion thou shalt not speak [evil (?)].

---

[1] See above, pp. 48 and 96.

[2] Published by K. D. Macmillan, "Some Cuneiform Tablets
Bearing on the Religion of Babylonia and Assyria," No. II., in
Beiträge zur Assyriologie, vol. v., pp. 557–562. See also *Cunei-
form Texts, etc.* Part XII., Plates 29, 30.

[3] The god of justice.

[4] We would say "learn from your books."

[5] The collective name for a lower order of gods.

Thou shalt not say low things, but (speak) kindness.
If thou promisest, give [what thou hast promised (?)].

.   .   .   .

Thou shalt not in tyranny oppress them,
For this his god will be angry with him;
It is not pleasing to Shamash—he will requite him with evil.
Give food to eat, wine to drink.
Seek what is right, avoid [what is wrong (?)].
For this is pleasing to his god;
It is pleasing to Shamash—he will requite him [with mercy].
Be helpful, be kind [to the servant(?)].
The maid in the house thou shalt [protect (?)].

Brief as the fragment is, it covers a large proportion of the relations of social life. The advice given
is largely practical, and the reward offered is ever of
this world—long life, happiness, freedom from misfortune—while errors, be they moral or ritualistic,
bring their own punishment with them. The ethics
taught is not of a kind to carry us upward into higher
regions, and the nearest approach to a nobler touch
is in the inculcation of the proper attitude toward
the gods, and of kindness and mercy toward fellow-
men; but in spite of these obvious limitations, the
ethical standards in the precepts show that it was
considered, at least, the part of wisdom to maintain
a clean morality. Worldly wisdom takes the precedence throughout in popular maxims and say-
ings, and it is from this point of view that we
must consider such a text as the present one. Whole-
some teachings, even where the motives enjoined are

not of the highest, may yet point to sound moral foundations and indicate that the ethical sense has had its awakening.   A nobler height may be gained in course of time.

VII

The spirit of Hammurapi's Code further illustrates the ethical standards imposed alike upon rulers, priests, and people.   The business and legal documents of Babylonia and Assyria show that the laws, codified by the king, and representing the summary of legal procedures and legal decisions down to his day, were not only enforced but interpreted to the very letter.   To be sure, the Code embodies side by side enactments of older and later dates.   It contains examples of punishment by ordeal, as, *e.g.*, in the case of a culprit accused of witchcraft,[1] where the decision is relegated to the god of the stream into which the defendant is cast. If the god of the stream takes him unto himself, his guilt is established.   If the god by saving him declares his innocence, the plaintiff is put to death and his property forfeited for the benefit of the defendant, wrongfully accused.   The *lex talionis*—providing "eye for eye, bone for bone, and tooth for tooth"—also finds a place in the Code;[2] but in both the ordeal and in the *lex talionis*, it does not differ from the Penta-

[1] §§ 1, 2.   [2] §§ 196–200.

teuchal Codes, which, likewise compilations of earlier and later decrees, prescribe the ordeal[1] in the case for instance of the woman accused of adultery; and if it be maintained that the principle of "eye for eye and tooth for tooth" is set up in the Old Testament[2] merely as a basis for a compensation equal to the injury done, the same might hold good for the Hammurapi Code and with even greater justification, since the Code actually limits the *lex talionis* to the case of an injury done to one of equal rank, while in the case of one of inferior or superior rank, a fine is imposed, which suggests that the *lex talionis* as applied to one of equal rank has become merely a legal phrase to indicate that a return, equal to the value of an eye or a tooth to him who suffers the assault, is to be imposed. This, of course, is a mere supposition, but at all events the underlying principle is one of equal compensation, and in so far it is ethical in its nature. On the other hand, there can be no doubt that the original import of the *lex talionis*, among both Babylonians and Assyrians (as among the Hebrews), involved a literal interpretation, as may be concluded from the particularly harsh and inconsequent application to the case of the son of a builder, who is to be put to death should an edifice,

[1] Numbers v., 11-28.
[2] Ex. xi., 24 (Book of the Covenant); Deut. xix., 21 (Deuteronomic Code); Lev. xxiv., 20 (Code of Holiness).

Pl. 34. Code of Hammurapi, King of Babylonia (*c.* 1958–1916 B.C.).

Found in 1901 at Susa, whither it was carried as a trophy by the Elamites (see comment to Pl. 8 and 22) in one of their incursions into Babylonia. Fragments of a second copy have also been found. The code was originally set up in the temple of Marduk at Babylon. Copies were probably prepared and set up in other centres. At the top is a design representing Hammurapi in an attitude of adoration before Shamash, the sun-god, who as the god of justice and righteousness is the presiding genius of the king as law-giver, and from whom in their ultimate analysis the laws are derived.

The inscription, covering originally 44 columns, running around the stone and comprising over 3000 lines, is almost perfectly preserved. Forty-four columns, aggregating 2644 lines, are intact, while five columns (approximately 300 lines) have been intentionally erased, presumably to receive an inscription of the Elamite plunderer who proposed to perpetuate his vandalism by inscribing his name and titles on the polished portion. For some reason he failed to do so. Through fragments of late Assyrian copies in Ashurbanapal's Library parts of the missing columns can be restored. After an invocation to the gods and an enumeration of what he did to beautify and enlarge the sanctuaries in various parts of his extensive realm and to promote the well-being of his subjects, Hammurapi proceeds to enumerate the laws which may conveniently be divided into 282 paragraphs. The last three columns are taken up with a concluding statement on the part of the king of his career, emphasising his purpose in preparing the Code, and closing with the usual curses against any one who defaces or injures the monument or who alters any of its decrees. The stone is a block of diorite nearly 8 ft. high. See Scheil, *Délégation en Perse, Mémoires*, vol. iv., pp. 11–162.

Code of Hammurapi
King of Babylonia
(*c.* 1958–1916 B. C.)

erected by his father, fall and kill the son of the owner.[1]

Another unfavourable feature of the Code, which illustrates the limitations of ethical principles, lies in the extreme severity of many of its punishments. The penalty of death is imposed for about fifty offences, some of them comparatively trivial, such as stealing temple or royal property,[2] where, however, the element of sacrilege enters into consideration. Even the claimant of a property, alleged to have been purchased from a man's son or servant, or of a member of the higher class, who is unable to show the contract, is held to be a thief, because of the fraudulent intent, and is put to death.[3] The law is, however, fair in its application, and punishes with equal severity, when there is a fraudulent attempt to deprive one of legally acquired property. He who aids a runaway slave is placed in the same category[4] as he who steals a minor son,[5] or as he who conspires to take property away from his neighbour, and is put to death for the fraudulent attempt. A plunderer at a fire is himself thrown into that fire,[6] and he who has broken into a man's house is immured in the breach that he himself has made.[7] In cases of assault and battery, a distinction is drawn according to the rank

[1] § 230. If the fall of the edifice kills the owner, then the builder is put to death (§ 229). Other examples below.
[2] § 6. [3] §§ 7, 8. [4] § 15. [5] § 14. [6] § 25. [7] § 21.

of the assailant and the assailed. If a person of
lower rank attacks a person of higher rank, the punishment is a public whipping of sixty lashes with a
leather thong,[1] whereas if the one attacked is of equal
rank, the whipping is remitted, but a heavy fine—
one mana of silver[2]—is imposed. If a slave commits
this offence, and the victim is of high rank, the slave's
ear is cut off [3] At the same time, an ethical spirit is
revealed in the stipulation that, if the injury be inflicted in a chance-medley, and the blow not intentionally aimed at any particular person, the offender
is discharged with the obligation to pay the doctor's
bill,[4] or, in the event of the death of the victim, with a
fine according to the rank of the deceased.[5] A lower
level of equity is, however, represented by the enactments that, in case a man strikes a pregnant woman
and the woman dies, a daughter of the offender is
put to death,[6] or in case a surgical operation on the
eye is not successful, and the patient loses his eye,
the surgeon's hand is to be cut off,[7] or in the
event of the death of a slave under an operation,
the surgeon must reimburse the owner by giving him
another slave.[8]

All such laws are variations of the *lex talionis*, and
unquestionably reflect a primitive form of social organisation, where advanced ethical principles are not

[1] § 202.   [2] § 203.   1 mana = 60 shekels.   [3] § 205.   [4] § 206.
[5] § 207–208.   [6] § 210.   [7] § 218.   [8] § 219.

to be expected. They must be regarded in the same light as many of the enactments in the Pentateuchal Codes and in other collections of ancient laws— as survivals indeed of even earlier regulations which, having been once accepted, were faithfully incorporated in the compilation made by Hammurapi, whereof the aim clearly was to furnish a *complete* survey of regulations for the execution of justice.

These crude statutes, therefore, constitute a valuable testimony to the process of development which led to the higher conditions that characterise the Code in general. This superior level is reached, *e.g.*, in the provision that a judge who has rendered a wrong decision is to pay a fine twelve-fold the amount involved in the suit; and in addition, he is to be removed from the bench and never again to be permitted to exercise the judicial function.[1] This regulation recognises a fundamental principle of justice that he who dispenses it must be beyond suspicion, and must be familiar also with the law to be administered. No distinction is made between a judicial error due to ignorance, and one due to improper motives on the part of the judge. He is not to change his mind, and it is assumed that if he has made an unintentional error, he has shown himself to be as unfit as though the erroneous decision had been prompted by maliciousness or a wilful disregard of justice.

[1] § 5. See above, p. 276.

The judge stands in the place of deity according to the general view prevailing in antiquity. If he fail in the proper discharge of his duties, he lowers the dignity of his office; and the deity, by permitting him to go astray, shows that he no longer desires the judge to speak in his name. Confidence in the probity and ability of the judge is the *conditio sine quâ non* of the execution of justice. Defective as this uncompromising attitude toward a judicial error may be from a modern standpoint in not recognising an appeal from a lower to a higher court, the ethical basis is both sound and of a high order. With such a provision, which speaks volumes for the standards obtaining in the days of Hammurapi, the integrity of the courts was firmly secured for all time. Equally noteworthy and more modern in its spirit is the provision that a false witness, whose testimony jeopardises the life of another, shall be put to death.[1] One is reminded of the Venetian law quoted by Portia that the life of him who places a citizen in jeopardy "lies in the mercy of the Duke only, 'gainst all other voice."[2] If the false testimony involves property, the false witness must pay the amount involved in the suit.

Passing to more specific subjects, the regulation of family affairs and of commerce may be regarded as a safe index of the standards set up for private and

[1] § 3. [2] *Merchant of Venice*, Act IV., Scene 1, ll. 350–51.

public ethics. No less than sixty-eight[1] of the two hundred and seventy-two paragraphs or sections into which the Code may be divided, or just one fourth, deal on the one hand with the relation of husband and wife, and on the other of parents and children. This proportion is in itself a valuable indication of the importance in the social organisation attached to the family. The general aim of the laws may be summed up in the statement that they are to ensure the purity of family life. The law is severe against the faithless wife—mercilessly severe, condemning her and the adulterer to death by drowning,[2] but it also protects her against false accusations. He who unjustly points the finger of suspicion against a woman—be she a wife, or a virgin who has taken a vow of chastity—is to be publicly humiliated by having his forehead branded.[3] Even the husband must substantiate the charge against his wife, and the wife can free herself from suspicion by an oath,[4] though, if the actual charge is brought by another than her husband, she must submit, at the husband's instance, to the same ordeal of the river god[5] as the one accused of witchcraft. But even if the charge be substantiated, the husband may exercise the right of possession and allow his wife to live; and the king also may grant mercy to the male offender.[6]

As a protection to the wife, a formal marriage con-

[1] §§ 127–194. [2] § 129. [3] § 127. [4] § 131. [5] § 132. [6] § 129.

tract must be drawn up, as is not infrequent in our days. A marriage without a contract is void.[1] A woman betrothed to a man is regarded as his wife, and in case she is disgraced by another, the offender is put to death;[2] from which we may perhaps be permitted to conclude that if she be not betrothed, the offender is obliged to marry her. The Code still recognises the wife as an actual possession of her husband, but, on the other hand, if he fails to provide for her support, she may leave him. A fine distinction is made between actual desertion or enforced absence on the part of the husband. In the former case,[3] the woman has the right to marry another, and her husband on his return not only cannot force her to return to him, but she is not permitted to do so. On the other hand, if her husband is taken prisoner and no provision has been made for her sustenance, she may marry another, but on her husband's return he may claim her, though the children born in the interim belong to the actual father.[4]

Inasmuch as the wife forms part of her husband's chattels, divorce lies, of course, at the option of the husband, but he cannot sell his wife, and, if he dismisses her, she is to receive again her marriage portion. Alimony was allowed for her own needs and those of her children, whose rearing was committed to her.[5] When the children reach their majority, a

[1] § 128.   [2] § 130.   [3] § 136.   [4] § 135.   [5] § 137.

portion of their inheritance must be given to the mother. Even in the case of a wife who has not borne her husband any children, he may not dismiss her without giving her alimony and returning her dowry,[1] but if she has neglected her husband's household, and as the law expresses it, has committed "indiscretions," he may send her away without any compensation or may even keep her as a slave, while he is free to marry another woman as his chief wife.[2] The dawning at least of the wife's liberty is to be seen in the provision that, if a woman desires to be rid of her husband, and provided on examination it is shown that she has good cause—the legal language implies a neglect of marital duties on the husband's part,—she may return to her father's house, and be entitled to her marriage portion.[3]

The prevailing custom in Babylonia at the time of Hammurapi was monogamy, but it was still permissible, as a survival of former conditions, for a man to take a concubine, or the wife could give her husband a handmaid[4]—as Sarah gave Hagar to Abraham (Genesis xvi., 1, 2), in order that he might have children by her. The Code endeavours, while recognising conditions that are far from ideal, so to regulate these conditions as to afford protection to the legitimate wife. It is provided that, in case the maid-servant has borne children, the husband

[1] § 138.   [2] § 141.   [3] § 142.   [4] § 144.

may not take an additional concubine.[1] It would, furthermore, appear that a second wife may be taken into the home only in the event that the marriage with the first spouse is without issue.[2] Even then, the first wife is protected by the express stipulation that she shall retain her place at the head of her husband's household. The manifest purpose of such regulations is to pave the way for passing beyond former crude conditions, such for example as are described in Genesis as existing in Hebrew society in the days of the patriarchs. Old laws are rarely abrogated—they are generally so modified as to lose their original force. Perhaps the most significant of these marriage-laws is the stipulation that the woman who is smitten with an incurable disease—the term used may have reference to leprosy—must be taken care of by her husband as long as she lives. In no circumstances, it is added, can he divorce her, and if she prefer to return to her father's home, he must give her dowry to her.[3]

Legal rights are assured to a woman even after her husband's death. Her children have no claim on property given to her by her husband. She may dispose of such property to a favourite child but, on the other hand, she is restrained from passing it on to her brother, which would take it out of her husband's clan.[4] Finally, there is a touch almost modern in

[1] § 144.　[2] § 145.　[3] §§ 148, 149.　[4] § 150.

the law that a wife cannot contract obligations in her husband's name, nor can he be held responsible for debts thus contracted.[1] The interesting feature of the provision is that it points to the independent legal status acquired by woman, who, as we learn also from business and legal documents, could own property in her own right, borrow money and contract debts independently, as long as she did not involve her husband's property, and could appear as a witness in the courts. The dowry of a wife who dies without issue reverts to her father's estate.[2]

That the laws against incest are most severe is perhaps not to be taken as an index of advanced moral standards, for we find such regulations even in primitive society where, while promiscuous intercourse with unmarried women is permitted, the severe *taboo* imposed upon a wife[3] is extended to every kind of incestuous relations. The Hammurapi Code ordains that a father who has been intimate with his daughter is to be banished from the city,[4] which means that he loses his position and rights of citizenship. If he enters into intimate relations with his daughter-in-law, he is to be strangled, and the woman is to be thrown into the water.[5] If this take place

[1] § 151.

[2] § 163—but the purchase money, given to the father-in-law at the time of marriage, shall be returned to the husband.

[3] See Frazer, *Psyche's Task*, pp. 30 *seq.*

[4] § 154.   [5] § 155.

26

after betrothal but before the actual marriage, the father is let off with a heavy fine and the woman may marry whom she pleases.[1] When a son is intimate with his mother, both are burned.[2]

It also betokens an advanced stage of society that a man can legitimatise the children born of his wife's handmaid, and they then receive equal portions of the estate with the children of the legitimate wife;[3] but even if he fail to legitimatise such children, they must be set free after his death. The legitimate children have no claim upon their half-brothers and half-sisters born out of wedlock.[4] Not only the wife but also the widow is amply protected by the Code, through the stipulation that a share of her husband's estate belongs to her in her own right and name. She is to remain in her husband's house, and if the children maltreat her, the courts may impose punishment upon them. If, however, of her own accord the widow leaves her husband's house, then she is naturally entitled to her own dowry only, and not to any share in her husband's estate; but, on the other hand, she is free in that case to marry whomsoever she pleases.[5] Daughters are given a share in their father's estate, and this is extended even to those who as priestesses have taken the vow of chastity. Such nuns have a right to their dowry, which they can dispose of as they see fit, but their share of the paternal

[1] § 156.   [2] § 157.   [3] § 170.   [4] § 171.   [5] § 172.

estate cannot be disposed of by them.   On the death of
a nun, her share reverts to her brothers or to their heirs.[1]

Lastly, as an interesting example of an older law,
dating from the period when a man could dispose of
his wife and children as he disposed of his chattels and
possessions, but so modified as to be practically
abrogated, we may instance the provision that, if a
man pledges, or actually sells his wife and children
for his debts, the creditor can claim them for three
years only.   In the fourth year they must be set
free.[2]   This stipulation assumes an older law, according to which a man could sell his wife and children
without condition.   Instead of revoking the law
(which, as has been pointed out, is not the usual mode
of procedure in ancient legislation), the limitation of
three years is inserted, and this changes the sale into
a lease.   We have a parallel in the Book of the Covenant (Exodus xxi., 2) which provides that a Hebrew
slave must be set free after six years.   This is practically an abrogation of slavery[3] by converting it
into a lease for a limited period.

Coming to the commercial regulations of the Code,
the fundamental principle underlying them is the
fixing of responsibility where it belongs, and the protecting of both parties to a transaction not only
against fraud on either side, but also against unfore-

[1] § 178.   [2] § 117.
[3] Though the provision applies to Hebrew slaves only.

seen circumstances. It is somewhat significant that, although many of the laws deal with cases of wilful fraud or deceit in one party, the general assumption is that both parties are actuated by honest motives, and that difficulties often arise through no fault of either, being due to the growing complications of business activities. As a protection to buyer and seller or to any two contracting parties, it is stipulated that there must be a written contract in the presence of witnesses. No claim can be made unless a contract can be found, and the assumption is that failure to produce witnesses in case of a claim is proof of attempted fraud. An interesting case is mentioned in a series of paragraphs,[1] of one who asserts that he has lost an article belonging to him, which he finds in the possession of another, which, however, the latter maintains that he has bought. The point is to find the guilty party. The purchaser must bring into court the vendor and witnesses to the sale, and he who claims the property must bring witnesses to establish his claim. If both sets of witnesses appear and their testimony is shown to be true, the vendor of the property adjudged to be lost is revealed as the thief and is put to death, this severer punishment being inflicted because the aggravating factor of fraud is added to theft. The article is restored to the lawful owner, and the innocent purchaser is com-

[1] §§ 9–13.

pensated out of the estate of the thief and fraudulent vendor. If the purchaser fail to produce the vendor and witnesses to the sale, and the claimant brings witnesses to prove his property, then the purchaser is put to death as the real thief, and the stolen article is restored to its lawful owner. If, on the other hand, the claimant cannot bring witnesses to prove his property, then he is considered to have made a fraudulent claim, and suffers the penalty of death. If the vendor—prove to be such—has meanwhile died, the amount is nevertheless to be restored to the purchaser out of the estate of the vendor. Finally, the law allows a term of six months within which to produce the witnesses in case they are not at once accessible.

The farming of lands for the benefit of temples or for lay owners, with a return of a share of the products to the proprietors, was naturally one of the most common commercial transactions in a country like the Euphrates Valley, so largely dependent upon agriculture. Complications in such transactions would naturally ensue, and it is interesting to observe with what regard for the ethics of the situation they are dealt with in the Code. If a tenant fail to produce a crop through his own fault, he is obliged, of course, to reimburse the proprietor, and as a basis of compensation, the yield of the adjoining fields is taken as a standard.[1] If he have failed, however, to

[1] § 42.

cultivate the field, he is not only obliged to compensate the owner according to the proportionate amount produced in that year in adjoining fields, but must, in addition, plough and harrow the property before returning it to the owner, besides furnishing ten measures—about twenty bushels—of grain for each acre of land.[1] In case of a failure of the crops, or a destruction by act of God, no responsibility attaches to the tenant,[2] but if the owner had already received his share beforehand, and then through a storm or an inundation the yield is spoiled, the loss must be borne by the tenant.[3] In subletting the tilling of fields as part payment for debt, it is stipulated that the original proprietor must first be settled with, and after that the second lessee, who shall receive in kind the amount of his debts plus the usual interest[4]. The ethical principle is, therefore, similar to that applying in our own days to first and second mortgages. The owner of a field is responsible for damage done to his neighbours' property through neglect on his part—for example, through his failure to keep the dikes in order, or through his cutting off the water supply from his neighbour.[5] A shepherd who allows his flocks to pasture in a field without permission of the owner is fined to the extent of twenty measures of grain for each ten acres. What is left of the pasturage also belongs to the owner.[6]

[1] §§ 43, 44. [2] § 48. [3] § 45. [4] § 49. [5] §§ 53–56. [6] § 57.

The same care, with due regard to the ethics of the situation, is exercised in regulating the relation between a merchant and his agent. The latter is, of course, responsible for goods entrusted to him, including damage to them through his fault, but if they are stolen or forcibly taken from him—after swearing an oath to that effect—he is free from further responsibility.[1] Neglect to carry out instructions in connection with a commission entails a fine threefold the value involved,[2] but, on the other hand, if the merchant tries to defraud his agent, he pays a fine of sixfold the amount involved.[3] According to the ethical principles governing the Code, the directors of a bank would be responsible to the depositors for losses incurred through the business transactions of the bank. The protection of the debtor in business transactions against the tyranny of the creditor is carried almost to an extreme; it would appear that the creditor cannot attach the property of his debtor without obtaining the authority of the court; and if, e. g., he has helped himself from the granary of the debtor without the latter's permission, although he may not have taken more than the amount of the debt, he must return what he has taken, and by his wilful act forfeits his original claim.[4] The courts[5] regulated the hire of cattle for ploughing or other purposes, the wages of mechanics and labourers, the hire

[1] § 103.   [2] § 106.   [3] § 107.   [4] § 113.   [5] §§ 257–277.

of ships for freight, the amount of the return for the farming of fields, and even the fee of surgeons for operations[1]—all with a view to affording protection against both extortion and underpayment.

VIII

There is, of course, also another side to the picture. The internal conditions of Babylonia and Assyria were at all times, naturally, far from ideal. The people, as a whole, had no share in the government, and, as we have seen, only a limited share in the religious cult, which was largely official and centred around the general welfare and the well-being of the king and his court. Slavery continued in force to the latest days, and, though slaves could buy their freedom and could be adopted by their masters, and had many privileges, even to the extent of owning property and engaging in commercial transactions, yet the moral effect of the institution in degrading the dignity of human life, and in maintaining unjust class distinctions was none the less apparent then than it has been ever since. The temples had large holdings which gave to the religious organisation of the country a materialistic aspect, and granted the priests an undue influence. Political power and official prestige were permanently vested in the rulers and their families and attendants. We hear, occasionally, of

[1] §§ 215–217; 221–225.

persons of humble birth rising to high positions, but the division of the classes into higher and those of lower ranks was on the whole rigid. Uprisings were not infrequent both in Babylonia and Assyria, and internal dissensions, followed by serious disturbances, revealed the dissatisfaction of the majority with the yoke imposed upon them, which, especially through enforced military service and through taxes for the maintenance of temples, armies, and the royal court, must often have borne heavily on them. The cruelties, practised especially by the Assyrian rulers in times of war, must also have reacted unfavourably on the general moral tone of the population.

But such conditions prevailed everywhere in antiquity; nor would it be difficult to parallel them in much later ages, and even among some of the leading nations of modern times. The general verdict in regard to the ethics of the Babylonians and Assyrians need not, therefore, be altered because of the shadows that fall on the picture that has been unrolled. A country that offers protection to all classes of its population, that imposes responsibilities upon husbands and fathers, and sees to it that those responsibilities are not evaded, that protects its women and children, that in short, as Hammurapi aptly puts it, aims to secure the weak against the tyranny of the strong and to mete justice to all alike, may fairly be classed among civilisations which, however short they may fall of the ideal commonwealth, yet recognise obedience to ethical principles as the basis of well-being, of true culture, and of genuine religion.

And yet how harsh is the judgment passed by the Hebrew prophets and psalmists on both Babylonia and Assyria! Prophet and religious poet unite in accusing them of the most terrible crimes; they exhaust the Hebrew vocabulary in pronouncing curses upon Assyria and Babylonia. All nature is represented as rejoicing at their downfall, and it has often been remarked that the prediction that jackals and hyenas would wander through the ruins of Assyria's palaces and Babylonia's temples has been fulfilled almost to the letter. The pious Jews of later ages saw the divine punishment sent for the many crimes of these empires of the East, in the obliteration of the vast cities of the Euphrates Valley and the region to the north, until their very foundation stones were forgotten.[1]

It was natural that to the Hebrew patriots Assyria and Babylonia should appear to be the embodiment of all evils; was it not through Assyria that Israel fell, and through Babylonia that Jerusalem was destroyed? Through the double blow the national life of the Jews was threatened with utter extinction.

[1] Xenophon actually passes by the spot on which Nineveh stood without knowing it.

Both empires, therefore, appeared to the Jews as incarnations of all that was evil and cruel and sinful.

Assyria *was* cruel toward her foes and, if Babylonia has a gentler record, it is because she never so greatly developed military prowess as did her northern cousin. Cruelty to enemies is indeed the darkest blot on the escutcheon of all nations, ancient or modern. The Hebrews are no exception, and one need only read the pages of their own chronicles to match therein some of the cruelties so vividly depicted by the Assyrians on their monuments. To judge fairly of the ethics of any people, we must take them at their best. War for conquest, while it may lead to heroic exploits, unfolds the worst passions of men. This has always been the case and always will be. The conqueror is always haughty and generally merciless, the conquered are always embittered and filled with hatred towards those who have humiliated them. Tested by their attitude towards rivals and foes, what modern nation can stand the judgment of an Isaiah or a Jeremiah? The culture that developed in the Euphrates Valley is full of defects, its ethics one deficient, the religion full of superstition. Assyria exhausted her vitality by ceaseless warring; Babylonia fell into decay through internal dissensions and through intrigues against her rival. The pages of the annals of both nations are full of abhorrent stains, but maugre all drawbacks, the tendency of culture, religion, and ethics was toward higher ideals; the movement was in the right direction.

Many-sided may be the touchstones of progress. Perhaps sharpest is respect for human life. Herein modern civilisations represent, and naturally, an advance beyond antiquity. We are become more humane, though the lowest instincts of man remain, and may always remain unconquered. None the less, the ancient civilisations, and not the least among them that which arose in the Euphrates Valley and spread its influence far and wide, have much to teach us. To the study of the religion of Babylonia and Assyria the summons is full of promise:—*introite, nam et hic dii sunt*. Ay, so indeed they are! The breath of the Divine sighs through that religion —as it does through all sincere religions, however various their forms, or humble and manifold their yearnings after truth.

IX

The mention of the Hebrew prophets and psalmists suggests a final question to which a brief answer may be presented in a general survey of some of the more striking elements of the religion of Babylonia and Assyria. To what extent do those elements stand related to the religion of the Hebrews? What are the influences, if any, of Babylonian and Assyrian beliefs and practices on those developed in Palestine during the centuries of Hebrew supremacy?

A vigorous school of thought has recently arisen in Germany,[1] which maintains that the civilisation of the Euphrates Valley has coloured the beliefs and practices of all antiquity—including those which we have been accustomed to regard as distinctively Hebraic contributions to the world's intellectual and spiritual life.   There is a tendency to trace a majority of the Hebrew traditions to Babylonian-Assyrian sources, to see in the myths of Genesis, in the legends of the patriarchs, and even in the accounts of historical personages in the Old Testament, the reflections of

[1] The founder and leader of the school is the distinguished and brilliant Prof. Hugo Winckler, who has set forth his views in numerous publications. Winckler has found in Dr. Alfred Jeremias his strongest and ablest ally, and in addition there are many other followers. As an outcome of the movement, a society for the comparative study of mythology has been founded in Germany which, in its publications under the general title of *Mythologische Bibliothek*, applies the method of Winckler-Jeremias to the myths and folk-tales of all nations; and while not directly stated, it is implied in all these special studies of particular stories that the astral character revealed in them originated in the astral-mythological system that had its rise in the Euphrates Valley. By "astral-mythology," the school means that all myths involve the personification of the heavenly bodies—chiefly sun, moon, and Venus—and that the explanation of all myths is to be sought in the phenomena of the heavens. For a criticism of the school, and indications of the chief literature on the subject see the present writer's Presidential Address before the Third International Congress for the History of Religions (Semitic Section), *Transactions*, i., p. 233 *seq.*

an astral-mythology and an astral-theology which were developed in the priestly schools of the Euphrates Valley.

At this late day it is no longer possible to question the kinship between certain elements of the Old Testament and what we find in the religion of Babylonia and Assyria, and yet it is difficult to resist the conviction that its closeness has been exaggerated.

It was natural and excusable in the first glow of enthusiasm over striking discoveries that their importance should be both overestimated and overstated. Tempting generalisations were hastily drawn of a direct borrowing by the younger civilisation from the older; and as more and more resemblances between the two were revealed, this discovery involved the originality of the later Hebrew civilisation to such an extent that there seemed to be little left that had not been taken from Babylonia or Assyria.

The thesis suggested by a more critical examination of the abundant material now at hand is that resemblances in myths and traditions are frequently as deceptive as resemblances in the words of different languages. Unless we have a tolerably complete chain of evidence of a direct borrowing and can also show that it proceeded according to certain principles, there is, at least, an equal probability for the existence of a common source, from which traditions may have spread in various directions—a supposition that has the advantage, moreover, of accounting satisfactorily for the *differences* among the traditions, as well as for their similarities.

That there is a stock of tradition common to both Hebrews and Babylonian-Assyrians is evident. The resemblances, for instance, between the Biblical tales of Creation and of the Flood, on the one hand, and the Babylonian-Assyrian myths, on the other, are too close to be accidental; and likewise in the beliefs and practices of the ancient Hebrews there are many analogies to those of Babylonia and Assyria. Some of these we have had occasion to point out,[1] and they can best be accounted for through the assumption of a common starting-point, while in other cases, to be sure, the analogies clearly point to a direct borrowing by the Hebrews. However, the contrasts between the two lines of religious development, as betrayed by the forms assumed by these traditions, beliefs, and practices, are no less striking. Even in the Biblical stories of the Creation and of the Flood, the significant feature is the minimising of the mythical element, whereas in those of Babylonia and Assyria myth is always in the foreground. Instead of a conflict between primeval chaos and the gods, representative of law and order, we have in Genesis the spirit of Elohîm breathing upon the waters. In-

[1] See above, pp. 72 *seq.*, 90, note 1, 266, 275, 284, note 1, 290, 332, 364, etc.

stead of a sun-god of the spring triumphing over the storms of winter, we have the conception of a mysterious Power behind and above creation, bringing the world and all the phenomena of nature into being by the majesty of his word. The divine fiat, "Let there be light," lifts the ancient myth out of the sphere in which it arose to the dignity of a sublime pæon in praise of a supermundane Creator. The language is still anthropomorphic, but the thought rises to the spiritual heights attained by the best of the Hebrew prophets, and evoked the praise of even the Latin critic, Longinus.

No less striking in the form assumed by the Biblical traditions is the ethical strain that diffuses through them, as salt is diffused through the waters of the sea. In this respect, likewise, they present a noteworthy contrast to the myths and legends of Babylonia and Assyria. Ut-Napishtim is saved from the general destruction merely because he is a favourite of Ea. Noah is singled out because of his superior merits. The Babylonian deluge remains on the level of the original foundation of myth—it is simply another aspect of the change of seasons from the dry summer to the stormy and rainy winter; in the Biblical story the setting is the same, but the tone is entirely changed by the fact that the storm which overwhelms mankind is sent as a punishment for sin and widespread corruption. In the same way, into the stories of the patriarchs—a mixture of legend and myth—an ethical spirit has been transfused that appears at its strongest in the prophets and in the best of the psalms.

In the same way also, the entire history of the nation is told from the standpoint of that ethical monotheism which represents the sublimest attainment of Hebrew aspiration. The ancient and later codes, combining the legal and religious practices of various periods, are welded into a fictitious unity by the conception that behind the laws stands a divine Lawgiver, governing the universe by self-imposed standards of justice, harmoniously blended with divine mercy and sympathy for the weakness of human nature. The kernel and true meaning of the monotheistic conception of the universe, as unfolded by the prophets, is lost by any endeavour to place the conception on a level with the monotheistic strain that is vaguely but unquestionably present in the speculations of the Babylonian-Assyrian priests.[1] Monotheism, in itself, is not specifically religious, but rather the outcome of philosophic thought—not necessarily even of a high order of thought, for even among people standing on a comparatively inferior level, we find faint suggestions of such a view of the government of the universe. Monotheism becomes religious only through the infusion of the ethical spirit. For the first time, in this combination, it

[1] See above, pp. 38 and 103.

makes its appearance in Hebrew history during the centuries which produced an Amos, a Hosea, a Micah, an Isaiah, and a Jeremiah—whose teachings may be summed up in the assertion that the government of the universe is an expression of the sovereignty of ethics. The question whether the assertion be true or not is irrelevant, but as it stands, it presents the line of demarcation that separates the later form assumed by the religion of the Hebrews, from other and earlier forms.

The exalted level attained by the prophets was not always maintained even by the Jews, for Talmudic Judaism, which begins to assume definite shape in the century before the appearance of the great successor of the old prophets, represents a reaction, reinstating and perpetuating many religious customs and rites that are merely survivals of cruder conceptions—for the most part, in fact, old Semitic practices that are not even specifically Hebraic or Jewish. Christianity, too, vitiated the pure atmosphere in which Jesus moved, by degrading extravagances which entered it from various quarters, but, none the less, the new factor introduced into the religious history of mankind by the Hebrew prophets, was never entirely lost to sight; and it is not difficult to trace in some of the religious movements of our own days the continued influence of that factor.

CHRONOLOGICAL LISTS

THESE lists, intended merely as a guide to the reader, are based on recent historical researches associated chiefly with the names of Eduard Meyer, L. W. King, François Thureau-Dangin, Arthur Ungnad, and Arno Poebel, but despite the considerable progress made during the past few years, the chronology beyond 2000 B.C. is still uncertain, while beyond 2500 B.C. it is quite hypothetical.

The sources[1] for our study of Babylonian-Assyrian chronology are (1) the votive and historical inscriptions and monuments of rulers, to which (for the later Assyrian and for the Neo-Babylonian period) are to be added: (2) the historical annals of the kings; (3) the dates attached to the thousands of

[1] The most satisfactory discussion of these sources will be found in Meyer, *Geschichte des Altirtums*, I., 2, pp. 313–346. This work and King's *History of Babylonia and Assyria*—both in course of publication—are the two standard works on the history of the Euphratean civilisation, replacing the older histories of Tiele, Hommel, Winckler, etc., while Rogers's useful *History of Babylonia and Assyria* now requires revision in order to be brought up to date. A great deal of valuable material with learned discussions is embodied in Hommel's *Grundriss der Geographie und Geschichte des Alten Orients* (in course of publication), but unfortunately in combination with many theories and conjectures, which though often ingenious are frequently extremely hazardous. It should perhaps be added that Vol. I. of King's work, above referred to, is generally quoted by its separate title "History of Sumer and Akkad."

business and legal documents of the various periods; (4) the lists of kings for Babylonia, and lists of Eponyms for Assyria, prepared by official annalists to whom we also owe: (5) a number of chronicles for both Babylonia and Assyria. Unfortunately, these lists and chronicles have come down to us in a badly preserved condition, which has greatly complicated the task of scholars in determining the sequence of the many names of rulers of political centres and districts for the earlier periods, as secured from the votive inscriptions and from the dates attached to documents. Finally, (6) we have the lists of rulers in the fragments of Berosus (embodying a curious mixture of legendary and traditional lore) and the lists and historical references in other Greek writers which, as a matter of course, can now only be used in connection with the data from the monuments. Of special value, however, is the so-called Ptolemaic Canon which extends from the middle of the eighth century B.C. to the end of Babylonian-Assyrian history.

The eight epochal events in Babylonian-Assyrian history from the chronological point of view are (1) the establishment of the Empire of Sumer and Akkad under the control of the Semitic kings of Agade-Sargon and his son Naram-Sin—c. 2500 B.C., (2) the Sumerian reaction under the Ur dynasty (c. 2300–2200 B.C.), (3) the final triumph of the Semites and the union of the Euphratean states under Hamurapi (c. 2000 B.C.), (4) the definite advance of Assyria which may be dated from the advent of Tiglathpileser I. (c. 1125 B.C.), (5) Assyria's complete control of Babylonia, beginning about

the ninth century, B.C., (6) the fall of the Assyrian
Empire in 606 B.C., (7) the rise of the Neo-Babylonian Empire with Nabopolassar in 625 B.C., (8)
the conquest of Babylon by Cyrus in 539 B.C.

Previous to the days of Sargon and Naram-Sin,
we find now one centre, now another—like Lagash,
Uruk, Kish, Larsa, Ur, and Umma—extending its
control, and the ultimate union of the southern
(Sumerian) states is foreshadowed by rulers who
call themselves "King of Sumer." The union of
Sumer with Akkad (the designation of the northern
section of the Euphrates Valley which was the stronghold of the Semitic settlements) is thus a natural
consequence of this movement, brought about through
the steady advance of the Semites, despite the temporary Sumerian reaction represented by the Ur
dynasty.

As the most convenient method of furnishing an
historical survey, the rulers of the various centres,
so far as known to us, are here grouped in separate
lists, while beginning with the so-called first dynasty
of Babylon—for which we have as our basis a long
(though unfortunately fragmentary) list of rulers
with indications of the length of each reign—the
rulers are arranged in ten continuous groups according to the dynasties as indicated by the official
annalists.

In Assyria, we have only one political centre
Ashur, replaced for two short periods—in the four-
teenth century (C. 1330–1130 B.C.) and again in the
ninth century (C. 850 B.C.)—by Calah, and finally
yielding to Nineveh as the capital in the days of
Sargon and Sennacherib (722–681 B.C.). The names

of Assyrian rulers—in the earlier days known as
patesis, later as kings—may therefore be arranged
in one continuous list, nor is it practicable for our
purposes (even were it possible) to indicate the frequent changes of dynasties through the rise of usur-
pers. For the neo-Babylonian dynasty and for the
Persian rulers, the task is a simple one since the
data for these centuries are complete.

The lists for the period before the first dynasty
of Babylon are still very incomplete. It must be
borne in mind that there are only a few sites in Babylonia at which extensive excavations have been
conducted. Important mounds like Mukayyar (Ur),
Abu Shahrain (Eridu), Tell Ibrahim (Cuthah), El-
Ohemir (Kish) have not been touched, others like
Warka (Uruk), Senkerah (Larsa), Abu Hatab (Kisurra), Fara (Shuruppak), Jokha (Umma) have only
been partially explored, or merely scratched on the
surface. In part, however, the fact that only a few
rulers have been found of certain places is due to
other causes. So the circumstance that the extensive excavations at Nippur have yielded the names of
only a few *patesis* is to be accounted for through the
position of Nippur as a religious rather than as a
political centre (see pp. 18, 66, etc.), controlled for the
most part by rulers of other centres. No doubt
there were many more *patesis* at Nippur than these
two, but on the other hand the political independence
must have come to an end at a very early date.
The "foreign" rulers either regarded themselves
as the *patesis*, or the position had become a merely
nominal one, not carrying any real authority. Again,
in the case of sites not far removed from another,

like Kish and Opis, or Shuruppak and Kisurra, the rivalry must have been particularly keen. The one or the other place would hold the supremacy, and during such a period the *patesi* of the one place would also control the other. Kish, *e.g.*, appears to have outlasted Opis and we should, therefore, expect more *patesis* of the former, though it is of course merely an accident that up to the present only one patesi of Opis should be mentioned in the material at our disposal, and that in an inscription of a *patesi* of Lagash. It is, however, entirely too early to base any definite conclusions on the relatively large or small number of rulers at present known to us. The *argumentum ex silentio*—always hazardous—is particularly so when so much material still awaits the spade of the explorer. Meanwhile, it will be useful to the general reader to obtain through the enumeration of the cities for which names of rulers have been recovered—even though the number of such rulers be few or only one—a view of the many political centres in the early period, and of the rivalry between them that lasted for so many centuries before a permanent union was effected.

Approximate dates are indicated by *circa*. Special attention has been paid to indicating all the "synchronisms" between Babylonian and Assyrian rulers; and it is hoped that this will be found helpful in determining the order and approximate position of rulers in regard to whom no definite dates can as yet be given for the period or duration of their reigns. Progress in Babylonian-Assyrian chronology during the last decade has been chiefly in the direction of obtaining more of these valuable synchronisms, which have been the main factor in reducing the entirely too high dates formerly assigned for the earlier rulers in the Euphrates Valley.

The few abbreviations used are (1) *p* for *patesi* (for which see p. 21 *note*), (2) *k* for king, (3) *s* for son, (4) *b* for brother, (5) figures within brackets indicate duration of reign, (6) an asterisk indicates uncertainty as to the position of a ruler in the list.

The following identifications of mounds with ancient sites (see the map)—arranged in alphabetical order—should be especially noted.

Abu-Habba	=	Sippar
Abu Hatab	=	Kisurra
Abu Shahrain	=	Eridu
Arbela	=	Arba'ili
Akarkuf	=	Dur-Kurigalzu
Babil (or Mujelibe), with el-Kasr, Amran-ibn-Ali and Jumjuma	=	Babylon
Birs Nimrud	=	Borsippa
Bismaya	=	Adab
El-Ohemir	=	Kish
Fara	=	Shuruppak (or Shurippak)
Jokha	=	Umma
Kaleh-Shergat	=	Ashur
Khorsabad	=	Dur-Sharrukin
Kouyunjik (and Nebi-Yunus)	=	Nineveh
Mukayyar	=	Ur
Niffer	=	Nippur
Nimroud	=	Calah
Seleucia	=	Opis (?)

Senkerah	=	Larsa
Sepharvaim	=	Agade
Tell-Ibrahim	=	Cuthah
Telloh	=	Lagash (Shirpurla, Girsu)
Tell Sifr	=	Dur-gurgurri(?)
Warka	=	Uruk (or Erech).

RULERS OF LAGASH

Lugal-shag-Engur (p.) contemporary with Mesilim, k. of Kish (c. 3050 B.C. (?))

*Badu (k.)

*En-khegal (k.)

Ur-Nina (k.) s. of Gunidu, grandson of Gursar (c. 2975 B.C.)

Akurgal (p.) (s.)

E-annatum (p. and k.) (s.)

En-annatum I. (p.) (b.) c. 2900 B.C.

En-temena (p.) (s.) c. 2850 B.C.

En-annatum II. (p.) (s.)

En-etarzi (p.)

En-litarzi (p.)

Lugal-anda (p.) (s.) (Fuller form Lugal-anda-nushuga.)

Uru-kagina (k.) usurper, contemporary with Lugal-zaggisi, k. of Uruk (c. 2750 B.C.)

En-gilsa (p.) (s.) contemporary with Manish-tusu, k. of Kish (c. 2700 B.C.)

Lugul-ushumgal (p.) contemporary with Sargon of Agade (c. 2500 B.C.)

Ur-Babbar (p.) contemporary with Naram-Sin of Agade (c. 2470 B.C.)

*Ur-E (p.)

*Lugal-bur (p.)

*Basha-Mama (p.)
*Ur-Mama (p.)
*Ug-me (p.)
Ur-Bau (p.) usurper (C. 2400 B.C.)
Nam-makhni (p.) (son-in-law.)
Ur-gar (p.) also son-in-law of Ur-Bau (?)
*Ka-azag (p.)
*Galu-Bau (p.)
*Galu-Gula (p.)
*Ur-Ninsun (p.)
Gudea (p.) C. 2350 B.C.—usurper
Ur-Ningirsu (p.) (s.) contemporary with Ur-Engur,
    k. of Ur (C. 2300 B.C.)
*Ur-abba (p.) (s.)
*Galu-kazal (p.)
*Galu-andul (p.)
*Ur-Lama I. (p.) (C. 2240 B.C.)
*Alla (p.)
*Ur-Lama II. (p.) (s.) contemporary with Dungi,
    k. of Ur (C. 2225 B.C.)
Arad-Nannar[1] (p.) contemporary with Bur-Sin, k. of
    Ur and his two successors, *i.e.* up to C. 2200 B.C.

RULERS OF NIPPUR

Ur-Enlil (p.) C. 3000 B.C.
Lugal-ezendig (p.)
Ur-nabbad (p.) (s.) contemporary with Dungi, k. of
Ur (C. 2260 B.C.)

---

[1] In addition to being patesi of Lagash, he calls himself *patesi* or governor of twelve other places or districts. See Thureau-Dangin, *Sumerisch-Akkadische Königsinschriften*, p. 148 *seq.*; King, *op. cit.*, p. 301 *seq.*

Dada (p.) contemporary with Ibi-Sin, last King of Ur. (C. 2200 B.C.)

RULERS OF ADAB

Esar (k.) C. 3000 B.C.(?)

RULERS OF SHURUPPAK

Dada (p.)
Khaladda (p.) } Period uncertain.

RULERS OF UMMA

*E-Abzu (k.)

Ush (p.)

En-akalli (p.) ⎰ contemporary with E-annatum
Ur-lumma[1] (k.) (s.) ⎱ of Lagash (C. 2925 B.C.)

Ili (p.) appointed by En-temena p. of Lagash (C. 2850 B.C.)

Ukush (p.)

Lugal-zaggisi (k.) (s.) See also under Rulers of Uruk—contemporary with Uru-kagina, p. of Lagash (C. 2750 B.C.)

Kur-shesh (p.) contemporary with (or generation before (?)) Manish-tusu, k. of Kish (C. 2700 B.C.)
*Galu-Babbar (p.)

Ur-nesu (p.) contemporary of Dungi, k. of Ur (C. 2240 B.C.)

RULER OF OPIS

Zuzu (k.) defeated by E-annatum, p. of Lagash (C. 2950 B.C.)

[1] Perhaps to be read Ur-khumma.

RULERS OF URUK

Lugal-zaggisi (k.) C. 2750 B.C. (also "King of Sumer")
*Lugal-kigub-nidudu (k.) (also k. of Ur.)
*Lugal-kisalsi (k.) (also k. of Ur.)
Sin-gashid (k.) ⎫
Sin-gamil (k.) ⎬ (C. 2150–2110 B.C.[1])
An-am s. of Bel-shemea[2] (k.)
Arad-shag-shag (k.)
Sin-eribam(?)[3] (k.)

RULERS OF BASIME

Ilsu-rabi (p.)
Ibalum (p.) contemporary with (or generation before
(?)) Manish-tusu k. of Kish (C. 2700 B.C.)

RULERS OF KISH

Utug (p.) son of Bazuzu—perhaps an usurper (?)
Mesilim (k.) contemporary with Lugal-shag-Engur
p. of Lagash (C. 3050 B.C. (?))
Ur-zage (k.)
Lugal-tarsi (k.) C. 2950 B.C.(?)
Enbi-Ishtar (k.) C. 2800 B.C.
Sharrukin (k.) C. 2750 B.C.

[1] These two rulers probably belong to a period contemporaneous with the earlier rulers of the first dynasty of Babylonia (see below p. 432). The reading of the second name is not certain. See Meyer, *Geschichte des Altertums* I., 2, page 505).

[2] During the closing decades of the Isin dynasty (below p. 430), Uruk secures its independence. How long it was maintained we do not know, but presumably a century at the most.

[3] According to Scheil, *Oriental. Litteraturzeitung*, vol. VIII., p. 350.

Manish-tusu (k.) C. 2700 B.C.
Uru-mush (k.) C. 2600 B.C.
*Ashduni-erim (k.) C. 2100 B.C.
Manana (k.) C. 2075 B.C.
Sumu-ditana (k.) C. 2060 B.C.
Jawium (k.) C. 2050 B.C.
*Khalium (k.)

RULERS CALLING THEMSELVES (ALSO) KING OF SUMER

Lugal-zaggisi, k. of Uruk and k. of "the land" (C. 2750 B.C.)[1]
Lugal-kigub-nidudu, k. of Uruk and Ur.
Lugal-kisalsi, k. of Uruk and Ur.[2]
En-shag-kushanna, lord of Summer, k. of "the land."
[These three before 2500 B.C.—perhaps before 2600 B.C.]

RULERS OF AGADE

Shar-gani-sharri (*i.e.* Sargon) (k.) (son of Dati-Enlil), C. 2500 B.C.[3]
Naram-Sin (k.) (s.) C. 2470 B.C.

[1] "King of the land" is a designation for Sumer.

[2] These two rulers, though they do not use the designation "king of the land," evidently belong to the group, Uruk and Ur being employed to indicate the extent of the control. Of another "king of the land" who defeats Enbi–Ishtar, King of Kish (c 2800 B. C.), four fragmentary vase inscriptions have been found at Nippur, but unfortunately in all four cases, the name of the ruler is broken out. See Hilprecht, *Old Babylonian Inscriptions*, I., 2, Nos. 102–105; 110.

[3] Nabonnedos (last king of Babylonia, 555–539 B. C.) gives the date of Sargon as 3200 years earlier, *i. e.* C. 3750 B. C. which, however, turns out to be about 1300 years too high. See above p. 295.

Bin-gani-sharri (s.)[1]

RULERS OF UR[2]

	Years	
Ur-Engur (k.)	(18)	C. 2300 B.C.
Dungi (k.) (s.)	(58)	C. 2280 B.C.
Bur-Sin I. (k.) (s.)	(9)	C. 2220 B.C.
Gimil-Sin[3] (k.) (s.)	(9)	C. 2210 B.C.
Ibi-Sin (k.) (s.)	(25)	C. 2200 B.C.

RULERS OF ISIN (16 KINGS)

	Years	
Ishbi-Ura	(32)	C. 2175 B.C.
Gimil-ilishu (s.)	(10)	C. 2145 B.C.
Idin-Dagan (s.)	(21)	C. 2135 B.C.
Ishme-Dagan (s.)	(20)	C. 2115 B.C.
Libit-Ishtar (s.)	(11)	C. 2095 B.C.
Ur-Ninib	(28)	C. 2085 B.C.
Bûr-Sin, II. (s.)	(21)	C. 2060 B.C.
Itêr-kasha (s.)	(5)	C. 2040 B.C.
Ura-imitti (b.)	(7)	C. 2035 B.C.
Sin-ikisha	($\frac{1}{2}$)	C. 2028 B.C.
Enlil-bani	(24)	C. 2027 B.C.

[1] Not certain that he succeeded his father.

[2] While from a list found at Nippur (?), we have the years of the duration of each reign for the dynasties of Ur and of Isin indicated, the uncertainty of the chronology of this period demands caution in following them too literally. I have, therefore, suggested approximate dates without too close adhesion to the exact figures in the list in question. The five rulers represent a regular succession from father to son.

[3] An official of this king, Lugal-magurri, calls himself patesi of Ur and commander of the fortress.

	Years	
Zambia	(3)	C. 2003 B.C.
[Name missing]	(5)	C. 2000 B.C.
Ea	(4)	C. 1995 B.C.
Sin-magir	(11)	C. 1990 B.C.
Damik-ilishu (s.)	(23)	C. 1980 B.C.

RULERS OF UR AND LARSA

Gungunu (k.)   C. 2085 B.C. contemporary with
Ur-Ninib, k. of Isin.

Sumu-ilu (k.)
Nur-Adad (k.)   C. 2030 "
Sin-Iddinam (k.) (s.) C. 2020 "
Arad-Sin (k.)   C. 1990 "   s. of Kudur-mabuk, a
ruler of a district
Emutbal border-
ing on Elam.[1]

Rim-Sin (k.)   (b.) C. 1970 "

RULERS OF KISURRA[2]

Idin-ilu (p.)[3]
Itur-Shamash (p.?) (s.)

RULERS OF ISHKUN-SIN[4]

Khash-khamer (p.), contemporary with Ur-Engur,
k. of Ur (C. 2300 B.C.).

[1] Kudur-mabuk must have held a good part of Babylonia in
subjection, and succeeds in placing two of his sons in control
of Larsa.

[2] Site of Abu-Hatab where, as at the neighbouring Fara (= Shuruppak the site of the Babylonian Deluge), some preliminary
work of excavation has been carried on. See *Mitteilungen der
Deutschen Orient-Gesellschaft*, Nos. 15-17.

[3] Probably later than the Ur Dynasty.

[4] In northern Babylonia (?). See King, *History of Sumer and
Akkad*, p. 281.

RULERS OF DUNGI-BABBAR

U.-Pasag (p.), in time of Dungi, k. of Ur (C. 2280 B.C.).

RULERS OF BABYLONIA[1]

I. Dynasty of Babylon. (11 Kings.)

Years

Sumu-abu   (14)   C. 2060–2047 B.C. contemporary of Ilu-shuma, k. (or p. ?) of Assyria.

[1] We now reach the great Babylonian list of kings (see above p. 421) as our main chronological source, the many gaps of which can be partially filled out through other sources. The founder of what the Babylonian annalist calls the dynasty of Babylon—with its seat in the city of Babylon—is Sumu-abu, but it is not until we reach the sixth member, Hammurapi, that the rulers of Babylon can lay claim to all of Sumer and Akkad. Indeed, it would appear that Sumu-abu started out as a vassal of the kings of Sumer and Akkad, but with him the movement of extension and conquest begins, which culminates in Hammurapi's overthrow (C. 1928 B.C.) of his most formidable rival, the Elamite warrior Rim-Sin, who was also the last ruler of the Larsa dynasty. This is also indicated by the names of rulers incidentally referred to in inscriptions (or other documents), who are contemporary with Sumu-lailu and other of the earlier rulers of the Babylonian dynasty, but independent of them, such as Immerrum, Anman-Ila, Buntakhtun–ila, who appear to have ruled in Sippar. Of others who also belong to this period like Mana-baltel, Rim-Anum, and Jakhzar-ili of Kasallu hardly anything more than the names are known, but their occurrence with royal titles, before Hammurapi and the other rulers of the first dynasty

	Years	
Sumu-lailu	(36)	c. 2046–2011 B.C.
Sabum (s.)	(14)	c. 2010–1997 "
Apil-Sin (s.)	(18)	c. 1996–1979 "
Sin-muballit (s.)	(20)	c. 1978–1959 "
Hammurapi (s.)[1]	(43)	c. 1958–1916 "
Samsu-iluna (s.)	(38)	c. 1915–1878 "
Abeshu (or Ebi-shum) (s.)	(28)	c. 1877–1850 "

} contemporary with Ilu-ma-ilu (2d Dynasty).

obtained control of Babylonia indicate that the local rulers at Sippar, and no doubt elsewhere, managed to maintain at least a partial independence.

On some still earlier rulers, of whom, however, only the names remain (Ilu-illati, En-men-nunna, Apil-kishshu), see King, *Chronicles Concerning Early Babylonian Kings*, ii., p. 47.

For the first dynasty, the names are wanting in the large list of kings, but can be supplied from a duplicate fragment for the first two dynasties. This duplicate also furnishes the length of reign of each king of the first dynasty, but the figures appear to be inaccurate. Those given by me follow the data derived from the dates attached to legal documents, and are the ones now generally accepted by scholars. In a few cases, they may however, be a few years out—so possibly the reigns of the last two kings for whom we have not as yet sufficient data from other sources. I follow the approximate dates as given by Meyer, *Geschichte*, i., 2, p. 507. From the third member to the end of the dynasty we have a continuous succession of father and son.

[1] According to Nabonnedos (last king of Babylonia 555–539 B.C. See Schrader, *Keilinschriftliche Bibliothek*, ii., p. 90; col. ii., 20–22), Hammurapi ruled 700 years before Burnaburiash of the Cassite dynasty (see p. 436), which turns out to be about 100 years too much, just as Nabonnedos' date for Shagarakti-shuriash (see below p. 437, note 1) is likewise 100 years too high.

Years

Ammi-ditana (s.)   (37) c. 1849–1813 B.C.
Ammi-saduka (s.)   (21) c. 1812–1792 "
Samsu-ditana (s.)   (31) c. 1791–1761 " ¹

II. Dynasty of the Sea-Land. (11 Kings.)²

Iluma-ilu	c. 1900–1870 B.C.	contempo- rary with S a m s u - iluna and A b e s h u (1st Dy- nasty).
Ittili-nibi		
Damik-ilishu	c. 1820	"
Ishki-bal		
Shushshi (b.)		
Gulkishar	c. 1800³	"

¹ Invasion of Hittites. See King, *op. cit.*, ii., p. 22.

² Its seat was in the region of the Persian Gulf, and it does not appear that the rulers ever extended their sway as far as Babylon. The first two (or three) kings of this "Sea-Land" dynasty are contemporary with the last five of the dynasty of Babylon; and the last three of the "Sea-Land" dynasty with the first three rulers of the Cassite dynasty. The large Babylonian list of kings furnishes the length of the reign of each of these rulers of the "Sea-Land," but the figures—a total of 368 years for 11 kings—are much too high. They are presumably guesses on the part of the annalist. The duplicate fragment gives no figures for this dynasty.

³ Enlil-nadinpal s. of Nebuchadnezzar I. (c. 1149–1130 B.C.) of the Isin dynasty (below p. 438) places Gulkishar 696 years before his time, *i.e.*, c. 1835 B.C., which may, however, be a little too high. See Meyer, *op. cit.*, ii., 1, p. 576, who thinks that the

Peshgal-daramash (s.)
Adara-kalama (s.)
Akur (or Ekur)-ulanna
Melam-kurkura
Ea-gamil   C. 1720 B.C.   contempo-
rary with
Kash - tili-
ash I., k.
of Baby-
lonia (C.
1712–1691
B.C.).

III.   Cassite Dynasty.   (36 Kings.)[1]

	Years	
Gandash	(16)	C. 1750–1735 B.C.

figures may be about 50 years too high; it may even be as much as 75 years out of the way.

[1] The first dynasty of Babylon was brought to an end through an incursion of the Hittites (see above, p. 434, note 1), and it would appear that a Hittite ruler actually sat on the throne of Babylon for a short time. At all events a period of some years elapsed before the Cassites came into control. As a minimum we may assume 10 years between the end of the dynasty of Babylon and the first of the Cassite rulers, though it may turn out to be as much as 20 years. Of the 36 Cassite rulers, only 20 are preserved on the Babylonian list and many of these only in part, but thanks to numerous business documents of this period and boundary stones, most of the defective names may be restored and others supplied together with approximate lengths of their reigns. Seven names, however, are still entirely missing and some of those entered between Nos, 5-20 are uncertain. I follow Meyer's indications, p. 338, with some modifications on the basis of the researches of Ungnad, Thureau-Dangin and Clay. The latter was kind enough to place his results of a special study of this period at my disposal.

	Years	
Agum I. (s.)	(22)	C. 1734–1713 B.C.

Kash-tiliash I., Usurper.
  b. of Ulam-buriash[1]
  and s. of Bur-naburiash
	(22)	C. 1712–1691 "

Ushshi (s.)	(8)	C. 1690–1683 "
Abi-rattash (b.?) of Agum I.?)		
Tazzi-gurumash (s.)		
Ayum II. (s.)		

[Gap of about two centuries.]

Kara-indash		contemporary with Ashir-rim-n i s c h e-schu, k. of As-syria (C. 1430 B.C.).
Kadashman-kharbe I. (s.?)		
Kuri-galzu I. (s.)		
Bur-naburiash[2] (s.)	(25)	contemporary with Puzur-Ashur, k. of Assyria (C. 1380 B.C.).
Kara-khardash		son-in-law of Ashur-uballit, k. of Assyria. (C. 1350 B.C.)

[1] Who defeats Ea-gamil, last ruler of the Sea-Land dynasty, but who does not appear to have actually occupied the throne. See King, *Chronicles Concerning Early Babylonian Kings*, ii., p. 22, and Meyer, *Geschichte des Altertums*, i., 2, p. 583.

[2] See above p. 433, note 1.

Nazi-bugash (usurper)

[Kings 5 to 20= about 340 years. c. 1682–1346 B.C.]

	Years	
Kuri-galzu II. (s. of Burnaburiash)	(23)	C. 1345–1323 B.C. contemporary with Ashur-uballit and En-lil-nirari, kings, of Assyria.
Nazi-maruttash (s)	(26)	C. 1322–1297 B.C. contemporary with Adad-nir-ari I., k. of As-syria.
Kadashman-turgu (s.)	(17)	C. 1296–1280 B.C.
Kadashman-Enlil	(6)	C. 1279–1274 "
Kudur-Enlil (s.)	(9)	C. 1273–1265 "
Shagarakti-shuriash[1](s.)	(13)	C. 1264–1252 " contemporary with Tukulti-Ninib I., k. of Assyria.
Kash-tiliash II. (s.)	(8)	C. 1251–1244 B.C.
Enlil-nadinshum (s.?)	·(1½)	C. 1243–1242 "
Kadashman-kharbe II.	(1½)	C. 1242–1241 "
Adad-shumiddin	(6)	C. 1240–1235 "

[1] According to Nabonnedos (last king of Babylonia, 555–539 B.C.) Shagarakti-shuriash, the son of Kudur-Enlil, ruled 800 years before him (Schrader, *Keilinschriftliche Bibliothek*, iii., 1, p. 106; col. iii. 27-29) which, however, appears to be 100 years too high.

	Years	
Adad-nadinakhi [1]	(30)	C. 1234–1205 B.C. contemporary with Enlil-kudur-usur, k. of Assyria. (C. 1240 B.C.)
Meli-shipak (s.?)	(15)	C. 1204–1190 B.C.
Marduk-paliddin (s.)	(13)	C. 1189–1177 "
Zamama-shumiddin	(1)	C. 1176 " contemporary with Ashurdan I., k. of Assyria.
Bel-nadin-[akhi]	(3)	C. 1175–1173 B.C.

IV. Isin Dynasty. (11 Kings.)

	Years	
Marduk	(17?)	C. 1172–1156 B.C.
[Two names missing]		C. 1155–1140 "
Nebuchadnezzar I. usurper (?) contemporary with Ashur - reshishi I., k. of Assyria.		
Enlil-nadinpal (s.)		
Marduk-nadinakhi contemporary with Tiglath-pileser I., k. of Assyria.		C. 1140–1086 B.C.
Marduk-shapik-zermati, contemporary with Ashur-bel-kala, k. of Assyria.		

[1] Or perhaps to be read Adad-shum-usur. See King, *Records of Tukulti-Ninib I.*, pp. 72 and 99.

Chronological Lists

	Years	
Adad-paliddin (s. of Itti-Marduk-balatu)[1]	(22), usurper, father-in-law of Ashur-bel-kala, k. of Assyria.	c. 1085–1064 B.C.
Marduk-akhirba	(1½)	c. 1064–1063 B.C.
Marduk-zer	(12)	c. 1062–1051 "
Nabu-shumlibur	(8)?	c. 1050–1043 "

V.   Sea-Land Dynasty.[2]   (3 Kings.)

Simmash-shipak (son of Erba-Sin)	(18)[3]	c. 1042–1025 B.C.
Ea-mukin-zer (s. of Khash-mar)	(5 months)[4]	c. 1024 B.C.
Kashshu-nadinakhi (s. of Sippâya)	(3)	c. 1024–1022 B.C.

VI.   Bit-Bazi Dynasty.   (3 Kings.)

	Years	
E-ulmash-shakinshum (s. of Bazi)	(17)[5]	
Ninib-kudurusur (b.)	(3)[6]	c. 1020–1000 B.C.
Shilanim-Shukamuna (b.)	(3 months)	

[1] See King, *Chronicles*, ii, p. 59, Note 2.

[2] A king of the Sea-Land—Marduk-paliddin is mentioned also in the annals of Tiglathpileser IV. (745–727 B.C.).

[3] Or 17, according to a Babylonian chronicle.   Uprising under the lead of a man of the Damik-ilishu Dynasty.   See above p. 434.

[4] Or 3, according to a Babylonian chronicle.

[5] Or 15, according to a Babylonian chronicle.

[6] Or 2, according to a Babylonian chronicle.

VII. Elamitic Ruler. (Name missing.[1]) (6 years.)
C. 1000–995 B.C.

VIII. (About 13 kings ruling c. 994–754 among them.)

Nebo-mukinpal   C. 994–959[2] B.C.
*Sibir

Shamash-mudammik Nebo-shumishkun I.	contemporary with Adad-nirari III. (C. 910 B.C.)
Nebo-paliddin[3] C. 888–854 B.C. Marduk-nadinshum[4] (s.)	contemporary with Shalmaneser III., k. of Assyria (858–824 B.C.)
Marduk-balatsu-ikbi Bau-akhiddin (to C. 800 B.C.)	contemporary with Shamshi-Adad IV., k. of Assyria (823–811 B.C.)

[1] Perhaps to be restored as Ea-apal-usur. See King, *Chronicles Concerning Early Babylonian Kings*, ii., p. 55.

[2] This long reign of 36 years is now extremely probable. See King, *op cit*, i., p. 222 *seq.*

[3] Ruled at least 31 years extending back, therefore, into the reign of Ashur-nasirpal II., k. of Assyria, 883–859 B.C. (See Schrader, *op. cit.*, i., p. 98, col. iii., 19.)

[4] Uprising under lead of his brother Marduk-bel-usati, but crushed with the aid of Shalmaneser III. (8th year = 850 B.C.) See Schrader, *op. cit.*, i., p. 134, ll. 73–84.

IX. Dynasty of Babylon. (About 5 kings.)

	Years	
Nebo-shumishkun II.		753–748 B.C.
Nebo-nasir[1]	(14)	747–734 B.C., contemporary with Tiglath-pileser IV, (745–727 B.C.)
Nebo-nadinzer (s.)	(2)	733–732 B.C.
Nebo-shumukin	(1 mo.)[2] (13 days)	732– B.C.

X. Various Dynasties.[3]

Mukin-zer	(3)	732–730 B.C.
Pulu (= Tiglathpileser IV.)	(2)	729–727 B.C.
Ulula (= Shalmaneser V.) (s.)	(5)	727–722 B.C.
Marduk-paliddin I.[4]	(12)	721–710 B.C.
Sargon	(5)	709–705 B.C.

[1] With Nebonasir (= Nabonassar) the Ptolemaic Canon begins.

[2] According to a Babylonian chronicle, a little over two months. (King, *op. cit.*, ii., p. 64, note 1.)

[3] After Mukin-zer (or Nebo-mukin-zer, as his full name appears on a tablet to be published shortly by Prof. Clay), who is designated as of the Shashi dynasty, we have Assyrian kings acting under special names (as Pulu and Ulula) as governors of Babylonia or appointing the crown prince (as Sargon and Sennacherib), or high officials until the destruction of Babylon by Sennacherib in 689 B.C., after which Assyrian kings themselves assume direct control with the exception of 668–648 B.C., during which Shamash-shumukin appointed by his brother Ashurbanapal, king of Assyria, is in command.

[4] Perhaps the son of Nebo-shum-ukin—if the line in the Babylonian chronicle (King, *op. cit.*, ii., p. 64—rev. 3) is to be restored accordingly.

	Years	
Sennacherib (s)	(2)	704–702 B.C.
Marduk-zakirshum[1]	(one month	} 702 B.C.
Marduk-paliddin II.	(nine months)	
Bel-ibni	(3)	702–700 B.C.
Ashur-nadinshum (son of		
Sennacherib k. of Assyria)	(6)	699–694 B.C.
Nergal-ushezib	(1½)	693–692 B.C.
Mushezib-Marduk	(4)	692–689 B.C.
Sennacherib[2]	(8)	688–681 B.C.
Esarhaddon	(12)	680–669 B.C.
Shamash-shumukin	(20)	668–648 B.C.
Kandalanu (in conjunction		
with Ashurbanapal)		647–626 B.C.
Ashur-etil-ilani		625–

RULERS OF ASSYRIA[3]

Ushpia

[1] Two pretenders in his short and evidently disturbed reign are Marduk-bel-u-she[zib (?)], and Marduk-balatsu-[ikbi (?)] See King, *op. cit.*, iii., p. 65.

[2] According to the Babylonian chronicle, however, an interregnum of 8 years (Schrader, *Keilinschriftliche Bibliothek*, ii., p. 280, and iii., 28). Within this period, perhaps, a certain Erba-Marduk, s. of Marduk-shakinshum and other aspirants whose rule was not subsequently recognized are to be placed. (See King, *op. cit.*, ii., p. 66, note 2.)

[3] *Patesis* up to about 1500 B.C., though later rulers, not distinguishing sharply between *patesi* and *sharru* (king), occasionally use *sharru* when referring to rulers before this date.

The chronology of Assyria beyond 1500 B.C. is still quite uncertain. Through the inscriptions at Kalah-Shergat (Ashur) many new names of *patesis* have been ascertained, but the sequence is not clear in all cases, and there are still gaps of uncertain length to be filled out. I have not included in the above list a certain Enlil-bani, s. of Adasi, whom Esarhaddon,

Kikia

Kate-Ashir, C. 2100 B.C. (?)

Shalim-Akhum (s)

Ilu-shuma—contemporary of Sumu-abu, k. of Babylonia (C. 2060–2047 B.C.)

Irishum (or Erishum) (s)–159 years[1] before Shamshi-
Adad I., *i.e.* C. 2030 B.C.

Ikunum (s.)

Shar-kenkate-Ashir

*Enlil-Kapi

*Shamshi-Adad I.[2] (s)—580 years before Shalmaneser
I., *i.e.* C. 1870 B.C.

Ishme-Dagan I.

Shamshi-Adad II. (s)–641 years before Ashurdan
I., k. of Assyria, *i.e.* C. 1820 B.C.

680-666 B.C., mentioned as his remote ancestor and to whom
he gives a royal title. (Schrader, *Keilinschriftliche Bibliothek*,
ii., p. 120). The specific manner in which Esarhaddon speaks
of this personage warrants us in believing that Bel-ibni was really
his ancestor. The statement that the latter was an actual
ruler over Assyria is open to the suspicion of being an invention
by the king to justify his dynasty, which we know begins with
Sargon, his grandfather. Until the name, therefore, is found
in an inscription of Assyria it is better to leave the name out
of any provisional list.

[1] So according to a statement of Shalmaneser I., while according
to Esarhaddon 126 years.

[2] There may be a third Shamshi-Adad son of Enlil-Kapkapi
(Rawlinson, i., Pl. 6, No. 1) in this early period who might be
the ruler of that name mentioned in a legal document (Ranke,
*Babylonian Legal and Business Documents fron the Time of the
First Dynasty of Babylon*, No. 260 bv. 12.) as contemporary with
Hammurapi (*i.e.* C. 1950), but that is uncertain; and it is not
likely that a *patesi* of Assyria should be mentioned in a Babylonian document. It is more likely that Enlil-kapkapu is
identical with Enlil-kapi.

Ishme-Dagan II.
Ashir-nirari I.

Ashir-rabi I., c. 1475 B.C.
Ashir-nirari II. (s)
Ashir-rim-nisheshu—(s)—contemporary with Kara-
   indash, k. of Babylonia. (c. 1430 B.C.)
Puzur-Ashur—contemporary with Bur-naburiash
           C. B.C. 1390
Ashur-nadinakhi
Erba-Adad (s)
Ashur-uballit (s) c. 1370–43 B.C.—father-in-law of
   Kara-khardash, k. of Babylonia.
Enlil-nirari (s)—contemporary with Kuri-galzu II.,
   k. of Babylonia (c. 1340 B.C.).
Arik-den-ilu (s)
Adad-nirari I. (s)–contemporary with Nazi-marut-
   tash, k. of Babylonia. (c. 1320 B.C)
Shalmaneser I.[1] (s)
Tukulti-Ninib I. (s)—c. 600 years before the conquest
   of Babylon (689 B.C.) by Sen-
   nacherib, k. of Assyria, i.e. c.
   1290 B.C.[2])
Tukulti-Ashur (s)

[1] See above under Shamshi-Adad I.
[2] See King, *Records of Tukulti-Ninib*, i., p. 60 *seq.*; 107 *seq.*
Sennacherib speaks of a seal of Tukulti-Ninib, once the property
of Shagarakti-shuriash, of the Cassite dynasty, who thus turns
out to be the contemporary of Tukulti-Ninib. The latter conquers Kash-tiliash II. and brings him as a captive to Ashur.
Subsequently Tukulti-Ninib is killed in a revolt organized by
his son and successor (*op. cit.*, pp. 87, 97, 991).

Enlil-kudur-usur— C. 1240 B.C.   contemporary with
Adad-nadinakhi,
k. of Babylonia.

Ninib-paleshar.[1]

Ashurdan I.[2] (s) c. 1185 B.C.— contemporary with
Zamama-shumid-
din, k. of Babylo-
nia; and *circa* 60
years before Tig-
lath-pileser I., k.
of Assyria.

Mutakkil-Nusku (s).

Ashur-reshishi I. (s)— contemporary with
Nebuchadnezzar
I., k. of Babylo-
nia. (C. 1150 B.C.)

Tiglath-pileser I. (s)—C. 1125–1100 B.C. Beginning of
reign con-
temporary
with Mar-
duk-nadi-
n a k h i—
5th k. of
I s i n dy-
nasty.[3])

Ashur-bel-kala (s)— contemporary with

---

[1] Son of Erba-Adad II., founder, therefore, of a new dynasty.

[2] See above under Shamshi-Adad II.

[3] According to Sennacherib (705-681 B.C.) 418 years elapsed between Tiglathpileser's defeat of Marduk-nadinakhi and Sennacherib's conquest of Babylon in 689 B.C. (See Schrader, *Keilinschritfliche Bibliothek*, ii., p. 118. Pl. 49–50.), which would therefore make Tiglathpileser I. still reigning in 1107 B.C.

Marduk - shapik zer - mati, 7th king of Isin dynasty and son-in-law of Adad-paliddin, — 8th king of Isin dynasty. (C. 1085–1064 B.C.)

Shamshi-Adad III. (b).
Ashurnasirpal I. (s).
Shalmaneser II. (s).
Adad-nirari II.
Tiglath-pileser II.
Ashur-rabi II.
Ashur-reshishi II. (s).
Tiglath-pileser III. (s).
Ashurdan II. (s).
Adad-nirari III. (s) 911–890— contemporary with Shamash-mudam-mik, k. of Babylonia.

Tukulti-Ninib[1] II. (s) 889–884.
Ashur-nasirpal II. (s) 883–859.
Shalmaneser III.[2] (s) 858–824— contemporary with Nebo-paliddin, k. of Babylonia (C. 888–854 B.C.).

[1] From Tukulti-Ninib II. to Ashurbanapal we have lists of Assyrian Eponyms in several copies. From Shamshi-Adad IV. to Shalmaneser V. we have the fragments of another list of Eponyms.
[2] See Delitzsch, in *Mitteilungen der Deutschen Orient Gesellschaft*, No. 42, p. 35 note.

Shamshi-Adad IV.[1] (s) 823-811— contemporary with Marduk-balatsu-ikbi, k. of Babylonia.

Adad-nirari IV. (s) 810-782.
Shalmaneser IV. (s) 781–772.
Ashurdan III. (s) 771–754.
Ashur-nirari III. (s) 753–746.
Tiglathpileser IV. 745–727— contemporary with Nebo-shumukin, k. of Babylonia (732 B.C.).

Shalmaneser V. (s) 727–722 B.C.
Sargon 721–706 B.C.
Sennacherib (s) 705–681 B.C.
Esarhaddon (s) 680–669 B.C.
Ashurbanapal (s).
(Sardanapalos) 668–626 B.C.
Ashur-etil-ilani (s) 626–c. 618 B.C.
Sin-shum-lishir c. 618 B.C., who is followed after a short reign by Sin-shar-ishkun, the brother of Ashur-etil-ilani. See Clay, *Babylonian Expedition*, viii., 1, p. 9.
Sin-shar-ishkun c. 616–606 B.C.
(Destruction of Nineveh 606 B.C.)

RULERS OF NEO-BABYLONIAN EMPIRE

Nabopolassar (also last governor of Babylonia under Assyrian control)   625–604 B.C.
Nebuchadnezzar II. (s)   604–561 B.C.

---

[1] Suppresses uprising of his brother Ashur-daninpal that had broken out during the closing years of the reign of Shalmaneser III. (See Schrader, *op. cit.*, i., p. 176; Col. I., 39–52.)

Evil-Merodach (s)[1]	561–560 B.C.
Neriglissor (brother-in-law)	559–556 B.C.
Labosoarchod (s)	–556 B.C.
Nabonnedos.[2]	555–539 B.C.

(Cyrus' conquest of Babylonia 539 B.C.)

Persian Rulers of Babylonia[3]

Cyrus	539–529 B.C.
Cambysses (s)	529–522 B.C.
Darius I. (Hystaspis)	522–486 B.C.
Xerxes I. (s)	486–465 B.C.
Artaxerxes I. (Longimanus) (s)	465–424 B.C.
Xerxes II.	(45 days.)
Darius II.	424–404 B.C.
Artaxerxes II. (Mnemon) (s)	404–359 B.C.
Artaxerxes III. (Ochos) (s)	359–338 B.C.
Arses (s)	338–336 B.C.
Darius III. (Codomanus)	336–331 B.C.

(Alexander the Great conquers Babylonia 331 B.C.)

[1] More properly Amel-Marduk, Nergal-shar-usur, Labashi-Marduk, Nebo-na'id. I give the more familiar forms of these four names.

[2] His son Bel-shar-usur, associated with his father in the government of Babylonia, is the famous Belshazzar of the Book of Daniel.

[3] I have omitted the numerous pretenders like Gaumata, Nebuchadnezzar III., etc., mentioned in the Behistun inscription of Darius I. and elsewhere.

INDEX

A

Abel, 289

Abraham, 28, 399

Adab, 36

Adad, 48, 105, 123, 125, 140, 271, 307; = Hadad, of Amoritish origin, 26, 117–120; storm-god, 38, 83, 103, 128, 182, 232, 249; "god of divination," 96, 120, 165, 297; = Ramman, 117; = Mar-Tu, 117; Anu-Adad temple, 118, 292; counterpart of Enlil, 120; eleventh month associated with, 238

Adad-nirari IV., King of Assyria, 99

Adam, 357, 367

Adapa legend, 366; parallel to "tree of life" story, 367 *seq.*

Adar = 12th month, 238. See *Month.*

Adon, a title of Tammuz, *q. v.*

Adonis, Tammuz-Adonis myth, see *Tammuz.*

Agade, 18, 19, 36, 175, 293, 294; early stronghold of Semites, 11; capital of Akkad, 21; capital of Sargon, 22; yields to Kish, 24

Agriculture, 405 *seq.*; in early Babylonia, 17; factor in establishing pantheon, 64 *seq.*, 114; in Palestine, 288 *seq.*

Ahriman, 60, 252

Ahura-Mazda, 60, 252

Aḳabi-ilu, 381, 382, 383

Akhula-galla, a quarter of Borsippa, 380

Akkad, = northern Babylonia, 3, 23, 25, 31, 356; kings of, 21; one of "four regions," 24, 235 *seq.*; months assigned to, in omens, 219; section of ecliptic assigned to, 228 *seq.*; represented by side of moon, 235, 239; represented by Jupiter, 236; days assigned to, 237

Akkadians = Semites, 5

Aldebaran, see *Stars.*

Aleppo = Hallab, 36

Alexander the Great, 34, 62, 255, 259

Ali, 108

Allatu, consort of Nergal, 368. See *Ereshkigal.*

Ama-Ushum-Gal = Tammuz, *q. v.*, 346

Amorites, 22, 43, 235; influence on Sumero-Akkadian culture, 25 *seq.*; ethnic character, 29 *seq.*; Amoritish elements in Assyria, 41; migration, 118; home, 120

Amos, 418

Amurru, 12, 76; claimed by Sargon, 22; one of "four regions," 24, 235 *seq.*; influence on Babylonia, 26; = Mar-Tu, 76, 117; months assigned to, in astrology, 219; section of ecliptic assigned to, 228 *seq.*; represented by division of full moon,

449

A Selection from the
Catalogue of

G. P. PUTNAM'S SONS

❦

**Complete Catalogues sent
on application**

AMERICAN LECTURES
ON THE HISTORY OF RELIGIONS

I. **Rhys-Davids—Buddhism: Its History and Literature.** By T. W. RHYS-DAVIDS, LL.D., Ph.D., Professor of Pali and Buddhist Literature at University College, London. Crown octavo. *Net*, $1.50.

" . . . An admirable handbook of Buddhism, written from a point of view at once scholarly and unprejudiced."—*St. Paul Pioneer Press.*

II. **Brinton—Religions of Primitive Peoples.** By DANIEL G. BRINTON, A.M., M.D., LL.D., Sc.D., Professor of Archæology and Linguistics in the University of Pennsylvania. Crown octavo. *Net*, $1.50.

" . . . No book has yet appeared which brings the religious thought of all races and times within closer range of the modern reader; and to the reader who revels in tracing the psychic history of man, no book can be more welcome."—*Boston Transcript.*

III. **Cheyne — Jewish Religious Life after the Exile.** By Rev. T. K. CHEYNE, M.A., D.D., Oriel Professor of Interpretation of Holy Scripture in the University of Oxford, and formerly Fellow of Balliol College; Canon of Rochester. Crown octavo. *Net*, $1.50.

"Few men are as well qualified as Canon Cheyne to discuss the Jewish literature and life of the period covered by this course, and the treatment of the subject before us in this handsome volume is all that could be desired. . . . The whole book is exceedingly interesting and instructive."—*Universalist Leader.*

IV. **Budde — Religion of Israel to the Exile.** By KARL BUDDE, D.D., Professor of Theology in the University of Strassburg. Crown octavo. *Net*, $1.50.

"The chief merit of Professor Budde's book is its condensation. He gives a distinct view of the subject, undistracted by details. While the book will take its deserved place in the estimation of scholars it is also a book for the general reader."—*The Outlook.*

V. **Steindorff — The Religion of the Ancient Egyptians.** By G. STEINDORFF, Ph.D., Professor of Egyptology at the University of Leipzig. Crown octavo. *Net*, $1.50.

"Presents in compact form and interesting style the latest information, and should find a place in every library of comparative religions."—*The Congregationalist.*

AMERICAN LECTURES
ON THE HISTORY OF RELIGIONS

VI. **Knox—The Development of Religion in Japan.** By GEORGE WILLIAM KNOX, D.D., Professor of the History and Philosophy of Religion in Union Theological Seminary, and Sometime Professor of Philosophy and Ethics at the Imperial University, Tokyo.

Crown, octavo, ... *net, $1.50*

"A notable addition to this excellent series."—*The Churchman.*
"The author is peculiarly qualified for appreciative treatment of his subject.—*The Outlook.*

VII. **Bloomfield—The Religion of the Veda. The Ancient Religion of Veda (From Rig-Veda to Upanishads).** By MAURICE BLOOMFIELD, Ph.D., LL.D., Professor of Sanscrit and Comparative Philology in the Johns Hopkins University.

Crown, octavo, ... *net, $1.50*

The reader of these pages will learn how the religion of Veda rests upon prehistoric foundation which is largely nature myth ; how this religion grew more and more formal and mechanical in the Yagur-Vedas and Brahmanas, until it was practically abandoned ; how and when arose the germs of higher religious thought, and finally, how the motives and principles that underlie this entire chain of mental events landed Hindu thought in the pantheistic and pessimistic religion of the Upanishads which it has never again abandoned.

VIII. **Jastrow—Aspects of Religious Belief and Practice in Babylonia and Assyria.** By MORRIS JASTROW, JR., Ph.D., Professor of Semitic Languages in the University of Pennsylvania.

Crown octavo. 33 Illustrations and a Map.

New York   **G. P. Putnam's Sons**   London